Kitty's People

Kitty's People is a biographical novel, an intimate portrait of Kitty Flanagan from her youth as the daughter of Irish immigrants, through her years as a young mother and businesswoman plagued by senseless tragedy, till her rise as the woman-in-charge—confident, organized, fierce, and supremely generous. Kitty was my grandmother and a role model for our times.

Her story lies at the heart of a multi-generational family saga, woven from oral histories and deeply researched. Despite their talents and hard work, life for the Flanagans in America becomes an epic battle, pitting the goals of prosperity and loving family life against the forces of disease, organized crime, alcoholism, fires, a wicked stepmother, abortion, and cold-blooded murder. Kitty survives to run a grocery business against the backdrop of harsh winters, wild river floods, war shortages, the Spanish Flu pandemic, Prohibition, and the Great Depression.

You know Kitty and her people—the Flanagan, Keville, Barrett, and Curran families. They are our ancestors, fleeing the Old Country for the promised land of America, hounded by death and disaster. Yet… here we are. They persisted. They endured. They found love and laughter. They are the salt of the earth.

For further information on the research behind *Kitty's People*, use the QR code or visit *http://madinpursuit.com/KittysPeople.html*

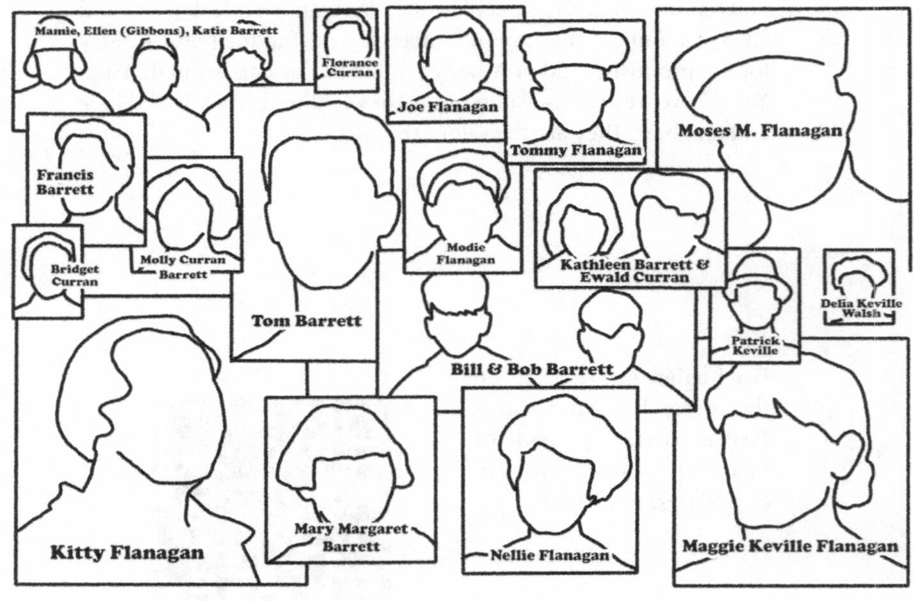

Key to Kitty's people illustrated on the cover

Kitty's People

An Irish Family Saga About the Rise of a Generous Woman

1885-1934

Susan Barrett Price

Mad in Pursuit, Ontario NY

Published by
Mad In Pursuit

FIRST EDITION
Revised August 1, 2022

Author's Note

This is a biographical novel, based on the best research available. The scenes and dialogue are imaginary, based on family stories or inferences from factual information to the degree possible. If you are a member of one of the families described here and have additional information or stories, please contact the author through Mad in Pursuit (madinpursuit.com) to contribute to future editions.

ISBN 978-0-9841292-6-3

To my mother, Kathleen Ellen Barrett Price
(1925-2020)

ACKNOWLEDGMENTS

I owe much to the fact that my Irish ancestors loved to tell their family stories. My memories were supplemented by memories from family members Kathleen McDermott, Ellen Stretch, Tom Price, Jim Hohmann, Carmen Haffer, and Barbara Holland.

It's astonishing to me that so much of our family lore has been verified in online archives. I am particularly grateful for genealogy archives, such as Ancestry.com, Family Search (familysearch.org), and Irish Genealogy (irishgenealogy.ie). In addition, Newspapers.com provided important real-time reporting on relevant events, as well as background color on popular culture, fashion, and weather. In particular, I relied on the archives of the *St. Louis Post-Dispatch, St. Louis Globe-Democrat, St. Louis Star and Times, Edwardsville Intelligencer*, and *Chicago Tribune.*

Missouri Digital Heritage (sos.mo.gov/mdh/) was invaluable for its online death certificates. It also provided online access to the St. Louis Mercantile Library at the University of Missouri-St. Louis, which contains early city directories. The Washington University Digital Gateway (digital.wustl.edu/) provided access to Whipple fire insurance maps in its "Unreal City: Historic St. Louis Maps" section, which helped me understand the buildings and neighborhoods where Kitty's people lived and worked.

It was thrilling to explore the online archives of the Friends of Leclaire [Illinois] (historic-leclaire.org), where I found the work history of my great-grandfather at Nelson Manufacturing Company.

Thanks to Daniel Waugh, author of *Egan's Rats: The Untold Story of the Prohibition-Era Gang That Ruled St. Louis,* which provided context for a great uncle's life of crime.

Thanks to Andi Cumbo-Floyd (andilit.com), who provided the professional review that helped give *Kitty's People* its final shape.

Finally, a bouquet of gratitude to my friend Pat Drum. For nearly two years, every Friday afternoon, she listened to me read draft after draft, revision after revision, providing feedback both kind and helpful. Along the way, she, too, fell in love with Kitty and her people.

Contents

"Call me Ishmael."
Herman Melville, *Moby Dick*

April 4, 1901.

Learn to labor and to wait.

Catherine.

I write not ~~wear~~ here for beauty
I write not here for fame.
Its only for rememberance,
That I record my name.

Catherine Flanagan.

Note from Kitty in the Flanagan family autograph book, dated April 4, 1901. She was ten years old.

Preface

I fell in love with Kitty's people that time the two of us sat in her kitchen, when she told me how her sister died.

And when my mother told me about the wicked stepmother and the cast iron frying pan.

And that afternoon on the picnic bench when Ewald told me about the gangsters.

I fell in love with Kitty's people when I saw the Edwardsville article about her papa's job.

And the first time I saw a 1910s newspaper ad for Barrett's Market.

And whenever my mother told the story of that deep scar along her arm and ribs.

Kitty Flanagan was my grandmother, known famously to the world of her grandchildren as *Kitty Mom*. Kitty's people and their tales of faithfulness and fortitude grabbed our hearts.

My mother Kathleen adored her Irish-American family and took great pride in her mother's *joie de vivre* in the face of hardship. She researched and organized the first set of information, then passed her work on to me.

What a gift.

Family history research became my meditation, its revelations strongest when my mind was quiet. And when the revelations came, I could feel the loving presence of Kitty and her people.

In 2020, my mother died just before her ninety-fifth birthday and just before the pandemic plunged us into isolation, leaving me to grieve with my folders full of notes and photos.

One evening, as I sifted through family documents for the umpteenth time, I stopped at a great-uncle's death certificate—cause of death: *delirium tremens*. I'd seen it before—the sad consequence of chronic alcoholism. But times being slow, I meditated on every line of the death certificate and consulted all my family timelines. What chain of events led him to despair and landed him in City Hospital, dying an agonizing death, with no family by his side? Suddenly, I knew. Suddenly, I felt a heartbreaking moment of communion with him. I hadn't known him before, but now I loved him.

Then came the question: Who can I tell? Who will share my insight and shed a tear with me? The timelines and fact-filled blog posts I'd uploaded over the years felt too bland for what my heart knew.

But I needed to share, not a single moment in time, not a single insight, not a single sorrowful profile, but the whole saga—*all* the moments, all the epiphanies, all the intertwined fates of Kitty and her people.

So many facts will be forever unknowable, but could I write the *legend*? Could I say, given what we *do* know, here's how the life and times of Kitty and her people *probably* looked and sounded?

Think of tapestry restoration.

Real people and actual events are the fragments of an ancient tapestry, excavated over time from the vast dig of old archives, and gently laid out on plain linen, waiting for the wise application of storytelling methods to complete the picture. The images and their stories are gradually reconstructed with the sturdy yarns of logic; background, filled in with the shape and movement of history; its figures, made vibrant again with the newly spun fibers of scenes and dialogue.

Was I up to this epic task?

Then, I had a dream. I sat at the dining room table with my mother and she took my hand in hers, a gesture of love and confidence. I knew she'd stick with me on this project.

For months, I wrote. For months, I checked my research and hunted for more insights. Mapped every address. Checked every weather report. Scanned old newspapers for popular clothing styles, from corsets to fur coats. I was surprised at how often I dug up another original patch of weaving for my tapestry, something that fit in and connected one ragged fragment of the legend with another.

Whether my "restorations" came from a mystical connection to my ancestors or from deep in my own unconscious, I don't know. Part of me wants to think the experience of my forebears is encoded deep in my DNA, slowly revealed by walking with them through fifty years of history.

Although the restoration storytelling is clearly mine, I tried to push aside any preconceived themes or messages about women, the Irish, the Catholics, big families, or small businesses. In letting Kitty's people become characters who tell their own stories, some mystery remains, some holes in the saga that neither the data nor the logic can fill in, mysteries that will continue to disturb and raise questions.

But here is the legend. And like many legends, it begins with a chance encounter.

BOOK 1. MAGGIE & MOSES

Part 1. Chicago Love Story, 1885-1891

:: 1 ::

Monday, November 2, 1885. On the corner of Cottage Grove at Thirty-Ninth Street, Maggie Keville huddles with a small crowd waiting for the Jackson Park trolley. The man next to her has a coughing fit, hawking up phlegm and spitting it into the darkness. She backs away from him, her ankles wobbling on the frozen mud.

The wind picks up. She tightens the scarf holding her bonnet in place, then curls her hand to make sure the nickel is still inside her glove.

Her old job was walking distance from her room—a basement crowded with immigrant girls making cloaks. Through the grapevine of Irish seamstresses, Maggie snagged a better job as a dressmaker's assistant up on State Street. She thanked Our Lady for the blessing, till she realized the work meant jumping onto a trolley every day before dawn, just as winter and its coal-dust fog were settling over Chicago.

Here it comes.

She checks her nickel again.

The trio of cable cars slows down and car number one pauses in front of her. The conductor stands ready to collect the fares, his brass buttons gleaming in the lantern light.

Maggie lunges forward to catch the narrow step. One foot up, her arms flail. The conductor reaches a gloved hand out to her, but she misses it, grabbing his coat sleeve instead.

His hand cups her elbow and floats her aboard.

Mother of God, it's a miracle she didn't fall to her death. Her heart is pounding.

"Easy there, Miss. Hang on. Here." He guides her hand to a pole, then turns to collect coins from other passengers, ringing the bell with each fare, his movement smooth as a juggler's. "Mrs. Keenoy. Miss Hennessey. The gout better, is it, Mr. Sweeney?" His greetings are lyrical, a litany sung by a priest to his congregation, the riders mumbling back their response, communicants in a workers' ritual.

"Morning."

"G'morning, sir."

"Could be worse."

Trembling, Maggie fumbles the nickel out of her glove and hands it over. With a clang of the bell, the car picks up speed.

She's on her way.

:: 2 ::

In the lantern light, Moses recognizes the young woman. From the neighborhood, yes, with that strong jaw, those sharp eyes, and that dark hair cut to a fringe across her brow. Glad that he took the time to wax his mustache this morning, he smiles at her.

"Moses McCarty Flanagan," he says with a tip of his conductor's cap, "welcome aboard, Miss—?"

The woman takes a beat before answering. "Keville," she says, then louder, "Keville."

"Why so fearful of my luxurious coach?" He has cultivated a stage actor's voice to cut through the whine of the wheels and roar of the wind.

"I'm no fool," she says with a brogue from the west of Ireland. "This monstrosity could kill me in the blink of an eye."

Moses throws his head back in laughter. "Oh my, that would be a pity. But did you know that the Jackson Park trolley is one of the great feats of American ingenuity? Did you know that these lovely cars are pulled along by miles of underground cable? That they are operated from a labyrinth of gears and clutches at the Fifty-Fifth Street power plant? What kind of imagination dreams up projects so monumental? What kind of engineering brings those dreams to life, every belt and cotter pin in its place?"

"But you hear stories every day," she retorts. "Trains and trolleys crushing people out of the blue."

"So much blather, Miss Keville. Not fashionable anymore to talk about the number of folks trampled by horses every day."

Mr. McManus, hunched next to Miss Keville, grunts and says, "The Lord giveth and the Lord taketh away. Praise be."

"Indeed," says Moses. "And we men roll on toward the twentieth century in our magnificent contraptions."

Finally, Miss Keville gives him half a smile. "You men indeed—always thinking you can invent a machine that outruns the reach of the Lord."

The trolley rolling into its next stop, Moses again performs his fare-taking, bell-ringing, passenger-greeting acrobatics, perfected after months on the job, repeated constantly ten hours a day, six days a week, with variations at any given moment to guide a drunk to his seat, lift a child onto the car, or catch packages slipping from an old woman's arms.

The work is demanding and poorly paid—by no means his life's calling. He arrived in Chicago a craftsman, but for years the only jobs available to him were pounding nails into planks, slapping together tenement housing with the cheapest materials possible to accommodate the tidal wave of immigrants. Last year, he leapt at the chance to work for Chicago City Railway, to be part of their grand mission to replace the filthy horse-drawn trolleys with modern cable cars. He admires the taut engineering of the system, but mostly he loves his trolley riders, loves coaxing smiles from faces too often clenched with worry, eyes focused on the sick child at home or the back-breaking job ahead.

And on this fine day, he meets Miss Keville.

:: 3 ::

By the end of the week, Miss Keville is hopping onto his car like a cat, always taking the seat next to his post, appearing to enjoy his patter between stops.

"I was living on Cottage Grove when the cable car started running in '82," he announces one morning. "The street was tore up something awful, but what a marvel watching them construct the cable-conduit, stone by stone. Like watching the pyramids of Egypt go up."

"I only arrived in '84, from Mayo, God help us," she says.

"Mayo, *God help us*. What is it about Mayo, Miss Keville, that everyone who mentions it implores the Lord's assistance?"

She looks away. "We are so very poor, Mr. Flanagan." Her voice is strong, like a teacher's. "God-forsaken, you might say. Those who survived the famine and the fevers are now forced to send their daughters to America. It wasn't my idea to leave a job I loved for the privilege of filling my lungs with coal dust and the stink of stockyards."

As the brakeman slows the trio of cars to pick up more riders, Moses performs his fare-collection duty, then turns back to Miss Keville.

"So you were the chosen one?"

Her eyes harden. "I got put on the boat because I could read and write, most qualified to find work or a wage-earning husband, to send home a wee bit of change every month. Boys are needed on the farm. Girls have strong arms to carry water from the pump, but are more valuable in Boston or Chicago."

She tightens the woolen shawl around her neck and tucks a blowing lock of hair under her bonnet. "Then, wouldn't you know, the minute I arrive, my papa is struck dead with typhus. Typhus! Mam was left running the farm with six sons and two unmarried daughters. She wrote, informing me that my sister Delia was on her way here because they needed another remittance. So here we are," she says, her sad eyes catching the lantern glow. "In El Dorado."

As the car rolls into the next stop, Moses helps Mr. McManus to his feet. The old man has a wheezy coughing fit and Moses gives him a thump on the back. *El Dorado, indeed.*

:: 4 ::

During Moses's ten years in Chicago, his Saturday night entertainment has usually revolved around the corner saloon, where he can listen to music and sing, and, with a little luck, pay for his drinks by winning at darts in the side room or horseshoes in the alley.

But he is beginning to long for a wife.

So, he gives up his rowdy, smoke-filled saloon for the church-sponsored hooleys designed to help immigrant girls find husbands. The dancing is strictly supervised, in lines or circles, lively enough to blow off steam but without the occasion of sin. Moses has been well-taught: intimacy is a frightening thing. Giving in to lustful temptation not only puts a man's immortal soul at risk of damnation but also carries with it the risk of uncomfortable infections, not to mention the inconvenient timing of children. Moses is a careful man.

He meets many women at these soirees, some bashful and backward, some plucky and bold, all anxious to find their men, to liberate themselves from domestic service or the shirtwaist factory, and to start their families. None hold his attention.

Now, here is this Miss Keville, keen-eyed and well-spoken, with an edge of darkness, not at all sure Chicago is where she wants to be.

Being a cable-car conductor as winter closes in on Chicago is no way to get to know her. He can raise his voice in the few minutes between each stop and his riders can shout back, but real conversation is impossible. After weeks of greeting Miss Keville at Thirty-Ninth Street, he gets an idea.

An early riser, Moses usually goes to the 5 a.m. Mass at Holy Angels, a succinct service geared to the servants who need to run back to their jobs before their employers wake up. But on the Sunday after Christmas, Moses sits in the back row through every crowded service till, finally, he catches sight of the woman whose pale eyes haunt him, heading toward the exit at the end of the eight o'clock Mass.

Trotting up to her outside, he removes his derby hat and takes a dramatic bow. "Miss Keville! It's me, Moses Flanagan, your humble cable-car conductor!"

After a surprised look, she smiles. "Well, hello! Let me introduce you to my sister Delia and her beau John Walsh."

Walsh doffs his hat and Delia curtsies. "Ah, Maggie has told me about her entertaining conductor," Delia says

So, her name is *Maggie*. And she has spoken of him.

"Aren't we lucky to see the sun this chilly morning," Moses says. "Perhaps you're going my way? May I walk with you?"

In a split second, Moses senses Maggie taking stock of him and he stands a little taller, knowing that his coat is brushed and his boots are polished.

With a twinkle in her eye, she says, "Of course you may."

:: 5 ::

Maggie isn't sure what to think when Moses Flanagan invites her to join him at one of the Catholic social clubs.

She hates the idea of merriment on a Saturday evening. After a week of sitting at a noisy sewing machine, easing sleeves into armholes and gathering skirts onto waistbands, she enjoys embroidering or painting china in the room she shares with her sister. Despite her growing collection of embellished linens and decorated teacups, she is not ready to be courted. Courting leads to marriage and marriage means children. How could she bring a child into such a dangerous city? What she sees of America is worse than Mayo, God help us. Babies catch diphtheria, men are trampled in stockyards, and women are casually molested by cigar-smoking employers.

Completely opposite is Delia—her "Irish twin," born nine months after Maggie and soon to be celebrating her twenty-first birthday—outgoing and fun-loving, comfortable in the crowded city and firmly attached to John Walsh. But what boon to mankind is John Walsh? A night watchman at the yards, reporting for duty at midnight. What kind of future does he have?

Maggie certainly didn't come all this way to raise babies in a tenement, with a night-shift husband shouting at everyone to let him sleep.

But she doesn't want to be a nun either. Reluctantly, she agrees to go out with Moses.

In their first conversation away from the dark clangor of the morning trolley, Maggie wants to know more about her new friend.

"Limerick-born and Dublin-bred. I'm the son of a sea cook." He chuckles to himself at the turn of phrase. "I can only guess my father Tim Flanagan was a drunk and a wife-beater. I can only guess that Mam's family, the McCartys, wouldn't hear of her moving back home with six boys. I was told she meant to get us all to America but only made it as far as Dublin."

"Good Lord, that must have been terrible!" Maggie says. Breaking up a family in Ireland, no matter what the conditions, is unheard of.

"I hardly remember. She claimed to be a widow, I think, and got herself a job as a cook on one of those paddle steamers that ferry wealthy passengers along the coast. And she turned us younger boys over to the

Christian Brothers to be educated."

"So you can read and write, then," Maggie says.

"I'm a wizard at math too. Being the best in my class saved me from many a paddling at the hands of the Brothers. Anyway, you have to know fractions and basic geometry to get anywhere in the carpentry trade."

"Carpentry?" Maggie is surprised. "I thought you were dedicated to entertaining trolley riders."

"Ha! I don't fancy being poor for too many more years in this land of opportunity. I went from primary school into an apprenticeship with a cabinet-maker. I was on my way to being a master joiner when Mam decided it was time for me to make my fortune in America. I was eighteen."

"But the trolley—?" she asks.

"A stepping stone. They were hiring conductors who needed to be both physically strong and quick-witted, but my real goal was to get a foothold in the railway shop where they hire only skilled craftsmen."

"And have you?"

"I have! A couple of nights a week, I work at replacing the wooden slats on trolley car seats. They take a beating. The other nights, I work with a carpenter there, learning to operate an industrial lathe and a couple of other big machines. Nothing like finding yourself an apprentice again when you're near thirty years of age."

Maggie is impressed with her new friend's ambition and his eagerness to learn.

She also likes the fact that he has a clean neck, starched white shirt collars, and trimmed fingernails. The soles of his polished boots have received the attention of a cobbler. And the patches on his old wool coat are nearly invisible, so skillfully darned.

Very soon, stepping out with Moses on Saturday nights becomes the highlight of her week.

Her pastimes change. Instead of embroidering dainty flowers on the corners of tea towels, she turns her attention to enhancing her silhouette and making herself feel pretty from the inside out. With a supply of scraps from her day job, she adds lace inserts to her store-bought shifts and corset covers. Strips of linen are gathered into ruffles to add volume to her petticoats.

She stuffs muslin padding into the voids around the top of her corset to round out her shape. Working-class women don't have the luxury of wearing bustles, but a bum pad worn at the back of her corset balances the look of her full bosom and helps support the weight of her wool skirt.

And her hair! She's never satisfied. She tries various styles that might look good with or without a hat. She takes special care of her hairpiece, which gives her bangs to hide the premature old-lady creases on her forehead.

As she dares dream of having a husband, it is Moses's face she sees. Delia can have her burly John Walsh and his night shifts. Moses will lead her to the promised land—not this America of crowded rooms and foul air, but one where she's the lady of the house, with a brood of fat happy children, and a garden—a garden not for cabbages and potatoes, but a garden for cut flowers, full of roses.

:: 6 ::

Maggie loves strolling through the neighborhood with Moses. The community anchor is Holy Angels Church, founded to serve Irish families exiled from home by the famine and mass evictions of the 1850s. They are the stable base of the parish. But nowadays, the Irish come as singles, sister by sister, brother by brother, cousin by cousin.

Unlike the Germans and Italians, who arrive as families and don't miss a beat organizing their domestic lives, the new Irish are wildlings, young people on their own, putting off marriage and children for as long as possible. They work and play without parents, free to be whoever they want—as long as they work their six ten-hour days a week, participate in the Holy Sacraments, and save a few pennies to support the farm at home or to pay for a sister's passage. They are free to enjoy Saturday nights, free to stay out late, free to sip whiskey till they reel along the sidewalk back to their shabby rooms—as long as they begin their fast at midnight so they can take Communion at Sunday Mass.

A young woman like herself is free to pair up with the future father of her children—as long as she is careful to avoid sin, but, if sinning, careful to know the difference between mortal and venial sin, mortal sin being a fast trolley to hell if she dies before saying her Act of Contrition at Confession.

On her precious Saturday nights, that winter of '86, Maggie Keville lets Moses hold her hand as they walk through snow and ice to their gatherings, where the lads share hip flasks of whiskey with colleens.

Maggie meets Moses's younger brothers Denis and Jeremiah, who followed him from Dublin and who live together on Halstead. Denis works his railroad job on most Saturday nights, but Jerry becomes an annoying fixture. He's a big lug who works in the stockyards and smells of sweat and cow dung. His girl is the chatty Miss Bridget Meehan, who shows too much petticoat when she dances and allows her hair to fall loose when she drinks too much—which is every Saturday night.

And every Saturday night, she drapes herself over Jerry or fakes a stumble near Moses to force him to help her up, despite the warning of chaperones.

One evening as Moses walks her home, Maggie can't help voicing her disapproval. "I don't get why such a beautiful girl would make such a vulgar display of herself."

"Oh, my darling," Moses says. "I've known Biddy since Dublin. When she was orphaned, the nuns took her in. Jerry tells me they sent her to a cousin in Chicago, but the cousin never showed up, so the nuns stuck her into the Industrial School on Van Buren. She learned too much from the wayward girls there, I'm afraid. But she's good at heart, lucky to have run into Jerry. She'll settle down."

Maggie walks faster when she hears the affection in Moses's voice, but he catches up with her. He lays his hands on her shoulders, pulling her close and bowing his head till his mustache tickles her ear and his breath warms her neck. "By now, you must know that my heart has room for no one but Margaret Keville."

She touches her gloved hands to his. "I love you near me," she murmurs.

Winter gives way to spring. Maggie finds she enjoys the effects of whiskey. Walking home with Moses becomes the favorite part of her week as they slip into darkened doorways to kiss and cuddle. Slowly, they come to an understanding: they will eventually marry but they have much to accomplish beforehand to avoid starting a family in poverty.

Maggie encourages Moses to quit his conductor job and devote himself wholeheartedly to carpentry and the booming building trades.

"You're thirty years old. Time to show the world who you are," she tells him.

He agrees. And, with his experience in the City Railway shop, he's able to get a job at a planing mill, operating a lathe.

For extra money, she brings home mending and alteration jobs to sew by hand at night. On Sundays, they attend Mass and have a quick breakfast together, but spend the rest of the day on their jobs.

Their precious Saturday hours together become more intimate.

While they kiss in the darkened doorways, they press together, hands roaming. As the months pass, swooning under the influence of her whiskey, Maggie becomes more generous about lifting her skirt and petticoats, allowing Moses's fingers to find the open seam in her bloomers. He leaves her shivering with pleasure and always wanting more.

"Soon," he whispers, "soon."

Each Monday before she catches her trolley, she stops at Holy Angels to confess her sins to Father Tighe or Father Callaghan, veiling her ecstasy in the bland language of impure thought and touch. Her contrition is sincere and she prays that her guardian angel will keep her safe from temptation. But when Saturday rolls around, as soon as she sees Moses's smile, her guardian angel is relieved from duty. There can be no sin with this man, this gift from God.

:: 7 ::

In the autumn of 1887, when Moses picks up Maggie for their Saturday night, he has an announcement.

"The planing mill promoted me to supervisor, with a big raise. Let's start planning our wedding!"

Throwing her arms around him, Maggie squeals, "Yes! Wonderful! I know just the style of dress I want to wear."

"We'll do it up properly," he says, holding on to her. "With what family we have here and with all the friends we've made, I want a bit of fanfare to signal our prosperity, not a rinky-dink tea party like the Walshes put on."

"I agree," she says. Delia and John Walsh got married last June and only served tea and cookies afterward. They claimed to be saving their pennies for a house, but it felt too humble for her exuberant sister.

"We can even wait till spring," Maggie says, "like the rich families do, so we can have fresh flowers and an open carriage."

They celebrate their decision that evening by dancing faster and drinking harder than any Saturday before.

On the walk home up Cottage Grove, buffeted by a harsh wind off the lake, the two dash into their favorite dark doorway, giddy with joy, desperately hungry for each other, scrambling to raise her skirts. In a new move, he guides her hand to that place between his legs that she's been so curious about. For the first time, he doesn't pull away, doesn't caution her that it's too dangerous. She tugs open the buttons on his trousers.

They do an awkward dance as they close the gap between them. Then Maggie gasps.

Moses pauses to whisper, "I don't want to hurt you."

"Don't stop! I want this!" She is surprised by the breathlessness in her voice and then by her sudden weeping when they must separate and rearrange their clothing as the sound of voices grows near.

Moses holds her close till the voices fade.

"You're all right?" he asks.

"I'm in heaven," she answers.

But by morning, her anxiety sets in. When Moses picks her up for Mass, she grabs his arm and looks him in the eye.

"We committed a mortal sin last night, Moses Flanagan. We can't take Communion today." They begin walking. As if it were as trivial as breaking their fast after midnight, they will keep their fingers pressed to their lips when the priest reaches them at the communion rail, a discreet signal to pass them by. But this is the least of Maggie's worries.

"What if I'm with child? Then what?"

"Oh, my darling!" He stops walking to look at her. "How can that be?" His gaze shifts to the horse-drawn carriages crowding the street, then brightly back to her. "We were standing up. You can't… you can't make a baby standing up."

"Where did you hear that bit of science?" she asks, praying that it is true.

But it isn't.

:: 8 ::

Windy November gives way to frozen December. On Christmas eve, with most of the rooming house residents out celebrating with cousins, Maggie and Moses snuggle together on a threadbare loveseat in the parlor. Maggie gives Moses a package wrapped in brown paper and scavenged string. He grins with pleasure when he sees the worn copy of

Moby Dick.

"I hear it's very popular," she tells him. "I found it in the used bookstore near work. Since we have both traveled the high seas..."

He laughs. "And we both chase the white whale of prosperity."

Then he gives her a necklace—a fashionable gold-plated book-chain with a small square cameo and two dangles. "From an estate in Evanston," he tells her. "That jeweler down the street—Cohen—he fixed the clasp and got it all polished up for me. For you. It will have to do till someday I can afford a diamond ring."

"It's too beautiful. You shouldn't have—" Her voice cracks as Moses drapes it around her neck and closes the clasp, his fingers brushing against her neck. She looks down at the floor. "There's something I need to tell you. Something—my monthly hasn't come. I need a tonic of some sort to bring it on. I can't have a scandal. I'll lose my job, my room. I'll be forced into one of those homes where girls in trouble are sent."

He puts his arm around her shoulders, pulling her close. Since that one time, they have been chaste, not only out of fear and caution, but also to purify themselves for the sacrament of Matrimony come May. He is quiet.

"Say something," she says.

"You've lost weight," he suggests. "You've had a cough since the weather turned cold. I wonder if we should be more worried about consumption—"

"Stop!" she says, her voice sharp as she twists around, pushing his arm away. "Is that supposed to comfort me? Don't you know my sister Mary died from TB? I was seven and she was nine. She wasted away, fairy-stricken, for two years at the center of our household before the angels took her. It was horrible. Don't talk to me about consumption."

The memory of those harsh years fills Maggie's eyes with tears.

"I'm so sorry. How terrible." Moses pulls her close again and dabs her eyes with his handkerchief. "But, Maggie, listen to me. You're not *in trouble*, no matter what. You have *me*. Forget harsh tonics. We'll get married tomorrow. If we have a baby, it will be a couple of weeks early, that's all. Not an eyebrow will be raised."

She pulls back to look into his eyes. "Seriously? What about the big wedding?"

"To hell with trying to impress everyone. All I need in this world is you by my side."

She sniffs and lays her head on his shoulder. "We'll find a little house," she says, "with a rose garden."

"And I will never again make you weep. Only tears of joy from now on."

After Christmas Mass, Maggie and Moses follow Fr. Tighe to the rectory.

In his parlor, Maggie asks, "Can you marry us today?"

He glances pointedly at her belly. "The rush?"

"Since her sister got married," Moses says, "Miss Keville can't afford her room. The two of us can live cheaply together and start our family, God willing."

Maggie glows at Moses's fine words, but resists the urge to grab his hand.

Fr. Tighe opens his 1888 Matrimony calendar, already crowded with names. "You need three weeks to post the banns. I can add you to today's list. How about Thursday, January 12, in the Blessed Mother's side chapel? You'll have to bring me your license from the County Clerk in the meantime."

That afternoon, Maggie pulls Delia aside to tell her about the change of plans.

Delia's eyes widen. "You're knocked up!"

Maggie rears back. "I swear to St. Anne and the Blessed Virgin I am not!"

She hates the look of mockery in Delia's eyes. She'll tolerate no whiff of scandal. "We're saving our money is all."

Delia grabs her hand. "You know I'm happy for you, no matter what. Flanagan is a brilliant man. So well read. Learn something new every time we talk. And he adores you, Maggie, that's what counts."

On January 12, the blustering west wind and four-degree air temperature do not keep Maggie and Moses from celebrating. Wearing a borrowed, ivory silk dress and fashioning a yard of lace into a veil, Maggie proudly takes her vows with Moses.

At the age of twenty-two, Maggie Keville becomes Mrs. Moses Flanagan. And because of the fine print in the immigration law, she also becomes an American.

:: 9 ::

Moses is disappointed that the only living space he can find for them is a one-room cold-water flat at 4446 Cottage Grove. He's used to living in buildings with a shared toilet and washroom down the hall, but wanted more for Maggie.

Maggie is a good sport. "I don't see a rose garden, but, look, a big stove and a full bucket of coal." She lifts the thin mattress to check for bedbugs before she sits down and bounces on the uneven, squeaky bedsprings. "Oh my, our first chore will be to retie these springs!"

They are both surprised when the announcement of their marriage results in Maggie's losing her job. The reason is curt: "Girls on their own need the work and can put in long hours. Married women are a pain in the arse."

Delia scolds her. "You were a fool to tell them! I still go by Keville at the shirtwaist factory and they're none the wiser."

But Moses is secretly pleased. It's a point of pride with him to accept the responsibilities of a husband, just as he has taken on the obligations of citizenship by registering to vote. And, no denying it, he is tickled to come home to a wife who cooks him dinner, darns his socks, and heats kettles of water for his baths. He is growing roots in America and loves the tender burden of family life.

After three missed cycles, Maggie invests a dollar on a maternity corset, with lacing up the sides to fit a changing figure.

"God willing, this garment will keep my back healthy through many childbearing years," she says to Moses.

When Maggie begins to hand-sew gores and gussets into her clothing, Moses barters a Sunday of woodwork installation for a second-hand, treadle-operated sewing machine, which he oils and polishes for her.

"I'll find you the softest white cotton for our baby's clothes," he promises, enthralled by the romance of fatherhood. "Or linen—that's cooler. It'll be the hottest part of summer when our babe arrives, about August fifteenth, I figure."

Maggie's eyes harden above her smile. "No, no, my dear. The due date is September 12, nine months from our wedding night. The Blessed Virgin and St. Anne blessed us with new life on the first day of our marriage, don't you remember?"

Moses understands and sweeps Maggie into his arms.

On August 22, 1888, a sweltering Wednesday afternoon, Maggie gives birth to a healthy daughter "just a few weeks early." She is baptized at Holy Angels on September 2, with the Christian name *Ellen*, after Moses's mother. They call her *Nellie*.

:: 10 ::

As the Flanagan's ring in 1889, they celebrate a year of marriage, their precocious little girl, and a better apartment down the street—one with hot water and a private toilet. They are both exhausted, but remind each other that prosperity is just around the corner.

But their optimism wears thin. With the never-ending demands of cooking, laundry, and childcare, Maggie begins to resent Moses's long working hours, sometimes topping eighty a week. She tunes into the hallway gossip that unions will soon force companies to adopt a forty-hour workweek. She's all for it.

One winter evening after another 10 p.m. dinner, she mentions the rumor to Moses.

"Do you want to put us in the poor house, Margaret?" he growls. "If my hours are cut in half, who's going to double my wages?"

"The unions will demand better wages. It's not like the owners aren't making more money than they know what to do with."

"I'm too weary to discuss it."

She sighs, longing for the days when he would jot bits of poetry on the pages of her autograph book; when he would tell her stories about growing up around the docks in Dublin; when he would help her make dinner, boil pots of water to wash their whites, and take in the laundry from the fire escape; and when he would rock their fussy Nellie while Maggie stole a nap.

Now, sweet times are reduced to Sunday mornings, when the Flanagans bundle up and promenade to Mass, where they catch up on family news.

In February, Moses's brother Denis hails them with the news that his wife Katie gave birth to a their first child, Timothy. The baptism will be after Mass in two weeks.

Delia tells her that she and John are sponsoring their brother Pat's passage to America. "He's done with farming," she says, "and wants to join us here in El Dorado. Passage booked for April. Now that we have the house, he'll live with us, help with the mortgage."

As they mingle after Mass, Moses seems to know everyone, greeting them with questions about their mothers and children, whose names he all remembers. No matter how tired and frustrated she is, Maggie beams with pride at her genius of a husband.

:: 11 ::

For his part, Moses worries that Maggie is too withdrawn, that she is losing her edge. Her world has shrunk to little Nell and brief exchanges with other mothers as she dashes around the neighborhood, through wind and rain, getting her errands done. He wonders if America really is better than the Old Country. In rural Ireland, Maggie would be surrounded by family, including a mother who raised ten children. They might subsist on potatoes and oatmeal, but he would be home at night. He would have time to learn the fiddle and time to teach Nellie the flute.

But there is no going back. His obligations are here. *This is who I am*, he tells himself, *a poor immigrant fellow, figuring out this damn new world on my own.* He is terrified that the two of them will grow distant and silent, like too many couples.

He gets an idea. On Saturday afternoon, when the mill finally closes for the week, he stops at the public library on the way home. A new ritual is born. He brings Maggie books they can talk about. *Tom Sawyer. Uncle Tom's Cabin. Little Women.* Stories and poems by Edgar Allen Poe. *Ben-Hur.*

At first, Maggie protests that she is too tired, too busy to read. Then one night, he comes home to find her absorbed in *Tom Sawyer.*

"When I taught school, the government gave us readers with excerpts from Mark Twain," she says.

"You taught school?" he asks.

"Didn't I tell you?"

Moses shakes his head. "Talking about home always seemed to make you sad."

"It does. I hated leaving that job—a tiny primary school I could walk to from Moyne. They told me I could be a teacher in America but, surprise, I had nowhere near the qualifications to teach here. I learned to read from a tattered copy of *Jane Eyre*, which I read and reread, but it was missing the final chapter, so I made up different endings." She runs her fingers along the firm binding of *Tom Sawyer* and murmurs. "Mayo, God help us."

❦

Maggie loves the library books but finds herself envying the characters, such as those in *Little Women*. She loves Louisa May Alcott's March sisters for their energy and ambition. Even when they squabble, their love shines through. Maggie had three sisters as well, but look at them. Her sister Bridget, who can't even write enough to compose a letter, lives a world away on the farm in Mayo, while her poor sister Mary is long dead. Delia still works at the factory, impatient for Walsh to give her a baby, yet prospering—buying a house on Union, sponsoring Pat Keville's passage. Their fresh-off-the-boat brother now has a steady job carrying bricks for city construction projects. Maggie envies them, too, for their roomy home and three paychecks.

So much for sisters. But what she wouldn't give for a Marmee or an Aunt March to teach her how to be a good wife and mother.

She envies Mark Twain's characters too. She wishes they lived in Hannibal, Missouri, with its whitewashed fences and boyish adventures. The more she is cooped up in this apartment, with its clanking radiator and sewage odors, the more she envies Huck Finn floating on his raft down the wide Mississippi.

:: 12 ::

When Christmas comes around in 1889, Moses surprises her with the news that he's found another, even better apartment for them. It's still on Cottage Grove but faces the lake, a corner flat with windows on two sides for cross-ventilation.

Maggie smiles, even though it means that once again she'll be surrounded by strangers. Her news for Moses is that she thinks another baby is on the way.

"We can do this," he says as he hugs her close.

On the first Sunday in January, 1890, after they miss Mass because of Maggie's morning sickness, Moses hires a wagon to move their few belongings three blocks down the street.

Maggie is frazzled. The flat is filthy. A dish and one of her hand-painted teacups are broken.

"I surely see no lake view," she says, standing at the east-facing window with her fists on her hips.

Moses steps beside her. Against the backdrop of heavy fog, they gaze out on the arse-end of another row of apartment buildings and a cobblestone alley dotted with ash pits and garbage pails.

"It was a clear day when…," he starts to say but lets the sentence trail off. She hears his sigh and feels his pang of regret. She knows how he loves sitting with his morning newspaper at a streetside window, watching the hustle and bustle along Cottage Grove Avenue. She knows he has sacrificed that so she can have a cross-breeze, a larger icebox, and gas lights.

He puts an arm around her, but as she starts to lean against him, Nellie lets out a holler, screaming for the ragdoll that went missing during the move. When the sixteen-month-old pitches herself on the floor in a fit of tears, Moses sweeps her into his arms.

"I'll take her to meet the neighbors and let you have some time to…" He looks around at the mess. "Some time."

As he exits with the crying child, Maggie shouts after him. "Bring back ice. We have no ice!"

:: 13 ::

1890 is full of unrest. Moses gets embroiled in union politics as the atmosphere heats up over working hours. As strikes sweep the country, many of his union brothers join the Socialist Labor Party. A Jewish neighbor takes him to one of the meetings, a lecture on the right of workers to share in the profits of their bosses. After the talk, Moses browses a table of free books and picks out a dog-eared copy of Looking Backward: 2000-1887 by Edward Bellamy.

The story is a utopian fantasy about Julian West, who wakes up after a hundred-year sleep in the year 2000, to find the world has become a worker's paradise. Instead of inspiring Moses, the book depresses the hell out of him. Wouldn't a tired working man just love to fall asleep like Rip Van Winkle and wake up in a fine community with all his problems solved?

He leaves it on the table next to the rocker, where Maggie is reading to Nellie *Around the World in Eighty Days,* a fantasy adventure by Jules Verne.

"Here's another fairy tale for you, dear," he says.

❦

Maggie reads *Looking Backward* through to the end, even though she too is disturbed by it. Her discontent with Chicago is growing as fast as the baby in her womb. Newly arrived Germans and Italians crowd several families to a flat in their neighborhood. Parents let their children play in the alley, where garbage piles up, stinking to high heavens and drawing rats. Every child she sees has a runny nose and a cough.

Too often, she hears the keening of a mother whose babe has died of some horrifying ailment. Last September, Moses's brother Denis and his wife Kate lost their dear little Timmy, only seven months old. The wail of heartbreak is everywhere.

Moses makes a decent wage, but he's stuck. He talks about finding a job with profit-sharing but has no time to look. Maggie starts reading his *Chicago Tribune*, hunting for an answer, a path forward. She collects names of companies with profit-sharing plans, companies that could benefit from a clever carpenter and shop supervisor like Moses.

Spring arrives. Moses takes up smoking and re-introduces whiskey into their Saturday night routine. He doesn't want to hear about her unhappiness or her ideas. He wants drink, smoke, and the warmth of his woman.

Then, on the first hot Saturday of summer, Moses's brother Jerry shows up with his boisterous girl Biddy Meehan and a bottle of cheap rye. Although it's understood they are bound for marriage, there is tension between them.

"Tell your brother it's time to quit living with Denis and Kate, for christsake," she says to Moses. "It's time to start our own family. I'm fed up with being a maid."

Jerry turns to Moses. "How can I start my own family after watching Timmy be taken by the strangling angel, choking to death in his mother's arms while another child was growing inside her. Since little Helen was born last month, Kate is back to weeping again every day and Denis himself is doing poorly, missing work."

Maggie jumps up from the table to chip ice for their drinks. Just hearing the story makes her feel cursed by it. How in the world will she protect her own children?

She turns to see Moses force the worry off his own face with a smile, as he sloshes the rye into glasses. "You're a big-hearted man, Jerry, being faithful to your brother in his time of need. Don't worry, Biddy, Denny and Kate will spring back. It's what people do, carry on. You'll get your own babies before long."

:: 14 ::

August of 1890 comes around with the hottest weather Chicago has seen in decades. People and animals are dropping dead in the streets, broiled in the hundred-degree heat. Outbreaks of diphtheria add the element of terror, as heat-exhausted parents watch their children succumb to the "strangling angel."

On the twelfth, with the help of a midwife, Maggie gives birth. Catherine Margaret announces herself with a healthy wail. The Flanagans decide to mark their good fortune with a combined christening party for "Kitty" and second birthday party for Nellie.

After the Baptism on the twenty-third, the family gathers in the Flanagan's small apartment. On the Keville side, Delia and John—Kitty's godparents—are joined by their brother Pat, now twenty-three and full of muscle from hauling bricks sixty hours a week. He lifts Nellie onto his shoulders, making her squeal with delight. On the Flanagan side, Jerry and Biddy arrive with Denis and Kate, who bring their four-month-old Helen. It is nearing the one-year anniversary of Timmy's death. Although Denis and Kate avoid the topic and join the laughter, Maggie still sees the darkness behind their eyes.

With two daughters to protect from lurking dangers, Maggie is reinvigorated. Even with her workload doubled, she is more determined than ever to find her family's way out of grimy Chicago to their promised land. Moses will get them there, even if he doesn't know it yet.

Autumn brings relief from the heat and rampant disease. But the days still fly by with no discussion of improving their lot. A few family gatherings at Delia's brighten the holidays—women in the kitchen preparing food and playing with babies, while the men smoke and drink too much in the parlor.

Maggie is looking forward to a quiet New Year's Eve, where she might introduce the idea of change using Moses's own imagery of progress and the wondrous world of the twentieth century.

But Jerry and Biddy show up.

As the liquor flows, their guests get louder and louder. Moses laughs at their uproarious stories of life around the stockyards. Long before midnight, bored with the silliness, Maggie retreats to the bedroom to check on Nellie and nurse Catherine. She falls asleep.

When she awakes, the family chatter has gone quiet. Maggie lies there for a few minutes, sorting through the noises of her neighborhood—a saxophone wailing from across the alley, a fiddle playing a jig down the hall, an accordion squeezing out a polka downstairs, all these sounds against a bassline of laughter, shouted arguments, tipsy singing, and children crying.

Buttoning her shirt, she leaves the bedroom. The flat is dark. She turns up the gas on the sconces by the bedroom door, then a lamp.

Jerry is slumped over the kitchen table, passed out. Slowly, her mind sorts out the puzzling vision on the settee. Moses is there, a stunned look on his face. And Biddy. Biddy is sitting on his lap, her hair loose from its bun, her shirtwaist open to show her frilly white corset cover. She is clutching Moses's hand to her bosom.

Maggie stares.

Moses mumbles, "Margaret. This isn't..."

Biddy giggles. "Mar-gar-et. This isn't *anything*." She tries to get off Moses's lap and winds up rolling onto the floor. "I'm drunk, Mar-gar-et, can't you see?" She puts a hand on Moses's knee and raises herself up. "Moze was just... I don't know..."

Maggie presses her lips into a hard line. She watches Biddy stumble to her feet. Watches her teeter over to Jerry and give him a shove.

"Come on, Jer."

Jerry grunts. "Is it midnight?" he slurs, stumbling to his feet.

"Nah, we wore out our welcome here," Biddy says, grabbing their coats and pushing Jerry out the door.

Moses weaves across the room, his arms outstretched to Maggie. "I nodded off. I nodded off and there she was—"

Spinning away, Maggie slams the bedroom door in his face.

:: 15 ::

As the new year is greeted outdoors with shouts and pops of gun powder, Moses slips into the bedroom, reeking of whiskey and cigar smoke. In the darkness, Maggie hears the rustling of his suit and shirt dropping to the floor and feels his weight against her as he crawls under the covers. In a minute, he is snoring.

Catherine begins to cry, a hungry baby, always wanting more.

For the rest of the night, Maggie sits propped against the pillows, cuddling her little sweetheart, sometimes dozing, sometimes staring into the darkness, listening to the sounds of Chicago fade, then begin again as Friday morning deliveries commence and the last party of drunkards passes through their alley singing tuneless rounds of *row, row, row your boat, gently down the stream; merrily, merrily, merrily, merrily, life is but a dream.*

January 1 is the feast of the circumcision of Christ, a holy day of obligation. Mass is required. Maggie rises, lights a lamp, and gets herself and her girls dressed. Then, she gives Moses a poke.

"Time for church," she says. "We're going to early Mass."

When he starts to speak, she can only say, "I don't want to hear a word from you."

❦

Moses was not so loaded last night that he can't remember what happened. He is horrified at how fast he caved in to Biddy's seduction. The booze—he swears to go on the wagon, at least till Maggie forgives him. Still, it amounted to nothing—a brush with Biddy's bosom, a few seconds of excitement. He was about to push her off him when Maggie turned up the light.

They walk to church in silence. Too much silence. Maggie finally gives him the elbow and mutters, "You'll talk to the neighbors like you always do, hear me? And you'll take Communion with me."

Moses musters a smile and tips his hat at the next passerby.

Back home, Maggie clatters the plates as she puts breakfast on the table. When they sit down to their ham and cheese sandwiches, she finally speaks.

"Here it is, Moses Flanagan. We are leaving Chicago. We'll pack up our belongings this weekend. Monday, you're quitting your job and we'll take the evening train to St. Louis."

He is dumbfounded. "Maggie, I'm so sorry—it isn't necessary—I'll cut Jerry off—we don't—"

She holds up a hand. "It's time. Last night was only the final straw.

We have to get out of this place, out of this city. We need a fresh start."

"I can't start over just like that. I have to plan, to line up a new job. We have no people in St. Louis."

She reaches through the side slit in her skirt, into the tie-on pocket beneath, where she keeps her rosary, a small scissors, a magnifier, her key, a small notepad, a hankie, and the gold necklace he gave her, among other necessities and valuables. Pulling out a small embroidered pouch, she slides it across the table to him. "We'll be the first. Pioneers. Isn't that what America is all about?"

He opens the pouch to find a thick wad of cash.

"I've been saving our money," she says. "Every spare penny since our wedding. We have train fare and enough to rent a room till you find a job, which I'm sure will be very soon." She retrieves a scrap of paper from her pocket and smooths it out on the table. "This company, Nelson Manufacturing, is located in St. Louis. They are hiring and they have profit-sharing."

Moses takes the paper. He's heard of Nelson a couple of times at the union hall—run by a rich fellow with progressive ideas. He knew of men who packed up their families for St. Louis. But was it really any better than Chicago?

"I don't know, Margaret. I can't promise you'll find rose gardens in another coal-fired city."

She reaches across and presses her fingers to his lips. "I don't need promises, Moses. I need hope."

Moses is surprised to feel tears well up in his eyes. He expected Maggie to punish him, to chain him to the doghouse. But instead, she has liberated him to dream again. He was once thrilled to accept the obligations of a family man, but no matter how sweet the burden, it is heavy. Suddenly, Maggie is not the dependent he vowed to care for, a passenger sitting in the back of his wagon, but a beautiful and clever partner, sitting beside him, holding the map, pointing out the road ahead.

Moses takes her hand. "Then we'll go."

Moses retrieves shipping crates from the alley behind the greengrocer's shop. He repairs and reinforces them while Maggie decides which of their scant possessions will make the trip. She pads her precious pieces of painted china with clothing as Moses dismantles and crates the sewing machine.

On Monday, Moses heads to the planing mill, still only half believing he's giving up his wages for a future unknown. But he does it.

That afternoon, as a gentle snow falls, they hire a wagon and two boys to haul them and their belongings to Union Station. At 6 p.m., with Maggie holding Catherine and Moses holding Nellie, they board the train for a new life in St. Louis.

Part 2. Workers' Utopia in Leclaire, 1894-1897

:: 16 ::

Spring, 1894. Kitty runs through the new house, loving the rhythm of her leather soles slapping the bare wood floors. The rooms smell of wallpaper paste and linseed oil. She stops to peek through the holes of the coal-burning stove and burns the tips of two fingers on the grate.

Her papa yells, "Get away from there, Catherine, you'll hurt yourself."

"No, I won't," she shouts back, as she curls the fingers against her dress and runs off to the kitchen.

She is three and a half years old.

Mama is holding Tommy in her lap while she snaps string beans into a bowl. "Pull up a chair, Catherine, and help with these beans."

Kneeling on a chair, Kitty breaks a couple of beans in half, but her burned fingers sting. "I want to go outside and play."

"Well, go find your sister." Mama calls out, "Nellie!"

A faint voice answers from upstairs, "What?"

"You're supposed to be watching Catherine!"

"Where is she?"

"I'm not a baby," Kitty says as she runs out of the kitchen and clambers up the stairs. She counts as she climbs—*one-two-three*—but keeps catching her feet in the skirt of the hand-me-down blue dress she's supposed to grow into. Getting the hang of holding both her skirt and the banister, she bumps her knees only twice. *Ten-eleven-twelve*.

Nellie is sprawled on their bed near the open window, gazing at *Treasure Island*. Papa has been reading it to them, interrupting it with stories of his own sailing adventure across the Atlantic. Nellie can read most of the words now and is teaching Kitty the letters.

"Where the heck have you been?"

Kitty raises her hand to show Nellie the shiny red spots on her fingers. "I burnt myself," she says, as her eyes fill with tears.

"Oh, that's nothing. I burned myself way worse than that. We might go on a treasure ship someday, so you have to toughen up."

Kitty frowns.

"Anyway, I thought we were going to read."

"I want to play outside."

"Well, come here. You're going to break your neck running around in that long skirt." Nellie takes the long ribbon out of her hair and ties it around Kitty's waist, blousing the dress over it. "That's better."

With a kiss on top of Kitty's head, Nellie spins her sister around toward the stairs.

Halfway down the stairs, Kitty's feet slip out from under her. She slides down the last few steps on her butt. Gulping down her tears, she races out to the front porch. The screen door slams behind her.

She looks down the winding street at the line of pretty, new houses, all different colors and all with rows of tulips and daffodils in front. She looks at each house and reminds herself who lives there, till the lump in her throat fades. Then, she straightens her dress and positions the ribbon-belt just like Nellie did.

Down the street, girls have chalked a hopscotch game onto the wooden plank sidewalk. They take turns hopping, jumping, and spinning in the air. Kitty runs out to join them. "I want to play, please? Pretty please?"

They give her a turn, but her legs are too short and she falls. Cinders, blown in from the street, tear through her stocking and skin her knee.

As one of the girls helps her up, she shouts, "It's nothing! I've been hurt much worse than this!"

She wishes Nellie had come out with her.

Kitty races back toward the house but veers away, afraid of upsetting Mama for messing up her spotless new dress.

Knee throbbing, hands stinging, she sits on the neighbor's front steps, choking back the little sobs that sound like hiccups.

The screen door slams and Mrs. O'Brien steps onto the porch. Even though Kitty tries to squeeze herself invisible, the neighbor sits next to her and hands her a damp washrag.

"I saw you stumble, Kitty. That must hurt."

Kitty tries to say thank you and wants to explain that she's not a crybaby, but her throat is too tight.

Mrs. O'Brien dabs at Kitty's knee and assures her that a few darning stitches will make her stocking like new. She wipes the dirt and cinders from Kitty's hands. Reaching into her pocket, she pulls out a fat chunk of white chalk, presses it into Kitty's hand, and folds Kitty's fingers around it.

"Don't you worry, sweetie, by next year you'll be the best hopscotch player in town."

Kitty takes the chalk and clutches it against her heart, smiling. *Yes, she will be.*

:: 17 ::

Maggie stands up, puts eighteen-month-old Tommy on the floor, and watches him toddle off toward Moses, who is reading the Sunday *Globe-Democrat* in the living room. She straightens her apron and runs a hand over her belly. Another summer baby is due mid-August, her fourth in six years.

After three years of crowded city living in St. Louis, the Flanagans have moved across the Mississippi to the pretty little village of Leclaire, Illinois, just south of Edwardsville. They live in a new six-room house on a third of an acre, every day full of beauty.

There are no rats, no roaches, no fleas. The family's perpetual coughs and runny noses have faded away. With plenty of clean, crime-free space for her children to play in, Maggie sets up her sewing machine again. She gets out her paints to decorate dishes again. And she can garden. Taking advantage of the community's free greenhouse services, she has already planted two rose bushes on either side of the porch steps, to complement the beds of spring bulbs planted when the house was built.

She thinks back to their long journey to get here. Her hope for easy access to St. Louis profit-sharing was dashed. Moses was turned away from a job at Nelson Manufacturing, told that all the open jobs were for metal workers.

They rented a narrow flat at 2130 O'Fallon, crammed into a row of fifteen two-story brick dwellings. The wooden sheds along the alley behind them were crowded with immigrants just off the boat and they all had to share a handful of flush toilets located in the crap-strewn and rat-infested yard in between. Their sliver of living space was located just west of the notorious Kerry Patch, once a haven for Irish squatters, now a crime-ridden slum, teeming with street gangs, saloons, and cockfights. The Flanagan's situation was ten times worse than Chicago and Maggie had only herself to blame.

After getting through the winter months of 1891 working day labor at several nearby lumber yards, Moses snagged a steady job at the Mississippi Planing Mill. They moved to a better flat on North Twelfth just through the alley from the mill. Moses quickly got promoted.

A year flew by and on July 31, 1892, Tommy was born.

In Maggie's mind, their son's arrival marked a turning point. Moses was recruited to run a crew at Crescent Planning Mill on Ninth and they moved yet again to a flat at 1326 Nineteenth Street across the alley from St. Vincent's Orphanage. At Crescent, the turnaround time for Moses's crew got the attention of a manager at Nelson Manufacturing, who invited him to the company's annual meeting, which included a chartered train across the river for a tour of the company's new factory town of Leclaire.

Maggie will never forget Moses's arrival home that Saturday evening, bubbling with excitement. He pulled her up from her chair and waltzed her around the room. "I have seen our future," he announced. "I have seen the promised land. Single-story factories, with state-of-the-art ventilation and *windows* looking out on *trees* and *gardens*. Quiet streets. Houses with yards for children to play in. The workers themselves named the village, after *Maison Leclaire*, a French experiment in profit-sharing. An amazing place!"

It was Moses at his finest, an enthusiastic believer in a progressive future.

"I spoke to Mr. Nelson on the train home," Moses continued, "and told him my ideas for improving the efficiency and quality control in planing mills and the importance of hiring men who are not just machine operators but artisans, men who know a beautiful curve from an unbalanced one. I think he's interested in me, Maggie."

It took months of negotiation and planning, but by the end of 1893, Moses was hired as the superintendent of the Cabinetry division at N.O. Nelson Manufacturing and the Flanagans received an interest-free loan to buy their new home in Leclaire. The future had arrived.

The screen door slams and knocks Maggie out of her reverie. Kitty marches in, her arms full of something wrapped in a tea towel. She lifts it up and dumps her burden onto the kitchen table. Fresh asparagus!

"Mrs. O'Brien says *here*," she yells.

"Use your indoor voice, young lady. And I can see by your red nose you've been bawling. Tell Mama what's going on."

"I wanted to play hopscotch, but I fell." Her eyes well up with tears.

Maggie wipes her wet hands on her apron and crouches to examine Kitty. The Sunday dress is dirty and stocking is torn.

"It's nothing to be crying about. Go put on your gingham dress and fresh stockings, then bring me my mending basket and the bottle of iodine for your knee. And tell Nellie to get herself down here."

Kitty takes after Moses, chatty and busy, a different personality altogether from Nellie, her artful dreamer. Maggie is thankful for the move to Leclaire, where Kitty can bring home asparagus instead of head lice and worms.

Before long, everyone is in the kitchen. As Maggie peels potatoes and punches down the dough for dinner rolls, Kitty snaps the ends off Mrs. O'Brien's asparagus. With a length of yarn threaded on a large blunt needle, Nellie concentrates on darning Kitty's torn stocking. At five and a half, she has a fine hand and is already learning to embroider linen handkerchiefs.

"This is boring," she says. "I want to run away on a sailing ship."

"And do you think sailors stitch pretty little roses over the holes in their socks?"

Nellie considers this. "But sailing would be more fun. Papa says he sailed all the way across the Atlantic Ocean before I was born."

Moses is bouncing Tommy on his knee, and Maggie catches his eye.

"A fine lot of fun it is to have filthy shipmates puking on your pretty shoes and howling delirious with fever," she says. "I made that very trip myself. There's nothing glamorous about it, not at all."

Nellie frowns and weaves yarn back through her long stitches. Then: "Papa says Granny Flanagan was a sea cook. I could be like her."

Moses cracks a grin. "She's got a spirit of adventure, that one."

Maggie laughs. "Ha! Granny Flanagan worked on those fine little steamers that took ladies to their country estates down the coast from Dublin. If you want that kind of life you can go back to St. Louis and serve tea on the big steamers going to New Orleans."

"I know how to make tea," Kitty says. "Can I go with you, Nellie?"

Nellie slams the half-darned stocking onto the sewing basket and stands up. "First, you have to know how to mend your own dang stockings."

"Miss Flanagan, mind your tongue," Maggie says.

Kitty giggles and looks adoringly at her big sister.

Maggie feels a little kick in her belly and is suddenly overwhelmed with joy. She imagines her family as a new rendition of *Little Women—Flanagan's Flock*. Her children are just as bright and spirited as the March girls she once envied, but they have a father. All they need now is a piano.

:: 18 ::

In June, 1894, the community buzzes with news that the famous New York *World* reporter Nellie Bly is coming to investigate how life in the company town of Leclaire compares to life in the company town of Pullman, Pennsylvania.

When Mr. Nelson escorts her into the cabinetry shop, Moses sees a woman about Maggie's age, a slim woman with a notepad and pencil, whose eyes scan the layout of brightly lit machinery. He joins the entourage.

As he finishes their tour, Moses can't help acknowledging Miss Bly's accomplishments. "My wife and I followed your round-the-world adventure in the *Chicago Tribune*. *Around the World in Eighty Days* is one of Maggie's favorite books." He hears himself gushing but goes on. "And *you* made it in seventy-two! We named our first child *Nellie* because we wanted her to be as smart and enterprising as you, Miss Bly." It's a fib, of course. Nellie was a year old when Bly began her adventure, but who could be a better hero for his girl to model herself on?

Glowing with the praise, Bly rummages through her bag for a publicity photo of herself in her famous checked coat and wool cap, carrying her leather duffel. She hands the cardboard rectangle to Moses. "For your Nellie. Good travels to her."

That evening, Moses ducks out of the house to hear Bly's talk about her round-the-world adventure. It is thrilling.

As he strolls home, the sunset pink fades and stars begin to twinkle. Suddenly, Leclaire seems too small a vessel to hold all the things his daughters could accomplish. In this quiet little town, will they get their education only to marry factory hands?

He and Maggie have none of the panache of Nellie Bly, but they did each travel on their own from Ireland to America, then halfway across America to Chicago. They did figure out the everyday puzzles of penniless immigrant life in overcrowded Chicago, then in St. Louis, and at long last in their tiny Eden of Leclaire.

Like princesses in a castle, would his daughters never meet a stranger, never worry about their next meal, and only hear about the world through lectures at the lyceum? He heaves a sigh at this dark thought, but can't chase it away.

:: 19 ::

Hot weather comes with an explosion of color in Leclaire as flowers bloom around every house. How often does Moses walk home from the factory to find his girls have planted another row of English daisies or columbines or violets. Nellie's kindergarten class is taught by a gardener and she's brimming with new words and know-how as the greenhouse boy delivers a flat of baby plants every few days. Maggie designs the flower beds and ties string between sticks to mark the rows, then Nell uses her artful eye to position the plants just right. Kitty is an energetic hole-digger who likes getting her work done fast. They sing as they work, their voices loud and gleeful. *Row, row, row your boat gently down the stream; merrily, merrily, merrily, merrily, life is but a dream.*

August is kicked off by Tommy's second birthday on July 31, followed by Kitty's fourth birthday on the twelfth. The day after that, Maggie sends Moses for the midwife, Mrs. Haag, and she delivers Joseph Timothy. In no time, Maggie is back on her feet, back in the kitchen, and instructing Nellie and Kitty how to keep Tommy out of her hair.

The evening before Nellie's sixth birthday on the twenty-second, Moses makes an announcement at dinner. He has received a raise. "So, in honor of Nell's birthday, a very special surprise will arrive tomorrow."

"Tell us, Papa!" Nellie begs.

"I hope it's a dog!" Kitty shouts.

"Doggie!" Tommy echoes.

"I'm keeping it secret. You'll just have to wait."

He is as excited as they are. He hasn't forgotten how Nellie Bly made him worry about the future of his talented girls in their tidy village. He thinks of his dear mother, working on the coastal ferries out of Dublin, a perpetual servant, invisible to those she served. Not his vision. He wants his girls to be as refined, skilled, and loving as Maggie but as bold and worldly as Nellie Bly. He made a frame for the cabinet card photo Miss Bly gave him and hung it in the girls' bedroom. He wants to feed their ambitions. He wants to make sure they understand that they will succeed in anything they set out to do.

He's not so worried for his boys. After a taste of factory work in Leclaire, Indian wars, gold rushes, and homesteading opportunities will draw them into the vast western states.

But his girls? They already love books and even little Kitty is beginning to read. How can he encourage them on their path into the world? The answer came to him quickly and he made arrangements.

In bed, Maggie whispers to him, "You're not even going to tell *me* what the big delivery is tomorrow?"

"I want it to be a surprise for you too, Maggie."

The baby fusses and Maggie reaches out to rock his cradle.

"It better not be a dog," she says.

Moses lies awake that night picturing the future in his mind, praying he'll always make good choices for his family.

The next afternoon, he arrives home in time for Nellie's birthday party, a picnic with three of her school friends on the front lawn. Maggie and Kitty serve them cherry pie and lemonade. Then, just as the girls begin a game of hopscotch, a horse-drawn cart drives up to the house.

Everyone squeals with delight. His surprise has arrived—a shiny black upright piano.

Both girls enroll in piano and voice lessons. Soon the piano bench is full of sheet music and evenings are full of practice.

"This feels very American," Maggie says to him. "A prosperous little town with flower beds and healthy drinking water. Now a piano in the parlor."

Maggie and the children are amazed that Moses can play a repertoire of jaunty tunes, learned by ear as a youth. He can approximate any song the girls challenge him with, disguising his mistakes with chords and ornamentation.

Maggie teases him. "Here we are in the heart of a new world and you can turn any song into an Irish reel."

He changes his tune to a familiar old lament. "But we should never forget," he says, "that the blood pumping through the marvelous mechanical heart of this new world is Irish."

:: 20 ::

1895. Moses is on top of the world. As superintendent of N.O. Nelson Manufacturing's planing and cabinet mill, his department turns out finished woodwork for builders—mantels, bathroom fixtures, decorative doors, window frames, and fine cabinet pieces. Despite the Panic of '93 and the two years of economic depression that follow, business is expanding. He spends much of his time hiring mechanics and artisans for the demanding work.

In November of '94, the metal shop was organized by the United Brotherhood of Brass and Composition Metal Workers. Then in April of '95, the International Woodworkers Union organized the men in Moses's shop. Mr. Nelson is adamant that union contracts be negotiated in the spirit of his cooperative working principles. To this end, he decides that all his plant superintendents need to meet monthly at the company headquarters on Duncan and Boyle in St. Louis. The men will stay overnight to boost the spirit of fellowship among them.

The October meeting is Moses's first time away from Maggie and his first trip back to St. Louis, which is an hour away by train. As they cross the Mississippi over the Eads Bridge, Moses is excited to see the jam of steamboats along the riverfront and to catch a glimpse of New Orleans barges unloading their merchandise into boxcars.

He thrills at the sight of black smoke billowing from chimneys, tinting the blue sky green. As they take the streetcar west to headquarters, he inhales the sweet old perfume of wood fires burning in ashcans along the avenue, despite how the soot makes his eyes water.

People in a hurry crowd the sidewalks, dashing in and out of shops. Two horse-drawn carriages collide, their drivers cursing one another. A policeman chases a group of boys down a side street, waving his nightstick.

Oh, how he misses city life!

At the end of the day's meeting, two men, colleagues from Leclaire's metal shop, invite Moses to go drinking with them. *Yes!* The founding citizens of Leclaire made it a dry town, so unless a man has the wherewithal for a special trip into Edwardsville, there is never an opportunity to hoist a pint and unwind with his comrades.

From Nelson headquarters, the men work their way east through several saloons, each one leaving Moses looser and more jolly, whistling old Irish airs to himself.

"Ah, here we are," Smythe says, as they stop in front of a saloon on the ground floor of a small hotel.

The neighborhood is unfamiliar. Moses knows Carr Square and the Kerry Patch, but his pals call these blocks between Chestnut and Pine *Chestnut Valley*. Instead of the pallid faces of Irishmen, he sees only blacks—children of slaves recently moved north from Mississippi, forming their own version of the nearby Irish ghetto. Moses is both terrified and curious.

"What the hell—?" he asks.

"Brown sugar," Smythe says, poking Moses with his elbow. "You born yesterday, Flanagan?"

Moses's cheeks burn. "I damn well know a bawdy house when I see one. You boys do what you want. I'm heading back to the hotel."

But he doesn't go straight back. He stops at another saloon and sits at the bar. He orders a beer and someone lights a cigarette for him. The piano player sits not ten feet away from him, banging out a tune that assaults his ears.

Moses watches the player's hands and the music starts to make sense. He taps his foot. The beats are off, all askew, but the sound is infectious, energizing, taking him somewhere he's never been.

He asks the bartender about the music. The big man shrugs. "I dunno. Comes from the fields. Work songs and spirituals. Someone calls, people call back. Offbeat summons the Spirit. Young guys makin' it ragtime."

On his walk to the hotel, Moses hears songs coming from alleyways and open windows, soulful laments, voices full of heartache and longing.

The next morning, riding the train home with a throbbing head and queasy stomach, Moses feels confused. Proud to be successful at his trade, he's nonetheless disturbed by the lewd hypocrisy of his colleagues, so prominent at prayer circles and Bible study groups in Leclaire.

Still, he loves being back in St. Louis. He loves the drink, the edge of danger, the novelty. He is captivated by the new music, humming what he can remember of the careening melodies and tapping out the unusual beat on his armrest, wondering if he can reproduce it on the piano at home.

:: 21 ::

Maggie is thrilled to see her Moses flourish. In September, he gets his name in the paper as the man in charge of renovating the retail space at the *Edwardsville Intelligencer* building. In the same paper, he wins plaudits for giving factory tours to summer-session students from the Edwardsville Teachers' Institute.

However, the monthly meetings in St. Louis make Maggie anxious. Moses drinks there. He makes no secret of it. She's appalled when he brings home a bottle of bourbon in his valise.

"Won't we risk our good name?" she asks. "Even at weddings, I've never seen so much as a drop of sherry in this town."

"The Unitarians who run this place are hypocrites," Moses responds. "Leclaire is perfect for wives and children, but the men race to wicked St. Louis every chance they get."

Maggie looks out the window, where the children are gathered around a neighbor burning autumn leaves. The thought that her promised land is an illusion troubles her.

By the new year, Moses has changed in Maggie's eyes. Maybe it isn't St. Louis. Maybe at thirty-eight, he's maturing, facing old age.

The newspaper celebrates a job his shop completed for Louis May's saloon on the square in Edwardsville. The article credits Moses for both designing the elaborate bar fixtures, but he shrugs it off.

Quieter now, he spends more time at the piano, with one of the boys on his lap, sounding out haunting tunes with flat notes and odd harmonies.

"What is this devil's music you're playing?" she finally asks.

"Listen," he says and picks out a tune, while he sings in a soft voice:

Sometimes I feel like a motherless child
Sometimes I feel like a motherless child
Sometimes I feel like a motherless child
A long way from home, a long way from home

Maggie frowns, unsure what to think.

"I hear it in St. Louis," he says. "New music coming up out of rural Mississippi."

"Negroes?" she asks. "Why would you be associating with African people, with descendants of slaves?"

"We have a lot in common, Margaret. They're poor migrants finding their way out of poverty into a white world. They have music, songs, their own voices, their own style."

"I think it's safer to keep with your own kind, Moses Flanagan."

His head snaps toward her and his voice sharpens. "You think Leclaire is filled with our own kind? I hear the snickers about *mackerel snappers* and *Paddies* and *Micks* and the size of our families, too stupid to know how to have sex without babies."

He looks at one of Maggie's prized possessions, a painted chalk statue of the Blessed Mother. "And they think we worship Mary as if she were a god. They call it *idolatry*, a *pagan* streak among god-fearing Christians."

"I don't want to hear such nonsense," she says in a tight, quiet voice as she turns away. "There's no place on earth like Leclaire. Look how your children are thriving. Isn't that what's important?"

"You're right, but—"

"But *what*?"

"What passes for culture are musty old Wordsworth poems, read by a preacher's daughter, served with lemonade. Or yet another Chopin recital. Or the town band playing John Philip Sousa marches, I don't care how popular they are."

Maggie crosses her arms and glares at him.

"Don't you remember our Saturday nights in Chicago? Don't you miss a good storyteller? Don't you long for some real music, in a smoke-filled room with enough liquor to open your heart to life's sadness and struggle—real music, whether made by a Negro piano player or an Irish fiddler?"

"Irish *culture* is a salve on the ass of poverty, disease, and early death. I want none of it."

"Don't tell me you aren't enjoying the bourbon I bring back from St. Louis."

"What of it?" She loves a nip of liquor at the end of the day, but she won't let Moses use it to get her to admit Leclaire is boring. Her children deserve life without melodrama around every corner. "Enough of this blather," she says. "I have ironing to do."

:: 22 ::

When Valentine's Day rolls around on a Friday in 1896, Moses makes sure the children are in bed early. Maggie has been prickly lately and pushing him away in bed. His fear is that they will eventually draw apart, like so many old Irish couples do, she in her kitchen, he with his manly amusements. Silence between them.

He needs her friendship. He needs her laughter.

Pouring two glasses of bourbon, he wishes they had gramophone to play those wax cylinders of music. Lacking that, he sings his version of "Bicycle Built for Two," as he dances Maggie around the parlor floor.

"*Maggie, Maggie, give me your answer, do. I'm half-crazy over my love for you…*"

She melts in his arms. They float. They drop onto the settee. They kiss. Moses quickly unbuttons her bodice.

"Not here," she whispers.

"Here," he says.

He lifts her skirt and petticoats.

"Not here," she insists, even as he can hear her breathy excitement. "It's dirty. I'm a proper matron now. We have a proper bed."

"You are twenty-one," he says. "And we live in Chicago and I'm walking you home on a cold winter's night and we slide into a dark doorway and you raise your skirts to give yourself to me, in pure unabashed love. Love is our featherbed, dear Maggie Keville, encircled by mountains of sugar and rivers of wine."

Sometime later, candles flickering, they lie together on the floor, half undressed. "If you've given me another son tonight," Maggie says, "we're naming him after you."

And sure enough, on Wednesday, November 25, 1896, the day before Thanksgiving, Moses Rafael Flanagan is born, named for her husband and for an angel.

:: 23 ::

By the time Moses Rafael is born, Maggie is exhausted. The child is two weeks late, forcing her to carry his stubborn weight throughout her preparation for the holiday. She spends Thanksgiving in bed, sleeping and nursing her newborn, to the lullaby of voices and piano-playing from downstairs and a west wind gusting outdoors. By late afternoon, she smells roasting turkey and watches falling snow through her window.

On Friday, Maggie looks forward to another day of rest, but Moses brings her a letter from Mayo, God help us. He sits on the side of the bed while she tears it open and scans the scribbled contents.

"From my brother James, the second youngest. Oh!"

"What is it?"

"My mam. Fairy stricken. Some kind of paralysis." She closes her eyes for a moment, knowing her mother only as a whirlwind of energy. Moses moves closer, to put his arm around Maggie's shoulders.

"He's telling me the court gave him legal ownership of the farm… and that he's taken a wife, Annie Walsh. My youngest brother, Charlie—they put him on the boat… going to live with Delia in Chicago." She looks up at Moses. "Delia must have known all this then. Why didn't she let me know?"

Moses shakes his head. "She has two babies now… busy… maybe she thought James already wrote you…"

Tears bubble into her eyes. "We could have helped… sent money for Charlie's passage. We could have taken him in with us."

Moses sighs. "He'd be a fish out of water here."

Maggie knows it's true. Immigrants blend easily into the streets of Chicago. He'll fit right in living with Delia and John, and their brother Pat.

Kitty pops into the bedroom. Maggie swipes at her tears, but Kitty sees.

"What's wrong, Mama?" She crawls beside Maggie opposite Moses and kisses her cheek. "Is it the baby? Can I hold him? Can I bring you food? Mrs. O'Brien made bread this morning and said she'd send over soup later."

"I'm just tired, sweetheart. Pull the cradle closer and you can rock little Moses to sleep."

Kitty jumps up to move the cradle. "Tommy can't say his *esses*, calls the baby *Modie*. So we've all been calling him *Modie*."

"I think it's a fine nickname till he's old enough to insist on something else," Moses says. "The name of *Moses* is too heavy for a wee one to carry."

Maggie lays the baby in the cradle. Kitty rocks him, singing *Are you sleeping, are you sleeping, brother Mo, brother Mo*. Maggie lies back against Moses's shoulder and closes her eyes.

Moses murmurs in her ear. "Your mam would be so proud of you."

:: 24 ::

Anxious to boost Maggie's spirits, Moses goes all out buying Christmas decorations for the house and presents for their children. He plans a christening for Modie at St. Mary's Catholic Church in Edwardsville on January 3. As a special treat for Maggie, he asks her brother Charlie, newly arrived in Chicago, to be Modie's godfather.

Neighbors stop by for cookies and tea after the baptism, while Nellie and Kitty take turns playing the piano. Uncle Charlie keeps disappearing into the kitchen for nips of Moses's bourbon. He decides it will be very entertaining to teach his nephews fisticuffs.

"Ya got to learn to throw a good punch wit yer bare knuckles, boys, like a good Irishman." He makes great sport of teaching them about jabs and hooks in the midst of the gathering. Finally, two-year-old Joe surprises his older brother with an uppercut, knocking the air out of his lungs and leaving him gasping on the floor till he catches enough breath to start wailing.

Charlie thinks it's hilarious till he hears one of the guests mutter, "Dumb mick."

"Who you callin' a dumb mick?" he shouts and throws a roundhouse punch at the guy, who falls backward, knocks over a lamp, and sends Maggie's precious Blessed Mother statue crashing against the wall, broken to pieces. Charlie bounces on his toes, poised to fend off a return punch, but the room is full of sober Protestants. The only sound is Maggie weeping.

Moses offers embarrassed apologies as the guests grab their coats and say hurried goodbyes. Then he sweeps the remains of the statue into the dustpan. Was it a mistake to invite his greenhorn brother-in-law to staid Leclaire?

But Uncle Charlie is unfazed. "Farewell to those stiffs. Let the hooley begin!" He sweeps Joe up onto his shoulder and parades around the house singing "*Whiskey you're the Devil, you're leading me astray; Over hills and mountains and to Amerikay. You're sweeter, stronger, decenter—You're spunkier nor tay—Oh whiskey, you're me darlin' drunk or sober.*"

Moses glances at Maggie and sees her start to smile.

The day dissolves into a pleasant fog as Moses sits at the piano pounding out drinking songs while Charlie teaches the children to sing along. With a couple of shots, Maggie's spirits lift and cranky little Modie drifts into a deep sleep.

It is a joy to be Irish again.

:: 25 ::

On a Sunday evening in January, 1897, after the children are all down for the night, Moses sets a bottle of whiskey on the kitchen table and brings up the issue that has hung between them for nearly a year—his desire to return to St. Louis..

Tears well in her eyes. "Is it because Charlie punched out Mr. Johansen? Are we pariahs now?"

"No, no," Moses assures her, even though he did endure a chill on the factory floor for a few days after. "No. I've gone as far as I can go here. To get ahead, we have to go back to the city, where they pay more."

"But the profit-sharing..."

"Isn't magic. The panic last year over the gold standard and the failure of the Bank of Illinois have Nelson's inner circle battling over what goes into the pool to divvy up among the men. I can reliably make more living closer to rich industrialists and their grand building projects— right now that's St. Louis."

"But Leclaire attracts the best talent in the region," she argues, "because men want to get their families *out* of the city."

"They're draftsmen, machine operators. I'll be forty this year. I can command a decent salary. We'll live in a good house, in a clean neighborhood, with a garden just like here. No more flats. And the children can go to Catholic schools."

"It's the children I worry about. The crowds, the coal dust, the constant coughs and runny noses..."

"The children are smart and healthy. They'll be fine out in the world, rubbing elbows with all types of people, jumping on a streetcar to get somewhere, hearing new music. If we're going to live on America's frontier, then let it be the leading edge, where a truly American culture is being born."

"St. Louis." Maggie heaves a sigh, then nods. "We'll need to be organized then."

Moses notifies Mr. Nelson of his intention to move back to the city. Nelson protests and offers Moses a job in management at the St. Louis headquarters.

"That's a kind offer," Moses responds, "and one I may consider. But you know I love the smell of sawdust too much to work any distance from a shop."

In St. Louis, Moses visits the office of Tom McMahon, owner of the Crescent Planing Mill, where he worked before Leclaire. McMahon greets him like an old friend.

"We've been expanding and reorganizing," he says. "Just say the word and you can have your old supervisory job back with twice as many men and a boost in pay over what you get at Nelson."

"I'm ready!" Moses responds, extending his hand for a shake. "But we need to work out the details. I owe it to Nelson to finish some big contracts and my wife would love it if Nellie and Kitty could finish the school year."

After touring the shop and giving McMahon some ideas for immediate improvement, they agree on a September start date.

When Moses announces his good fortune to Maggie, she grabs his hand. "I'm proud of the man who makes his dreams come true," she says, "even if I'm worried to death about leaving Leclaire behind."

Part 3. Rebuilding in St. Louis, 1897-1898

:: 26 ::

Moses planned to start work in St. Louis at the beginning of the school year but a big job in Leclaire delays him till October. Meanwhile, he finds a fine little two-story house to rent on Kossuth, just three blocks from Fairground Park, where there are big annual agricultural and mechanical fairs, as well as a lake and a private zoo. Six blocks to the west is Holy Rosary Church.

When it comes time to say goodbye, his friends and colleagues throw a going-away party for him. The *Edwardsville Intelligencer* publishes his departure, with the note that he "has the friendship of all the men who worked under his supervision, and also of citizens generally." He notes that Maggie clips it out and slips it into the pages of her autograph book.

The move goes smoothly. Local merchants—enterprising Irishmen and Italians—stop by to get the Flanagans on their delivery routes for dairy, meat, produce, dry goods, and ice. Nellie and Kitty are outfitted in their navy-blue serge uniforms and enrolled in Holy Rosary parochial school.

Moses's dream of return to city life is fulfilled, but is not the musical, cosmopolitan experience he fantasized. His return to Crescent Planning Mill was a brutal eye-opening.

Yes, the business expanded over the past four years, but the factory building did not. The air is choked with sawdust and the lighting, too dim. The ventilation fans are too small and rarely cleaned so that breakdowns are frequent and the threat of fire always lurks.

While Leclaire attracted the finest mechanics and artisans from the region, the workforce at Crescent is a hodgepodge of mediocre talent, often grabbed off the surrounding lumber yards. Every one of them needs instruction and supervision. Moses organizes crews and tries to put the most skilled men in charge, but the shop steward complains to McMahon that Flanagan is violating union seniority rules.

At Nelson, Moses had his own projects and walked the floor as a peer, kidding with his men and learning about their families. At Crescent, Moses walks the floor like a beat cop. He tries to teach but often winds up yelling and demanding a job be done over. Too many men are reporting to work with whiskey on their breath and too many fingertips are lost to sharp blades with no safety shields.

It is tough on Moses not to be popular, not to know the names of his men's children, not to be greeted with a handshake and a howdy-do.

The mill shuts down over Christmas, giving Moses a needed pause, a chance to think through some strategies, even if it was at 3 a.m., while his houseful of children slept.

He reassures himself that returning to St. Louis was the right thing. In America, problems are solved with action, with bold decisions, with movement, not with old-world prayers and humility. In the Old Country, a man runs from poverty, like young Charlie Keville, beating it out of Mayo. Like young Moses Flanagan beating it out of Dublin. In America, a man runs toward opportunity. The boundless open spaces of the West are the perfect metaphor. The solution lies just over the next rise.

In the new year, he will work on better hires and to be more forceful with McMahon about working conditions. Or maybe he'll give the shop steward an education about what the union should be demanding, aside from their drone for higher wages.

He'll make it work.

:: 27 ::

Adjusting to a new school has been tough on seven-year-old Kitty. She was in trouble from the very first day, when she told Sister Mary Michael that she could read *Tom Sawyer* and the nun scolded her not to be impertinent.

Kitty shouted, "I know what *impertinent* means and I'm *not*!"

The nun grabbed her pigtail and shoved her into the cloakroom for a ten-minute standing punishment.

She and Nellie are in the same crowded classroom of primary-school girls.

"You're getting off on the wrong foot," Nellie tells her. "Use your loud voice to make friends in the schoolyard and keep your mouth shut in the classroom."

Kitty listens to her sister's advice.

By winter, all the girls want to be friends with the Flanagan sisters. With Nellie, because she carries yarn and a needle in her coat pocket and can darn closed the worn finger of a knit glove in five minutes and because she hands out clever drawings on scraps of paper. With Kitty, because she can make them laugh, is the best at calling out jump-rope jingles, and loves leading them in singing games, like "Ring around the Rosie."

Still, Kitty winds up in the cloakroom every week or two.

Kitty knows that Nellie's pocket-sized sketchbook is her prize possession, a ninth birthday gift from their parents. She hides it among her textbooks and sneaks it out while Sister Michael is busy with other children. She does her schoolwork fast, so there is always time for drawing.

One day in February, Sister Michael catches her and snatches away the pad. She flips through the drawings of flowers and faces and ornate letters. She yanks Nellie to her feet, makes her stand at the wastebasket, and commands her to tear each of her drawings into shreds.

Tears stream down Nellie's face. Their classmates are deathly quiet. When she is done, the nun makes her hold out her hands and starts cracking her fingers with a ruler—penance for her sin of pride.

Kitty is horrified, frozen in pain and embarrassment for her sister. But when the nun starts snapping the ruler across Nellie's fingers, Kitty snaps.

"Stop it!" she screams, as she flies between them.

The nun grabs Kitty by her braids and slams her against the chalkboard. Then she boxes Kitty's head so hard it makes her ears ring.

The girls are sent to the principal's office to wait for dismissal time. They walk home taking turns crying and comforting each other.

"No matter what, we can't tell Mama or Papa," Nellie says. "They'll kill us."

"But what did we do wrong?" Kitty is mystified.

"You *hit* a *nun*. You have to go to confession for that. And you might have to do time in Purgatory when you die."

"But she was hitting *you*. You're a little girl!" She mops up the tears with her gloves.

It seems magical to Kitty that Mama is standing on the porch, like she is waiting for them, like she knows they are in trouble. The moment they turn toward her, she says, "Jesus, Mary, and Joseph. What in God's name happened?"

"Nothing," they say in unison.

"Catherine Margaret, speak to me."

Kitty blurts out the story, in full detail, getting louder and louder as she speaks.

Mama pulls off Nellie's gloves and gasps at the welts across her fingers.

"Mother of God," Maggie says. "Nellie, go get the perambulator from out back. Kitty, help me get the boys bundled up. We need to go sort this out immediately."

"No!" shouts Kitty. "We'll get into more trouble!"

"Do as I say, young lady."

With her children in tow, Maggie marches to the school. Why did Moses think St. Louis and Catholic schools would be an improvement for his family?

When they arrive at Holy Rosary, Maggie pulls a blanket around Modie and Joe, then instructs Nellie, Kitty, and Tommy to sit with them on the steps outside while she talks to the principle. "And stop your bawling, girls. You've done nothing wrong."

With no time to waste, Maggie barges into the principal's office. "My name is Margaret Flanagan and one of your nuns injured and humiliated my daughters Nellie and Catherine."

The principal, a stout woman in a medieval black veil, stands with her fists on her hips. She begins to lecture Maggie on the discipline needed to educate children from poor and ignorant families.

Maggie cuts her off. "We're not poor. And we certainly aren't ignorant," Maggie pulls herself tall, chin out, and moves toward the door. "If you can defend striking children and tearing up their creative work, their personal property, then my daughters will not be returning to school here."

She marches back to the street and the five children she will protect forever.

When Moses gets home, Maggie sends the children upstairs and tells him what happened. When he jumps to his feet in anger, she says, "Calm down. I've taken care of it. I informed the principal that our girls don't need any kind of education that involves pain and humiliation. You can confirm this with Father Lavery after Mass on Sunday. Let him know he won't be seeing any more monthly tuition envelopes from the Flanagans."

"But their education—"

"They can go to Ashland on Natural Bridge in the fall. Tommy will start there too. Meanwhile, they'll help me with the housework in the mornings, then I'll supervise them reading books, drawing, and playing the piano. We'll go to the library tomorrow for books."

Moses squints at her plan, then nods. "I can give them math problems and check them after work. And, yes, I'll give Father Lavery a piece of my mind on Sunday."

:: 28 ::

Kitty learns what a telegram is when one is delivered to their door on the night before St. Patrick's Day.

"Mother of God," Papa cries as he reads what's on the thin yellow paper. He looks at Mama as he plops onto a chair. "Denis is gone. Killed in a railroad yard accident."

Kitty watches from the kitchen table, where she is working through a sheet of multiplication problems and Nellie is struggling with long division. Mama has been reading *Tom Sawyer* to Tommy and Joe, while Modie sleeps in her lap. Her rosy cheeks turn paste-white.

"Like John Walsh," she says. "Another widow with babies…"

Kitty remembers her Uncle John dying last summer before they moved back to St. Louis. Mama was terribly upset. But they got to take the train with her to Chicago, she and Nellie and baby Modie. Kitty got to meet her godmother Aunt Delia and her cousins Mary and Peggy. She got to meet her Uncle Pat who picked her up with his enormous strong arms. Uncle Charlie was there too, remembered from Modie's christening. The days were a strange mix of tears and laughter that Kitty enjoyed very much.

Denis, Kitty figures out, is Papa's younger brother, a railroad worker with three little girls. This upsets Mama more than anything.

"How will Kate get by? That poor woman, losing her little Timmy, then her little Katie—remember that? After we moved to Leclaire, right after Joe was born. Only fifteen months old." She hugs Modie close to her. "How does a woman survive loss after loss? How will she protect those girls?"

Moses stares at the floor as Joe climbs into his lap. "She has a couple of single brothers there. Maybe they'll do what Delia did, throw their lot in together. Maybe a married sister, too, I forget."

Uncle Denis's death rattles the household for days. Mama is fretful. On Thursday night, Papa takes the Midnight Special up to Chicago for the funeral and is home by Saturday morning, collapsing into bed. Mama doesn't want to leave his side.

:: 29 ::

May comes. Both Kitty and Nellie are worried about hearing their mother puke every morning. Walking to the library for their weekly book exchange, they hold hands and recite Hail Marys, so that the Blessed Mother will keep Mama from dying.

But before long, Maggie tells them that Christmas this year will bring them a new little sister or brother.

"That's why I may seem sick, my dears, but I'm really not. It's a blessing from God."

Kitty believes Mama that another baby is good news, but in bed that night, Nellie seems put out. "Why does she have to go having more babies? It will only make us poorer and more crowded."

Kitty agrees that they don't need another brother but maybe a baby sister would be fun.

"Fun, my eye," Nellie says. "We'd have to share our room with her and she'd get all Papa's attention. We'll be back in school by then and he won't do arithmetic with us at night. He'll be all about the boys and a baby."

Kitty reaches out to pat Nellie's hair. "We have each other, Nell. Let's practice piano more together. We can learn more duets."

"We'll stick together," Nellie says as she hugs Kitty close.

On December 21, 1898, Mary Ethel Flanagan is born.

Part 4. Maggie's Pain, 1903

:: 30 ::

"The thing is, Catherine, come rain or shine, the wagonloads of cured wood arrive at my factory door all day, if not from the lumber yard, then up from the river barges. I group my orders by type. Some days it might be windows, the next, wainscoting. The men and the equipment are ready to transform that lumber as fast as possible into woodwork, out the other door of the shop, onto another wagon to be delivered up to Forest Park." Papa nudges six-year-old Modie off his lap. "Go get me the bottle and two glasses."

Papa was late again and Mama is bristling. She sits at the other end of the table holding the baby and instructing Nellie how to beat the lumps out of the gravy she made a big mess of. At fourteen, Nellie should know better than to add cold broth to the grease before the flour's all absorbed.

"Like I was saying to your mother, the whole thing has to go like clockwork and when a few men show up all puffy-eyed from too much celebrating after the St. Paddy's Day parade, the whole operation goes to hell."

Tommy and Joe giggle at Papa's saying *hell* and Mama snaps at them to finish their work or go upstairs without dinner. Shelling peas is normally Kitty's job, but the boys are being punished for fighting in the living room and knocking over a lamp. It's taking them forever, while Kitty sets the table and four-year-old Ethel places the silverware at each plate.

"Fork on the left," Maggie reminds her.

Papa pours a finger of whiskey in each glass and passes one to Mama.

"Tell us what happened," Kitty says. "Did someone saw his fingers off? Was there blood everywhere?"

Moses laughs. "Nothing that terrible, my dear."

Kitty loves hearing Papa talk about the World's Fair preparations: the thousand temporary buildings for Forest Park, new hotels for millions of visitors, new streets for transportation to and from, more efficient sewerage systems to keep the city smelling sweet, and improved water purification so visitors don't wind up spreading cholera or some such horror.

And she loves hearing about his work: how fast the clerks do the paperwork; how mechanics keep the planers, molders, saws, and other machinery in tiptop shape; how the carpenters shape wood according to spec without deviation; how he inspects everything and plans the next day's work. And of course, she loves hearing about the disasters, too.

"When is your work going to make us rich, Papa?" Nellie asks. "Then we can hire a cook and a housekeeper and Mama will get all better."

The kitchen falls silent for a moment, as all eyes jump to Mama, who shoots a glance at Papa before she throws her head back in a laugh. "Nothing wrong with me that seven obedient children can't cure."

They lapse back into their dinner routine, but Kitty has noticed the glance and knows all is not well.

Ever since Loretta Julia was born in January, 1901, Mama has been touchy. Yes, Julie was underweight and sickly. Yes, the tiny house on Kossuth finally got impossible with seven children.

Papa found them a five-room rental nearby at 4221 Farlin. Mama's irritable moods should have been cured with more space, but they only got worse.

It didn't help that in October of 1902, Mama got word from Ireland that her mother, long paralyzed from a stroke, passed away. The letter from Uncle James told Mama the death was a blessing, but she collapsed into tears, so sad that she hadn't been there to hold her dying mum in her arms. Papa consoled her and said how proud her mother-in-heaven must be of her daughter and seven beautiful grandchildren in the great city of St. Louis. But the darkness never left her eyes.

She heard Papa whisper to her about seeing a doctor, but Mama hushed him.

Tonight, after dinner, while Mama supervises Tommy and Joe doing dishes, Ethel brings Papa his mail.

"Chicago," he mumbles as he slices an envelope open with his pocket knife. It's a letter on black-bordered stationery. He shakes his head, the rims of his eyes redden, and he passes the letter to Mama. "Jerry..."

Kitty pauses her sweeping.

"*We lost our Jerry*," Mama reads. "*March 5... work at the yards... heart attack*. Oh, Moses! *Funeral delayed till I get insurance money... April 6*."

"I'll wire Biddy tomorrow." Papa pulls a small calendar from his shirt pocket, his calloused hand shaking. "The sixth is a Tuesday. I'll take the train on the fifth, go to the wake and funeral, and catch the evening train back."

"But your work," Mama says.

"I can miss two days," he says, resting his head in his hands. "There's time to plan. It'll be fine."

The children gather round, their faces full of questions.

Mama digs into her skirt pocket and counts out some change. "Tommy, darling, run and get us some ice cream. We'll have dessert tonight."

Nellie picks up the letter. "I don't understand. I thought parents were supposed to live to see their children grow up, keep them off the streets and out of the poorhouse. This is the third uncle we've lost. We have seven cousins now growing up without a father—*all* of them by my count. In *America*! Why go to the trouble to be an immigrant if you're going to drop dead anyway!"

"Enough." Papa grabs Nellie's hand. "Terrible things happen, it's true. Families pull together is all I can say. We do what needs to be done.

"Don't you go worrying," Maggie says pulling Julie up onto her lap. "Your papa doesn't do the kind of labor that puts men in an early grave. You'll graduate from Ashland in June, then go on to Visitation Academy for a fine education. Don't fret about Uncle Jerry's boys. Aunt Biddy is very resourceful."

:: 31 ::

Kitty isn't at all consoled by her mother's words, She can tell when her parents are rattled. And she can tell something isn't right with her mama. Nellie knows too.

Lying in bed together, they compare notes. Nellie says she overheard Mama tell Mrs. Kennedy that Julie would be healthier if her milk hadn't dried up so fast, and with her milk dried up she was surprised not to be expecting again.

"*Like clockwork*," Kitty says mimicking Mama's favorite description of herself. "Never a sick day in her life. A baby every two years, *like clockwork.*"

"Her clock has gone haywire," Nellie says. "Her monthlies have become dailies. Have you noticed, she uses sanitary towels every day. Washes them out in the bathroom and hangs them on the clothes tree behind their bedroom door so we don't see. But I caught on. I don't think that's normal."

"We should help her more after school," Kitty says.

"And mornings. I think I can finally make enough porridge for us all without scorching the pot."

"And I'll line everyone up to wash their own bowl."

Kitty grabs Nellie's hand and they drift off to sleep.

❦

Maggie stares into the dark. The window is open and she smells lilacs. Are they blooming already? She has no time to notice. Moses leaves the house at 6:15, leaving her to the morning melee of getting five children dressed, fed, and out the door to school, always worrying about their long trek to Ashland, wishing she hadn't rejected school at nearby Holy Rosary. The nuns may be harsh, but the children learn to behave, a big help to Catholic mothers coping with full houses.

And the endless laundry and scrubbing! How did her dear mother do it with ten?

She tries to forget the gnawing pain in her belly, but it keeps her awake at night and saps her energy. The bloody discharge worsens by the day.

She consulted her midwife. "I suspect it's an eighth child whose soul has gone to heaven and whose wee body needs to return to earth."

Maggie was horrified by the image, and drank the midwife's turpentine purgative. The cramps that night dropped her to her knees, making her beg to the Blessed Mother to keep Moses from noticing.

Nothing changed. The soulless child hung on.

Last week, the midwife gave her a tonic for the pain, but it made her loopy. Why not just drink whiskey?

Tonight, after the children were in bed, while she scoured a burnt saucepan, Moses brought it up again, acting more concerned for her bellyache than for his brother's fatherless boys.

She snapped at him. "How many times do I have to tell you, it's wear and tear. I'm out of spec, like one of your big machines, off my rhythm, tolerances in need of adjustment. Make love to me tonight, Moses, and we'll have another baby by Christmas. Perform your quality control magic. Give me another child to cure me from the inside out." She flipped the pot over onto a towel to dry.

Moses set his strong hands on her shoulders and turned her toward him. He hugs her close, not minding her wet hands on his shirt. "For the love of God, Margaret," he murmured, "see a doctor."

She yanked away. "I'm dealing with it."

But she isn't dealing with it. It's making her crazy, the pain all the more ferocious tonight with Jerry's sudden death.

What cruel God takes men from their families?

Jerry leaves two sons, Timothy and James, about eleven and nine, leaves them with a mother Maggie still remembers as a loudmouth floozy who tried to seduce Moses on that terrible New Year's morning in Chicago.

She never cared much for Jerry, so different from her Moses. Tall and rough-spoken, forever carrying a whiff of the stockyards, blood and shite. A big lug, like her boy Joe is growing up to be.

"No," she says aloud and curls around the nastiness in her belly. *Joe won't be like Jerry*, she tells herself, *not if I'm around to teach him manners and respectful behavior*. But she knows the pain—the belligerent, soulless child—is going to kill her, that it is some terrible malignancy she will never escape.

As she admits to herself that it's time to see a doctor, sleep washes over her. She dreams of Chicago, of running for the trolley, of reaching her hand up for Moses to catch, but doubling over with the pain and falling back, the world turning black.

:: 32 ::

On Monday, April 5, Moses arrives in Chicago with his small overnight bag. Bridget has had time to arrange an elaborate funeral for Jerry and Moses walks in on day three of a three-day wake at Jerry's home. The house is a mess. While a couple of women friends gather up empty bottles, dump ashtrays, and wash dishes before the final day of mourning begins, Bridget stumbles around in her black dress, slender and pale, her eyes unfocused.

She greets Moses with an off-balance hug, reeking of alcohol.

“What will I do now?” she asks him. “The insurance won’t last forever. I’ll have to go work in a factory.”

Moses looks for comforting words but finds himself wishing he’d never come.

Kate Flanagan, Denis’s widow comes by in the evening, looking gaunt and shabby.

As she stands next to Moses, staring at Jerry’s corpse in the wooden coffin, she says, “Did Biddy ever tell you I was with child when Denny was killed? Baby Ita was born but couldn’t face the world fatherless, so she joined Denny—and Timmy and Katie—in heaven.”

“I’m so sorry to hear that,” he says. “How are you getting by now?”

She takes a sip of her whiskey and grabs his coat sleeve to steady herself. “Managing,” she says. “My sister rented a house—you know her rake of a husband ran off to California. We all live together. Our two brothers, our five children. She cares for the children while I work as a washerwoman. It’s a life.”

Moses pulls away from her to greet Delia Walsh, with her brother Pat Keville. In contrast to Kate, she is rosy and well-dressed. Like Maggie, her sister is clever and well-organized. Turning her home into a boardinghouse for her brothers and a couple of other laboring men suits her. Seeing the Kevilles makes him want to speed home to Maggie.

The next morning a high Mass is held at St. Gabriel’s, followed by a long carriage procession to Mt. Olivet cemetery, then back to the house for lunch and more drink. Moses is anxious to catch his train, but Bridget clings to him. “We need more time to talk, Mose. Tell me what to do. How can you help your poor nephews? Your poor brother’s widow?”

Moses has to remove her hands from his hips, gripping them firmly to keep her at arm’s length. She is still a gorgeous woman with full lips and dewy brown eyes, her skin still unblemished after all these years.

She gazes into his eyes and whispers. “Don’t leave just yet. The party is over and I’m so alone.”

He can only shake his head, as he gives her a gentle push away. “You’re a clever woman, Biddy. You’ll work it through.” Grabbing his valise, he catches his carriage to the train station.

:: 33 ::

Maggie asks a few women friends for the name of a doctor and comes up with one nearby. Still, she finds excuses not to visit him. Eighth-grader Nellie needs help with her application to Visitation. Six-grader Catherine has been home with an earache. Then second-grader Joe and kindergartener Modie come down with scarlatina and she needs to do all she can to isolate them from the others, making Tommy sleep on the couch.

Fourth-grader Tommy finds himself in a different kind of hot water. While she is home, Kitty confides to Maggie that Tommy is being bullied by larger boys. Instead of going out for recess, he hides out with the janitor. And that the janitor stinks of whiskey. And sometimes Tommy does too.

Maggie keeps Tommy home for a few days, makes him scour the stove and scrub floors with her, all the while telling him stories about the ill fate of drunkards in the townlands around her small village in Mayo. She encourages him to work on his skills with marbles and other games played by the quieter boys.

The night Moses spends in Chicago going to Jerry's funeral, Maggie lies awake with cramping pain. Tomorrow, she'll quit delaying and see the doctor.

It is Tuesday of Holy Week. Moses will arrive home from Chicago late tonight. Pushing Julie in the pram, enjoying the bloom of magnolias and redbuds, she and Ethel walk to Mass. Then, she leaves the babies with Mrs. Kennedy while she walks around the corner to Dr. Broder's office.

He is fat and friendly, a general practitioner who has delivered many of the neighborhood children. He begins their visit with five minutes of gossip and inquiries about Mrs. So-and-so and the Whatsit family. Then he leaves her to undress.

She lies back on the exam table in her shift and stockings, covered in a sheet, feeling like a platter of turkey. No man but Moses Flanagan has ever touched her. Broder looks out the window as his rough hands press and poke around her belly through the sheet. He quizzes her about why she used a midwife for her deliveries. "It's twentieth century America, my dear," he says. "Half those women are in league with the devil, helping whores with their abortions. Time to leave Old World customs behind."

He finds a spot that makes her gasp.

"Aha, there is your painful mass. Might be nothing more serious than a fibroid tumor—quite common, completely benign. But I want you to see a gynecologist—a women's specialist—to check it out. Meanwhile, a shot of morphine now and a bottle of laudanum to take home with you should give you some respite from the pain."

Maggie feels faint. She closes her eyes, wishing she hadn't come, wishing she had stronger faith in the love of God to keep her from the rough hands of doctors.

But the morphine gives her immediate, miraculous relief.

On her way out, Broder hands her the card of Frank A. Glasgow, a member of the American College of Gynecology and Obstetrics. She frowns. Help with births and female problems should be a woman's domain. What do men know?

But she is thankful for the lack of pain on her walk home.

Maybe all she needs is the morphine and the laudanum.

No, she wasn't born yesterday. She has read newspaper articles about the scourge of morphine addiction, how it binds up a person's system and sets off an ever-increasing craving.

No. She'll use the family's new telephone to call Dr. Glasgow for an appointment.

Unfortunately, he doesn't have an opening till May, so she carries on, performing her duties mechanically, trying not to think, and stopping by Dr. Broder's office for refills of her laudanum.

:: 34 ::

Dr. Glasgow has posh offices on Washington Boulevard, near Vandeventer. There are leather chairs in his waiting room and paintings of rivers and rolling fields. A nurse escorts her to his office—more leather and framed diplomas. The gray-haired physician asks a thousand intimate questions from behind his oak desk before the nurse takes her to the exam room.

The exam is painful and humiliating. Her legs are spread, his fingers are everywhere. Something cold is inserted into her, then his hand. The mechanical device is removed and clatters onto a tray. Glasgow disappears, leaving the nurse to help her clean up and get dressed.

In his office, he is blunt.

"You need surgery, Maggie. A tumor. Can't say if it's cancerous or not, but in any event, it has to come out. A hysterectomy will get you back in action in no time."

Maggie is stunned.

Glasgow continues to speak but she is thinking of Moses, how to tell him, how to tell the children. Each child appears to her in turn, each with a special need requiring her attention. She knows she is going to die and the thought of seven motherless children paralyzes her with grief and terror.

The physician dips his pen into a bottle of ink and writes on a large desk calendar. "So, we will see you on June fourteenth at Mullanphy Hospital, get you all prepped, and conduct surgery bright and early on the sixteenth. After a week or two of recovery, you'll go home to your children right as rain. Meanwhile," he continues, "please have Mr. Flanagan stop by to work out the financial arrangements."

❦

The children have dinner early, which Kitty knows is a sign that Mama has something bad to discuss with Papa.

When he arrives home at six, Kitty and Nellie park themselves at the bend in the stairs, so they can eavesdrop. Ethel joins them. Kitty pulls her close and whispers for her to stay quiet.

Maggie speaks first. "The pain—I went to the doctor today. I need to have surgery. A hysterectomy. I saw a Dr. Broder around the corner while you were in Chicago. He gave me laudanum—that's why I've been okay these weeks. But he referred me to a gynecologist. Dr. Glasgow."

"Margaret," Papa says, then his voice drops low. The girls lean forward to hear but can't make out anything.

Nellie peeks around the corner. "He's hugging her," she whispers. Then she grabs Kitty's hand. "She's crying."

Hearing her mother sob, Kitty jumps up and runs down the stairs, flinging her arms around both her parents. Nellie and Ethel follow.

"We'll take care of everything, Mama, don't you worry," Kitty says. "I don't have to go to school. I can take care of the babies and cook."

"And I'll do laundry and housekeeping," Nellie adds.

"And I'll comb your hair," Ethel chimes in as she brushes strands of Maggie's hair away from her tears.

Mama's sobs go deeper. She buries her face in Moses's jacket. The girls rub her back and her arms, just like she has comforted them a thousand times. Slowly, their mama stops crying and the shudders subside. She pushes back from Papa's arms and pulls a handkerchief from her skirt pocket. Papa is wiping his face too.

"I'm sorry, girls. I don't want you to worry," Mama says, her voice thick but strong. "I'm not going to the hospital till school is out. Then, yes, you can help me all you want."

❦

As Maggie hugs the girls, her thoughts careen through all the scenarios of family disarray—burnt food, unwashed clothes, thickening dust and grime, infections passed from child to child… Then, she hits upon an idea.

"I'm going to write Delia, Moses, to see if she can come down while I'm in the hospital."

Delia is smart and strong. The Keville brothers Patrick and Charles could easily manage the boardinghouse while she's gone. Her daughters could squeeze in here with the Flanagan children, no problem.

"You remember Aunt Delia, girls. We went to visit her when we lived in Leclaire, when Uncle John passed away. You all loved her."

"I remember she's my godmother," Kitty says. "And she has two sweet little girls."

Then Maggie's thoughts turn dark. When she dies, maybe Delia will stay on, to take care of Moses and rear her children. Delia always wanted a big family.

No. She banishes the thought.

Maggie writes Delia that night.

Within a couple of days, Maggie receives a postcard. *Of course I'll come*, Delia writes. *Will arrive on 11th with Mary (already 7!) and Peggy (9 and bookish like her Auntie Maggie) to help you prepare.*

Maggie spends her days now cleaning cupboards, mending summer clothes, writing schedules and chore lists, and labeling boxes. With Nellie's graduation coming up, she orders a frilly white summer dress for her beautiful girl.

Maggie is preparing to die.

:: 35 ::

Moses is relieved when Delia arrives. The Keville sister brings fresh energy and the authority of a boardinghouse operator, helping

Maggie give the house a final polish, everything in its place, before hospital time. It allows him to spend time playing games with the children, reassuring them that everything will feel normal while Mama is away.

On Sunday, June 14, he arranges a large carriage so that they can all accompany Maggie to Mullanphy Hospital. When the hospital won't allow the children in, they have to shower her with kisses and hugs at the door. While they wait, Moses walks Maggie to the surgical ward.

"It looks very clean," she manages to say, looking around at the white walls and bleached sheets.

He holds her in a long embrace, hating to leave her here.

Tuesday, June sixteenth. The children are half-asleep and all on their best behavior when Moses leaves the house for the hospital. The surgery is scheduled for 8 a.m. and the hospital is two miles away, so he hires a carriage and arrives at the hospital by seven. Maggie is awake but he is surprised to find Father Lavery in her room. The priest is administering last rites.

Moses feels the blood drain from his face and leans against the door jamb. The priest finishes anointing her with small crosses of blessed oil, then takes off his stole, kisses it, and packs it with his oils and holy water into a leather satchel. As he brushes past Moses, he says, "Don't worry, Flanagan. It's routine before every operation."

Still, Moses is shaken and has a hard time putting on a cheery face for Maggie. They both have tears in their eyes as they exchange kisses.

"In a couple of short hours," Moses says, "the ordeal will be over and we'll be all smiles."

"Mountains of sugar and rivers of wine," she whispers.

At noon, Dr. Glasgow enters the waiting room, mopping the sweat off his face with a towel. His white surgical gown is stained with blood. Moses stands to greet him.

"Mr. Flanagan, she is sleeping in the recovery room now. The lab will examine the tissue, but I'm sure it was cancer—a large growth in her womb."

Moses drops into a chair. "What next?"

"Hysterectomy went well. Got her patched up. She's young, should easily spring back from the surgery and then… time will tell."

Moses senses his world wobbling and shaking, feeling like a passenger trying to change cars on a speeding train. He steadies himself for a tomorrow unknown.

It is late afternoon before Moses is escorted into the surgical ward and shown to a chair next to his slumbering Maggie. Slow fans rotate in the high ceiling, circulating fresh air from the open windows. She is so pale, so sepulchral, with her chestnut hair pinned up under a white cap. Her eyes flutter open as he presses his cheek against hers.

"Moses," she whispers.

"We're on the other side," he says, raising his eyebrows to force a brighter smile. "Mountains of sugar and rivers of wine from here on, Maggie mine.

"Thirsty," she whispers.

A nurse appears. She puts a thermometer between Maggie's lips and fiddles with a contraption attached to Maggie's arm.

"What might that be?" Moses asks.

The young woman explains that it's an intravenous set-up, a bag of sterile saline solution dripping into a vein, through tubing and a hypodermic needle. "*IV* they call it."

Moses frowns. "The purpose?"

"Mrs. Flanagan lost a lot of blood during the operation. The saline—salty like blood—brings the volume back up. Avoids shock. Dr. Glasgow knows all the latest procedures."

At home, Moses puts on a good show for the children and is grateful for Delia's cheerful but no-nonsense organization of dinner and bedtime. Julie and Ethel are thrilled to be assigned to their parents' bed and Moses sings them to sleep.

He lies on his side with a hand on Julie's thin little shoulder wondering how she would possibly do without her mother's loving care. He forces his thoughts away from envisioning doom to the puzzles of his job.

Luckily, work at the mill this week is moving at a snail's pace because the river is flooded, inundating the riverfront and much of East St. Louis, disrupting barge traffic, and redirecting the wagon drivers into emergency hauling of debris. He can take a few days away without the enterprise careening out of control.

:: 36 ::

As visiting hours open the next morning, Maggie is talkative, asking a hundred questions about the children and how Delia is managing. Moses can't take his eyes off the way the light catches her eyes and how her hair curls around her face. Pale pink roses return to her cheeks. He sits so he can hold her hand in his and feel the strength of it.

But by noon something changes. Maggie is sitting up for her bowl of broth but her first swallow catches in her throat and she spits it out with a cough.

"I must have taken too big a gulp," she croaks.

Her shoulders twitch and she massages her jawline. "In bed too long," she says. "Seizing up like a rusty gate."

Moses sees beads of sweat on her forehead and takes her hand. It is hot. His finger finds her pulse and it is racing.

"Nurse!" He calls to one passing by. "My wife has a fever."

"Oh, Mr. Flanagan, don't you be worrying. We checked Maggie's vitals an hour ago and she's doing just fine."

He stands up. "I haven't reared seven children not to know a fever when I feel one."

The nurse takes Maggie's wrist, then lays the back of her fingers against Maggie's brow. Maggie has a sudden spasm that makes her scream. As her face blanches white, her hands fly to the surgical bandages, knocking away her food tray and spilling the broth. She tries to say something but the words don't come out right.

"Be right back," the nurse says, racing out of the ward.

Within seconds she returns with the head nurse—a nun. As soon as the nun touches Maggie, she says to the other, "Call the attending. Tell him we have a tetanus case."

Tetanus? Lockjaw? What kills children who run around in bare feet over rusty nails, or men on battlefields showered by shrapnel—*tetanus*?

"How can that be?" Moses asks. "In a modern hospital?" He grabs Maggie's hand and looks into her terrified eyes, while the nurse removes the IV.

"It happens. We need to make sure she doesn't rip out her stitches and hemorrhage." The nun turns to Maggie. "I'll give you a sedative, dear, and a muscle relaxant."

"There's antitoxin for tetanus," Moses says. "I've read about it. You'll give her antitoxin too."

The nun glances up at him. "We'll do whatever we can to get her through this." The other nurse returns with a tray of syringes.

Maggie grabs Moses's arm and gasps when another spasm shakes her. "I don't… understand." She receives the shot. Her eyes flutter and close.

The nightmare begins.

Maggie disappears into a twitchy sleep. Moses smooths her hair, dabs her face with a cool compress, caresses her arms, massages her legs—anything to command his life force into her, to bring her back to him and their children.

Before long, they take her back to surgery.

"They'll try to find the source of infection," the nun tells him, "and bathe it with the antitoxin to bind up as much of the poison as possible. Pray that it helps, Mr. Flanagan."

Late that afternoon, Maggie is wheeled back to the ward, heavily sedated.

Dr. Glasgow appears, confers with the nurses out of earshot, then stands at the end of the bed "The prognosis is not good for tetanus, Mr. Flanagan. Treatment is tricky—"

"Tricky problems are my business," Moses says. "How can I—"

Glasgow raises a hand to hush him. "There is some talk of experimental treatment, but it involves getting the antitoxin directly into the brain. We're searching to see if someone local understands the procedure. It is only the slimmest thread of hope, I'm afraid."

"Give me numbers. I can make calls," Moses says.

"You need to go home to your children now. When you come back in the morning… in the morning, we'll know better what lies ahead."

It is agony to leave Maggie's side. He walks the two miles home along Grand and Natural Bridge to clear his head and to gin up some optimism for the benefit of his children.

At home he is vague and cheery, confiding only in Delia that there are "complications" that must be dealt with. After a sleepless night, he repeats the pattern in reverse, cheering his children off to school, setting off on his walk humming a tune, then filling with dread as he nears Mullanphy. He prays Maggie will be awake and smiling at him.

She is not.

:: 37 ::

On Tuesday, June 23, at 9:45 a.m., after six tormented days, Margaret Keville Flanagan dies. All efforts to reverse the explosion of toxin throughout her system failed. No miraculous brain treatment materialized. They could only manage to reduce her wrenching muscle spasms with heavy sedation and, at the end, a flood of morphine.

Moses is smoothing her hair as Maggie's twitching suddenly stops. He collapses across her frail shoulders.

She is only thirty-six years old.

How does this happen?

Someone in white helps Moses stand, hands him a handkerchief, and escorts him to a room, where he talks to a man whose name he doesn't catch. He signs papers. He is given a page of instructions that he folds unread into his jacket pocket. The man walks him out to the street and hails a cab to take him home.

On Farlin, he pays the cabbie and trudges into the house. Delia is cleaning up after lunch for Ethel and Julie, Mary and Peggy. One look at him and she knows. Tears spring to her eyes as she pulls out a chair for him. Ethel and Julie crowd against him, full of kisses. He puts his arms around them and lets his tears flow.

:: 38 ::

Kitty knows there is bad news when she and Nellie get home after school. Papa's eyes are all bloodshot and Aunt Delia's lips are a tight line. They call all the children into the parlor. Kitty sits on the floor with Julie in her lap. The day is sunny and warm, so the windows are open. Mama's roses are in full bloom, and their scent drifts in on the breeze.

Papa starts to speak, then can't. Aunt Delia tells them. Mama is dead. Her soul has gone to heaven. She will no longer be in pain.

Six-year-old Modie is the first to cry. Moses leans out and pulls the boy into his arms.

Nellie goes and sits at the piano and pounds out a series of angry chords. Delia puts her hands on Nellie's shoulders and asks her softly to please stop.

"It's not fair!" Nellie screams and collapses her head and shoulders across the piano, sobbing.

Tommy begins to sniffle. Joe punches him, then runs outside. Kitty holds Julie closer, shuddering and watching everyone through a blur of tears.

Mary Walsh speaks in a small voice. "Is it like when our papa died?"

"Yes, sweetheart," says Aunt Delia.

Then Ethel asks, "Can we see her?"

The question raises the hairs on Kitty's neck, but Aunt Delia says, "Yes. Her body will be brought here tomorrow afternoon. Father Lavery will come by to help us pray for her. Then friends can come by on Thursday morning before we all go to church for a Mass and then to the cemetery, where she will be buried.

"What good is prayer now?" Nellie asks.

Aunt Delia blinks. "Maybe you need to pray to St. Joseph to help your father. Maybe a prayer to—"

Nellie slams down the piano lid and runs upstairs.

The day goes on like this—a rotating drama of tears and temper tantrums. Papa sits on the settee with a glass of whiskey at hand, offering hugs and backrubs as each child takes a turn snuggling next to him.

Aunt Delia makes a phone call to Papa's employer, notifying him of the tragedy. She wires the Keville uncles and the Flanagan aunts, too, and tells them to stay put in Chicago.

"You don't want everyone descending on you for a big wake," Kitty overhears Aunt Delia tell Papa. "The children need you more."

Neighbors show up with fruit and flowers, cakes, and kind words. Delia sorts through the family clothing for their most somber attire, including a black dress of Maggie's for herself.

The next afternoon, under gray skies, a horse-drawn hearse from Cullen and Kelly Undertakers parks in front of the house. Bert Cullen introduces himself, then directs his assistants to carry the casket into the parlor. One of them runs back out to the hearse for a pile of black crepe, which they begin to drape on the windows and mirrors, but Moses says *no*. He consents only to a crepe ribbon tied on the doorbell pull. When Father Lavery arrives, Mr. Cullen opens the casket.

There is Mama, looking waxen, in a purple shroud that clashes with the color of her hair, hair that has curled with the day's humidity, as if she were still alive. The rosary that she took to the hospital is wrapped around her hands. Everyone cries. Ethel is loudest, so Moses lifts her into his arms.

The priest booms out a prayer in Latin and holds a thing in his hand that sprinkles holy water on their dear mama. Then he makes them all say Hail Marys with him.

Mr. Cullen leaves candles, which they light after Father Lavery leaves. The family sits the evening in a sort of vigil, eating from platters of cakes and bowls of fruit on the kitchen table.

:: 39 ::

Thursday, June 25. It's a warm day with a sprinkle of rain. Moses is up first and wakes the children. Delia helps them each dress in the most subdued of their Sunday best clothes. Nellie and Kitty braid their long hair, then put braids in Ethel's and Julie's hair. Delia starts to object when Nellie ties a bright red bow at the end of each braid but lets it go after a sharp glance from Moses.

His Maggie stolen from him, Moses can now only manage the process of her burial. He instructs his children to bow their heads and sit absolutely still during the visitation hour.

"Your mama is watching from heaven," he says.

He assigns Nellie to be in charge of Ethel and Kitty in charge of Julie. Modie is fragile and tearful, so Moses tells him to stand by his side. The Walsh girls will sit between Tommy and Joe to keep them from poking each other.

At 7:30 a.m. Delia opens the front door to a stream of neighbors who pay their last respects. Many bring small bouquets cut from their gardens and lay them on the casket. For an hour, Moses shakes hands and accepts the pity of the neighbors.

At 8:30, Cullen herds the visitors outdoors. When no one is left but the family, he removes the rosary from Maggie's hands and passes it to Moses, who drops it into his jacket pocket. Before the coffin is closed, Cullen directs the family to the pair of carriages waiting for them at the curb. From their seats in the carriages, they watch six men from the parish carry the casket out, leaving a trail of flowers. They slide it into the hearse.

Father Lavery meets them at Holy Rosary. The requiem Mass is long, with clouds of incense and songs of choir boys filling the air. Delia's stomach growls, causing Ethel to break out in giggles. Moses taps her skull with his knuckle.

When the Mass is over, they move out to the carriages again, and again watch his dear Maggie being moved to the hearse. The horses slowly clip-clop in the drizzle past their house on Farlin, past their old house on Kossuth, north on Newstead, and on and on, nearly four miles till they reach the burial plot at Calvary. They stand under umbrellas while Father Lavery says more prayers. Then the gravediggers lower the casket. One of them hands Moses a shovel and he lifts the first shovelful of dirt into the grave. *Dust to dust*.

Every member of the family is sobbing.

When the long goodbye is finally over and the family begins its walk back to the carriages, Moses approaches Father Lavery. He thanks him and hands him an envelope—the expected donation after such elaborate sacraments.

As Lavery folds the envelope into his pocket through a slit in his cassock, Moses makes a request. "Many years ago, in anger, we pulled our children out of the parochial school. Now, with this..." He nods toward the grave. "I think it would be a boon for them to return to Holy Rosary. Kitty will be in seventh grade. Ethel may be ready for kindergarten in the fall and the three boys are in between. That's five tuitions I can find the money to pay."

"I'm sorry for your loss, Flanagan. Your little one is welcome, but we don't take transfers from Ashland. The children are undisciplined. It's too disruptive for the sisters to deal with public school bad habits." He shakes his head. "You made your bed, Flanagan." With that, he turns away toward his carriage.

Feeling hollow, Moses stares after the supercilious son of a bitch.

:: 40 ::

The house dissolves into chaos after the long day's rituals. More neighbors stop by with dishes of food, while the younger children run wild in their good clothes, grabbing cakes and cookies off the kitchen table instead of having a meal.

In the late June twilight, Kitty begins cleaning up, packing the sweets into tins and deciding what needed to be refrigerated.

When the last neighbor leaves, Papa and Aunt Delia join her.

He is saying, "You can stay, you know. We can make room."

She sits at the table, slathering a slice of soda bread with soft butter. "Don't be daft," she answers.

"Oh, please stay," Kitty says. Without Aunt Delia, Mama's absence will crash down on them. None of them will know what to do.

"You must be lonely without Walsh" Papa says. He splashes whiskey into two glasses and hands one to her. "And it must be hard to make ends meet."

"I do very well, haven't you noticed?" She takes a sip. "I own a house with four boarders, including my two brothers Their contributions pay the mortgage and Catholic-school tuitions for my girls. It's a fine life."

Julie toddles past and grabs another square of cake from the table, trailing crumbs behind her.

"You'll get through this. Nellie is out of school. She can't fill Maggie's shoes, but she'll learn fast how to run a household."

Kitty's not so sure. They'll make it through summer, but what happens when Nellie starts school at Visitation in September? Maybe Kitty can leave school. Ashland can't give her any arithmetic problem she can't solve and she's already memorized enough poems for a lifetime. What good is sitting in a boring classroom when her family needs her?

:: 41 ::

On Friday morning, Moses feels a jab and awakes to Kitty standing by the bed.

"Something's wrong with the baby," Kitty says. "She won't wake up."

Moses twists to see Ethel slumbering next to him and remembers Nellie taking Julie to bed with Kitty and her. Slipping on his trousers and shoes, grabbing a shirt, he follows Kitty downstairs, where Nellie is sitting in the rocking chair with Julie in her lap. His two-year-old is awake but stuporous, with an odd perfume-y body odor.

Over the years his children have run through the usual gamut of childhood diseases but this is different. No spots. No puking. He takes the baby from Nellie's lap and presses his cheek to hers. Not feverish, but cool and clammy. Moses is stymied.

He is tired of feeling helpless against God's trickery.

He feels a jolt of anger at Maggie for abandoning him like this. It feels spiteful, as if her child-bearing parts had revolted against him, his sex, his children. She had enough of houses and washing machines and ironing boards and America. Pain became her lover and she ran away with him.

"Lord help us," he murmurs, holding Julie close, bouncing her slightly to a silent tune.

Delia appears in the doorway, still in her robe, her hair unbrushed, her eyes puffy. "What's the matter?"

"We tried to wake you up, but you wouldn't budge," says Nellie as she jumps up from the chair. "Our mother would have never slept through a daughter's cry for help!"

Nellie stands as tall as her aunt. When did that happen?

"I'm sorry," Delia says, rearing back as if her face was slapped. "I don't know—tell me what's the problem?"

"You're not our mother, that's the problem." Nellie's voice is harsh. "You boss us around but you don't hear us when we need you. What good are you?"

Delia puts her hands on her hips. "Don't you speak to me like that, young lady."

Now Moses snaps. "Shut up, Delia. Shut up and make yourself useful. Nellie doesn't need a scolding from the likes of you."

Delia folds her arms and glares back.

He hands the baby back to Nellie, looking her in the eye. "Get a grip on yourself. Please."

He buttons his shirt and pulls up his suspenders.

"Without Mama, we need a doctor," Nellie says. "Mama's doctor, Broder, is just around the corner. We can call him to come over. Or I'll get the buggy and take Julie to him now."

"I'll go with you, honey," he says softly, lifting Julie from her arms. "Get some clothes for her and find the baby buggy." His eyes meet Delia's. "You can go back to Chicago now, to your fine boardinghouse. We can take care of ourselves."

"Oh Moses, don't be an old fool. I was planning to stay for a couple of weeks while Maggie was in the hospital. I can still stay. Teach the children some basic skills… get Nellie organized."

Nellie appears again and takes Julie. "Mama wrote lists. And instructions. I can do anything." She quickly pulls stockings onto Julie's legs and exchanges her nightgown for a wrinkled dress. "We don't need you here."

When Moses and Nellie take Julie out the front door, Kitty is horrified by the sudden breakdown, by the trail of smoky anger that lingers in the room.

"That damn Irishman. Too proud for his own good" Aunt Delia mutters. "To hell with him and his—"

"No!" Kitty throws her arms around her aunt. "Please don't go. Papa's just upset. Nellie too. But *I* want you to stay. *I* want to learn skills. We need help!"

Aunt Delia hugs her, and Kitty hears her auntie's heart beating fast through her dressing gown. "Your papa's right, darling girl. You need to work on things as a family, together. Plot your course. Then, maybe the girls and I can come back later in the summer to check up on you before school starts."

"Mary and Peggy miss their friends, don't they?" Kitty asks.

Aunt Delia smiles. "And when was the last time you played hopscotch or jumped rope?"

Kitty shakes her head. "I don't remember. Last week—a century ago."

Aunt Delia kisses the top of her head.

Dr. Broder examines the listless Julie, while Nellie pets her hair, telling her not to be afraid, just like Mama would have. But none of them have been to a doctor before. Mama always knew what to do. The doctor unfastens Julie's diaper and takes a sniff.

"Ah. We'll do a blood test, but by the scent of her, she's suffering from sugar sickness. No more sweets for this young lady."

"Jesus, she's had nothing but cookies and cake for the past two or three days," Papa says. "We've been preoccupied with—"

"Yes, yes, of course, Mr. Flanagan, my condolences. A pity the missus didn't see me sooner. Maybe… Glasgow tells me the cancer was quite advanced. But then tetanus, my, my, what a wretched way to die, with spasms enough to break your bones and twist your face into a frozen grin."

Nellie goes lightheaded. "What?" she whispers.

"My God." Papa pushes a chair behind her knees, pulling her down to sit, then bending her forward so that her head is between her knees. "Jesus, Mary, and Joseph," he says, as the ringing slowly fades from her ears. "Where the hell is your good sense talking about that in front of my child?"

"Sorry, Flanagan," he says. "I didn't see a child here, but a young woman."

Nellie sits up straight to look at the doctor.

"You're lady of the house now," he says to her. "Responsibilities! This baby needs three square meals a day, lots of spinach and slabs of roast beef. You bring her back to me in September for a checkup, if she doesn't have one of these spells again sooner."

"I…" She starts to protest, to tell him that she was admitted to the prestigious Visitation Academy, but suddenly realizes there is no way she can go to high school now.

As they walk home, Papa pushes the buggy and Nellie clings to his jacket.

"You told us she went peacefully," Nellie says.

"She struggled, it's true. It was a tough week but she had a lot of strong medicine and her passing brought peace."

"Was it because she had so many children? Did we destroy her insides? Would she have been better without the hospital, without doctors cutting into her? I feel like this was a cosmic error, that it was not 'God's will' like Father Lavery keeps saying, that it was a mess of terrible mistakes made by men who think they know better than God."

Papa slows his walk and gives her a look. "You are a woman now, aren't you? I have to agree. Her passing was not part of any heavenly blueprint. It was a wrecking ball. No messages, no meaning, no moral to the story. It's shite is all. And it is now part of who we are, people with holes in our hearts, like your Aunt Delia and her girls, losing their John Walsh too young." He heaves a sigh. "All we can do now… all we can do now is put one foot in front of the other."

They stop at the front steps of their home.

"I won't be going to high school, will I?"

Papa lifts the baby out of her buggy. "Maybe next year."

Nellie fiddles with the buggy latches, collapsing it so she can lug it up into the house. A light breeze rustles the leaves of the elm trees along the street and her nostrils are flooded with the fragrance of Mama's roses, all in full scarlet bloom. "Is this where we're all supposed to be courageous now?" she asks.

"Courageous?" The rims of Papa's eyes redden. "Courage is for soldiers. And the likes of Nellie Bly, Lewis and Clark, Kit Carson. Regular people like us—let's just get up these six steps and get some oatmeal on the stove for Julie."

:: 42 ::

Late Saturday morning, a carriage comes by to take Aunt Delia and her girls to Union Station. Papa has apologized for his sharp words, but to Kitty's distress, they both agreed it was time for her to go. Kitty loves her bossy aunt and the order she brought to these terrible two weeks.

Yesterday, she helped Aunt Delia make a pot of beef stew, enough to last the weekend. This morning, the two of them cut and boiled more potatoes.

After their goodbyes, Kitty takes charge of the kitchen, mashing the potatoes with milk and gobs of butter for a simple lunch. Everyone sits at their usual places, trying not to look at their mama's empty chair, but watching Papa for his lead. His eyes bloodshot and dark, his long mustache untended on his upper lip, he nevertheless blusters with cheery energy.

He addresses her brothers. "The shed could use a good cleaning! Chase out the mice and sharpen our tools! We'll get it shipshape, lads! I'm the captain and you'll be my crew. Two scoops of ice cream for the most hardworking mate!"

That afternoon, Kitty climbs the stairs to the bedrooms, warm and muggy, as rain drums on the roof. Nellie sits on their bed, Ethel and Julie curled against her. Twenty-four hours of no sweets and wholesome food have brought the light back to Julie's eyes. Nellie is reading aloud from *Around the World in Eighty Days* by Jules Verne, a family favorite. The photo that Nellie Bly gave Papa eight years ago still hangs over their bed, despite two moves since Leclaire. Nellie loves telling her friends that someday she will go around the world too.

Kitty tiptoes into her parents' room. The bed is made, but the babies' dirty clothes are piled on a chair and the furniture is covered in dust.

She'll do the housekeeping, but first she opens the bottom drawer of her mother's dresser and takes out the small box containing her mother's hairpiece, a set of bangs Mama had woven from eight-inch strands of her own hair. Mama had the hairpiece made for herself before she was married, she said, because she didn't like her high forehead and its premature creases. Among the family treasures is a cabinet card photo of young Maggie Keville, taken with her beloved bangs.

Kitty sits on the upholstered bench by the window and opens the box. There it is. The only remaining part of her mother. Thick chestnut hair, with glints of dark cherry, cut when she was twenty years old. In the June humidity, the ends curl and frizz.

"Oh, I miss you!" she says, clutching the hairpiece, pulling her knees up to her chin, and allowing herself to sob.

Her tears slowly play out, leaving an ache in her chest.

Remembering Mama's autograph book, she wipes her face on her sleeve and gets the book out of the nightstand drawer. Occasionally, Mama would let Kitty and Nellie write love notes to her in it. Glancing through it, Kitty stops on a page she wrote just a couple of months ago when Mama wasn't feeling well and rested in bed. In the four corners was written *for get me not*, with a wavy line under each syllable. In the center she wrote:

> Mar. 31, 1903
> Dearest Mother:
> I will always love and pray for you and, dearest mother, I hope you will never forget me. When I am dead and gone pray for my soul.
> From Catherine

Tears flooding her eyes again, Kitty wants to write more, to tell her mama how much she misses her already and to swear that she will never forget. But her mind is too jumbled.

The pages fall open to four lines entered by Papa in 1888, fifteen years ago, written in his fine decorative script:

> I wish there was mountains of sugar
> And rivers of wine
> Plantations of tea leaves
> And you to be mine.
> M.M. Flanagan

She touches the hair again, petting it, smoothing it. "I wish you mountains of sugar." Her voice cracks and she starts again, making her voice strong against the catch in her throat. "I wish you mountains of sugar and rivers of wine."

Wanting a better box for the precious hair, Kitty searches the dresser, opening and closing drawers till she finds a walnut box with oak inlays containing a few embroidered hankies. Gently, she folds Mama's hair into it. "Mountains of sugar and rivers of wine," she repeats.

Suddenly inspired, she pulls a pair of scissors from the top drawer, looks into the mirror, and, as carefully as she can, cuts off her own two braids, braids long enough to rest on the collar of her shirt. Her hair is darker than her mother's, the color of bitter chocolate. With the red ribbons still tied to the ends, she folds the braids into the box with Mama's.

"Mountains of sugar and rivers of wine. We will always be together, Mama."

The box is big enough for the autograph book too, so she lays that on top. She'll hide the box in her bedroom drawer for safekeeping.

She's smiling now but makes the mistake of looking into the mirror again. Her remaining hair is sticking out in all directions. She picks up a brush and smooths it down. *Where has little Kitty gone?* Who she sees is a red-eyed young woman with a lump of a nose and a crooked front tooth, almost thirteen years old. She opens her eyes wide. They are a dull green color, but her eyelashes are thick and her eyebrows arched. Squaring her shoulders and tucking the ragged ends of her hair behind her ears, she raises her chin and speaks in a clear voice, "Hello, Catherine M. Flanagan. I wish you mountains of sugar and rivers of wine."

BOOK 2. ENTANGLEMENTS

Part 1. Meet Me at the Fair, 1903-1904

:: 43 ::

Life without Mama begins. They drift through summer. Yes, they drift, Papa says, like a barge without its tugboat, bouncing from shore to shore on the flooded Mississippi. Kitty likes the image. Hot days rush by like towns along the big river, as the boys disappear to the Ashland playground, and as she and Nellie figure out how to keep house and how to care for non-stop Ethel and cranky Julie.

With Papa working all evening to pay for Mama's hospitalization and funeral, they are clueless tugboat captains, trying to steer a rudderless family barge.

Amid shouting and tears, meals get put on the table. Bowls of oatmeal. Peanut butter and jelly. Warmed up cans of Campbell's soup poured over boiled potatoes.

But there is something seductive about not having a mother and hardly having a father. They sleep till ten. Linens turn gray. Laundry piles up. Cobwebs collect in the corners. Weeds choke Mama's garden.

Kitty looks to Nellie for leadership, but Nellie retreats into learning to use Mama's sewing machine, bristling at anyone who interrupts her.

They've become their worst selves.

A crisis comes in August.

From the start, Nellie has struggled with Julie. One minute, she adores the thin little two-year-old and invents toys and games to occupy her time. The next minute, she is scolding her for wandering off or spilling her milk or picking at the paint chips on the windowsill.

One sweltering afternoon, Nellie flies off the handle at Julie for leaving her diaper somewhere and soiling her dress.

"You spiteful little brat," Nellie screams. "What did I ever do to be cursed with you? No wonder Mama left us—you drove her away! I hate you! I wish you were never born."

Julie wails.

"Nellie!" Kitty scoops up Julie to wash her at the spigot outside.

Nellie runs after them. "I'm sorry! I didn't mean it!" She collapses on the back steps, hunched over her sobs. "I'm sorry, Kitty, I'm sorry. Why did she have to leave us? Why? I don't know what I'm supposed to do. She made it all look so easy. Why did she have to die?"

Leaving Julie to splash around in the shallow washtub, Kitty slides next to Nellie and rubs her back.

"I'm thirteen now. I've learned all I can from school. You go take your spot at Visitation next month. I'll figure it out. Mama made lists. So can I. And papa—I'll ask him to teach me more about management. You need school more than me. You'll find a rich husband then."

Nellie chokes back her weeping and lays her head on Kitty's shoulder. "Don't be a dunce," she says. "Visitation already filled my spot and we can't afford it now anyway. *You* have to stay in school in case Papa gets rich again. Then, you can go to an academy. I'm the oldest. This is my obligation, my curse."

In bed that night, to the lullaby of crickets outside their open window, Kitty wants to talk more.

"We're too poor for a housekeeper, but what if we help Papa find a wife? The parish has a lot of nice widows, ladies who've already grown their children and know what they're doing. There are some old maids, too, nurses and teachers. I bet they'd love a handsome man like Papa and we children can promise to be on our best behavior."

"A stepmother? Sleeping in Mama's bed? Pawing through her stuff? What a revolting thought. And what if she beat us and made us do the dirty work?"

"Wicked stepmothers are for fairy tales. Why would anybody be mean to us?"

Nellie scoffs. "Why did I flip out at Julie this afternoon? We get worn thin and the devil jumps in."

"Nellie?" A soft whisper comes from the doorway. Modie appears at their bedside. "I'm hungry."

Nellie groans. "That'll teach you to stay out with your little gang of hoodlums past dinner," she says.

Kitty lays a hand on Nellie's shoulder. "I'll get you something," she says to the six-year-old, "but only if you promise to be at the dinner table tomorrow."

"I promise."

Moment to moment, things get better. Kitty adopts Mama's habit of waking up early to get a head start on the day. She uses her loud voice to assign chores to the boys before they disappear to the playground. To Ethel's delight, Kitty teaches her how to fold clothes "like a big girl" and how to stack them in the correct drawers. She talks with Nellie about how they can divide the work once school starts.

Labor Day is on September 7. It is Papa's only day off since Mama died, and his last day off till Christmas, and then till the World's Fair opens next spring.

"Find the old picnic basket in the shed, Tommy," Papa says. "We'll pack sandwiches and boiled eggs and join the festivities!"

The Flanagans join 200,000 other St. Louisans watching the parades of the Central Trades and Labor Union and the Building Trades Council where their paths cross at Washington.

Papa is in his glory. Proud of his own carpentry trade and impressed by the skills of others, he lectures the children on the work of machinists, broom makers, blacksmiths, furnace workers, trunk makers, hack and cab drivers, and more, as their costumed representatives march by.

As they walk to Forest Park Highlands, where the Trade Council is having its big picnic, Ethel grabs his hand and says, "Tell us again about

Marconi."

At the breakfast table he read them the *Post-Dispatch* story about the Italian inventor Guiglielmo Marconi, in town to plan a station for his new wireless telegraph on the fairgrounds.

"Isn't it exciting!" he says. "Before long we'll be able to send messages to someone a thousand miles away without any wires strung on poles, right through the air. The twentieth century will be full of such marvels, wait and see!"

Classes begin the next day with a line of thunder showers. The boys race out of the house to meet their friends in the schoolyard. Kitty gets Ethel dressed for her first day of kindergarten and they trot through the rain to catch a streetcar. The marvels of the twentieth century seem far away.

.

:: 44 ::

June 1904. The Flanagans have made it through a year without Maggie. Moses looks up from his evening newspaper, tuning in to the domestic hum. The clatter and splash of dishes being washed in the kitchen. A giggle—Ethel's. The metallic whirr of Joe's pushing the lawnmower across their patch of grass and Modie's begging for a turn.

Gradually, their lives have settled into new a new order, not all of it good, but less of it unpredictable.

Fifteen-year-old Nellie bears the brunt of running the household and caring for their sickly three-year-old Julie. How he regrets not sending her to Visitation High School with the other smart girls. She is more artful than organized, more interested in romance novels than cookbooks, but she manages. A genius on Maggie's old sewing machine, by Christmas she left behind the short dresses of a schoolgirl and altered Maggie's matronly skirts and shirts to resemble the "new woman" fashion, with its pigeon silhouette. Her long hair is always neatly pinned into a pompadour. She is too soon a woman.

Thirteen-year-old Kitty has become his old reliable. She packs lunches and takes Ethel and Modie to school with her, while Tommy and Joe ride their bikes. She stops at the butcher's and grocer's on the way home and Ethel reports that Kitty always treats each of them to a chocolate-covered cherry. Ethel also shows him how Kitty taught her to jump rope.

Over the year, he watched Tommy and Joe, only eleven and nine, assert their individuality and become defiant against the sisterly rule. Grey-eyed Joe is tall and strong, a sportsman, his teeth already tobacco-stained. Black-eyed Tommy prefers to shoot marbles, or so he says, smelling too often like a saloon. Moses suspects he's become one of those boys who hang around pool halls after school, running errands and fetching drinks for gamblers waiting to hear how their horses did at the track. And yet they are full of boyish affection for their old papa. Modie too. They tease him that, yes, one of these days he can teach them how to sit quietly on the front porch, whittling twigs into spoons with their pocketknives.

Now a year has gone by. Maggie's scent has faded from her pillow. Her medical and funeral bills are finally paid off. They made it. Time to reward the family with the grandest fair the world has ever seen.

Moses looks forward to visiting the Fair as a customer, not as a foreman troubleshooting a wagonload of window frames that don't fit or ordering the removal of wainscoting that cracked because the pine wasn't cured properly. A month after opening day, the volume of work at the planing mill has finally slowed down.

He announces the plan at dinner. "Wait till you see the Ivory City palaces! People from all over the world! You've never seen such a wondrous thing!"

Kitty, Tommy, and Joe exchange glances. Joe giggles. Then Kitty giggles.

"Oh, Papa," she says, "We've already been to the Fair, me and the boys." Her cheeks turn pink. "We played hooky and snuck in. Lots of children do it. Nobody has fifty cents to pay for admission."

"We saw the gigantic Ferris wheel, Papa!" Tommy says. "Same one that got built for the Chicago Fair. Each car as big as a trolley—holds forty people! Can we go on that?"

"I saw twenty-foot-high sculptures, made of butter, no lie," Joe adds. "And a statue of King Cotton some thirty-odd-feet high."

Nellie throws down her napkin. "So now you miscreants have ruined the experience for all of us!"

Modie's face crumples into a tearful scowl. "I didn't go! How come you didn't take me?"

"You're just a squirt," Kitty says. "Anyway, I didn't stay long the times I went because I had to hitch a ride back to school to walk you and Ethel home."

"We're not babies," Ethel pipes up. "We know our way home!"

As the children squabble, Moses changes his plan.

He takes seven days off work and gives each child their own special day with him at the Fair. They draw lots to see who goes first.

On the sprawling grounds of Forest Park and down the Pike, each child takes a ride on either elephants or camels. Each child gets treated to scoops of ice cream in sugared waffle cones. Each child gets a photo taken and chooses a souvenir.

The week is so successful, he does it again for their birthdays, one in July, three in August, and one in November, before the Fair shuts down December first.

Going to the Fair is a moment of grace for Moses and his children. Their lost Maggie is an emptiness they share. Seeing the world—its diverse cultures and promises for the future—is a thrill they share. For a day, he is the perfect father. For a day, each child is the perfect child, sunny and curious.

His last outing to the Fair is the day after Thanksgiving, November 25, Modie's birthday. Forty-six-year-old Teddy Roosevelt has just been re-elected President and Moses has just turned forty-seven. The temperature is in the thirties, with a brisk wind out of the northwest. They explore many of the indoor exhibits, watch Scott Joplin play the piano, have their photo taken at the automobile exhibit, and eat hotdogs for lunch.

In the late afternoon, exiting the last exhibit hall, they sit for a few minutes on its steps. Moses gazes at the towering wireless telegraph station, the first local installation of Marconi's marvelous invention, radiating its messages to other towers, out past the fair's manmade lagoon, past the hemp and plaster-of-Paris buildings that will be torn down by spring, on past the Mississippi River, on past his worker's utopia in Leclaire, on and on to Chicago where somehow he still exists as a young greenhorn, falling in love with Maggie Keville. He puts his arm around Modie and pulls him close against the wind.

Modie is as handsome and bright as any eight-year-old can be.

"Think of all we've seen here," Moses says to him, "all that the future holds."

"I liked the cars," Modie says. "Can we get one, Papa? Can you teach me to drive?"

"One of these days, one of these days..."

"I liked learning about the Spanish-American War and how we captured the Philippines. Do you think we'll have more wars? I'd like to be a soldier. I could be a Rough Rider and shoot my gun from a horse."

"You wouldn't like war."

"I would, Papa. I think I would."

Moses adjusts Modie's cap to cover his ears and makes sure his coat is buttoned up before they walk to the streetcar stop. He swears to himself that he will be a better father, more attentive, more patient, more encouraging. He prays to Maggie that she will stay by his side and protect her dear children through whatever the new century brings.

Part 2. Disasters, 1907-1908

:: 45 ::

As 1907 draws to a close, Kitty doesn't mind being in charge of the household, but now that she is seventeen, a certain misery has stolen over her.

The problem is not the children. Nine-year-old Ethel and eleven-year-old Modie are happy-go-lucky in school. Six-year-old Julie stayed healthy enough to make it through the first half of second grade with good report cards and no absences. Tommy and Joe, fifteen and thirteen, are no problem since they quit school and got jobs as apprentice mechanics. After buying their tobacco, they hand over the remaining pennies to help with groceries.

No, Kitty's misery is in the mirror. Who can look good when they're cleaning and cooking all day? She dresses for comfort, in easy-to-wash fabrics, and pins her hair into a tight bun. Unless she has shopping, she doesn't bother with a corset. Her reflection tells her she's dowdy. Her heart tells her she's lonely.

The delivery boys flirt with her, of course. She's always ready for a chat, but the last thing she needs is to fall in love with a dope whose only asset is a strong back. She and Nellie have been accumulating a stack of used romance novels and, on this they agree: they each deserve a man with a princely nature, handsome and brilliant, destined for wealth. No brawny laboring men for them, leaving them poor and bored or, worse, turning them into thirty-year-old widows, like their aunties, with children to raise crowded into houses with their brothers. Life has already punished them enough.

She was happy to take over the house from Nellie when she graduated from eighth grade, but now she is envious. Nellie has a job downtown—a dreadful one, transferring numbers from one ledger to another six days a week—but she dresses up every day, creating ensembles over a well-fitted corset and frilly white undermuslins for a stylish silhouette on her willowy frame. And her hair is always coifed to perfection, with added hairpieces and pretty hats. She is being courted by at least three young men.

Kitty removes her stained apron and takes stock of herself in the mirror. She stands on her toes to look taller and puts her hands around her waist to pull the baggy dress in, sticking out her chest to see if she can look buxom.

She wasn't Cinderella. She had no fairy godmother to outfit her with a silk gown and glass slippers.

"Mother of God!" Nellie surprises her.

"Don't look!" Kitty says.

"You know, there are women up and down this street, with umpteen children, who manage to look shapely even when they're washing windows or taking out the ashes."

"Well, I can't work in a corset. The boning stabs and pinches."

"Your corset was meant for a fourteen-year-old. You desperately need an update."

"I know." Kitty groans. "But I don't know where to start."

"I'll be in charge of this project, Catherine," Nellie says. "We'll give you a new look. And we'll throw a big Christmas Eve open house, inviting all the neighbors, especially the ones with handsome unmarried sons.

Kitty hugs her sister. "*You'll* be my fairy godmother."

:: 46 ::

On the Friday before Christmas, 1907, Moses sits at the bar of the Rosebud Café with his half-empty pint of beer and the remains of his catfish sandwich, while the piano player reinvents traditional holiday melodies to the syncopated beats of a rag.

Moses is making good money now, boosted by his successful work on the World's Fair. Based on his reputation, Gedney Lumber across the river in East St. Louis, hired him to upgrade their planing mill. Within six months, Gedney was competitive with the city planing mills and Moses was recruited back across the river by St. Louis Mill Work and Supply.

Shortly after taking charge of the St. Louis mill, his boss offered him a promotion.

"You know the business inside and out and know how to get it all down on paper," he said. "But you also have that twinkle in your eye, that Irish charm. You tell a good story. Plus, with that walrus mustache of yours!" He slapped Moses on the back. "You remind people of Teddy Roosevelt—a man with big ideas."

So Moses took on the job of estimator, putting together bid packages.

He was thrilled to be on the ground floor of new projects, where he could influence architects and builders to lose the old Victorian curlicues for the sleeker American Craftsman styles. Even more exciting, since he needed to move quickly around the city, they gave him a vehicle—a jaunty Ford S Runabout.

Tom Turpin, the Negro musician who owns Rosebud, is working behind the bar this afternoon. As he clears Moses's plate, Moses launches into the story of how crazy his children went when he brought home a car.

"My daughter Kitty, she screams, 'We're rich!' and the seven of them pile on, hugging and kissing me. The girls squeeze in next to me, with the babies on their laps and the lads brace themselves on the running boards. They insist on a ride. For the life of me, I didn't think such a small vehicle had the power, but we made it around the block, the children whooping and hollering the whole way. I'll never forget it."

He did feel rich. He got a mortgage for $1,650 to buy their Farlin Avenue home and refreshed the first floor with new carpets and furniture.

And yet he is melancholy. He takes a letter from his jacket pocket, rereads it, and folds it away. Since a business trip to Chicago, his sister-in-law Biddy—Bridget—has been writing. Her voice, her words, her playfulness make him feel young again and remind him how lonely he is.

Maybe it's time for a change, but he doesn't want to tip the apple cart.

And yet… Julie will need mothering for another decade, till she can manage her own eating. Kitty already looks like an old washerwoman. He doesn't want to be that parent who chains a child to the hearth.

He turns his ear to the music, drawn into the plangent melodies, syncopated beats, and lively rags. It makes Moses itchy to play the piano again but the one they brought from Leclaire now has a cracked sounding board and can't be tuned.

"Say, Tom, where can I get a good buy on a first-class, used upright piano, delivered by Christmas Eve?"

"You're in the right place, Mr. Flanagan. I got one in storage for you." He squints his eyes. "Let's say a hundred bucks, delivered and tuned, old one hauled away."

"Oh, a hundred will set me back too much."

"How about if I swear it was the very piano where Mr. Scott Joplin composed "The Entertainer" and the "Gladiolas Rag," sitting right here in this saloon? Wouldn't that magic make it worth a few extra bucks?"

Moses smiles and reaches out his hand to shake on the deal.

:: 47 ::

With Nellie's help, Kitty starts updating her look and plans to greet the new year with panache. They make an expedition to the Scruggs-Vandervoort-Barney sale to update Kitty's undermuslins and buy her first swan-bill corset, which cinches her waist, pushes her bust out in front, and boosts her derriere in back. Together, they construct Kitty a tight-fitting ivory dress full of ruffles and trimmed with red ribbon. Then, they splurge on a pair of dainty button-top boots, with Cuban heels and pointed toes.

Finally, Nellie shows Kitty some easy ways to style her hair into a soft upsweep instead of a dreary old bun.

"Now you need to alter those raggedy housedresses you wear, like

I showed you. But even if you don't go anywhere during the week, you can dress up for Sunday Mass," Nellie says. "If the only chance you have to meet worthy boys is at church, you better look smart," she says. "This Gibson Girl style will help your petite figure stand very tall—everyone will notice and respect you."

The delivery of their new piano on the morning of Christmas Eve thrills Kitty and promises a perfect Christmas. Once the old piano is hauled out, the new one is rolled into place on its metal casters, which are then seated into wooden caster cups. The tuner stops by so that it's ready to play by afternoon. It is taller and richer sounding than the old one.

That evening, as dozens of neighbors and old school friends squeeze into the little Farlin house, the piano gets a good workout as she and Nellie play from their collection of sheet music and Papa joins in with the Irish airs he learned by ear. Everyone sings.

After the last guest leaves, the family sits around the tree to open their gifts from "Santa"—fur-trimmed leather gloves for Nellie and Kitty, sleds for Ethel and Modie, toolboxes for Tommy and Joe, and a teddy bear for Julie. Aunt Delia has sent two beautiful quilts for the family, which will stay in the living room for all to use.

For Papa, the children have chipped in "according to their means" for a portrait of their mother, painted from her 1880's photograph.

"This is a treasure," he says, immediately hanging it in place of an old Maxfield Parrish reproduction.

On Christmas Day, they sleep till nine, then bundle up against the forty-degree chill to stroll as a family to the ten o'clock Mass at Holy Rosary. Kitty and Nellie wrap themselves in shawls instead of long coats, so that all the world can see how stylish the Flanagan sisters are.

:: 48 ::

Thursday, January 23, 1908. After dinner, as Kitty opens a box of Zuzu gingersnaps, Nellie sits at the kitchen table with the *Post-Dispatch*, browsing the sales and laughing at some of the stories.

"Listen to this one. A despondent *chicken* commits suicide by catching her neck between the staves of an old barrel. Look, there's a diagram and everything."

"What's so hilarious?" Papa pokes his nose into the kitchen.

"You're back from Chicago!" Nellie says. "How was it?"

"Wonderful. Very successful." He takes off his overcoat and drapes it over a chair. "Our bid on woodwork for a large tract of housing in Evanston was accepted. And there's more. Let's have a drink together, girls. Sit down, Kitty, sit. Bring those cookies."

His eyes glittering, he pours them each a glass of beer. "Cheers, my dears!" He pulls up a chair. "I had a wonderful idea on the train ride home."

"Tell us everything, Papa," Kitty says.

"Now, you know I want nothing more than the two of you to be happy and prosperous," he begins.

Kitty raises her glass to that. "Yes, yes."

"You two have kept this family together and functioning during our darkest days." He looks down at his beer. "It will be five years in June since your mama passed away. Five years that you have sacrificed your education and your personal lives for us. It's tradition in Irish families that at least one child will commit his or her life to the support of an aging parent."

Nellie butts in. "What are you saying, Papa? Do you need a promise from one of us to stick by you?"

"Quite the opposite. Your mother and I had the alternative experience. We got pushed out of our nests to emigrate to America, to make our own way, free of family obligation, except to send a bit of cash when we could. We loved the serendipity of finding each other on the streets of Chicago, the craziness of moving to St. Louis, the adventure in Leclaire. We swore to each other that we wouldn't strap our children with old-world expectations."

"So…?"

"So, I want you to be Nellie Bly. To have adventures, to take risks, to meet life on your own terms. You won't know the world, you won't know yourselves until you live among strangers."

"Wait," says Kitty. "Are you kicking us out?"

"No! Well… yes. Wouldn't it be a fine experience for the two of you to get a flat together? To be liberated from the drudgery of this household? The boys are getting to the age where they won't listen to you and the baby girls—well, they need a full-time mother."

Kitty stands up. "I'm full-time! I mend their clothes. I cook their meals. I watch over their health. Julie's sugar is under control. She's growing! Now you want me to live in some roach-infested room over a shop like I just got off the boat and have no family, no home?"

Moses grabs her wrist. "Sit. I'm not saying you don't do a fine job, Catherine. But you'll be eighteen this August and you should get a job, like Nellie, out in the world. Develop your wonderful talents. Meet a young man and be free to plan your own future."

"So what then? You'll hire a big old housekeeper to manage around here?" Kitty's voice rises.

"Please. Let me finish. Sit down." He gets up for the whiskey bottle and pours two fingers in his empty glass, then lights a cigarette. "Chicago was more than a business trip. I spent some time with your aunt—"

Nellie interrupts. "Aunt Delia? What advice is that busybody filling your ears with?"

"Aunt Delia, yes. I visited with her and your uncles. I think Uncle Pat is moving down to St. Louis, in fact. Better pay for a bricklayer here." He gets up again, for an ashtray. "Aunt Delia's doing well but to tell the truth I stayed with your Aunt Bridget."

"Uncle Jerry's widow?" Kitty asks. She only knew of Bridget as someone whose name raised Mama's hackles. "You mean 'Biddy'?"

"Her name is Bridget. Did you know we've been friends since I was a boy in Dublin? She has two sons, about the ages of Tommy and Joe. Did you know she was an orphan? Not as fortunate as Delia to have her brothers jump on the boat from Ireland to help her out. She's hit on some hard times."

A horrified look strikes Nellie's face. "Don't tell me she's moving *here*! Don't tell me she thinks she's going to take over this house. And that you're kicking *us* out to make room for *her* and her stupid boys. Please don't tell me."

Kitty stands up again. "You had *sex* with her!"

Moses's face reddens and he grabs her wrist again, but she pulls away. "You're fifty years old, Papa! An old man! That's disgusting!"

Tears spring to his eyes. "Try to understand. A man gets lonely..."

Nellie pops out of her chair and covers her ears. "Oh my God, I can't hear this." She rushes out of the room and pounds up the stairs.

"My father has lost his mind," Kitty mutters, as she stomps out of the kitchen into the dining room, where the sewing machine and ironing board are set up. She plugs in the iron and yanks a dress from the laundry basket. Her heart is pounding. Yes, she wants a job out in the world—someday. Yes, she wants Papa to be happy—someday. But *now* she is comfortable. Their home is organized. Tommy and Joe are taller than she is, but her voice is loud and clear enough to maintain their respect. And she likes their crowded little house, with its piano and all the furniture and carpeting they got since Papa's new job. And she can't wait till spring so she can tend Mama's rose garden again with eggshells and coffee grounds, just like Mama taught her.

She chokes back tears as she presses Julie's dress for school tomorrow.

Moses is still at the table, about to pour more whiskey.

With the dress in one hand, she returns to the kitchen and seizes the bottle, stowing it in the cabinet and slamming the door shut.

"Don't make it worse," she huffs and heads upstairs.

Nellie is sprawled on their bed, crying. Ethel and Julie are asleep. Kitty hangs up the dress, sits next to Nellie, and rubs her back. They talk quietly and decide to speak with Papa again before work tomorrow.

:: 49 ::

Friday morning, 6 a.m. Kitty drags into the kitchen in her stocking feet, a shawl wrapped around her chemise. Papa has already boiled water for coffee and she hears it dripping into the pot. The front door slams and he comes in red-faced, with his morning *Globe-Democrat.*

"Jesus, it's cold out there. He glances at the weather report in the upper left of the paper. "Hoo, eighteen degrees they say. Hope I can crank the car." He pours his coffee and sits down.

Kitty puts on a pot of water for the Cream of Wheat, happy not to continue last night's conversation.

Papa sniffs and makes a face. "Whosever in charge of coal this week, make sure he minds what he's doing and not using wet coal."

Kitty smells it too. "I'll tell Joe."

Nellie sweeps in, dressed for work. In an automatic gesture, she pulls a stack of eight bowls from the cabinet and eight spoons from a drawer, and clatters them onto the kitchen table.

"What's that godawful smell from the dining room?"

They look. The iron is still plugged in and has fallen into the laundry basket. It is smoldering.

"The plug! Pull the plug!" Papa yells. But before he can get to his feet, Nellie grabs the handle on the pot of cereal water and flings the liquid into the basket.

There is a crackle and explosion as flames erupt and the electric lights blink out, leaving them in the dawn twilight. Nellie shrieks.

"Everybody out!" Papa shouts to the top of his lungs. "Kitty! Blankets! Smother it! Everybody out!"

She manages to toss him her shawl and Aunt Delia's quilts before she picks up the phone for the fire department. Then she grabs the broom to beat down the flames crossing the carpeting. "Oh my God, this is my fault. How could I be so stupid? The plug! The door slam! How stupid!" The words keep tumbling out as little fires pop up all over.

The children are screaming as they rumble down the steps. They want to see what's going on, but Nellie pushes them out the front door.

"Out, out, out!" she cries. "The baby! Where's Julie? Oh, God!" She dashes through the acrid air back upstairs.

"I think we got it out," Papa yells to Kitty.

But suddenly the window shears burst into flame.

Kitty hears the sirens in the distance. They are at least a minute away, a minute too late. She begins to feel dizzy as the fire sucks her breath away.

"We have to go," Papa shouts, as the world goes black.

❦

Meanwhile, Nellie finds Julie in bed. She won't wake up. Nellie lifts the frail child into her arms and carries her down the steps and out the front door. She can hear Papa and Kitty shouting as they put out the flames.

Mrs. Kennedy from next door is at the bottom of the porch steps, where other neighbors are bringing coats and boots to the four Flanagan children on the sidewalk. She rushes Nellie into her home. The cold air revives Julie, so Nellie leaves her with Mrs. Kennedy and runs back outside.

She grabs Joe and Tommy by their hands. "The piano! Come on! We'll push it out!"

The three of them pull the piano out from the wall, dislodging the caster cups, and begin to push it toward the porch. Two neighbor ladies appear at the door, calling for them to get out. But Nellie keeps crying out, "We have to save the piano! Move! Push! Push!"

The women see no alternative but to help by pulling it from their end. The piano finally bumps over the threshold and slides out onto the porch just as the fire trucks pull up.

"Mama's portrait! Her china!" Nellie shouts. She turns to re-enter the house but sees the flames climbing up the wallpaper now. Across the room, the portrait falls to the floor and catches fire. "No!"

Joe grabs her by the shoulders and pulls her down the steps, out to the sidewalk. Someone throws a blanket around her.

As firemen set up their hose, the captain thunders, "Is everybody out? Is everybody out of the house?"

Ethel screams. "Papa! Kitty!"

Tommy shouts, "Our father, our sister! Where are they?"

With that, Nellie hears Papa's voice. "We're safe! We're safe! Turn on your pump!"

He appears from around the side of the house, carrying Kitty, her arms looped around his neck, her bare toes poking through her ripped stockings, the hem of her shift scorched.

As water hits the flames and smoke billows into the gray skies, Nellie throws her blanket around Moses and Kitty, hugging them, breaking into sobs.

In moments, the blaze is extinguished.

To the east, Moses sees daybreak, the sky turning pink. The firemen disappear into the house to finish their work. Suddenly, the world is quiet, except for the sound of his children crying. Their cozy little house is a sad, dripping mess. Then he sees the piano on the porch. Tears spring to his eyes and he laughs. "We have our music, girls. We have our music."

:: 50 ::

Moses braces himself for a terrible day. When the fire captain gives the all-clear, Moses and the children traipse through the ruins, gathering what can be salvaged and carrying it out to the shed. Kitty retrieves her treasure box, with its family heirlooms and photos. Neighbors help drag ruined furnishings to the curb. To clear the smell of smoke, Joe opens the windows that aren't already broken. Tommy stokes the boiler and opens all the radiator valves full force to help dissipate the icy dampness that permeates everything.

A flirtatious young reporter follows Nellie around, asking her dozens of questions.

"Get out of here or make yourself useful," Moses yells at him.

As the air clears, he assesses the damage. He can see the parts amid the horrible whole. Broken windows and electrical, first. Gutting the first floor, next. The upstairs is okay, except where the firemen axed the wall in the boys' room to make sure the electrical fire was out.

He aches for the terrified neediness of his children, wishing he could tuck them into warm beds, and sing them lullabies. But the brain of a lifelong carpenter and project manager pulls him forward, scolding him that it's no time for fantasies, no time for fairy tales. Everyone is alive. Get to work.

After a couple of hours of salvaging what they can, Moses shoos the children next door to the Kennedy's, to get fed. An electrician friend shows up to begin the rewiring and Moses starts tearing the wallpaper and plaster off the walls. A neighbor brings sheets of glass to replace the broken window panes.

Everyone is alive.

The sun sets early in January. Kitty stares out the window of the Kennedy living room at her dear old home. The lights are on now and she sees that their piano on the porch is covered with a canvas tarp.

Her father is there alone.

She puts on her smoke-smelling coat and is about to ask Tommy to come with her when Mr. Kennedy walks through the front door.

"You won't believe who made the front page of the evening paper!" He spreads the *Post-Dispatch* on the dining room table. A striking photo of Nellie stares out, with the headline: "Miss Nellie Flanagan Heroine During Blaze Which Destroys Home."

Nellie is standing across the table flushed with excitement. She is truly beautiful, Kitty thinks, maybe even more so after the day's ordeal. Her hair is still in a perfect pompadour. Her clothes are spotted with soot and her hand bandaged from a burn, but she still projects elegance and poise. Everyone congratulates her on her heroism.

"But look," says Tom. "It says she rescued the wrong sister—Ethel!"

Julie chimes in. "You carried *me*, not Ethel!"

Joe starts laughing. "Look, Modie, they got your name wrong. Called you *Maud*." He gives Modie a shove. "Must have thought you was a little girl, haha! *Maud*!"

Modie shoves him back and stomps from the room.

At that moment, Kitty loves Nellie more than anything. Her quick thinking saved Julie. But as Kitty runs after Modie, the bubble of heroism bursts. It was crazy impetuous for Nellie to go back into a burning house for the piano, yanking Tommy and Joe with her. The same brainless impulse that made her toss a pot of water on a plugged-in iron. They would all be in the kitchen washing up after dinner now if she had paid attention to Papa yelling at her to *unplug* the iron.

Eleven-year-old Modie curls under a quilt on the sofa, hiding his face. As Kitty sits next to him and runs her fingers through his hair, she is suddenly angry at her sister for being the center of attention, petty as it is. Her stomach aches and her heart feels heavy in her chest.

"Don't be upset," she says to Modie. "The newspaper misspelled my name too."

Turning toward her, he wipes his snotty nose on a sleeve. "It made me sound like a girl."

"I know," she says. "They wanted to get the story in tonight's paper so they were sloppy with their facts."

"And we saved a lot more than that piano, too."

"Yes, we did. Let's go over there now and see if Papa can use our help."

Modie puts on his shoes and coat and they walk next door.

Papa, his eyes red, his sooty clothes now white with plaster dust, has roughly stripped the dining room walls down to the lathe. Kitty spies the near-empty whiskey bottle on the kitchen table.

"We came to help," Kitty says.

Modie adds, "Nellie got her picture in the paper for saving Julie but they said *Ethel* instead. Then they said she saved the piano but that wasn't the only thing."

Papa gives Kitty a dark look. "That's all we need, our business spread all over town. Boy, get your brothers over here to help haul this crap out to the alley. Mr. Kennedy has some tubs. Bring those. You boys will sleep here with me tonight. The heat's on and nothing's wrong with your beds."

Modie dashes away.

"What can I do?" Kitty asks.

He is sweeping the broken plaster and torn wallpaper toward the back door.

"This isn't working anymore, Catherine. It's been nearly five years since your mother left us. And here we are. Ashes to ashes. Dust to dust."

"That isn't true!" she protests, even as she looks at the shambles around her.

"The school called me last week," he says. "Modie was caught stealing some model cars from one of his classmates."

Kitty is shocked. "Why didn't they call *me*?"

Moses speaks slowly. "You… are not… his mother."

The words feel like a slap. Her heart races. This is the unfinished conversation, the insanity that made her forget to unplug the iron.

"So…" She hesitates. "So, you think Aunt Bridget will be better? Better than me?"

He pauses his work. "You need to take care of yourself, Catherine. You're too young for this burden. I love you too much."

"And you think Aunt Bridget will have all the answers?"

"She's raising two boys of her own. We can share the responsibilities, give the young ones both mother and father."

"Do you love her?"

Papa looks toward the kitchen, toward the whiskey bottle. "Bridget and I have always had a great deal of affection for each other. She's outgoing, fun-loving. She'll bring joy to our family."

Kitty notes that he avoids the word *love*. It sounds like a business deal. An arrangement. But she keeps her mouth shut.

Instead, she asks, "Does she play the piano? Does she sing?" She is trying to be sympathetic toward her poor papa, but she feels the anger rising again. The knot in her stomach tightens.

"Go see what's keeping the boys," is all he says.

On the porch, she meets the boys running up the steps, carrying empty tubs. They are laughing at some joke, hardly seeing her as they blaze through the front door.

The cold feels good on her face. She stands there and remembers her days in Leclaire when she would stand on the porch and count houses to calm her nerves. She looks down the street. Homes have their lights on. Shadows move across their curtains. The neighbors are winding down, confident that tomorrow will be the same as today. Everyone thinks tomorrow will be the same as today.

She shakes her head and walks slowly down the steps.

:: 51 ::

Kitty can't believe how fast Papa is moving to bring them a stepmother. As their downstairs walls are replastered, Papa is adamant that the fire was a signal for change. He and Bridget exchange daily letters and he announces a wedding date of April 19. *Bridget likes the symbolism of Easter.*

She watches as he supervises the hanging of a bright and overpowering William Morris wallpaper in their living and dining room. *Bridget picked it out.*

During March, Papa organizes the conversion of the attached shed into a dormitory for their brothers, so that Timothy and James can have their own room upstairs. *Bridget decided.*

One evening, when Papa tells Kitty that she can't keep her ironing board up in the dining room, she breaks down.

"You're doing everything you can to squeeze me out of your life, aren't you?" she cries.

"Catherine, stop this sulking." His voice is low, but clear. "I am liberating you. Go back to school. Get a job. Find a husband. Make hats and sell them on a street corner. Can't you see what a gift I'm giving you?"

"No, I can't!"

She marches out the back door, slamming it behind her. She sits on the steps and focuses on trying not to cry. The chilly spring air makes her shiver.

The gate creaks and Mrs. Kennedy from next door slides next to her and drapes a shawl around her shoulders.

"What is it, dear?"

Kitty tries to explain but her words make her sound stuffy and selfish.

"How about this," Mrs. Kennedy says. "You know my mother just moved in with us. She's close to bedridden, not long for this world, and needs a lot of attention. Maybe you can help me out. We can move cots into our screened-in porch. You and Nellie can easily stay there through the summer. She can go to work and you can watch after my girls and help with the housework. It would be a tremendous help to me and you can keep an eye on your family. It will buy you some time."

Kitty hugs her. "Thank you, thank you."

Watching Aunt Bridget move into their mother's bedroom is agony.

At the same time, Kitty is fascinated by this new woman. Mama had little time for fashion. They only knew her to be pregnant or nursing or, at the end, in pain. Her corset was structured for bust and back support beneath her simple skirts and shirtwaists. But their Aunt Bridget, even in her late forties, uses her corset to create an hourglass curve and elegant posture. Her skirts are silk taffetas layered over ruffled petticoats. Her shirtwaists, with their leg-of-mutton sleeves, are trimmed with netting and lace. Her thick, henna-dyed hair is styled into a youthful pompadour. And her hatboxes take up a whole corner of the bedroom.

Papa gave his girls the impression that Aunt Bridget was penniless. Kitty can only guess that, while she and Nellie scarred their fingers sewing and altering clothes, Papa has been treating their aunt to shopping trips, letting her amass a grand trousseau for their new life together.

Kitty gives her aunt credit for being vivacious, as she sweeps into the Flanagan home with her trunks of finery and box of cookbooks. But she takes charge without asking a single question about the family's normal routines. Immediately after inspecting the pantry, she is on the phone with the grocer ordering roasts and expensive spices. While she is chummy with Kitty and Nellie ("We're going to be *such* good friends!"), she really only has conversations with Papa.

The men her papa works with make a big deal of their lonely colleague getting married again. Someone in the front office feeds the story to the *Globe-Democrat*. It is published on Saturday, April 18.

> CHILDHOOD SWEETHEARTS TO WED AFTER MANY YEARS
> *Mrs. Bridget Flanagan to Marry Moses M. Flanagan*
> Moses M. Flanagan, employed by the Saint Louis Mill Work and Supply Company as estimator, will be married Sunday afternoon to Mrs. Bridget Flanagan, his boyhood sweetheart in Ireland. That was twenty-six years ago, and since then both have been married and left free to marry again by the death of their mates. Flanagan has seven children and the woman who will become his wife two. He met her in Chicago a year ago, and the old engagement was renewed. She arrived from Chicago a week ago and is now stopping at his home at 3221a Farlin avenue, where they will keep house. He is 45 years old and she is 40. Her husband has been dead four years and his wife six. They will be married at the Holy Rosary Church by Rev. Father Daniel Lavery at 6 o'clock.

The article is full of errors—the address, Papa's age, how long Uncle Jerry and Mama have been gone—but Kitty has to concede that the world sees the event as romantic and worth celebrating. Papa is happy.

Still, she feels a little guilty that Mama has faded as the heartbeat of their family. Kitty digs out the autograph book from her treasure box, finds some blank pages, and copies into it a love poem about never forgetting, promising to think of her mama every day.

The wedding is an Easter Sunday afternoon extravaganza in a church full of white lilies and the heady aroma of incense from the preceding Holy Week services. The Flanagan children all have new store-bought clothes, the five boys—including the two step-brother/cousins—in suits, the four girls in ivory frocks with large bonnets full of feathers and silk flowers. Bridget is stunning in a high-fashion dress of pale jade silk damask and creamy lace. Her hair is crowned with silk flowers and a silk organza veil.

The church is packed with friends and neighbors. After the nuptial Mass, the gathering adjourns to the Church hall for an evening of catered food and dancing. Many toasts are made to the joy of resurrecting love from tragedy.

:: 52 ::

Kitty watches Aunt Bridget and the reconfigured family from the Kennedy house. Timothy and James are signed up to continue their Catholic education at the expensive Christian Brothers College high school on Kingshighway and Easton.

Tommy and Joe spurn the idea of C.B.C., preferring life in the unionized mechanical trades. With an apprenticeship under his belt, sixteen-year-old Tommy already makes a wage that outstrips Nellie's office job. Joe will soon follow.

Modie rides his hand-me-down bicycle with a new circle of friends at school. Ethel enjoys being the big sister traveling with Julie to and from school. Whenever he can, Papa drives the baby girls to school, ignoring Bridget's admonition that he is spoiling them.

Bridget is not as organized as Kitty. Dinners are chaotic. With the windows open, she and Nellie can hear the boys roughhousing, Julie crying, and Ethel looking for attention by rambling on about a story she read or some irrelevant event at school. Bridget screeches for them all to sit down, shut up, and say grace. Typically, no one pays attention till Papa begins to bark orders. One night, after dinner, Kitty and Nellie spy Bridget sitting on the back steps weeping.

"I wish I could give her a talking to," Kitty whispers. "Mama gave everyone a task when she was getting dinner ready. I can't remember all hell breaking lose like this when she was alive."

"She won't listen," Nellie says. "I'd rather convince Papa to boot her back to Chicago."

"He wouldn't listen!" But then Kitty wonders, "Do you think he'd listen?"

"To use his language, he's not getting much return on his investment, is he?"

"He's spending a lot of his money for mediocre housekeeping, that's for sure. But I think he'd need a stronger argument to reverse course. He's too proud. Let's think about it."

When school lets out in June, the situation at the Flanagan house gets worse. Timothy and James disappear early with Modie to hang out at the Ashland schoolyard, the hub for sandlot baseball and other games, but Ethel and Julie are under foot. And it's hot. Kitty overhears Bridget telling Mrs. Kennedy that "Mose" better buy her a new house soon.

Kitty has pity on her baby sisters, encouraging them to come play with the Kennedy children, so she can check their ears for wax and their underclothes for stains.

When the Kennedy strawberry patch is full of bright, ripe berries, Kitty and her sisters pick a big bowlful to take home to Bridget.

"Ethel, make sure she knows not to put sugar on them for Julie's sake. Do you hear that, Baby? These strawberries are plenty sweet as they are."

Julie nods and the girls disappear through the back door of the Flanagan house.

Kitty lugs a load of laundry out of the Kennedy basement and begins hanging it on the line.

The next thing she hears is Bridget yelling and Ethel's little voice arguing. She catches the word "sugar."

Jesus, Mary, and Joseph, Kitty thinks and starts toward her old home to clear up the misunderstanding, for Ethel's sake.

Then she hears Julie scream. And scream and scream. Kitty races through the gate, up the back steps, and through the back door. Bridget is standing there with an iron frying pan raised above her head.

"Shut up or you're next!" she screeches at Julie.

Julie sees Kitty. "She killed Ethel! She killed Ethel!"

Bridget turns toward her, wild-eyed, sweating, her hair askew. Ethel is lying in a heap on the floor.

"Mother of God," Kitty says as she rushes to Ethel's side. Her sister is not dead, but unconscious, with a bloodied forehead. Strawberries are strewn everywhere. "Call the doctor!"

Bridget stands there, the frying pan frozen in her hands like a baseball bat. "I'm so sick of that little brat. Doesn't she ever shut up?"

Kitty can't believe it. Damn Biddy is out of control. Hands shaking, voice quavering, Kitty calls the doctor herself.

"Chip some ice for her head," Kitty instructs as she gently repositions Ethel to lie flat on the floor.

But Bridget keeps ranting in a low voice. "She doesn't shut up. She thinks she can tell me what to do. There's no arguing with her. She doesn't shut up."

Ethel's eyes flutter open, then roll back into her head. She stiffens then begins to twitch like a fish flopping on the bottom of a boat.

"The devil's got her!" Bridget screams. "She's possessed by the devil!"

Kitty knows it's a fit. In school she saw children fall and twitch like this, usually because of a fever. Unsure what to do, she lies next to Ethel and tries to hold her still. Julie copies her and lies down on Ethel's other side. Kitty puts her lips close to Ethel's ear and, in a cracking voice, she sings, "Daisy, Daisy, give me your answer do..." Julie joins in. By the time they finish the song, the seizure has subsided. Ethel is sobbing and speaking incoherently as Dr. Broder rushes through the front door.

Helping her up to a straight-back chair, he dabs the forehead abrasion with iodine.

"She had a fit," says Kitty and glares at Bridget, who has pinned her hair back into place.

Bridget says, "She rushed in with those strawberries and must have hit her head on the edge of the icebox."

Julie grabs onto Kitty's skirt and mumbles something into the folds.

As the doctor shines a light into Ethel's eyes and holds up fingers for her to count, Kitty tells Julie to speak up, but the child will only whisper. Kitty leans over to hear.

"Ethel told Auntie not to put sugar on the strawberries." She pauses to swallow her tears. "And Auntie Bridget slammed the frying pan into her head and knocked her down. I thought she was dead!" She buries her face again in Kitty's skirt.

Broder, who hasn't heard Julie's revelation, turns to Bridget. "Concussion," he says. "See them nearly every day during the summer, boys beaning each other with bats and balls. Keep her up and about till bedtime. An ice pack will help." He pats Ethel on the knee. "You'll have a shiner, young lady. Your brothers will be jealous."

Ethel stares blankly at him. He tips his hat to Bridget and leaves the house.

The room falls silent.

Finally, Bridget says, "She's a very clumsy girl."

Kitty is speechless in the face of Bridget's lie.

"You can go now, Catherine. Julie and Ethel need to clean up these strawberries."

Ethel tries to get up from her chair, teeters, and sits back down. "I'm…" She loses the word and points to her head with a twirling gesture.

Kitty helps her to her feet. "Let's go sit on a blanket in the backyard where there is a cool breeze. Come on, Julie. You too."

Outdoors, Kitty sets up a game of jacks on a picnic blanket and runs into the Kennedy house for an icebag. Her heart is racing. Her brain is a fog. What the hell has just happened? And what is she supposed to do about it?

Mrs. Kennedy picks up on Kitty's distress.

"Ethel had an accident," Kitty starts to say, then bends over at the terrible knot in her stomach. "Bridget smashed a frying pan into Ethel's skull. She's lying about it. And I don't know what to do. Ethel has a concussion."

Mrs. Kennedy grabs Kitty's arm. "Listen to me. You'll find out if she's beating any of the others or if today was a fluke, You'll tell your father when he gets home. Whether he believes his children or that woman will tell you what kind of man he is. Meanwhile, you bring the girls inside here at dinnertime."

Back in the yard, Kitty sits with her sisters and asks them questions.

Ethel is frustrated that her jacks game is off and won't answer, but Julie does.

"She slaps us when we're naughty. Or yanks us by the arm." She shows

Kitty the line of faded bruises.

"That time she beat Modie," Ethel finally says, "when the police brought him home. When he got caught pickpocketing on Easton. She whupped him. With Papa's belt. On his legs. She called him a… spoiled little bastard."

Kitty struggles to stay calm even as anger tenses every muscle in her body. She prays to the Blessed Mother to tell her what to do. After sitting quietly for a few minutes, she says, "I think I have to move back home."

That evening she watches for Papa to park his car in front of the house, calling him into the Kennedy's, to tell her story.

❦

Moses finds Bridget in the kitchen, fussing over a pot roast. Smashed strawberries dot the edges of the kitchen floor. He confronts her.

"You gave Ethel a concussion with the frying pan. You've been hitting my children."

"What a horrid lie!" she exclaims. "Catherine hates me! She spies on me!"

"Catherine doesn't lie to me," he says. "And neither do the babies. I'll be speaking to the boys before the evening is out."

It doesn't take long for Moses to gather his facts. Sitting next to Tommy on Joe's bed, he listens. They each describe run-ins where Biddy has boxed their ears or banged their knuckles with a wooden spoon or smacked their legs with a belt. Modie claims she tossed a saucepan of hot water at him and scalded his arm. And yes, she did belt him that time when the police brought him home.

"She told us you were grateful that she took charge, that you wanted us to be like her good boys," Tommy says.

Moses puts an arm around Tommy's shoulders and kisses the boy's black mop of hair, for once in his life speechless.

The grease has congealed on Biddy's pot roast by the time Moses marches into the kitchen. The whiskey bottle is open and she's been crying.

"Why the hell are you hitting my children?" he roars.

Her hands fly up to cover her ears. "Your children despise me. And I'm trying my best to love them, to act out of love." She turns to the counter and pours more whiskey into her glass, spilling half of it on the counter. "I thought you brought me here to be a mother, to discipline your house full of unruly brats. Every one of them is spoiled rotten. Children have to be taught to do as they're told, without any lip. Don't tell me your mother didn't use a razor strop on you when you needed it."

Moses stares at her. No, his mother did not strop him. Was that her mistake? Has he been a weak parent? Has he done it all wrong? It is a shattering thought, to be examined at a later date.

For now, he is only sure of one thing. Pulling himself tall, he states it in a clear voice: "If you ever again lay a hand on or take an instrument of any kind against any of the children in this house, I will kill you. I swear it, Bridget."

She throws her head back but doesn't say a thing.

:: 53 ::

That night, Kitty and Nellie move back into their old room with Ethel and Julie.

"Lord have mercy," Nellie complains as she stuffs her clothes back into the old drawers and the tiny closet. "I thought I was done with this place, done with being a daughter and a big sister. Now I'm back, with the bonus of a shrewish stepmother."

After dark, when they are tucked into bed with the familiar old ceiling fan tick-ticking overhead, Papa enters. He stoops over to kiss his sleeping babies, then sits on the side of their bed.

"I'm sad that you had to come home," he says to Nellie and Kitty, "but relieved. I was stupid to think her adjustment to a new city, a new family, a busy husband would be easy. Give her time. If we can make it through the summer, till the weather is cooler and the babies are back in school, I think we'll be all right."

"I'll do some housekeeping here," Kitty says. "But I still want to help out Mrs. Kennedy, at least till her mother passes away."

Papa stretches out beside Ethel and Julie and soon Kitty hears his snore.

With Kitty back home, Aunt Bridget abandons housekeeping altogether, leaving the sweaty work to Kitty, calling her a lazy dunce if the laundry isn't folded just so or if dust bunnies gather under the furniture. Her focus is on Papa now, keeping herself pretty for him, keeping the whiskey flowing in the evenings, and ordering expensive prepared foods to minimize her time in the kitchen.

Kitty keeps herself pretty too. Her house dresses are shaped with proper foundation garments now and she always wears shoes with heels to make herself look taller. She will be no Cinderella to Bridget's wicked stepmother.

Her heartache is not so much for herself as it is for Ethel. Her chatty, effervescent little sister does not spring back from her head injury. She is quieter, avoids playing jacks and jumping rope, and every few days has another terrifying fit.

Dr. Broder has nothing to offer. "You may have to keep her home from school this fall," he suggests. "The brain heals slowly."

But Kitty doesn't see healing. She sees a fearful little girl retreating from life. Kitty tries to be upbeat. She gets Tommy and Joe involved. Tommy teaches the two younger girls how to play craps and Joe plays evening games of catch with them. Kitty has no idea what else to do. All she knows is that every day, she hates Bridget more. And she is determined to drive Bridget back to Chicago.

But how?

Papa seems to be digging in. In August, he announces that the house is up for sale and that they will find a more spacious home with a bigger kitchen and two bathrooms. He and Bridget have been saving every penny to afford something grand.

Kitty is suspicious.

One afternoon, while Bridget is out shopping, Kitty pokes into the desk where Papa keeps the account books, account books that Bridget is now in charge of. There is a stack of unpaid bills from the greengrocer, the butcher, the iceman, the dairy, a seamstress, a milliner, and more. She sees Papa's pay stubs. And she sees check stubs for large amounts written to the bank where Papa has a passbook savings account.

On another day, she searches for the savings passbook. She finds it stuck in an envelope of bank statements. The last deposit was in November of 1907, followed by a big withdrawal in May of this year. It now contains ten dollars.

"Maybe they have another account," Nellie says when Kitty shares her information. "A joint account."

"We have to find that other passbook," Kitty says.

It takes her days, but she finally finds it, tucked into the palm of a glove in the top drawer of what used to be Mama's dresser. Kitty quickly flips through it. Here was all the money. It takes a minute for her to realize that the only name on the account is Bridget's.

She keeps it and shows it to Nellie that night to make sure her eyes are not deceiving her.

"I knew she was a gold-digger!" Nellie says. "Let's show this to Papa right now. I want to hear what excuses he makes for her this time."

"No," says Kitty. "I'm going to confront her myself. She has too much power over him. She'll tell him some cock-and-bull story and he'll buy it."

The next day, Kitty puts on a fresh house dress and fixes her hair just so before she marches into the kitchen and throws the passbook on the table.

Bridget grabs it. "You little busybody! You little sneak!"

"I'll give you a week," Kitty says, pulling herself tall. "A week to put all the money back into the checking account and to tell Papa that you're leaving him to go back to Chicago. Make up whatever story you want about us *brats*. Just go. Or I'll spill the beans. If Papa doesn't report you to the police for theft, I will."

"You're an ignorant little fool. Wives can't steal from their husbands."

"You were planning to leave anyway, weren't you? With all our money. There wasn't going to be any grand house with two bathrooms, was there?"

"I tried to make this work out! No one has any respect around here!"

"Respect?" Kitty has to choke back her tears. *No crying.* "Respect? You hit my little sister with an iron frying pan. She still isn't recovered. She's having seizures because of you."

Bridget turns her back on Kitty, grabs her handbag, and stomps out of the house.

Before the week is up, on the Friday before Labor Day weekend, Bridget and her two boys disappear, their absence unremarkable till dinnertime.

"Where is she?" Papa asks Kitty.

Kitty shrugs. "I've been helping Mrs. Kennedy all day cleaning up after her mother's funeral. Everyone else was at the schoolyard carnival."

"Get something on the table."

He goes upstairs and returns in a few minutes with a note in his hand.

I have no choice, it says. *Your horrid children have finally driven me away. Send everything to the old address on 48th Place—or don't. Biddy.*

As Kitty throws her arms around Papa, she feels a rush of triumph. But it is followed by the panic of realizing she's made a horrible mistake. A horrible, horrible mistake.

She knew, as sure as she knew her mama loved her, she knew that Aunt Bridget did not return the money to the family's savings account.

Leaving Papa to stew with his glass of whiskey and his astonishment, Kitty recruits Joe to grind cold leftovers into hash. She runs upstairs to face reality: Papa's savings passbook still had only ten dollars in it.

As she stands there shaking, Nellie walks in.

"She's gone? She's really gone?"

"You were right," Kitty says, hearing the tremble in her voice. "I should have told Papa about the money. Why did I think I could bully her into putting the money back? Why? I'm such an idiot, such a goddamn idiot."

After dinner, Papa sends Modie to buy ice cream.

Kitty sits with him and Nellie on the porch steps with their bowls.

"I'm an old fool," he admits to them. "Don Quixote, thinking I found a Dulcinea to mother my children and to make me feel like a man again."

It takes all Kitty's courage to reveal Bridget's treachery.

After she tells the whole story of finding the money transfers and confronting Aunt Bridget, he is silent, finishing his ice cream and staring at the sidewalk.

"Can we have her arrested?" Kitty asks.

Papa scoffs. "She's across the state line. There'd have to be extradition papers filed and I doubt any charges would stick. I don't have the energy."

"What a gold-digger," Nellie says, scraping her bowl for the last melted spoonful.

Moses shakes his head. "Latching on to a St. Louis man with seven children is surely digging for gold the hard way. She was as much a fool as I was." He sighs. "And yes, Catherine, you should have told me immediately. We'll have a long winter ahead of us."

:: 54 ::

The wicked stepmother is gone. The house is Kitty's again. Her dear papa is not only broke but broken. In the weeks that follow, he comes home late from work, drinks too much, and is short-tempered. He goes out two or three nights a week, to hear some music, he says.

The family drifts again, like those weeks after Mama's death.

On Tuesday morning, October 6, Moses is late coming downstairs. The younger children are at the table eating oatmeal. Ethel has the morning paper in front of her.

"Look! Papa's in the news!" she says suddenly. There on page twenty-two, between ads for Blanke-Wenneker Gum Drops and Dr. Price's Baking Powder, is an article with the headline *HIGHWAYMEN AND BURGLARS BEAT VICTIMS AND ESCAPE.* She reads aloud. "*Moses Flanagan. 50 years old. 4221 Farlin Avenue, captured one of two highwaymen who attacked him early yesterday morning near Twelfth and Morgan streets. Robber who escaped had $6 of Flanagan's money. The prisoner being held at the Carr Street Station pending application for a warrant.*"

With that, they hear Moses's footfalls on the stairway and he makes his entrance, limping and sporting a swollen jaw.

"Papa!" Modie cries. "You captured a bad guy!"

"And he was a nasty son of a gun!" Moses responds, with jovial bluster. "Had him by the leg, I did!"

"Mother of God," Nellie mutters. "What next? What in the world were you doing in that neighborhood?"

"The saloons there have good piano players, sometimes a trio or quartet. It soothes my soul."

"How soothed is your soul with a busted jaw?" Nellie scolds.

"I may be old, young lady, but I'm lifting and moving wood all day with these hands. I grabbed hold of his leg like a vice till the police came."

Tommy slaps him on the back. "Nice work, Pop."

That evening, Papa's back is stiff and the side of his face is a mass of purple and red. He had promised to take the girls to see the Veiled Prophet parade, with its glittering floats of St. Louis debutantes in their magnificent gowns, but Nellie persuades him to rest and Tommy volunteers to take Julie and Ethel on the streetcar.

At the kitchen table, Nellie pours a beer into three glasses for Papa, Kitty, and herself.

"I have news," Nellie says, lifting her glass. "I got a new job. Working the switchboard at Hotel Jefferson downtown. It pays better than the office girl job." She takes a breath. "And, because the hours are so variable, they provide free rooms to the operators. I can start right away. I may never fly around the world like Nellie Bly, Papa, but it's one step out to experience the world on my own, like you always tell me."

"Congratulations, my dear!" Papa clinks his glass against hers. "Now, what about you, Catherine? You need to be out there in the world too."

Her eyes widen. "No! I mean, the girls—they need me. Ethel is still recovering, still having fits. Julie is so fragile. Neither of them is back in school."

"I've had a few conversations with Mrs. Kennedy," Papa says. "She has some nurse's training and can watch them during the day now that her mother has passed on. I'll find a girl for laundry and tidying up. We'll make it work. I owe it to you."

Kitty looks from her father to her sister. Moses has sad, beaten eyes. But Nellie's eyes glint with the boldness of choosing her own life over service to her family. Can Kitty take off her apron and do likewise? She imagines herself dressing for a downtown job, wearing her pretty boots with the Cuban heels, carrying a handbag full of cosmetics and streetcar tokens. Having a collection of hats. She imagines having a boyfriend and packing for carefree picnics in the park or sitting by a fireside not surrounded by chattering children. But it is such a leap.

"I'm scared," she whispers and looks at her father. "What if I fail?"

He pats her hand. "You will fail. You will start over. There's no magic to it."

She gives him a hug and kisses his bruised cheek.

Within a week she has a job as a switchboard operator at Bell Telephone.

Part 3. Hellos & Goodbyes, 1908-1913

:: 55 ::

October 1908. Becoming a Bell Telephone operator is a huge transition for eighteen-year-old Kitty. For years she has been the stay-at-home sister, bossy and organized, scolding when scolding is due, and interrupting her chores on a whim to sit at the piano or play a game.

But at Bell Telephone, she is a humble worker bee in the great hive of twentieth-century telecommunications. She is lucky to land a job on the day shift. She begins work at exactly 6 a.m. and ends at exactly 6 p.m., with four fifteen minutes breaks scheduled in between.

The first day is hell. She fumbles with cords, asks callers to repeat themselves, and worries how long it will be till she gets to use the bathroom. But by the end of the week, she masters the flow. Her mind hums with voices and her hands never stop moving. She learns to speak clearly in the standard Bell phrases. *Operator... one moment, please.* She finds her rhythm. It's like playing the piano, where there is joy in hitting the right notes and not missing a beat.

By quitting time, her ears hurt from the pressure of the headset and her shoulders ache from her constant arm movement. She finds her groove, but no concert pianist has ever put in a day's work with such concentration. She is satisfied.

As the dark, cold days of November begin, she needs to wake up at 4 a.m. in order to get dressed, eat something, pack a lunch, and walk to the streetcar stop for the slow ride downtown. Despite a neighborhood girl helping out, the kitchen is always a mess. Every morning she clatters around, griping out loud that nothing is where it should be or dishes were put away dirty or someone forgot to buy bread. Her banging around wakes the others and they complain.

Within a couple of weeks, she decides it will be less hassle all around if she pays for a cot to sleep next door at the Kennedy's. Mr. Kennedy is a factory worker on the same schedule, so there is always coffee and oatmeal ready when she comes downstairs. And for a penny extra, Mrs. Kennedy is happy to pack her a sandwich.

If the weather is nasty, Kitty envies Nellie her room at the Hotel Jefferson, an elevator ride away from the switchboard, with a coffee shop in the lobby. But most days, she is invigorated by her streetcar ride. She is out in the world, rubbing elbows with other working people, getting to know the conductors, seeing the same riders day after day. She nods and smiles at friendly faces, sleepy in the morning, exhausted in the evening.

On the ride home, she begins to notice a tall young man eyeing her. He has clear blue eyes and sandy hair.

"Do I know you?" she finally says to him.

"You're one of the Flanagans, right?" he answers.

She nods.

"Francis Barrett," he says as he tips his hat. "We live on Lexington. I've seen you at Mass and at some fish fries."

Kitty thinks. "Is your sister a dressmaker?"

He smiles. "Mamie. She's a real pro. Works for a skirt maker now in Wellston."

At a church social, Mamie once admired one of Kitty's homemade dresses and gave her some finishing tips. They spoke about fashion and Kitty wanted to get to know the older girl, but life pulled them in different directions.

Kitty and Francis begin sitting together. They chat about their families and compare the similarities and differences. His family is Irish too.

"My mother came from Mayo. Mayo-God-Help-Us," he tells her. "Arrived in Chicago right in time to witness the Great Fire. When was that, about 1870?"

"Mayo-God-Help-Us. My mother always said that too. She also came by way of Chicago, but later, in the '80s. She fell in love with my papa on a trolley." With her coat sleeve bumping against Francis as their streetcar chugs its way west, she feels her cheeks burn.

He continues with his story. "Barretts are from Mayo-God-Help-Us too. Got driven out during the potato famine in the 1840s. Worked their way up to St. Louis from New Orleans, then wound up in Franklin County. I was born on a homestead in Catawissa. Moved to the city here when I was ten. So, kind of a country boy at heart."

"What brought your family back to St. Louis?"

"Mother hated the farm," Francis said. "She swears Granny Barrett put a curse on her for having a mind of her own, say, for refusing to ride a horse side-saddle like a proper young woman. Mamie was a twin, but her sister died at birth—a curse, Mother insisted. She campaigned for Daddy to take us away to St. Louis."

"Oh, my! She must have been really scared."

His blue eyes drift off to some distant place and time. "We jumped out of the frying pan, into the fire." He heaves a sigh. "Two more babies lost, then Daddy dies of a heart attack, all within three years."

"That's terrible," Kitty says. She has never considered *curses* as a source of misfortune. "I was twelve when my mama died. How old were you when your father died?"

"Fifteen."

The streetcar ride with Francis becomes the highlight of her long day, an interlude of conversation between the focused frenzy of the sixth floor of the Bell Telephone building and the unsettled homelife on Farlin Avenue.

Francis is a clerk with the big wholesale hardware company Norvell-Shapleigh on Washington. She is surprised to hear that he's going to be twenty-five in January and that he's had his name in the City Directory as a working man since 1900, nearly nine years.

"Mother made Tom and me get jobs when Daddy died. She was already forty-eight years old. No one pays old women what they pay young men."

Kitty grasps the sad truth of losing the breadwinner. Papa had a management job when Mama died and never missed a paycheck. If it was Papa who died, she and Nellie might have been pushed into factory labor. Or maybe the family would have wound up living in the poorhouse, next to the insane asylum on Arsenal, laboring on the county farm as paupers.

Kitty snaps out of her nightmare vision, as Francis goes on.

"You'll meet Tom one of these days," he tells her. "He takes himself *very* seriously. We both started work at Luyties—you know, the big mercantile. They have a grocery operation on Sixth and Franklin." He shakes his head, eyes softening in a memory. "So there we are, fifteen and sixteen, Catholic school boys, father dead, mother hysterical, tossed out into the business world, and Tom says to me, he says, *Francis, we have to buckle down. If we can't go to St. Louis University, we'll have to turn our clerk jobs into a college education.*" Francis laughs. "Intense! Instead of joining us in a game of Parchesi, he's the fellow who'd rather sit in his room inventing his own game. You have to meet him to believe him."

Kitty and Francis get a kick out of the fact that they are both second children, each with an older sibling, smarter, better-looking, and more ambitious than they are.

The holidays are a blur. Office clerks like Francis Barrett get time off for the holidays, but switchboards have to keep running. Their junior status requires both Nellie and Kitty to work on Christmas and New Year's Day. Papa, Joe, and Tommy are exhausted from working extra hours to make up for Aunt Bridget's larceny, so little is planned except to play games and to rein in Modie from his growing fascination with street gangs.

On Christmas Eve, Nellie rides the streetcar home with Kitty, so they can attend midnight Mass together before heading back to work. Kitty tells her about the daily conversations with Francis.

"I'd like a boyfriend," she says. "I think about him in bed at night. But he's almost twenty-five. He might want too much of me, too fast."

Nellie asks, "Does he touch your hand? Ever give you a peck on the cheek when you part? Does he look at you all dreamy when you talk?"

Kitty wrinkles her brow. "No. None of that. We talk and laugh, that's all."

"How do you know he isn't already married?"

"Oh, my!" This possibility makes Kitty reconsider every conversation she's had with Francis.

Nellie continues. "You'd be surprised at the eye-opening I've had working in a hotel. I thought it would be a good place to meet a rich husband, but all I see are Don Juans. The only women striking it rich are the midwives, selling their tonics and their procedures to girls who miss their monthlies."

Kitty is aghast. "I don't think Francis Barrett is any kind of Don Juan. He's a complete gentleman."

"All I'm saying, Catherine, is be smart. They are all complete gentlemen—until they're not. A word to the wise is sufficient."

Kitty admires Nellie's savvy when it comes to boys. Her pretty face and curvy figure attract lots of flirtations, but she is careful, owing to her love of dime novels, where virtuous young women always protect their honor against villainous suitors and false lovers.

"No one's pulled any of those shenanigans with you, have they?"

Nellie straightens herself on the seat. "Of course not. I'm nobody's fool."

Kitty grabs Nellie's gloved hand and they ride the rest of the way home in silence.

:: 56 ::

It is mid-January before Kitty sees Francis on the streetcar again. He is all smiles and launches into a long story about having to work every night on Norvell-Shapleigh's year-end inventory process.

Kitty is cautious and forces herself to say, "I imagine that made your wife awful lonesome."

"What? My *wife*? Haha!" He has a full-throated, hearty laugh. "Do I look like an old married man to you? An old lecher with a straying eye for beautiful working girls? Haha!"

Kitty pulls her coat tightly around her and tucks a strand of hair under her hat. She looks straight ahead. "You never know."

Francis folds his hands together on his lap. "Well! I'm a devout Catholic. Nuns all through school. Altar boy till I was thirteen. I've hardly had a girlfriend. Too busy really."

Kitty gives him a sidelong glance. "I got booted out of Catholic school for hitting a nun." She tells him the story of Nellie's sketchbook and plays it for laughs. They both wind up in stitches.

Kitty is relieved. She likes Francis and wants a beau but is unsure about the kissing and touching parts. She is better at attracting pals and running with groups of friends.

"Say, Kitty," Francis says. "What do you say we meet after ten o'clock Mass this week and you join me and my family for dinner?"

Kitty hesitates for a moment, surprised, then accepts.

Sunday is unseasonably warm. Kitty decides to wear her plaid taffeta skirt with a frilly shirtwaist, a fitted bodice, and her high-top shoes with the medium heel. Her stylish felt chapeau sports a hatband with a couple of long pheasant feathers. It is exciting to be promenading down the street after church with such a good-looking and mature young man, even though her stomach flutters at the idea of meeting his family, who have all gone to eight o'clock Mass before them.

Mrs. Barrett is an ancient woman with leathery skin and steel-gray hair pulled into a tight bun. While sisters Mamie and Katie set the table and serve their guest tea, Mrs. Barrett grills Kitty about her family and her work. Kitty has no problem being chatty and polite, but she senses disapproval from the old woman.

"I want my children to be successful," Mrs. Barrett says. "Well-to-do. You need skills to get there. And you can't marry young. Having children too young kills all a woman's dreams."

Kitty is too polite to assert that her family used to be well-to-do before her father lost his fortune to Aunt Bridget, so she simply nods and smiles.

Mrs. Barrett goes on. "My Mamie is barely twenty-four and already supervises a room of fifty seamstresses. Katie is teaching herself typing and shorthand and will take a course at Bryant and Stratton when she finishes eighth grade. And my boys! Look at them, learning business and getting more accomplished by the day. No time for tomfoolery."

As Kitty wonders whether Francis's inviting her to dinner falls into the category of tomfoolery, the brother Tom runs down from upstairs into the dining room. He's carrying an accounts ledger.

"This is driving me crazy," he says, as he moves a place setting to spread the ledger open on the table. "I can't get these figures to come out right."

Starting to feel inferior to the ambitious Barretts, Kitty blurts out, "I can do math. Do you want me to try?"

"Who are you?" He stares at her with piercing blue eyes.

"Kitty Flanagan," the mother says. "From the parish. Works a switchboard for Bell Telephone. Francis's friend."

"Do you know double-entry bookkeeping?" he asks.

"I can add," Kitty states, sensing the defensiveness in her voice.

Without so much as a howdy-do, Tom delivers the ledger to Kitty's lap and hands her his pencil.

The wide page has a list of food vendors in the first column, then a column for every month of 1908. The page is filled in from May onward, the numbers added up both horizontally and vertically.

"The vendor subtotals and the monthly subtotals should add up to the same number, but they won't," he tells her.

"In May, Tom opened his own grocery business," Mrs. Barrett says, beaming.

It takes Kitty less than five minutes to find the two addition errors.

"Jesus," is all he says as he takes the book and disappears back upstairs.

"You're welcome," Kitty calls after him.

The dinner is pleasant enough, with Francis and Mamie leading a lively conversation about local events, including the ongoing police crack-down on lid clubs, which, Kitty finally figures out, are after-hours joints that illegally serve liquor. She decides to introduce a new topic.

"Not to change the subject," she dares say, "but this is the one-year anniversary of our house fire."

She has their attention as she tells the thrilling tale of her family's battle against the flames. She makes a big deal of Nellie's defying the inferno to push their prized piano onto the porch and then getting her picture in the paper. "The newspaper said it was a total loss, but my Papa has a lot of contacts in the building trades, so he rebuilt it better than it was before."

Kitty amazes herself that she can turn the disaster into something to brag about over dinner with strangers. The Barretts are impressed. Tom asks an inconvenient question about how the fire started, but Kitty ignores it to go on about the piano.

"We love that piano," she says. "Papa got it second-hand from the owner of the Rosebud Café and it's the very piano where Scott Joplin wrote some of his first published tunes." Kitty has always doubted this pedigree for their old piano but realizes on the fly how entertaining the story is.

After dessert, as she gets ready to leave, she sees that Francis is preparing to walk with her.

"Oh, don't you bother," she says sweetly. "I'd like to see myself home."

He walks her out to the sidewalk. "Did you enjoy yourself?" he asks. "I know Mother can be tough—and Tom, well, I told you he was awful serious."

Kitty squeezes his arm. "Your family is amazing. Thank you for introducing me to them. We'll talk more tomorrow, right?"

He nods. "Yes, of course! Till tomorrow!"

Enjoying the sunny respite from dreary winter, Kitty walks slowly from Lexington to Farlin. She loves the energy and purposefulness of the Barretts. She is tickled that she might have a beau. But she needs the time to think. How fast does she want to leap from being a Flanagan to being a Barrett? Her recklessness in confronting Bridget lost the family fortune. She likes having a job but how long does she want to work a twelve-hour day for a fraction of what her brothers make as mechanics? What is she good at?

Nellie calls her 'the organized one.' Is there more? She makes a mental list. Organized. Quick, loud, nosy. Reliable. Responsible. Affectionate. Excellent at hopscotch and jumprope, but where had that gotten her? She thinks. What she loved about schoolyard games was getting all the girls involved, the more the merrier. What do you call people who do that?

Today, as intimidated as she was by the Barretts, by the time they passed around their platter of tiny lamb chops, she found herself in command of the table by turning her family drama into entertainment. What do you call that?

Being Kitty, she decides. Yes. Being Kitty.

:: 57 ::

August 12, 1909. Kitty turns nineteen during a withering St. Louis heatwave. But it's a day like every other—at her post at 6 a.m., out the door by 6:05 p.m. The air circulation on the sixth floor of the Bell building is well-engineered to keep the equipment and the operators from breaking down and her layers of clothing are made from loose-woven linen to keep her skin dry and cool. But outside the heat shimmers on the hot sidewalks and the city smells like rotting garbage.

On the streetcar home, she stands to get the maximum effect of air blowing through the windows between stops. She pulls out a fan that Francis gave her when he quit his job downtown and said goodbye to their long streetcar rides together.

In June, Francis joined Tom's grocery store business, which moved from a tiny shop at 4832 Easton to a more spacious building across the street at 4841. Tom got a loan to buy the whole building and moved the family into the apartment upstairs, efficient for the brothers and handy for Mrs. Barrett and the sisters to be on the streetcar line. Renting out their home on Lexington gives them extra cash to invest in the business.

The plan, Francis told her, is for Tom to open a second store, which will become Francis's operation. With two stores, they'll have the advantage of greater buying power with the wholesalers. Kitty is happy for them but misses her daily conversations with Francis.

Today, as she walks the final block toward home, she sees Ethel and Julie sitting on the Kennedy family's front steps.

When they see her, Ethel says, "Papa told us to stay here till he finishes reading the riot act to the boys."

"Modie got in trouble," Julie adds. "He didn't come home last night."

Now Kitty can hear her father's voice and hurries into the house. Her three brothers are squeezed together on the settee, Tommy and Joe stony-faced, Modie in the middle, with tears streaming down his cheeks.

"I'm at the end of my rope," Moses bellows. "I've had it!" He glances at Kitty. "Go take care of the girls." His voice shakes with rage. He yanks the starched collar off his sweat-soaked shirt and throws it on the floor. "Do you hear me, Catherine?"

"No," she says as she raises a couple of windows. "I want to know what's going on. Julie says Modie didn't come home last night."

"I spend the day searching for this little bastard at every hospital and precinct station in town, when there's a stack of estimates on my desk that need negotiating." He glares at Modie. "I stop back at the office and they tell me the Carr Street station called. They've been holding a kid who calls himself Jimmy Maroney and I guess when he gets hungry he admits he's Moses R. Flanagan and wants his papa."

Kitty looks at Modie. "Why did they pick you up?"

His eyes well with tears. "I didn't do nothin'! The coppers rousted a bunch of us kids just cuz we was hangin' out on the wrong corner."

"Jesus wept," says Moses. "Speak like you have an education, young man. I'm not raising a thug. And quit lying." He turns to Kitty, with disbelief and exasperation in his eyes. Sweat runs down the side of his face. "He was picked up driving, *driving* the getaway car for a couple of safecrackers who robbed one of the clubs downtown. They would have pressed charges except that he's *twelve* bloody years old."

Now he turns to Tommy and Joe. Tommy has just turned seventeen and Joe will turn fifteen tomorrow. "I'm paying the bills around here, so which one of you is going to take charge of your brother and keep him off the streets?"

Tommy jumps up. "The little bastard isn't my problem. I gotta get out of this house. I was going to tell you tonight. I got a room a few blocks from here, free if I take care of the property after work. I want my own life."

Papa pauses his rant, surprised by the news. "Good for you. Showing some initiative. That's fine." He turns to Joe. "Can you take him with you to the mill tomorrow? He can sweep and run messages."

"I will," Joe say, punching Modie on the shoulder. "But I'm looking at a new job. *Globe-Democrat* is looking for an office boy—starts at 2 a.m. but I'd be home by mid-afternoon. Modie and I can hang out together—how would that be, kid?"

Pushing Joe away, Modie snivels and rubs his eyes.

"Sit up straight, young man." Moses tosses him the handkerchief from his breast pocket. "Wipe your face and apologize."

The boy stares at the floor. His voice is soft. "I'm sorry, Papa."

"For—? Speak up now."

"For getting picked up… for lying… for being bad." Tears well up in his eyes again.

Papa takes a deep breath. "Catherine, go get the girls." He takes a dollar out of his billfold and hands it to Tommy. "Run down to the corner and get a couple half-gallons of ice cream. Drop one off at the Kennedy's. We'll sit on the porch and have ice cream for dinner, for Kitty's birthday. Joe, you better make a sandwich for the baby so she doesn't have more than a taste of sweets. Modie, get out bowls and spoons."

:: 58 ::

The next thing Kitty knows, Papa announces that he has sold the house. It's after dark on Saturday, September 4, still a muggy eighty-four degrees. Kitty is sitting with him on the front porch steps. They are sipping on cold beers.

"It will pay off all the bills," he says, "With the renovations after the fire and the improvements to the shed, it sold quickly. We'll rent for a while." He takes a drink. "I sold the piano too. A saloon on Easton liked my Scott Joplin story and paid a pretty penny."

The crickets in the overgrown rose bushes nearby begin to chirp, while Papa lights a cigarette.

Oh, what a bitter moment, Kitty thinks. The Flanagans without a piano. The world is a sadder place.

He goes on. "For the time being, we'll move to a small flat on Newstead, till I find something better. You can stay with the Kennedys or get a room elsewhere, maybe on a streetcar route. It will be good for you to experience the world with fresh eyes. Being a stranger forces you to solve a dozen small problems a day, makes you savvy."

Tears spring to Kitty's eyes and she's glad it's dark. Him and his damn immigrant experience. She doesn't want to be a stranger. She can get plenty of savvy surrounded by friends and family.

"What about the girls, Papa?" School is starting on Tuesday. Ethel has a fit once or twice a day and she's good as a ragdoll afterward. Julie's sugar is under control only because we're all watching what she eats."

"I know," he says. "I've spoken with Mrs. Kennedy. Neither is fit for the rough and tumble of schoolyards and classrooms of fifty assorted ragamuffins. But they can't grow up unschooled. They can't grow up with no skills. And I won't live forever."

Kitty has never thought about her baby sisters as adults, disabled and dependent. Her mind goes blank with alarm. But then she has a thought.

"I'll get married, Papa. And I'll take them in."

"What nonsense is that?" he asks.

"Sure, I'll get married to Francis Barrett. He's a good Catholic and he's on the way to having his own business. His sister Katie is just a couple of years older than Ethel."

"Has he asked you to marry him?"

"No," she says, with a sudden flutter in her belly. "But I can see it coming. And you can't want me to work at Bell Telephone forever."

He pats her knee in the dark. "Drink your beer, Catherine. I'll hear none of it. I was thinking of boarding school for them. Where they can be well cared for, while they get some education and learn a trade. It's what a rich father would do, don't you think?"

When the deed is transferred on the Farlin Avenue house, Papa and the four children move to 6227 Newstead, way north, near Calvary Cemetery. At the same time, he quits his estimator job at St. Louis Mill Work to work as a draftsman for Marvin Planing Mill on the west side, in Wellston, which means giving up his company car to become a streetcar rider again. He says that, with money in the bank, he needs the easier job so he can pay more attention to Modie, Ethel, and Julie.

Meanwhile, Kitty finds a room with kitchen privileges at the Flynn family home on 3861 Kennerly, near Vandeventer, a shorter ride to work each day. When she stops by the parish rectory to give Father Lavery her change of address, he raises an eyebrow.

"St. Matthew's," he says, looking at her note. "Abandoning your father and his motherless young ones to go out on your own? The Church doesn't approve—"

She cuts him off. "It's what my papa wants."

He scoffs. "That father of yours, thinks he knows everything."

:: 59 ::

As the first crocuses of 1910 bloom, Kitty receives a card from Papa telling her they have moved again, to a small rental house on 4245 Lexington, within walking distance from her room and just two blocks from the now-rented Barrett house.

On the next Sunday, Kitty and Nellie visit to pitch in with the organizing.

"How will this work, Papa?" Kitty asks when she and Nellie get him alone for a minute in the kitchen. "Ethel says you're leaving the two of them alone during the day."

"Modie looks in on them between his errand-boy runs. Ethel's eleven, Julie's nine—quite capable of looking after each other." He waves his hand at Nellie's frown. "It's only temporary. I'm arranging for them to board at Guardian Angel Industrial School."

"Papa!" Kitty says. "That's an orphanage!"

"Nonsense," he replies. "They board plenty of students from motherless families, who pay to give their girls what they can't get at home. The Daughters of Charity have a good reputation for teaching girls." He moves a couple of bowls from the table into the sink. "That isn't the only news. St. Louis Mill Work wants me back, at my old estimator job, with a pay raise. It's only a mile and a half from where the girls will be. Everything is working out."

The sisters bundle up for their wintry walk to Kitty's room, where they share a can of soup before Nellie heads back downtown. They tell each other that their father is doing his best given the circumstances. No doubt the girls will be able to join the family for Sunday dinners. Nellie thinks the school is only about a mile from Hotel Jefferson and Bell Telephone, so she and Kitty can visit them once a week or more after work, maybe for dinner.

They agree on all these things but look glumly into their bowls.

"Breaking up the family," Nellie says. "It makes me sad as hell. Makes me grieve for Mama all over again."

On Sunday, April 3, 1910, a week after Easter, Kitty and Nellie join the rest of the Flanagan family for ten o'clock Mass at Holy Rosary—a Mass offered in memory of their mother Maggie. The boys in suits, the girls in frilly dresses, they join the procession to Communion like perfect lambs of God.

After church, they walk to a restaurant on Newstead for brunch.

Papa raises his glass of grape juice. "Here's to our babies, Mary Ethel and Julia Loretta, who start their adventure in the world this afternoon."

His voice is cheery, but Kitty hears the catch in his throat.

"You'll make such good new friends," Kitty joins in.

"And learning to sew!" Nellie adds. "I wish I'd learned to operate a machine at such a young age."

Ethel and Loretta manage little more than wan smiles in response.

The joviality continues as they promenade back home. Ethel grabs Kitty's hand, holding on tightly, not saying a word.

At 2 p.m., a limousine pulls up to drive the whole family across town to the Guardian Angel Industrial School, where they will leave Ethel and Julie.

A nun meets the family and shows them around—dormitory, kitchen, workrooms, school rooms, play rooms—all sunny and clean. The girls who live there crowd around the Flanagans, asking questions and inviting Ethel and Julie to join their games.

When it's time to go, Papa hands the nun an envelope with the first of the monthly ten-dollar fee and says he'll be by tomorrow to check in on them. Nellie and Kitty promise to visit on Wednesday evening.

"And next Sunday," Nellie says, "I'll come by for you and we can ride the streetcar up to the house for dinner."

They are at the door when suddenly Ethel has a seizure. Julie bends over her to perform her usual first aid, left arm across Ethel's chest and her right hand stroking her hair, her lips near Ethel's ear singing her calming song, "Bicycle Built for Two."

The nun makes a move to pull her away, but Tommy says, "Stop! Julie knows what to do."

The seizure ends. Ethel sits up and hugs her dear sister. The spell of false cheer is broken. The family runs to them and smothers the two with another round of hugs and kisses, everyone in tears.

They finally get to the door again and, amid loud *See you soons*, the Flanagans pile back into the limo.

As the vehicle pulls away, Kitty says, "I think they'll be happy there." Tears stream down her face.

Modie begins to sniffle and Papa pulls him close, a distant look in his eyes. "They'll be just fine," Papa assures him as his voice cracks. "You be my good boy now, hear me?"

Modie nods and hugs his papa back.

:: 60 ::

Leaving Ethel and Julie at Guardian Angel is the hardest decision Moses has ever made. Despite putting on an optimistic face, he feels defeated, a terrible father who can't rescue Julie from her stupors or Ethel from her fits. A power beyond him, whether it is God or the devil—the same power that stole Maggie—pulls all the strings and he has neither the wit nor the virtue to fight back.

He reads the papers for news of medical advancements. This is America, after all, and the twentieth century is already ablaze with technical triumphs. Surely, treatments for diabetes and epilepsy will soon come along and free his smart little girls for normal lives.

But for now, there is nothing.

He takes consolation in his old habit of talking to Maggie as a form of bedtime prayer, easing him to sleep. He begs her to let him know somehow if he makes bad choices. To give him a sign if Guardian Angel turns out to be like the institutions in Ireland, where young women are abused by their guardians and live out their short lives in servitude.

He goes on to tell Maggie that he feels old at fifty-three, with a hint of rheumatism creeping into his joints. That he is putting together a bid for windows in a tract of new houses near Tower Grove Park. That he hates Nellie living at that businessman's hotel and wishes she'd settle down with a nice boy from the parish. That he's worried about Tommy's drinking.

That Joe and Modie got brought home by the police after a raid at the Typo Press Club downtown. That Kitty talked her way into a promotion as an assistant shift supervisor at Bell. That he misses music.

Conferring with Maggie over the early weeks of summer, to the soft croaking of tree frogs outside his bedroom window, he works out another problem. Bridget has not filed for divorce and he is afraid that, when she does, he will have to admit to some cruelty he never committed and will be forced to pay her alimony. A path lights up: since she is the one who spurned her obligations to him and his family, who left St. Louis with all his money, he will sue her—for abandonment.

Maggie seems to be listening. As Nellie considers turning twenty-two, she moves back home. *Temporarily,* she says, claiming she'll never find a husband living in a downtown cubby hole with three roommates. She begins to attend the evening concerts at the bandstand in Fairgrounds Park and the socials in the parish schoolyard.

Kitty moves too, to live with her Uncle Pat Keville and his new wife Delia.

During the Bridget fiasco, Maggie's brother Pat Keville moved to St. Louis for better money laying cobblestones for the city. In his forties, he surprised everyone by falling in love with Delia Lavin, a Roscommon woman about his age. They married at St. Edward's last year on November 3. It wasn't long before the strong-willed Irishwoman raised an eyebrow at Kitty's rooming with a family of strangers.

"Surely, you'll move in with us, darling girl," she said one Sunday, when she and Pat were visiting the Flanagans for roast chicken. "Unless you're in domestic service, an unmarried woman should be living with her family." She shot Moses a disapproving glance.

To Moses's surprise, Kitty accepted the offer eagerly. He wondered if, for all her independence and capability, he underestimated how much Kitty missed having a mother.

As for Moses, looking for company, he goes to Mass on Sundays and takes evening strolls. He is a rarity in the Irish-American neighborhood—a single father of seven, twice cursed, both widowed and abandoned. Even with his good income, available widows and spinsters steer clear of him.

The bright spot is May Gaines.

:: 61 ::

About the same time Moses began his job at St. Louis Mill Work at the end of 1906, May took over a little no-name lunchroom around the corner on Chouteau at Jefferson. In those days, she was May *Rakestraw*, a shapely woman in her late thirties, a childless widow full of enterprise.

On days when Moses needed to be in the office, he'd have lunch there. She made a decent meatloaf and enjoyable chitchat. He was attracted to her, to the point of fantasizing about whether she would be game to take on a family of seven children. But she was a Lutheran. To his eternal regret, he decided that his brother's Catholic widow Bridget would be a more appropriate second mother to his brood.

He didn't see much of May during the disastrous 1908 but learned she got remarried, to Sam Gaines, a widowed plumber who lived above the restaurant with his two children.

Now, in the autumn of 1910, he learns that Sam Gaines is dead. When the lunchroom reopens, some weeks after the burial, Moses sits at the counter and May tells him that a stroke did Sam in.

"He went a little nutty for a couple of months before," she says. Her grey eyes have acquired purplish half-moons and strands of silver streak her black hair. "Scared me half to death. Must have been all the lead pipe and chemicals he was careless with—the fumes, you know. The doctor called it something else, but who can keep track of all that lingo, right?"

Sam's sister took custody of his children, to May's relief.

"So here we are again, Moze, a couple of lonely hearts."

In November, when a judge grants his divorce petition, Moses is finally freed of Bridget. With that worry behind him, his usual quick lunches become longer. Instead of using his Irish charm on business clients, he spends too much time entertaining May. It doesn't take many afternoons like this before she invites him upstairs after work.

Her apartment is spare. The windows are open and a breeze makes the white sheers billow into the small rooms. It reminds him of the apartment he and Maggie had in Chicago so many years ago, when there were just the two of them.

May pours shots of whiskey. When the world begins to blur, May disappears to the bedroom, returning without her somber black bodice and skirt. In her frilly white petticoat and camisole, arms bare, she sits beside him, running her fingers along his cheek and across his mustache. They kiss. Her touch is too much for a lonely man to resist.

:: 62 ::

Taking a lover is a notion that Moses can barely deal with. As exciting as it is, on the drive home, he panics. At fifty-three, he can't start over with another child. Brushing off his embarrassment, he stops at three pharmacies before he finds one that sells reusable German condoms, a luxury item he only knows about from overhearing whispers among wealthy builders who hint at keeping mistresses. Preventing pregnancy hadn't been an issue with Bridget. She adhered to Church teachings about not interfering with God's will, but also claimed to be well into her change of life. May is another story.

When he gets home, Nellie is sitting on the settee reading the newspaper. He can see that dishes are still scattered on the kitchen table.

"You missed dinner," she says without looking up. "I didn't move back here to be the *hausfrau*. You'll have to get after the boys to clean up their own mess."

"Of course, dear. I'm sorry. Work, you know." He drops his overcoat on its hook by the door.

Nellie puts down the paper and stares at him. "You reek of perfume." She sniffs the air. "*La Rose Jacqueminot* from France. I know it from dabbing on the testers at Grand Leader. Popular with older women who like those cloying floral scents."

"Really," he says, his mind racing to come up with an explanation. But Nellie is too smart for a lie. He drops into a chair. "All right, I've been seeing a woman. Known her for years. Operates a little lunchroom five days a week near work. Lost her husband over the summer."

Nellie rolls her eyes. "Needing a daddy for her children?"

"Stop it. She has no children. She's lonely. I'm lonely. There's no crime in it."

"Will you at least introduce us before she moves in?"

Nellie's words sting, but they make Moses think. May delights him, but he needs to use his head, be systematic, keep everyone happy. He and May work out an arrangement: he stops by for a drink on Tuesdays and Thursdays, then on Saturdays he takes her to a musical matinee downtown. He visits with his babies at Angel Guardian on Mondays and Fridays and is home every night to see that dinner is put on the table. On Sundays, all his children gather for his roast chicken.

He's making it work.

:: 63 ::

"He's seeing a woman," Nellie tells Kitty as they walk to Guardian Angel for their Wednesday dinner with Ethel and Julie.

"Here we go again. Is she a clothes horse like Aunt Biddy?"

"I haven't caught a gander yet, but she wears expensive perfume. I wangled out of him that she's a widow two times over and barely thirty-five. No children."

"Holy mackerel," Kitty says, "she could be a murderess like that Bell Gunness, who poisoned her suitors with strychnine and buried them in her yard. They were hacked to bits!"

"Don't scare me, Kitty! Bad enough she could be another swindler like Biddy."

Kitty pulls her scarf closer against the damp wind blowing down Twelfth Street.

"Okay, we need a plan, then. It's time for us to have a big old Christmas Eve party like we used to. We'll tell Papa to invite her and we can check her out. And she'll see what she's in for if she hitches her wagon to the Flanagan wild horses."

"Great idea. You'll invite the Barrett brothers too?" She grabs Kitty's coat sleeve. "Do you think Francis will ask you to marry him—a ring for Christmas?"

"Oh, wouldn't that be the icing on the cake! That damn switchboard is turning me into an automaton." Kitty holds her hat down against a gust of wind. "Hey, do you have eyes for Tom Barrett?"

"He's tall and good-looking, somebody with a brain in his head and ambition in his hands. Why not? It might be fun to marry brothers." Nellie gives her a wink.

"Francis says Tom is looking for a college girl, someone with an education to help their business grow."

"Then he'll be a bachelor forever. Those girls aren't looking for someone who bags groceries for a living."

Kitty stiffens. "It's not 'bagging groceries.' They're businessmen, started from scratch. Tom got accepted into the Knights of Columbus, bought a house for his family. Both of them have had their names in the City Directory since 1900!"

"Don't get huffy at me, Catherine. I'm just saying those girls don't read the City Directory. They read the Social Register."

Christmas Eve falls on a frigid Saturday. In the small Flanagan house, lights twinkle off the frost accumulating on the windows. Papa fetches May from her apartment and the babies from Guardian Angel.

May Gaines is a thin woman dressed in black silk. Kitty wonders whether it's improper for a woman whose husband is less than a year gone to be seen with another man. When Kitty takes her fur coat, she can't help glancing at the label as she lays it on Papa's bed.

"Muskrat," she whispers to Nellie. "And it's old. The lining is worn."

"She brought a tin of homemade nut bars," Nellie whispers back. "No sugar, she says, for Julie. Have to give her credit for that."

"She has a tremor, did you see that? In her hands."

The doorbell rings and guests arrive—old friends from the neighborhood, Uncle Pat and Aunt Delia, and finally the Barrett brothers, who bring a basket of goodies from their store.

The Flanagans have no piano, no Victrola for music, but as the beer flows, Moses leads the group in singing a few Christmas carols. Twice, Julie pulls Kitty into the boys' room where Ethel is having a seizure.

"She can smell them coming," Julie says, as they hold on to Ethel and comfort her.

Kitty is already agitated that Francis's gift to her was a small box—a minuscule box—of chocolate-covered cherries, which she eagerly opened in hopes of finding a ring inside. It was not her night. She tossed the open box on the table and let the guests devour the candy.

Nellie flirts with Tom Barrett, who looks particularly handsome with windburned cheeks. She nudges him to sing along with the group, but he looks uncomfortable.

"Mother is waiting for us at home," Kitty overhears him telling Nellie. "We're having a late dinner. Francis and I need to head out."

With that, the brothers grab their coats and disappear into the night.

It is late. The boys have taken Julie to enjoy the pomp of midnight Mass, and Papa is driving May home. Kitty and Nellie sit on the settee, with drowsing Ethel sprawled between them. Kitty runs her fingers through the twelve-year-old's hair, while Nellie massages her feet.

"So, that's that," Kitty says. "The only romance here tonight was Papa's. I thought she looked old for thirty-five. What do you think?"

"Because she's so skinny. And her hair is turning gray. Of course, she wouldn't be the first woman to lie about her age." She sips her tea. "Papa's all gray now too."

"I guess he could do worse," Kitty says.

:: 64 ::

For Moses, the pleasure of his well-ordered life collapses with the start of 1911.

First, his boss collars him.

"I need you back in the mill, Flanagan. Lowell Bleacheries is locating a big cotton mill on the river in Carondelet. We got the contract for the woodwork. Need to upgrade our equipment. Need you to oversee the installation and retrain the men. Long hours, but you'll be well-compensated."

Moses is happy to work with the men and machinery again, even though he has to give up his Ford. But no one else is. May sulks over their lack of afternoon trysts and hates having to take the streetcar downtown to meet him for their Saturday matinees. Nellie sulks because she is left organizing dinner every night for Joe and Modie, which she barely does anyway.

To make matters worse, Guardian Angel Industrial School notifies him that they will be closing their doors within weeks. Unless Moses makes other arrangements, Ethel and Julie will be transferred temporarily to one of the Daughters of Charity family homes, where the children have to walk to the local parochial school. However, both the nuns and he agree that neither of his girls is fit for regular school. Ethel needs a vocational program that can also manage her mental issues. Julie continues to be sickly and is unlikely to tolerate traditional school. Another soul-nagging problem to solve.

At the end of the second week in February, Moses shuts down the mill, as the old machinery is hauled out and floors are reinforced and repaired before the new machinery arrives.

He has time to spend with May, though there is much on his mind.

On Saturday, February 11, he stops by the mill to check progress, then walks to May's apartment. No matinee today. He is feeling like crap—feverish and achy. His throat is sore and swollen. A mild rash has popped up on the palms of his hands. Is it something about the solvents they are using on the floor of the shop?

"Oh, I've seen that before," May says. "I had something like it a while back, let's see, not long after Sam and I got together. Dermatitis. Didn't last long. But looks like you have a touch of the flu as well, poor dear. Stretch out on the sofa and I'll take care of you."

He tells her about needing to find other arrangements for Ethel and Julie. She gives him a hot toddy and wants to know more.

"I have an idea," she says, as she snuggles beside him.

In spite of the winter's turmoil, Moses still expects the children to gather home on Sundays. He likes to roast a chicken, but today Kitty is bringing cold cuts.

He is grateful. He still has this grippe or whatever it is. With his paper and coffee, he can doze in his living room chair and put together his words for the announcement he needs to make when the children are assembled.

Nellie dresses for Mass, still hoping the perfect young man will bump shoulders with her and fall in love. Joe and Modie prefer to sleep late. Tommy was supposed to pick up Ethel and Julie for the long streetcar ride to Lexington, but the school is suffering from an epidemic of chicken pox and home visits are canceled.

Just as well.

At the table, Moses piles horseradish on his sandwich, hoping it will clear his head.

"Look here," Moses says after everyone is chewing their first bites. "I have something to tell you." He has their eyes. "May and I plan to get married."

The children stare at him.

Joe chuckles. "Runs a lunchroom—at least she can cook." says Joe.

"Did you knock her up?" Tommy asks. "Are we going to have a little brother?"

"No! God, no. You children are the only jewels in my crown, always and exclusively."

His dark eyes squinting, Modie asks, "Is she going to beat the crap out of me?"

Moses snaps back, "Why would you say that?" But he remembers Bridget and her defense of the belt against Modie's legs. He puts a hand on his son's shoulder. "No, my boy, she'll never lay a hand on you."

Joe stares at his plate. "I don't get it. I mean, I guess you must be lonely. But a wife… a wife marries all of us. We barely met her. She'll be like Aunt Bridget, barging in, taking charge, thinking she's our damn mother."

"I know a lot of older guys," Tommy says. "Guys who got a babe on the side and don't bother their families with the details."

"I'm not that—she's not that kind," Moses protests, indeed bobbling his juggling act.

Kitty reaches over and touches his forearm. "Are you happy, Papa? Does the idea of marriage thrill you?"

Moses takes a sip of his beer. "*Thrill* me? May thrills me, if you want to use that word. With Guardian Angel closing, she is willing to close her lunchroom and take the babies home with us. I'm worried about Ethel, but Julie would benefit from May's cooking."

"It sounds like you've thought everything through," Nellie says. "Except this house isn't even big enough for the four of us. I'll move—I'm feeling like a nomad—but there still isn't room."

"That's a problem I will tackle tomorrow, assuming I can shake this bug I have." He massages the swollen glands in his neck.

"So when is the big day?" Kitty asks.

"May wants to get married on Valentine's Day. Tuesday."

"Tuesday!" Kitty says. "We're all working. What about the bans? The waiting period after the license? Have you already spoken to Father Lavery?"

Moses holds up his hand. "There will be plenty of time to celebrate. We're going out to Clayton—no waiting, license and justice of the peace in the same building."

"Oh, Papa," Kitty says. "We have to have *something*! We'll meet up here after work. I'll get a cake. Tommy, you figure out the drinks. I'll invite

Uncle Pat and Aunt Delia. Did you hear their big announcement? Aunt Delia is going to have a *baby*!"

"God help us, she's older than May," Moses says.

"Talk about thrilled," Kitty continues. "They're over the moon with joy, an old couple like that, thinking family life passed them by. Nellie, come share my room with me there. A baby will be so much fun!"

Nellie scoffs. "I'd like to think for one minute I have more important things to do than goo-goo-gaga over someone else's infant."

Moses can't help a laugh. Maybe everything will work out.

:: 65 ::

Kitty is not surprised to hear that, within days, Papa rents a recently built house at 4229 Athlone, north of Lee, still in Holy Rosary parish. It is two stories, with a larger kitchen and three bedrooms.

During the week of the move, Kitty devotes her spare time to helping. She gets to know May, a fussy woman who likes everything in its place. But overall, she is good-humored, has fun joshing with the boys, and listens to Kitty's advice about Flanagan family habits and quirks.

Nellie opts out.

"I'm sick to death of family life, having to worry about meal after meal after meal. Dishes, shopping, laundry. I'm going back to the Hotel dorm. I'm thinking of starting my own seamstress business. You don't mind if I take the sewing machine, do you? It will be easy to start with the girls at the hotel. Their clothes always need updating or altering and a lot of them can't even thread a needle."

"That's new," say Kitty, folding undergarments into a large carpetbag. "What happened to your plan to find a husband this year?"

"Anyone who gave me a second glance was all dewy-eyed about starting a family. Out of the frying pan, into the fire. I wish I was a man, like your Barrett brothers, bold enough to open a retail store, go out on a limb for my dream."

"Who says you can't?" asks Kitty, as she stuffs Nellie's summer shoes into the bag's side pocket. "Women run shops. May had her own business, a lunchroom Papa says was very popular with the area businessmen. Maybe we can learn something from her."

Nellie rolls her eyes. "Sure. She's successful at finding husbands and cashing in on their assets when they drop dead. And how many tips did she make by inviting all those businessmen to 'stay a little while' after closing? How much money did she collect for fake abortions or pretend visits to midwives for make-believe potions? Don't think I haven't met her type and learned the lessons she has to teach."

"Nellie! Are you joking? Am I supposed to laugh or cry?"

"Well, there's no point in crying if you don't have someone to comfort you, to kiss you and 'make it all better,' Nellie says with a wry smile.

"That's true. Anyway, go ahead and take the machine."

"I want to have a business of my own," Nellie says, "but I can't see how a woman rises beyond tenement living without a man backing her. However plucky May is, she still got insurance money from her string of dead husbands, so I better keep looking for a man. Someone successful, who I adore and who adores me. But no children till I'm at least twenty-five."

"How do you avoid children if you're married?" Kitty asks. "Mama always said that if God wants—"

"God, shmod," Nellie interrupts. "You don't see rich women saddled with seven, eight, nine children," she says. "Catholics and poor people are kept in the dark about birth control so that the rich don't run out of servants for their big houses and low-wage workers for their big factories."

Kitty hears the wisdom in Nellie's words. She would have been thrilled to get an engagement ring at Christmas, but unlike Nellie, she still enjoys the carefree single life, admittedly supported by the generosity of her Uncle Pat and his backbreaking labor repairing streets.

Could she ever be single and not poor? She could go back to school. She might make a good teacher, but that would take years to qualify for certification.

It would be easier to marry Francis. Someday.

:: 66 ::

Once the chaos of moving has subsided, Papa brings Ethel and Julie home for a trial weekend.

In the months she's been away, twelve-year-old Ethel has grown gangly, all legs and arms. The new house confuses her. She has one fit after another, resulting in broken dishes and a bloody nose for Tommy. Where ten-year-old Julie used to be able to calm her sister, now she is frightened of her.

While the Flanagans focus on Ethel's deterioration, Kitty is surprised to see May bonding with Julie, fixing her plates of food and taking her outdoors during the seizure crises.

After work on Monday, Kitty visits the new house again. Julie is helping May in the kitchen.

"This is wonderful," Kitty says. "But Ethel—"

Moses shakes his head. "Long talk with the good nuns this morning. Her fits are getting more frequent and more violent. Only one option for her now, I'm afraid—the City Sanitarium."

Kitty sags into a chair. "How awful!" The St. Louis Sanitarium on Arsenal has a terrible reputation as the overcrowded last resort for people with the most severe mental disabilities and most profound retardation. "What can I do to help?"

"Pray to your mother in heaven that they find a remedy for her," he says, handing Kitty a glass of beer. "Pray they find a medication to calm her poor terrified brain."

"I will, Papa, I will."

:: 67 ::

Spring and summer slip by. The economy in 1911 is booming. Nellie tells Kitty that her off-hours alterations and mending business keeps her busy every spare minute. At Bell, the switchboard operation expands and Kitty works extra shifts whenever she can.

When Peggy Keville is born in August, Kitty's aunt and uncle rent one half of an airy duplex at 1957 Semple. For a break on the rent, Aunt Delia agrees to manage the property. The location is just a few blocks north of 5530 Easton Avenue, where the Barrett brothers have opened their second store, the one Francis is slated to operate—the one that keeps Francis so busy that he can't stop to think about marriage.

Kitty tells herself it doesn't matter. Nevertheless, she makes it her business to see him nearly every day. After work, she takes the Easton Avenue streetcar to Belt, stops at the store to pick up a few things for Aunt Delia, and has a quick laugh with Francis. On Saturday nights, she strolls the mile to the Barrett apartment above the 4841 store to join them for parlor games or cards. And on Sundays, she sits with Francis at Mass.

But, suddenly, it's winter. Kitty is working an extra shift downtown on

Saturday, November 11, when the unusually warm day turns frigid and high winds begin knocking out phone lines. She barely makes it home without being blown over or hit by flying debris. Sunday brings an early snowstorm.

Through the holidays and into January, an unrelenting weather pattern of record low temperatures and paralyzing snowstorms settles over the entire upper Midwest.

Pipes freeze and explode all over the city. People are letting faucets run all night to avoid catastrophe but officials plead with them shut off their main valve instead. Too many open faucets are reducing the water pressure at the Chain of Rocks pumping station. If the pump fails, the city will lose its domestic water supply and all hell will break loose.

Life becomes a ritual carried out in a deep freeze. Kitty is constantly cocooned in her felt hat, wool coat, and thick stockings. Work is stressful as power outages across the Bell system cause lost calls and angry customers.

The Keville household is thrown into disarray as Uncle Pat works double shifts to replace cobblestones dislodged by pipe explosions.

As snow accumulates and temperatures plunge, the Barrett brothers struggle to keep up with deliveries through snowbound side streets. As Thanksgiving nears, they work through the night setting up gasoline-powered backup generators to keep their refrigeration and freezer units functioning during the frequent blackouts. They fill extra water tanks in case the main explodes.

After their own long workdays, Kitty and Mamie Barrett pitch in at the 5530 store during the busy pre-dinner hour, stocking shelves, filling customer orders, or working the cash register.

Working with Mamie is the highlight of Kitty's day. They talk nonstop. As a dressmaker, Mamie is always up to date with the latest fashions and coaches Kitty on how to stay stylish by altering and updating clothes from second-hand shops.

"Being poor is no excuse for dowdiness," she says from atop a ladder for all the customers to hear. "Staying fashionable is a sign of self-respect. Like having good manners, it shows you aspire to polite society."

Mamie enjoys poking fun at her family and her fate as the spinster daughter.

"Oh, it's all worked out," she says, with a chuckle, as they empty a twenty-five-pound bag of beans into a bin. "I'll stay with Mother all her days, whether it's at the house on Lexington or the apartment above the store. It's very Irish—lace curtains on the window, daughter in the kitchen."

"I'm counting on May to take care of Papa," Kitty says, folding up the burlap sack, "but I have my doubts. She's a good housewife, easygoing with the boys, attentive with Julie, but—" She lowers her voice. "*But* she's nutty as a fruitcake. One time, she told me people were following her and looking in the windows. Ridiculous. Papa just laughed. Another time, she blanked out for a few seconds and forgot where she was." Kitty makes light of Moses and May, but she prays the slightly off-kilter woman won't break her dear papa's heart.

:: 68 ::

Kitty doesn't catch up with Nellie till late February when they agree to visit Ethel after work. There are still piles of soot-covered snow lining the street, but the arctic temperatures have moderated.

"I'm so anxious to hear how your sewing business is going," Kitty says as they huddle at the streetcar stop.

"Business is great." Nellie laughs. "The hotel cottoned on to my work and gives me all the quick repairs needed by guests—you know, split seams, torn pockets. I get back to the room after my shift and there are a pile of orders on my bed needing to be finished before dawn."

"You must be tired, but isn't that great?"

"Between the hotel work and the girls' alterations, I'm making a few cents, but not enough to give up the switchboard, not enough to get a private room, much less a flat."

"Can't you charge more?"

"The hotel acts like they're doing me a big favor. Says the women at the Chinese laundry down the street will do their mending for less. And the girls give me their business because they can't afford a dressmaker."

The streetcar pulls up. They gather up their skirts, climb aboard, and find seats.

"Why can't you become a bonafide dressmaker then? Move back to Papa's with your sewing machine for a few months and get word-of-mouth going till you can open a tiny storefront on Easton. You can do anything you put your mind to, I know you can. Mamie Barrett has made a good career out of her stitching abilities."

"Ugh, you're proving my point, Catherine." Nellie lays her head against the streetcar window. "Mamie is a master craftsman who makes money by supervising a factory-floor of nimble-fingered women making skirts and earning less than I do. And where does Mamie live? In a household wholly supported by her big brother. And, like you say, starting anything 'on my own' means moving back with Papa. You can't do anything without a man!"

They get off the streetcar and hail a cab for the drive west on Arsenal.

"Speaking of the Barretts," Nellie says, "what's going on with Francis?"

"Nothing," Kitty answers. "We have what I guess they call an 'understanding,' but that's about it."

"Then he's taking advantage of you."

"Well, not in any confession-worthy way. When he walks me home on Saturday nights, he'd be satisfied giving me a goodnight peck on the cheek if I didn't hold his head and find his lips myself." Kitty can't help giggling at this pathetic admission.

"Oh, that's boring," Nellie says. "Maybe you need to show him a little ankle. And get your hair up off the back of your neck. You don't want to be one of those old couples who drift along for decades, still living with their families." She grabs Kitty's gloved hand. "You're too vivacious for a man who's just your good old cocker spaniel. Francis will lose you. Someone with fire in his belly will sweep you off your feet, I know that for sure."

When the freezing pipe emergency fades, Kitty stops her dinner-hour work in the store, but volunteers on Saturdays so she can stay at the center of Francis's attention. Following Nellie's advice, she alters her skirts to the slimmer new fashion, shortening them to show off the pretty turn of her ankle, and she makes sure her foundation garments fit just right. She moves her hair bun from the back of her neck to the top of her head, with a proper hat to complete the look.

In theory, 5530 is Francis's store to manage, but both brothers are in and out on any given Saturday, supervising the pickers, keeping the canned goods perfectly stacked, refilling barrels and bins, making repairs, and dealing with invasions of rats, roaches, and weevils.

Francis is thrilled when Kitty offers to run the cash register on Saturdays but seems clueless about her new look. It is Tom she catches giving her the once-over as she hangs her coat up, but when their eyes meet, he glances away.

She smiles to herself as she unlocks the cash register and greets the first customer of the day.

Working at the store is so much more fun than plugging cords into switchboards and saying the same pat phrases over and over. She chats with the customers about their cooking and what brands their families prefer. She laughs at their funny stories and sympathizes if they've had a streak of bad luck.

She also has her father's eye for efficiency and speaks up with her suggestions, like keeping the popular cereals near the cash register. Again, it is Tom who pays attention.

His sharp blue eyes focus on hers. He squints as he visualizes what she's describing, then tries it out.

Her ideas work.

"Where did you learn to think like that?" he asks one Saturday as they are closing up.

"Must be in my blood," she answers, pleased to have found the secret door into his mental fortress. "I've been listening to my father's stories about organizing planing mills all my life. The lumber gets dropped off in the yard and, if you don't have your jobs organized, the equipment set up, and men ready, you have a giant mess on your hands. He spends a lot of time breaking down new designs into small steps, standardizing procedures, and training the men to do things right the first time. Rework is the bane of the milling industry because properly cured lumber is expensive."

He nods and gazes up to the cans on shelves only a clerk can reach. "I get it. Inputs." His eyes shift to the front door. "And outputs. What's the shortest route between?" Then he smiles. "Of course, I've known that all along, back from my days at Luyties."

She smiles back and tucks a stray lock of hair behind her ear. "Of course."

:: 69 ::

On March 30, the Saturday before Palm Sunday, Kitty calls her father to ask him to attend Mass with her. "You can do your Easter duty with me, Papa," she says, referring to the Catholic obligation to take Communion between Palm Sunday and Pentecost.

"Thank you, my dear Catherine, but you know I'm not in a state of grace. A divorced man remarrying—it's the unforgivable sin."

"You should have spoken with Father Lavery about an annulment. Looking back, you had no real marriage with Aunt Bridget, no children, just a few months of—"

"That Irishman would rather see me burn in hell than petition Rome on my behalf. No Easter duty is going to save me from the fires of hell."

Hearing her father's disembodied voice say this feels like the most terrifying, most lonely thing Kitty has ever heard.

"Papa, you aren't going to hell. I don't care what the Church says. Whatever sins you've committed in your life—don't you think you've done your penance by being a good father and a hard-working citizen?"

There is silence on the other end of the line.

"Papa, are you okay?"

She hears his sigh. Then, he says. "Don't you worry. I feel old and my brain grows fuzzy."

The conversation leaves Kitty unnerved and then angry at the Church for pushing her papa out. At Mass the next day, as she joins Francis in their usual pew, she is still irate and barely acknowledges Tom and his mother in the pew behind them. She stands with her shoulders squared and her chin up, striking a defiant pose against all the holy hypocrites who can't leave a good man to his happiness.

The sermon is about Jesus' triumphal entrance into Jerusalem, but Kitty can only think about how the same people murdered Christ the following week. Her Church.

As she turns to join the Communion line, she notices Tom staring at her and wonders if she's been muttering her diatribe out loud.

That afternoon, carrying an umbrella in the chilly rain, Kitty walks the three blocks from the Keville apartment to 5530, where she plans to mark prices on cans.

Because it's Sunday, the store is closed and Tom is there alone. Francis, he tells her, got caught up fixing a plumbing problem at 4841.

Using a china marker, Kitty begins scrawling the price on the top of each can before she shelves it. "I think stickers would be faster," she muses out loud as she works. "If you standardize your prices and have gummed labels printed up, you'd have more time to set up your displays."

Suddenly, Tom is standing in front of her, towering over her, setting his big hands on the shelf to either side of her. She can feel the warmth rising from his shirt and the scent of Palmolive soap. She looks up into his serious blue eyes.

He starts to speak, stops, then starts again. "You are the most brilliant woman I have ever met," he says.

He is standing too close to her and her heart begins to race. "I don't think using stickers is a very original idea," she says.

"But you're always thinking, always problem-solving, always looking for better ways."

"Well… thank you," she says.

"And the customers love you."

She thinks she needs to duck out from under his arms, but finds her knees trembling and doesn't want to move. Her voice is breathless. "That's just me, good ol' Kitty, always chattering away, the human teletype."

He glances away for a second, then gazes back into her eyes. "I watched you at Mass this morning. You had this massive… presence. You're so petite and yet you looked like the tallest woman in the church. I've been worried, you know. Kroger is looking to expand in the West End and, if I'm not smart, they can run me right out of business. I prayed to St. Joseph to help me figure out what to do to keep my business going and to support my family. Then there you were, right in front of me. Kitty Flanagan. A vision of strength and ingenuity. And I realized this: that I have loved you for months. For years." He smiles. "Ever since you found the math errors in my account book that strangely warm winter day. I need you to be my partner. I want you to be my wife."

"What? Oh!" What just happened? "What did you just say?"

He laid his hands on her shoulders. "I asked you to marry me."

"That's what I thought." Kitty feels she might faint and grabs onto his arms. She has never held a man's arms like this, through the thin cotton of his shirt sleeves, all bone and sinew. A bolt of electricity blasts through her. *This is wonderful*, she thinks. *This is perfect*. She is floating on a cloud. She nods her head and says, "I think—I think you should kiss me."

Tom bows his head to meet her lips and his hands fall to her waist. *Oh, this is no St. Francis polite brush of lips.* Tom devours her. Her hands reach for his head. Her fingers feel the shape of his ears and run through his hair. *Don't stop, don't ever stop.*

They twirl around and he lifts her up on the counter. He hugs her close. "Oh, Kitty, I'm the happiest, luckiest man in the world. I swear to you all my love, forever and ever. I will give you a home and every beautiful thing you ever desired. I will give you as many beautiful, healthy children as you want and send them all to college. I will worship you through all eternity."

Tears spring to her eyes. When she can speak, she says, "And I promise I will make Barrett's Market a household name, an institution in every neighborhood." They laugh. She rubs her nose against his, then whispers, "I love you too, Tom. I didn't know it. But here I am, overflowing."

And they kiss again.

When Kitty's heart rate finally slows back to normal, she has one question: "What about Francis?"

:: 70 ::

Kitty and Tom come up with a plan. As anxious as Tom is to pull Kitty into his business, they agree to take one step at a time. Kitty will break it off with Francis. And then when Tom thinks Francis is recovered, he'll ask if Francis minds that he wants to see Kitty.

That plan lasts one week.

On Easter, after Mass, Kitty visits her father on Athlone. All the children are dressed up and present for Easter pastries. Nellie arrives with Ethel. Lagging just behind her is Uncle Pat and Aunt Delia, with little Peggy.

Kitty has been walking on air all week, bursting at the seams to tell everyone about Tom's proposal and their plans for growing the grocery business. But, until Francis is taken care of, all she can do is glow.

May has done a beautiful job baking and setting out her good china and silverware for the occasion. The family has learned over the course of this year to keep their gatherings short and lighthearted to limit the stress on May, who repeats the story of her grandmother's china each time she puts it out and collapses into a depression if her baked goods aren't declared the finest anyone has ever eaten.

The family fawns over Peggy, who is beginning to crawl. They chat about baseball and politics. The boys have discovered Zane Grey novels and talk about moving out west and becoming cowboys.

May has introduced Julie to *Anne of Green Gables* and Julie proposes that she and Ethel travel north to Prince Edward Island as soon as they're old enough to buy train tickets. Everyone pretends that's a great plan, ignoring Ethel's stupor, caused by the heavy dose of potassium bromide that helps curb her seizures. As Uncle Pat tells a story about life on the family farm in Ireland, Kitty catches Papa looking sadly at his Ethel, taller than Kitty now, but at thirteen, still dressed in a baggy knee-length dress meant for a younger girl. She wasn't following the conversation at all.

When they exhaust all their fantasies about life on a cattle ranch out west or a farm in eastern Canada, Papa tells them that his job has changed. The big hardware stores and mercantiles are selling stock woodwork components now, much of it by mail order to farmers and townsfolk in rural Missouri and Illinois, some as far away as Iowa and Arkansas. He has moved to sales, keeping retail outlets stocked with the mill's most popular designs.

May interrupts Papa's dissertation on mail-order woodwork and says to Nellie, "What about you, dear? What good fortune does this Easter bring *your* way?"

"Not much," Nellie says. "Trying to build a little mending and alterations business from my room at the hotel. Keeps me very busy."

"Oh, you'll never make a dime that way. No repeat customers. No word of mouth. You need to open shop in a neighborhood, on a busy street. Middle class customers, like yourself, not poor washerwomen whose ass has gotten too big for their britches." May laughs at her own image. "Beautiful girl like you ought to have a husband to stake her in business. Any prospects?"

"Well, I…" Nellie is speechless.

Kitty jumps in. "You had a business on your own, May. How did you do it?"

"Oh, I did it the hard way, hon. My first husband Rakestraw worked in the yard at Union Station. Had some kind of spell and fell in front of a train. Railroad paid me a little insurance. The lunchroom was on a good corner, I could tell, but Ben Clearwater, who ran it before me, he wanted to move out west, so I took a gamble." She pats Papa's hand. "And here I am today."

Nellie catches Kitty's eye before she looks at May. "I have my admirers, but…"

Aunt Delia laughs. "But you don't want a laborer with a sun-baked face and broken fingernails!"

She pokes Uncle Pat, who takes his elbows off the table and hides his hands on his lap.

He looks at his old wife with adoring eyes. "Ay, you're lucky no one else would have me."

"That I was." Aunt Delia laughs again. "But there's lots of brewery money, lots of shoe-factory money in this town now. Pretty girl like you—smart to wait for a refined man with a good education. But don't wait too long!"

Kitty senses Nellie's nerves jangling and reaches out to grab her hand under the table. She shifts the focus.

"No one's asked me about *my* beau. I'll be visiting with the Barretts this afternoon for dinner." She looks around at her family's faces, all taking life so easily as they devour May's treats. "But I'm planning to break up with him."

Nellie squeezes Kitty's hand. "What's the trouble?"

Kitty furrows her brow and tries to look serious. "Nothing," she says, and presses her lips together to keep from grinning.

"Your eyes are dancing! Don't be coy now. You can't tease us!" Nellie insists.

Kitty blurts it out. "I'm in love with someone else!"

Everyone sits back in their chairs, mouths open.

Nellie jumps up. "Who? Who is it?"

Kitty jumps up too. "Oh, me and my big mouth. It's supposed to be a secret. We're already engaged. There are just a few things that need to be taken care of before we announce."

"He isn't married, is he?" Nellie demands. "He doesn't have to get a divorce, does he?"

May is suddenly aflutter, standing up and gathering plates, clattering them as her hands tremble. Moses puts a hand on her back and an arm out to steady her. "Let me help you with that, dear," he murmurs and gathers up the dishes himself.

"I really have to go," Kitty says as she grabs her jacket and umbrella. "I'll tell you all as soon as I can, promise!"

She flees, wishing so badly to shout the news about her and Tom. Nellie runs down the porch steps after her and takes Kitty by the arms. "Tell me who it is."

Kitty can't resist. "Tom Barrett."

Nellie gasps then hugs Kitty close to her.

Kitty continues. "You knew it wasn't going anywhere with Francis. The flame has flickered out. He's not the *one*. Tom—we just fell into each other's arms working at the store last Sunday. He says he thinks I'm brilliant, that he wants me as his partner and the mother of his children." Tears are making her nose run. She sniffs. "But now—we don't want to hurt Francis, so we aren't planning anything, till he's okay with it, till he understands, anyway."

Nellie kisses her cheek. "Oh, you brave girl. I love you!"

As rain begins, Kitty pulls back to open her umbrella. "I love you too!"

:: 71 ::

Kitty is mad at herself for spilling the beans. But maybe it's out of her system and she can now visit the Barretts as usual until she can get Francis by himself for a talk.

Easter dinner goes well. Or so Kitty thinks. As soon as she is alone with Mamie and Katie in the kitchen doing dishes, Mamie confronts her in a conspiratorial tone. "What the heck is going on between you and Tom?" Her eyes are wide and full of mischief.

Kitty looks down at the dish she is scraping into the garbage pail.

"Catherine Flanagan, you and Tom could not keep your eyes off each other all during dinner."

Sixteen-year-old Katie chimes in. "I saw too! And I saw him slide his foot across the rug under the table to touch your shoe!"

Kitty's cheeks begin to burn as Mrs. Barrett bursts through the swinging door into the kitchen, her wrinkled face in a terrifying scowl. She looks at Kitty, but before she can speak, they hear a crash from the dining room.

They hear Francis yell, "You bastard! You son of a bitch! You cold-hearted lizard demon of a brother! How could you do this to me?" There is another crash. "You get everything! You take everything! You could have a different girl every day of the week, but you take mine!"

Kitty covers her mouth in horror.

Mrs. Barrett gives Katie a nudge. "Go find me two ice bags."

As Katie runs through the door, Kitty sees Tom sitting on Francis. The door swings shut and their voices become unintelligible. Mrs. Barrett rushes over to the icebox for a small block of ice, drops it into a wooden bowl, and chips it into chunks. As Katie dashes back through the door,

Kitty sees the brothers still grappling on the floor.

"Pack them with ice and take them out to your brothers. Sure one will have a black eye and the other a knot on his head," Mrs. Barrett says. Then she pulls out her bottle of whiskey and a tray of six shot glasses. She pours two and hands one to Kitty.

"The boys are working it out," she says, raising her glass, her eyes twinkling. "Welcome to the family, darling. You're going to make a fine wife."

:: 72 ::

The following Sunday, while helping out Tom at the store, Kitty asks about Francis. The Barretts ended their Easter day with shots of whiskey all around and with Francis wishing Tom and Kitty the best, but his eyes were hard and wouldn't meet Kitty's gaze.

"Francis will be fine. He's very outgoing," Tom says, as he punches numbers from credit slips into the adding machine. "But look, I'm more worried about keeping our customers from leaving us for Kroger's." He reaches out and runs his fingers down her sleeve. "You're a vital part of that effort, Kitty. We need to get married right away."

Kitty lays her hand on his. "If you want to be king of Easton Avenue, we have to start behaving like royalty. No rushing off to a Justice of the Peace. People will talk. We'll have a Church wedding. Small and tasteful, but an event."

She envisions herself in a white silk suit. But already the St. Louis air is muggy and she's sweating through her layers of cotton, so she adds: "We'll marry in the fall after the weather cools. At Holy Rosary. Papa is still in that parish and they have a hall we can use to entertain our friends afterward."

Tom's brow furrows. "If that's what you want. I suppose Mother would love a family gathering. Still…"

"Still, Kroger," she says. "Kroger is lurking in the wings to destroy you."

He nods. "There aren't enough hours in the day."

Kitty squeezes his hand and glances around the store, where each can is stacked into precise pyramids, a visible testament to Tom's iron will. She has an idea.

"I'll tell you what," says Kitty. "I'll give my notice at Bell and start working with you. But, till we're married, you have to pay me what I get there as a shift supervisor."

He looks down at his calculations, letting the thought register, then smiles. "Terrific idea. It'll give me time to get the tenants out of the Lexington Avenue house and put up some fresh wallpaper, so we can move right in."

"Wait a minute. Lexington?"

"Well, sure. I always thought that would be the house I raised my children in."

"Why in the world would we live way down on Lexington when the business in here? The two of us would have to commute two miles every morning, every night. Then children? A logistical nightmare. All while the rest of your family is still squeezed into the apartment over the store." She shakes her head. "How about this—move your family back to Lexington. Your mother can have her vegetable garden and her chickens again. We'll live above the store. Let Francis do the commuting."

Tom reaches out to take her hand. "I heard you say once that you loved tending your mother's roses on Farlin. I thought you would want roses. I thought—"

"Later," she says. "When you have a chain of stores and we're rich, we can buy a country house and I'll tend roses to my heart's delight. But till then—" She reaches over and pats his arm. "We have many miles to travel."

:: 73 ::

The wedding is set for Friday evening, November 22. Kitty and Tom intend to keep it small—a few old friends from the parish, a few congenial business associates, and family. They limit the family to those who live in St. Louis, except for Kitty's Chicago godmother Aunt Delia Walsh. She's surprised when Mrs. Barrett reminds Tom of his relatives on the south side.

First is his Uncle John Barrett and his wife Catherine, who gave up farming and moved to St. Louis after the old parents died. They are in their sixties and live near Tower Grove Park.

"And of course their six children," she reminds him. "There's Mayme—she must be in her mid-thirties now, a hat maker—you should see her work!. Jane. Kate—she's a dressmaker who does all her work for one single family. Maggie. And, let's see, the baby Tom, about your age, Kitty. Those five are still living at home. The sixth is Martin. He works as a chauffeur and just married Anna. Are you getting these down?"

Then there is his Uncle Peter Gibbons—her brother—and his wife, Ellen. He's a laborer for a chemical plant in the Carondelet neighborhood, near River DesPeres. Also in their sixties, they have three grown children living with them—Tom, Annie, and Harry. Their daughter Mary Ellen is married to Roy Dunlop and they have a four-year-old.

"Mamie will have their addresses," Mrs. Barrett adds, as Kitty jots everything down.

But the summer is less about wedding plan and more about figuring out the retail grocery business. Kitty is forced to push beyond her good instincts to learn the intricacies of managing inventory and ordering from a variety of wholesalers. Tom believes in the growing trend of one-stop shopping, with meat, dairy, produce, and dry goods all in one convenient storefront. Kitty quickly realizes that the smaller the store, the more deeply she needs to understand the neighborhood's habits and preferences. For the Irish Catholics, they have to be ready for fish on Fridays. For the Russian Jews, they can't run out of beets.

It is October before her attention turns back to the wedding.

To minimize expenses, everyone pitches in. Katie Barrett writes out all the invitations in her beautiful hand. Mamie volunteers to make Kitty a white suit of silk shantung, copying a pattern she saw in a magazine. For the reception, they will have wine punch and sweet treats. Mrs. Barrett organizes her sewing circle friends—nearly all widows like herself—to bake. May joins in to make *petit fours.* Aunt Delia, struggling to manage her toddler and finding herself with-child again, signs on to make four loaves of Irish soda bread.

One afternoon Papa calls Kitty to give her the news that the Flanagans have moved from the house on Athlone to a large apartment at 4241 Evans, near the Easton Avenue streetcar.

"Tommy moved back home because he likes cleaning up May's leftovers, but we hardly see anything of him or Joe. So it's down to Modie and Julie."

"I like that you'll be closer to me after the wedding," Kitty adds, but then it dawns on her: "You're out of Holy Rosary parish. Can I still have my wedding there? Heaven help me!"

"That old cuss Lavery won't know the difference," Papa says. "He doesn't see me at Mass anyway. Now, what about your sister? I don't hear a thing from her."

"I assume she'll be my maid of honor, but my gosh, I've been so busy. We haven't coordinated a thing. I wish she had a private phone. I better get cracking."

Kitty puts a postcard in the afternoon mail asking Nellie to call as soon as she can.

Nellie calls the next evening. "I don't know where the time goes. How are the wedding plans coming along?"

"We're trying to keep it simple to save money," Kitty says, thrilled to hear her sister's voice. "Mamie is making me a silk suit. One of her cousins is a milliner, so she's designing a matching broad-brimmed hat covered in small feathers."

"Very high fashion!"

"I'm so excited." Kitty peeks around the corner to make sure her aunt and uncle are out of earshot. She speaks softly "I didn't think anyone would ever fall in love with me. You know, really, really in love, like men in books. But Tom burns so bright, as intense in romance as he is in his business. Such a surprise. I adore him!"

Nellie's silence makes Kitty rush on.

"Oh, listen to me babble. Say, I'm assuming you'll be my maid of honor, right?"

"Seriously?" Nellie sounds surprised. "Doesn't that entail a bunch of responsibilities? It's not that I—well, really, Mamie Barrett has been at your side since the engagement, helping you plan, working on your trousseau. And she's been such a friend to you. Shouldn't she be your attendant?"

"But you're my sister." Kitty feels a tremble in her chin. Asking Mamie hadn't occurred to her.

"I'm so exhausted. And this job is killing my back. You know, I stopped doing the hotel mending. Hate to admit that May was right, but I'll never stitch my way out of being an operator. So depressing. I'm just not in the mood for all the wedding rituals. Mamie is much more, you know, into the whole Catholic family thing."

Kitty suddenly misses her mother. What a different occasion this might be if her own artistic but firm-handed mother were managing the event. Nellie wouldn't dare beg off if Mama were in charge.

"All right," she says, hearing the whine in her voice. "I understand.

I'm sure Mamie would love to stand up for me." As she says this, she feels like she is not only marrying into the Barrett family but being adopted by them.

"Look, I'll still be there for you," Nellie says. "I'll still do something special for the occasion." She pauses. "I know! I have a trunk full of beautiful undergarments. Come visit me and try on the best of what I have for your new style. Oh, I know you hate hand-me-downs, but most have scarcely been worn. I'll tailor what you choose to fit your petite frame and embroider them with roses. I can do that lying in bed. It will be my wedding present to you."

"That's a lovely idea!" Kitty feels better. "Can't wait to see you!"

:: 74 ::

On the evening of November 22, old Father Lavery says a nuptial Mass, consecrating the vows between Catherine Margaret Flanagan and Thomas Patrick Barrett. At the reception in the church hall, Kitty is swept into the whirlwind of meeting Tom's uncles and cousins and glad-handing the business associates. She hardly has a moment for her own family, except to see that everyone is fine and looking their best. May outdid herself dressing Ethel and Julie in ivory silk frocks with pink sashes and pink bows in their hair.

Nellie arrives in a fashionable taupe wool suit with a straight, button-trimmed skirt and long, fitted jacket, topped with a large plumed hat. On her elbow is her escort, introduced as Harry-something. Kitty pulls Nellie close and whispers in her ear. "I'm wearing the whites you altered for me. The embroidery is luscious. I can't wait to show Tom."

Nellie squeezes Kitty's hand and kisses her cheek. "For my luscious sister."

An hour into the chatty reception, Papa surprises Kitty with his gift of music: three Irish musicians with fiddle, bodhrán drum, and concertina. Now they have a party. The church hall is quickly clouded with cigar smoke, the lights are dimmed, and someone spikes the punch with gin. The trio plays popular American melodies as well as sentimental Irish-American tunes, like "My Wild Irish Rose." The guests push aside tables and chairs and begin to dance.

Kitty takes off her prim jacket and oversized hat and pulls Tom Barrett into the cleared space. He is reluctant to dance, but Kitty takes the lead, making him laugh as he tries to follow her steps. Out of the corner of her eye, she sees her father say something to the fiddler. The band starts playing "Let Me Call You Sweetheart" and Moses belts out the words.

> Let me call you "Sweetheart," I'm in love with you
> Let me hear you whisper that you love me too
> Keep the love-light glowing in your eyes so true
> Let me call you "Sweetheart," I'm in love with you.

Papa's familiar baritone makes Kitty choke up. Tom pulls her close, catching the rhythm of the tune. Everyone joins Papa in singing.

While the cookies and cakes dwindle, Joe and Tommy Flanagan keep the punch bowls filled from an unknown and magically intoxicating source.

The musicians revert to more traditional Irish music. To Kitty's amazement, old Ellen Barrett pulls her brother Peter Gibbons onto the dance floor, lifts her skirts away from her feet, and begins a traditional step dance. The other old immigrants line up with them. Papa, Aunt Delia Walsh, Uncle Pat and Aunt Delia Keville, Peter's wife Ellen, a few neighbors, and even Father Lavery. Their feet aren't always dancing the same steps, but they move as one to the beat, as the younger guests clap and tap their toes. Before long, all the guests are dancing their own improvised versions of the traditional sets.

It is late by the time Kitty and Tom say their farewells.

Francis has given them the gift of a carriage ride and borrowed fur coats for the two miles between the church hall and their apartment over the store. The weather being fair for November, Tom asks the driver to fold back the roof. Beyond the city lampposts, they see twinkling stars.

As Tom pulls Kitty close, she realizes her big hat got left behind. No matter. Nothing matters except the adventure ahead.

"We'll have a grand life together, won't we?" Kitty says.

"I can't imagine being happier than I am at this moment," he responds. His hand caresses her cheek and she turns her face toward his.

They kiss.

:: 75 ::

Thursday, February 6, 1913. As they work, Tom and Kitty debate which five of the twenty-one flavors of Campbell's soup they'll order this month

"Don't forget a couple meatless selections for Lent," Kitty says.

"Yup. Tomato. Maybe asparagus?" Tom studies his list.

"By the way, I told Uncle Pat I'd have a basket delivered to Aunt Delia. He's working overtime again." Uncle Pat called last Thursday to tell her Delia had given birth to their second daughter.

As Kitty heads for the back of the store, the phone rings. Reaching for the pad and pencil in her apron pocket, she answers the storeroom extension.

It's Nellie.

"I'm glad you called," Kitty says. "Did you hear Aunt Delia had her baby? I stopped by on Sunday. Cute little doll, baby Delia. The christening's on Palm Sunday. We can go in on a gift together if you want."

Nellie scoffs. "I'll never understand how those old fogeys are having babies like they're in their twenties. Those girls will be orphans before they're ten years old."

"Stop. The two of them are ecstatic."

"All right," Nellie says, "I'm happy that they're happy, okay? I'll go in with you on something. But listen, I called because I have news of my own."

Kitty hears a slight tremor in Nellie's voice.

"I'm all ears," Kitty says.

"I want you to be the first to know that yesterday Harry and I got married."

"What?" Kitty is stunned. She met this Harry at her wedding reception in November and didn't even catch his last name. He clung adoringly to her sister during the festivities, but Nellie looked pained at his attentions. The family gathered over Thanksgiving and Christmas, but Nellie came alone. Kitty assumed she sprang loose from the lopsided relationship.

"Married!" Nellie says. "At long last! Isn't it wonderful?"

Kitty hears the words, but not the joy. "Of course! I'm thrilled for you. But no wedding? No celebration? I can't even remember his last name. I figured you dumped him because—"

"We had our ups and downs," Nellie cuts in, "but we'll be fine. Kralemann's his name. I'm Nellie Kralemann now. We decided over the weekend. What the hell, you know? Monday, he found a little rental on West Belle. We took a couple hours off work yesterday to go out to Clayton and get the deed done. Easy as pie."

"So tell me about him." Kitty glances through the doorway to make sure Tom can manage without her for a few minutes.

"He's a bookkeeper or something for the railroad. Lives—*lived* with his mother and his sister, up on Hebert near where Papa used to work at Crescent. He's a little younger. Your age. They're Germans. Lutheran or something, not Catholic."

"So why didn't you bring him to any Christmas festivities?" Kitty asks.

There is a pause on the other end. "Okay, I did dump him. But, but he wouldn't take no for an answer. He adores me. Isn't that what counts?" Kitty hears Nellie take a sharp breath. "Anyway, things heated up pretty good and the next thing you know, we decide to get hitched, minus all the falderol."

"Heated up? Do you mean 'confession-worthy' kind of heated up?"

Kitty expected Nellie to laugh at her reference to their old conversations, but the line was silent. Kitty pressed on. "I'm bowled over. It's all so sudden. It took me months to figure out the logistics of getting married and look at you—just like that." *People will talk*, she almost added, but bit her tongue.

Nellie changed the subject. "Jefferson will give me the boot—they like single girls—so I want to get my mending and alterations business going again, from home. Lots of work to do there. Harry is still supporting his mother, hoping he can wangle a promotion. I'll let you know when we're settled. You and Tom can come by."

In bed that night with Tom, Kitty shares Nellie's news and her worry about why they ran out to Clayton to get hitched by a Justice of the Peace. They lie in the dark, the wind rattling a loose window.

"Papa would have been in seventh heaven to pay for a church wedding, to walk his first-born down the aisle, to sing at her reception." She pulls the cover up to her neck. "Maybe she just didn't want all the grief of marrying outside the Church, the pressure on Harry to convert or swear to baptize their children Catholic. She hates that crap. Just like her to reject the whole brouhaha."

"Or should we expect a well-timed announcement that she's in a family way?" Tom asks.

"Shut up!" She gives Tom a light jab with her elbow. "That's exactly what I'm afraid of. And she'll be stuck with a poor Lutheran railroad clerk she doesn't love."

Tom pulls her close and gently massages the day's knots from her back and shoulders. "It happens more often than you think," he says. "Doesn't mean she can't be happy." He kisses her. "Not everyone is as lucky as me."

He kisses her again—her lips, her ear, her neck. His hand finds her dreamy parts, floating her up and away from the world and all its problems.

:: 76 ::

Wednesday, March 26. Kitty is taking advantage of a lull between customers to mop up puddles on the floor. Tom finishes a phone conversation and stares at his notepad. He's been talking with his wholesalers every chance he can get since Monday.

"Honest to God," he says, "it feels like the end of the world. Not one supplier knows when his next shipment will arrive."

For days, rain and wind have wreaked havoc on the Midwest and South. First, windstorms and tornadoes disrupted shipments of produce from New Orleans, already slowed by the annual flooding along the Mississippi. To the west, a large swath of Omaha—a hub for grain transportation—was leveled by a tornado followed by a snowstorm, a combo that knocked out the telegraph and telephone system. To the east, on Easter Sunday, wind and rain caused the Great Miami River to break through Dayton's levees, drowning the city and throwing Ohio's shipping routes into chaos.

St. Louis is also getting its share.

"Did anybody check on your Uncle Peter?" Kitty asks. "People are saying everything along the River Des Peres from Forest Park south is inundated. Ten or twenty feet of water in some areas."

"Ugh. I better ask Mother."

The phone rings. Tom answers and holds up the receiver.

"Your father. Sounds upset."

Kitty scoots behind the counter to get it.

Papa's voice is tight and urgent. "Catherine, I'm at Nellie's. Do you have her address? Mother of God, you need to come here now. Can you get here immediately?"

Her heart begins to race. "What's is it?"

Kitty saw Nellie three days ago, after Easter Mass on Sunday, when she and Tom joined the Flanagans for pastries. Nellie came alone, as she did to baby Delia's christening, saying that Harry had to take his mother and sister to services at their Lutheran church. Kitty found her pale and quiet, mentioning a backache as she picked at the sweet roll on her plate.

But Kitty's attention was pulled to her little cousins, Aunt Delia's and Uncle Pat's daughters. At seventeen months, Peggy Keville energized the room, bouncing from lap to lap, running through the apartment, and making everyone laugh. Kitty held baby Delia in her arms, mesmerized by the infant's sweet fragrance. Kitty had missed her monthly and was dying to tell them all that she and Tom would also have a child by the family's Thanksgiving celebration, but she held her tongue. As the conversation caromed from cute anecdotes about the Keville babies, to the relentless cold rains, to books, to local politics, Nellie was left to her silence.

Now, something was wrong.

Papa continues. "It's 4149 West Belle Place, between Sarah and Whittier. Jesus, get here now." He hangs up.

Kitty whips off her apron, grabs a hat and jacket from the coat rack, and replaces her shoes with rainboots. "Something's wrong at Nellie's," she tells Tom.

"Are they flooded out?" he asks.

"Dunno," she says, retrieving her pocketbook from behind the counter. "Papa sounded bad. I have to go."

She hails a cab for the mile-and-a-half ride to Nellie's. There is a police car in front. Papa is standing on the porch with the officer and the tall, pale-eyed man she remembers as Harry. Her hands tremble as she fumbles out some change to pay the fare.

Papa rushes out to meet her, taking her by the arms, tears streaming down his face.

"What is it, Papa. What's wrong?"

He shakes his head. His words won't come. She tries to pull away so she can run to the house, but he won't let go.

"Catherine," he finally says. "Nellie is dead."

Steadying herself on her father's arms, Kitty is too stunned to speak, but he answers the question in her eyes.

"I don't know, I don't know what the hell happened. The young man—Harry—he called me at work. I got here—" He chokes up again and fumbles for his handkerchief. "My baby. Maggie's first joy. Gone."

"Where is she?" Kitty cries, pushing away from Papa and racing up the steps into the tiny bungalow. A foul odor assails her. In the small bedroom straight ahead, she sees Nellie stretched out on the bed in her lacy chemise, her skin bleached white as the cotton. There are bloody sheets and towels on the floor.

"Nooooooo!" she howls. "Noooo! It can't be. Oh, Nellie!"

Bracing herself in the doorway, Kitty fights off a wave of nausea, then rushes to the bedside. She drops to her knees next to her sister, brushes the tangled hair away from her sister's face, and presses her lips against the cold cheek. "I'm so, so sorry," she says through her tears. "I didn't follow up. Something was wrong and I didn't follow up. I was so self-absorbed. I should have made you talk to me. I should have come by. What happened to you?"

"Catherine."

She turns to see her papa, handkerchief pressed to his nose and mouth. With him is a man dressed in a black suit, holding his Homburg.

"Why is she still lying here in all this filth? Can someone get these sheets out of here? Help me clean her up?"

Papa puts his hands on her shoulders. "Catherine, come away, sweetheart. Mr. Cullen from the funeral home is here to take care of her."

"In these circumstances," Mr. Cullen says, "the law requires us to wait till the coroner's office signs off on the scene. Dr. Fath is on his way."

These circumstances?

Scrambling to her feet, Kitty pushes past Papa and lunges at Harry Kralemann. He raises his arms to protect himself, then twists away, cowering.

"What did you do to her, you black-hearted villain? How did you murder her? Tell me!" She shoves him again, flashing back to all the dime romances Nellie loved, full of false lovers and treacherous husbands.

"I did nothing! I loved her! She's been sick. The doctor was here—last night and before dawn this morning. I did everything—her kidney..." His voice trails off and he runs outside.

The fact that Harry Kralemann is sobbing now only makes Kitty angrier. Not a villain, but a poor excuse for a man, his personality too feeble to make her Nellie happy, too weak to protect her Nellie from whatever horrible thing killed her.

Papa puts his arm around Kitty's shoulders and they both steady themselves against the porch railing. A motorized hearse is now parked in front, its back doors open, two attendants standing solemnly by. The sky is overcast and a chilly breeze ruffles the leaves in the elms along the street. More rain coming.

Another official with a small bag dashes up the porch steps.

"Dr. Henry Fath, Deputy Coroner." He hands Harry a card, then disappears into the house.

When he returns, he says to Kralemann, "Since your wife passed away unattended, there will be an autopsy and an inquest. I need you to present yourself at the Coroner's Office in City Hall at 9 a.m. tomorrow. We'll talk to you privately and the inquest will begin at 10. Officer Dowling said there were two witnesses." He consults his notes. "Dr. Keim and Mrs. Wondracheck. He'll notify them as well."

Kralemann sags into a rusty wrought iron chair, mindless of the wet leaves on the seat. He covers his face with his hands.

As Fath leaves, the two young men standing by the hearse trot into the house with a stretcher.

Within a few minutes, Nellie's wrapped body is carried out. Staring at the scene in horror and disbelief, Kitty feels her father begin to crumple and guides him to the porch steps, where they sit together and weep.

As their tears subside, Kitty hears Kralemann speak.

"She's been sick," he says from the iron chair. "Pauline was here for her. And the doctor. She was in terrible pain all night. I stayed home from work. And then…" He shrugs his shoulders. "She was gone."

Kitty glares at him. She has never seen a lonelier look on a man's face, but she hates him for letting her sister die.

That evening the family gathers at Papa's place. The Flanagan siblings are in shock. May is befuddled. Papa keeps repeating that some terrible cosmic mistake has been made. *He* is the old sinner. *He* should have been the one to die.

The Barretts bring food and sympathy.

Mr. Cullen stops by. Papa was the one who called Cullen and Kelly to Belle Place, instinctively wanting to ensure Nellie got a Catholic funeral. Instinctively freezing Kralemann out of the process. It is Papa and Mr.

Cullen who decide the funeral will be Saturday, with visitation at the Flanagan apartment, a requiem Mass at St. Ann's, and burial at Calvary.

:: 77 ::

In the morning, Kitty and Tom get a cab and pick up Papa on their way to the coroner's inquest at City Hall, where they are ushered into the hearing room.

Inside the small hearing room, at ten o'clock, six jurors and a stenographer take their seats and Deputy Coroner Fath sets up his papers on a large table. He is joined by another man who Kitty doesn't recognize.

The police officer James Dowling is sworn in.

Dr. Fath reads from Dowling's report,

> About 10:45 o'clock this a.m. Nellie Kralemann, 23 years old, married, residing with her husband Harry Kralemann, at 4149 West Belle Place, died at her home at above number without medical attendance. Her husband states that he called Dr. J.P. Keim of 2033 Lynch Street last night. Her husband was present when she died. The body is at above number.
>
> Witnesses: Pauline Wondracheck, 4049 N. Newstead Ave. Dr. J.P. Keim, 2033 Lynch St.
>
> Witnesses have been notified to be in the Coroner's office at 9 o'clock a.m.

"Is that all the information you got?" Fath asks.

"Yes, sir, that's all I got. I got that from the husband." The officer's voice is flat and impersonal.

"Didn't he state what was the trouble?"

"He said she had been troubled with kidney trouble for some time."

"Didn't he tell you what Dr. Keim said was the trouble?"

"No, sir, he did not."

"That is all, Officer."

Dowling leaves the courtroom with a polite nod to the family.

Papa nudges Kitty. "Did he say that doctor is on Lynch Street?" he asks in a stage whisper. "That's way the hell down in Benton Park—Soulard neighborhood. Flooding's made a mess of it this week. What in God's name—"

Kitty puts a hand on his arm as Fath calls for Dr. Keim, who is ushered in through the back of the hearing room. "Let's listen to what he has to say."

Keim is a young man, no older than Nellie herself, with darting brown eyes, a receding hairline, and a paunch. After Keim is sworn in, Fath asks, "Doctor, what do you know concerning the cause of death of Mrs. Kralemann?"

"I was called to the home Tuesday evening, sometime between five and six o'clock, and on arriving, I examined the case. The temperature at the time was 100.8, pulse of about 100, respiration was slightly increased to 24, and she complained of severe pain in the lower part of her abdomen. Abdominal muscles were rigid, had been flooding for some few hours. On gynecological examination, I found an abortion had been performed."

"Oh!" Kitty gasps loud enough for the whole room to hear. Did he say *abortion*? *Abortion*?

The deputy coroner shoots her a look as Tom takes her hand. Papa bows his head, covering his eyes.

Fath continues, "How often have you seen this patient, Doctor?"

"Well, I packed the patient that evening and I saw her again yesterday morning."

Kitty digs her fingernails into Tom's hand. Can she believe her ears? In her mind's eye, she pictures Nellie, after some terrible desperate act, lying in that squalid little bedroom, feverish, filling with fluids, and bleeding from between her legs, while Kitty was… doing what? Making small talk with customers about recipes and weather as she tallied their groceries and counted out their change. She begins to feel sick to her stomach.

"That is the first time you saw this patient?"

"Yes, sir, first time." The doctor massages his stomach as if he is in pain too.

"How did these people come to send for you?"

"The husband called me up. I treated him on a prior—for a cold."

Now Tom is shaking his head.

"You were acquainted with the family then?"

"Yes, sir, with the husband."

"What statement did this woman make to you, Doctor? Mrs. Kralemann, what did she say was the trouble? What happened to her?"

"She didn't confide in me at all. All I learned she had something performed on her."

"Did she say?"

"Yes, sir."

"Said what?"

Keim looks down at his hands. "Said something had been performed on her—induced abortion."

"When did she tell you that, the first time that you called there?"

"Yes, sir."

"Anyone present hear that?"

"Why the husband was there."

Papa mutters, "This is insanity."

"Well, did she state whether she had any other doctor or whether she had gone to some midwife?"

"She didn't state any name or any doctor. I was called yesterday morning about 6 o'clock. The husband called up. I went out and I called Dr. Frank. I had a brief consultation with Dr. Frank on the case."

"Well, did you ask her why she had this done or why this was performed?"

"Why, she wouldn't answer any question in regard to that."

"Have they any other children?"

"No, sir."

"However, Doctor, from all the evidence and from your investigation there, there is no doubt that an abortion had been performed?"

"Yes, sir, I know absolutely."

"That is all."

Dr. Keim leaves the courtroom, eyes downcast, without acknowledging the family. Papa is cursing under his breath. Tom wears his most perplexed face, his squinted eyes staring into the distance, lips pressed together. Kitty's mind is reeling with the revelation of what her sister went through.

Immediately, Pauline Wondracheck is ushered in. Kitty recognizes her, a fatter version of the young mother she knew from the old Farlin Avenue days, the Mrs. Wondracheck who brought the family loaves of her homemade bread and *kuchen* for a long time after Mama died—till Aunt Biddy entered the scene. She must be forty now. Kitty didn't realize Pauline and Nellie kept in touch.

Pauline is sworn in.

"Are you related to these parties?"

"I was a good friend to the lady, a dear friend, that is all." Her voice trembles. She glances around the hearing room, catching Kitty's eye before looking back at Dr. Fath.

"Now, state what you know about this case, Mrs. Wondracheck."

She looks at the floor. "All I know is I was sent for Tuesday. She sent for me and said she was sick. Would I come over and stay with her."

"Tuesday this week?"

"Yes, sir, day before yesterday. And I asked her what was the matter, and she said, 'oh, I don't know.' She said, 'Mrs. Wondracheck, I am awful sick.' I said, 'where are your pains,' and she said, 'all over.' So I said, 'shall I rub you?' and she said, 'yes,' and so I took liniment and rubbed her back and limbs, and I took towels and applied hot towels to her stomach and back. Then she suffered all afternoon like that until about five o'clock, little after. Then I said, 'I will have to go.' There was no one with her."

"Did she complain of very severe pains in her abdomen?"

"Yes, that's mostly where the pains are, and her back, she said, too."

"What else did she tell you, Mrs. Wondracheck?"

"She didn't tell me anything else. I asked her, I said, 'Only tell me what it is.' I said, 'Is it anything serious? I'll get a doctor.' She said, 'No, I'll be all right.' She said, 'I just feel bad all over. I don't know where my pains are worse.' So I said, 'I'll telephone for your husband. I have children coming home from school.'"

"Were you present when the doctor came?"

"I just left."

"Did you hear the statement she made to the doctor?"

"No, sir, I did not. I went to put on my rubbers and coat and hat and then I left. I was late then."

"Did you stay until the doctor left?"

"No, sir, I did not. I went home."

"Didn't she tell you at all what she had done?"

Pauline pulled at the hem of the handkerchief in her hands. "No, sir. I asked her to tell me, and she said she wouldn't tell me anything. I said, 'Did you take anything?' She said, 'No.' She wouldn't tell me anything. I told her I'd come back before Harry went to work yesterday, and when I got over there she was dead." Pauline glanced toward the family with tears in her eyes.

Tom reached for Kitty's hand again.

"You say you saw her Tuesday?"

"Yes, sir, I was there Monday and Tuesday. I called there Monday just to see how she was, and she said she wasn't feeling well, and I said, 'If you aren't feeling well and I haven't anything to do tomorrow, I'll come over.'"

"When did you see her before Monday?"

"Well, the week before that Sunday, she was at my house. They were there to dinner. That was the last I seen of her until Monday when I went over."

"Did she say anything then?"

"No, she never said anything then."

"Had she been feeling badly?"

"Oh, yes, she had stomach trouble and her kidneys were bad. She was a neighbor of mine, oh, about two years, and she always did. She used to get hysterical spells at times."

Hysterical spells? Kitty is needled by this expression. Who was Pauline to be throwing around psychological terms, to be making pronouncements in front of a jury about Nellie's health? Besides, that was back when Nellie was managing the household in the wake of Mama's death. She was fifteen, sixteen. Of course she had *spells*.

Fath continues. "Did she tell you she was in a delicate condition?"

"No, sir, she did not."

"Never mentioned that to you?"

"No, sir, she never mentioned it."

"Did she say she didn't want any children?"

"No, she loved children." She looked at her hands again, shaking her head. "No, she wouldn't tell me that. I was a good friend of hers, but she was deep."

Deep? Kitty doesn't like this pronouncement, but she has to admit—Nellie is dead. Six weeks into a marriage, she couldn't face having a child. If that isn't *deep*, nothing is.

Fath dismisses Pauline. "That is all."

As Pauline heads out of the hearing room, she stops to hug Kitty and Papa. Kitty wants to follow her out, ask her a million questions, and thank her for trying to help. But the hearing room officer is escorting Harry Kralemann in and she needs to hear what he has to say.

After Kralemann is sworn in, Dr. Fath asks, "And what do you do, Mr. Kralemann?"

"I am a railroad clerk, sir."

"This your wife, Nellie Kralemann?"

"Yes, sir."

"How old was she?"

"She was almost twenty-four years old."

"How long have you been married?"

"Since February fifth."

"Of this year?"

"Yes, sir, of this year."

Dr. Fath walks toward the witness chair, arms crossed. "Now, state what you know about this case, Mr. Kralemann. What was the trouble with your wife?"

Kralemann stares down at his hands. "Why about two weeks ago, she complained about having a backache, an awful backache, continually paining her, and she was taking home remedies and everything, don't you know, until finally, night before last, between five and six o'clock, they called me from the office. So I called up Dr. Keim. The doctor waited on me on several occasions. And I called up Dr. Keim and he came out there, and she seemed to be relieved after she got the first dose of medicine. The next morning about three o'clock, she began hollering with pains in her back."

"What kind of home remedies had she been using?"

Kralemann shrugs. "She used turpentine, hot toddies, and everything for the cramps in her stomach and calomel and everything."

Papa mutters, "Jesus, Mary, and Joseph, who drinks turpentine for a backache?"

"Do you know whether she had gone to any doctor before?"

"No, sir, not to my knowledge."

"Did she go anywhere?"

"Not to my knowledge, no, sir."

"Did you know she was in a delicate condition?"

"Yes, sir, I knew that." He looks at the jury, then back at Fath. "I knew it before we got married. She often mentioned to me she had those pains in her back."

"I mean, did you know she was *in a family way*?"

Kralemann blinked. "Oh. Yes, sir, she told me she was taking some of this medicine to draw that on."

"To bring her menses on?"

"Yes, sir."

"You were intimate with her then before you were married?" Fath's voice was sharp.

"No, sir. I don't understand." Kralemann's eyes dance around the hearing room.

"Did you have any *intercourse* with her?"

"No, sir."

"You say you were only married since February?"

"Only married since February."

What was Fath suggesting? Kitty felt a chill. That Nellie must have been pregnant when she got married? That Kralemann didn't have the courage to own up to his sins? Or was there something else, too *deep*, in Pauline's words, too deep for Nellie to bear?

"Now, when the doctor got there, Dr. Keim, what did he tell you was the trouble?"

"Why, he told me that acute kidney trouble was the cause."

"What else?"

"That was all. And that she couldn't pass urine, don't you know."

"And didn't he tell you anything else that had happened to your wife?"

"No, sir, that was all."

"Were you there when she told the doctor that she had something performed?"

Kralemann looks down at his hands. "I never heard a word. I didn't hear a word like that." His voice drops to a mumble. "Didn't tell the doctor she had anything performed or that she tried to do something."

"How did you know that your wife was pregnant?"

Kralemann looks back up at Fath. "Why, she told me herself."

"Just simply because she didn't come around?"

"Just because she didn't come around."

"How often did she miss, did she say?"

"No, sir."

"Once or twice since you were married?"

"Why, this is the first time. She came around right before we got married." Beads of sweat appear on Kralemann's forehead. He dabs his head and neck with his handkerchief.

"And didn't come around anymore after that?"

"No, sir, not after that."

"So that was the only thing made you believe she was pregnant?"

"Yes, sir." His eyes drop again.

"Well, now, didn't you hear her say to the doctor that she had something performed?"

"No, sir, I never heard a word."

"Did she ever tell you she was going somewhere to have this brought about?"

"No, sir, I forbade her to do that."

Forbade her? So they discussed her getting an abortion? Kitty is impatient with Kralemann's muddled testimony.

Fath says, "She told the doctor that and the doctor made an examination and found such to be the case." He consults his papers. "Do you know of any midwife she had gone to?"

"No, sir, not to my knowledge."

"That is all." Fath sits down and confers with the other man at the table.

That's all? Kitty can't believe that's all Kralemann has to say about her sister's hell and his part in creating it. Kralemann looks around, confused, then rises from his witness chair.

Fath stands up. He tells the jury that the post-mortem will be conducted this afternoon. They will need to reconvene tomorrow at the same time to hear the findings and render their verdict.

As Kralemann walks toward the door, Papa stands, holds on to a chair back to steady himself, and waves Kralemann over. "The funeral," he says. "From our apartment early Saturday morning. Evans Street. We've arranged for the burial at Calvary. We put a notice in the paper. Cullen and Kelly will bring her over tomorrow night for the wake if you want to pay your respects."

"Yes, sir. Thank you, sir. Mr. Cullen contacted me."

"But I'm warning you, son," Papa goes on, his tone changing. "If I have a drink in me, I'm likely to take a swing at you. You're the goddamnedest moron I ever heard speak the English language."

:: 78 ::

On Friday morning, Kitty, Tom, and Papa return to the Coroner's hearing room. Mr. Fath convenes the jury and begins reviewing the autopsy results, conducted at one of the Cullen and Kelly funeral chapels on North Taylor. It is hard for Kitty to follow. After reading out the status of each organ, Fath finally gets to the uterus.

"*Three times its normal size*," he reads. "*Lining of the fundus of uterus irregular and rough. Also, debris of placental tissue, which has an offensive odor. Ovaries. Congested. Corpus luteum present in left ovary. All evidence of recent evacuation of uterus present. Endometrium of uterus inflamed.*" He pauses. "This brings us to the cause of death, which Dr. Hachdorfer has concluded is *acute peritonitis due to abortion*."

He goes on to instruct the jury on the decision they have to make.

Kitty, Tom, and Papa wait on their bench in the hearing room, assured by Dr. Fath that the jury would not take long. They sit silently for a time, overwhelmed with all they heard.

Finally, in a low voice, Tom says, "Did you listen to the autopsy? Her kidneys were apparently fine."

"She complained about them for years. Every backache, blamed on the kidneys," Kitty says, staring at the floor.

"She was perfect," Papa adds, his voice soft. "Beautiful, strong, smart. Healthy. Recovered quickly from childhood diseases. I wanted her to go to high school, to Visitation. I wanted her to go to college, to travel. But then Maggie. Maggie—the pain, the heroic intervention, the nick of a blade, the wicked infection—leaving behind seven children and a fool of a husband. Now Nellie— her own unique pain, the desperately heroic intervention, the nick of an instrument, the wicked infection. Suddenly gone. It feels like a curse. The sin of pride. We think we can outsmart nature. But the big river still floods every spring, the tornadoes still rip through our towns, sweeping away all our cleverness..."

Kitty pulls her handkerchief from her pocketbook and presses it to her eyes, gulping back the tears, trying to avoid making a spectacle of herself. She feels Tom's arm around her shoulders.

Shortly, the jury returns with their verdict.

One of the jurors stands to read it. "*Upon full investigation of the facts in the case and hearing the evidence, we find that the deceased came to her death on the twenty-sixth day of March 1913, at about ten o'clock a.m. at her residence, from acute peritonitis, following an abortion at the hands of a party unknown. We find this to be a homicide.*"

"Mother of God," Kitty murmurs. "My dear Nellie."

The jury is dismissed and they exit through the front of the courtroom.

None of this seems real to Kitty, but she pushes herself to approach Dr. Fath and the other man before they leave the hearing room.

"What next?" she asks. "Will you search for the devil who butchered my sister?"

"I'm so sorry for this tragedy, Mrs. Barrett," he says. "This is Bill Fitzgerald, an attorney for the state. His office will get a copy of the inquest. They can direct the police to investigate further, but, frankly, this kind of case rarely gets very far. When we spoke privately to Mrs. Wondracheck and Mr. Kralemann, they simply wouldn't cough up any information about who she might have been seeing for her tonics or for this intervention. They led us to believe Mrs. Kralemann was very private about who she sought help from. Either that or they know something they aren't saying. It's a pretty common scenario, I'm afraid."

Kitty starts to ask another question, but Tom jumps in. "I didn't see any reporters here. Can you see this isn't picked up in the newspapers?"

Fath raises an eyebrow. "This kind of hearing happens every day. With no fingers being pointed, it won't get attention." He checks his watch. "We'll let you know if there are any developments." The two men rush from the room.

Kitty, Tom, and Papa walk in silence out the big doors of City Hall. In the biting cold air, they pull their coats tighter as they walk down the broad steps to the cab stand.

Kitty's thoughts shift from *how* to *why*. Papa was right. Why would Kralemann call a doctor from south St. Louis, not even from the north side where his family lives, not even from near his railroad office on Cass? Why? Unless he knew what was happening and wanted to avoid the gossipy docs nearby. Maybe Keim himself performed the abortion.

She was sure Nellie didn't love Kralemann. Was the blood Kralemann witnessed before their marriage not her menses but her virginal blood as he forced himself upon her? Kitty shivers at the thought. What woman mentions her flow to a man if there isn't sex involved? Nellie loved her old romance novels where young women performed heroic feats to protect their virtue against the assaults of unworthy men. She would have never given herself freely to a half-wit Lutheran railroad clerk. But apparently it happened. And then she was pregnant. Nellie agreed to the quick marriage but was also desperate to reverse her dismal fate, was that it? *Oh, my beautiful, brilliant, angry, desperate sister*, Kitty thinks. *How will I ever make this up to you?*

:: 79 ::

When she gets home after the inquest verdict, while Tom checks in with Francis about store business, Kitty digs out her black dress for the ritual of "laying Nellie to rest." What rest is there for restless souls like Nellie's? Kitty is sad but also irritated. In the cab from City Hall, her father and her husband made the decision between them to keep the abortion secret and to tell family and friends that a chronic kidney condition had taken a sudden and fatal turn for the worse. Kitty doesn't like the decision. It forces her to appear less angry than she is and somehow obliterates a part of who her sister was. It makes Nellie seem more diseased than defiant.

After a bite to eat, Kitty and Tom head over to the Evans Avenue flat.

Bert Cullen and his assistants arrive. While the family watches in a daze, they rearrange furniture in the small living room, set up a portable bier, and carry in Nellie's casket. Cullen opens the coffin. And there is the unbelievable sight of Nellie's girlish face, her mouth forever frozen into a humorless line, her eyes forever closed to the eye rolls and sidelong glances they knew so well. The Flanagans fall into one another's arms, weeping in grief and in anger. This should never have happened.

As the family tears are spent and numbness settles over them, Harry Kralemann shows up with his mother and sister. He carries an arrangement of white lilies. "From her friends at the Hotel Jefferson," he murmurs.

Tommy Flanagan pokes his brothers to get off the couch and let the Kralemanns sit. No one offers to take their coats.

Harry Kralemann's eyes are puffed nearly shut. His mother and sister sit beside him, patting his arms. Kitty can't muster any sympathy for his devastation. He knows what really happened. He knows that, one way or another, he murdered Nellie.

Papa whispers something to May and she fetches a tray with his bottle of whiskey and assorted glasses.

He addresses the Kralemanns. "Anyone like a shot?"

"We don't imbibe," the mother says.

Papa pours himself one. "I want to hear more about the physician, Harry, this Dr. Keim you sent for." He belts down the shot and pours a second. "Is he some kind of boy-wonder kidney expert, summoned as he was all the way from his posh little Benton Park neighborhood, an hour's drive or more from where my poor Nellie lay dying, through diluvian rain and flooded streets?"

Kralemann looks at Papa without an answer.

"I looked him up in the city directory and he's not listed among the physicians." His voice sharpens. "So forgive me if I have to wonder what kind of defrocked shite is taking care of my daughter."

Kralemann shakes his head. "He has a diploma. Washington University."

"And does he pay his rent by providing *kidney* cures to the riverfront ladies of the evening, who stroll down Broadway half a mile from his office, offering their goods to the brewery workers?"

"Papa!" Kitty tries to shush her father's rant, even as she wants these answers too.

But he goes on. "And just how did you meet this young physician? What kind of *cold* forced you to travel all the way to the south side for treatment and then made you think he was the one to call when my daughter was howling in pain with *kidney* trouble?"

Kralemann seems to crumple, but his mother scrambles to her feet.

"Mr. Flanagan," she says, "what in God's name are you implying about my son? The boy is crushed, heartbroken. It was your daughter who—" She glances around at the assembled family. "Nevermind. May the Lord have mercy on all your souls. Come along, Harry. There'll be no peace for you here with this madman."

As soon as the Kralemanns rush away, the pastor of St. Ann's shows up. Without much ado, Father Walsh performs a blessing and leads the family in prayer. After accepting Papa's offer of whiskey, he asks why no one called a priest to Nellie's deathbed to administer last rites.

Papa stiffens. "No one was expecting her to die, you damn fool."

With a sniff, Father Walsh says, "I pray she died in a state of grace."

It dawns on Kitty that if the priest knew the truth, he would be condemning Nellie to hell for the abortion and possibly refusing her a Catholic burial. The thought unnerves her. Maybe it is smart for the family to keep quiet about the actual cause of death.

Before the priest leaves the apartment, Kitty shows him her clipping of the 1908 housefire and tells him how Nellie saved Julie's life and then led the effort to push their piano out of harm's way. She asks him to celebrate Nellie's bold spirit and her bravery when he delivers the eulogy.

But the next day at church, Kitty is disappointed. From the pulpit, Father Walsh simply yammers on in platitudes about illness, and suffering, and the will of God. Kitty wants to scream.

She looks around and catches the eye of Pauline Wondracheck. Pauline knows the real story about Nellie and the risk Nellie was willing to take to live life on her own terms. Pauline will whisper the story to her women friends and the word will get around, woman to woman to woman, mother to daughter to sister to cousin. It underscores to Kitty that women and men live in different worlds, with different sets of facts, and different lessons learned.

:: 80 ::

March 27. The funeral is over by noon and the family convenes at the Barrett house on Lexington. It is a quiet spring afternoon. Over sandwiches and beers, the Flanagans indulge in storytelling about their dear Nellie and then about their dear Maggie, the two great family tragedies.

Fourteen-year-old Ethel is withdrawn, under heavy medication. After lunch, Tommy takes her back to her dormitory. Tom heads back to the store, still dealing with catastrophic delays in restocking their shelves. Sixteen-year-old Modie drifts away on his own. At about four, when Papa starts nodding off in his chair, Joe calls for a cab and takes his father, May, and Julie back to Evans Avenue. Exhausted, Kitty curls around a throw pillow on the couch and fades into a deep sleep.

It is dark when Kitty awakens and joins Mother Barrett in the kitchen. Francis, Mamie, and Katie are upstairs in bed and Tom is asleep in his chair. The lights are out except for a single bulb over the sink.

"Sit down, dear," Mother says. "I'll make you some tea."

Both in their stocking feet, sitting at the round oak table with their tea, Kitty begins to reminisce about the utopian life the Flanagans enjoyed in Leclaire, Illinois—her earliest memories.

Mother asks, "Did Nellie have kidney trouble back then, as a girl?"

Kitty is tired of the kidney story and shakes her head. "She had a perfectly healthy childhood. No kidney trouble. She complained of some back pain in recent years, but the autopsy showed a healthy pair of kidneys. Who knows. Pauline Wondracheck said she had 'hysterical spells' at the inquest."

"Well, I don't like *that* phrase," Mother says. "You know *hysteria* comes from the Greek *hystera*, which means *uterus*."

Kitty raises an eyebrow.

"I've learned a thing or two in my sixty-odd years. It's an annoying term doctors use to describe women when they aren't patient enough to figure out what the real problem is." She squints her eyes. "And women don't die from *hysterical spells*."

"No, they don't." Kitty stares into her teacup. "Nellie had an induced abortion. She died from peritonitis, not a kidney infection."

"Mother of God." Mother's hand flies out to grasp Kitty's.

"Why?" Kitty feels her emotions rising. "Why would a newlywed woman in her twenties have an abortion? Kralemann knew. He described her drinking tonics to bring on her monthly. But when they failed, she went to some amateur who performed a savage procedure that wounded her insides, got them all infected. The inquest jury labeled it a homicide."

Mrs. Barrett heaves a great sigh. She stands up with a soft grunt, rubs her hip joint, and fetches the bottle of whiskey and two jam jars.

"Women do awful things to themselves when they can't face a pregnancy. Desperation leads them to take terrible risks." She splashes whiskey into each glass and slides one over to Kitty. "I've known women to throw themselves down stairs or take boiling hot baths. But it's very hard to shake a thing lose once it latches on."

"Kralemann claimed she only missed once and not till after they were married. But the way they described it, from the autopsy, I think she must have been further along."

"In the old country, days gone by," Mother says, "it was always up to the women to do what they needed to do to bring on their flow. It was not a sin till the quickening. When you feel movement, well, then you have a child to protect no matter what the consequences. But before then, you act in the best interests of yourself and your family. It wasn't till the men got involved— doctors and the damn priests —then everything was murder and a mortal sin. I believe in the old ways, when women had the intelligence of their own bodies. Your dear Nellie is in heaven, Kitty. She was as wise as God could make a woman. It was the meddling of men that killed her."

Kitty's heart opens wide to Mother Barrett in that instant. She looks so ancient, with her deep wrinkles and white top knot, made all the more severe by her faded black shirtwaist. Kitty's idea of a mother has always been the luscious beauty of her own thirty-something mama at the time of her death, the mama she was never able to have an adult conversation with.

"I'll never understand what happened," Kitty says.

Mother hoists herself again out of her chair and retrieves a partial loaf of soda bread from the breadbox. She sets it on the table with a knife. "Finding out you're with child, then getting married—that's more common than you think." She smiles to herself as she takes her seat. "The Irish have a saying: most children take nine months in the womb, but the first child comes whenever it pleases."

Kitty loves the old woman's worldliness. "Okay, I get that. They did the right thing, even though I don't believe she loved him. But then why the panic? Or was it just Nellie? She could be very bullheaded. She wanted what she wanted. Just like saving our piano during a fire. Her passions overrule her good sense."

Kitty gets the pot of butter from the counter and sets it next to the bread.

Mother takes a sip of whiskey and slowly butters her bread. "So, she suspects she's with child. Tells the young man. He insists they get married. But she still wants to reverse course?"

Kitty adds, "And he apparently goes along with it. Knows she's drinking toddies made from turpentine, from calomel."

"Those are strong purgatives," Mother says. "A typical brew women use to get the blood flowing. She would have had violent belly cramps. Terrible diarrhea."

"But then he forbids her from going further, forbids her from seeing anyone for a procedure."

"She's scaring the hell out of him," Mother says. She takes a bite of bread and another sip of whiskey. "Does she have a dream? Does she read omens? Does she have a premonition that something has gone wrong with the thing inside her?"

"She wasn't superstitious. But.." Kitty nods her head. "But she was leery about having children." While she butters the slice of bread, her mind drifts back to their childhood. "After Julie was born, Mama got a pain that never stopped. Then she bled every day for months. The womb that gave seven children our lives turned ugly and killed her. Nellie was just starting her own womanhood then. I think it scarred her worse than it did me. Then suddenly, she was the mother and no good at it—a child thrown into a woman's job. Who can blame her for not wanting to start a family yet?"

Mother reaches out to hold Kitty's hand again. "You're having a baby, aren't you?"

Kitty sits up straight.

"Oh, I know it's bad luck to tell anyone before you've missed three times, but a mother knows."

Kitty understands she will be facing motherhood without her own mama's counsel, not that millions of immigrant women didn't do the same. Now it suddenly strikes her as something awful that she and her sister could have taken this road together, but Nellie bailed out.

She nods and squeezes her mother-in-law's hand in return.

INTERLUDE

Ellen Barrett's Story: Motherhood

"I was thirty-one by the time Tom was born," Mother says. "Too old. I was having a helluva good time working for the Knight family here in St. Louis, a wonderful, rich life, with no time for courtships. But my sister Cecelia married Tom Timlin, who lived out west along the Meramec in an area they said looked like Mayo, God help us. She wanted me to join her and fixed me up with Frank Barrett. What a damn disaster that was. Do you think I ever saw my sister? That Barrett log cabin was miles from anywhere. We lived cheek by jowl with Frank's parents and three of their grown children. Mary, Katie, and Martin. There was an adjoining cabin with a covered carriageway in between. That's where brother John and Catherine lived, with little Mary Ann—you met them at the wedding. Mary Ann made your hat. Anyway, the minute Frank hangs his pants on the bedpost, I'm in the family way."

Kitty has to smile at the thought of independent, citified Ellen Gibbons finding herself in a crowded log cabin in the middle of nowhere.

"You think Nellie was strong-willed. Maw Barrett ruled that household like the warrior-queen Maeve herself. They were refugees from the potato famine, you know, and broke their backs getting land under the Homestead Act. All the Barretts ever knew was work and she cracked the whip, harder on the women than the men, if you can believe it. For all her prairie toughness, she was terrified of losing old Pa and her boys. Terrified of starving again. So whenever extra hands were needed, the women labored alongside the men, but we also grew a kitchen garden, milked the cows, churned the butter, put on three meals a day, skinned our knuckles scrubbing clothes on washboards, and had babies."

She gazes off into a distant memory. "Six weeks before Tom was born, November thirteenth—I remember like it was yesterday—Frank's eighteen-year-old brother, Martin, the baby, was killed in a farm accident. Oh, the keening that went on in that household, like the howling of the winds that swept across those rolling hills. It was one thing for Maw to lose her handsome lad, but she was also sure I was carrying her first grandson and warned that he could be cursed with an untimely death like Martin's if I didn't take precautions. She made me stay next door in John's cabin during the services and forbade me from going to the cemetery."

Kitty loves the stories of Tom's family but doesn't buy into the old wives' tales. It's bad enough that the child inside her has lost a cousin to grow up with, but the idea that seeing Nellie's dead body or traipsing through the cemetery might carry a curse—she can't think about it. "You must have been very anxious," she says, slicing more bread, "then very happy when Tom was born so healthy,".

Mother gets up and finds a jar of marmalade in the cabinet and sets it on the table with a spoon. She picks a caraway seed from between her teeth.

"It's not the half of it, darlin.' Francis came along. Then Mamie. Mamie had a twin, but the infant was stillborn. That was it for me. John and Catherine had five children by then and the place was a madhouse. Yet they begged Frank to stay. They offered him his own patch of the farmland and logs to build our own cabin." She scoffs. "We'd have jumped from mayhem to utter loneliness miles away. I couldn't do it. I didn't have Maw's tough energy. I insisted we move back to St. Louis."

She shakes her head, her eyes glistening with tears in the soft light of the kitchen. "So often I wonder if we should have stayed, if all the sorrow that came after might have been avoided if only I had swallowed my pride and lived humbly under Maw's rule. John and Catherine hung on till Maw and Pa Barrett passed away before they moved to St. Louis and look what a lovely family they have."

"But you have a wonderful family," Kitty says.

Mother slathers the marmalade on her bread and nibbles the edge. "Has Tom told you about his brothers John and Martin?"

"No. Francis mentioned a couple of lost babies when we were getting to know each other, years ago. I'd forgotten, to tell the truth." Kitty takes a swig of her whiskey.

Mother leans forward. "No sooner had we arrived in St. Louis, I found I was with child again. That was in '89. Our sweet little Johnny was born. A couple years later, on January twenty-seventh, I gave birth to Martin. Tom had just turned nine. I thought it was bad luck to name him after Frank's brother, who died so tragically, but it was also his grandfather's name, so he insisted. Oh, dear."

She sighs deeply and takes a gulp of whiskey. She pauses while the burn in her throat passes. "It was such a bitterly cold day, but the sky was cloudless and so blue. The older ones—Tom, Francis, and Mamie—were all home with scarlet fever. While I was in labor, John developed the rash and fever. With a squalling baby in my arms, I watched Johnny slip away from me. The next week, February seventh, Johnny died in my arms. Three and a half years old, such a bundle of good cheer."

"Oh, no," Kitty whispers.

"Martin should have been okay. Nursing babies don't often get sick, but he was colicky. I don't know. I was so broken up by Johnny's death, I probably poisoned my milk with the grief. Martin was only ten months old when he died of pneumonia. It's a terrible thing to lose a child, Kitty, a dreadful, terrible, accursed thing. And then to lose another just as you're beginning to breathe again..."

She pauses for a moment to cross herself.

"I was good for nothing. I don't know how the other children got along." She takes another sip. "Years passed before I let Frank touch me again. I was forty-five years old when I let him hang his britches again on the bedpost and nine months later my beautiful Katie was born, fat and healthy. She brought me back to life."

"Oh, what a sad story," says Kitty. "I wonder why Tom never told me."

"He took it very hard. He blamed himself for Johnny's death, for bringing scarlatina into the house. He was inconsolable. And again, when Martin died, just before his tenth birthday. I remember him scolding us for not staying on the farm, where we would have all been safe. He was in school at St. Thomas and took his faith very seriously. He thought Frank and I must have been punished for something we did because God would not just take two little souls away like that. Poor child. I think that's when he threw himself into his schoolwork, as an escape."

Kitty is impressed that her Tom would struggle to make logical sense of death at the age of ten. When her mother died, she remembers only being sad and confused.

"Did Tom tell you he won a scholarship to Christian Brothers College for high school?"

"Francis told me. You must have been very proud of him."

"Frank was so tickled. He thought Tom would be an engineer or an architect, he was so good at thinking things through. But of course, Frank dropped dead in '99. And I found I had turned into Maw Barrett. A domineering old crone, terrified of being penniless without a man to support me. Guilt-ridden. I had not only failed at protecting two baby sons, but I had pressured Frank to work extra hours. I should have been kinder to him. I should have taken in laundry when we had trouble making ends meet. But I pushed him. Then he was gone. I was desperate. We had to move from the house on Chippewa to the tenements on North Seventh. I made Tom and Francis drop out of school and sent them to Luyties Brothers to work as clerks."

"I don't know what else you could have done," Kitty says. "But you have to be proud of how they turned their jobs into apprenticeships and learned the grocery business."

"Of course. But it took its toll. Not so much with Francis. He was always a happy-go-lucky child. School, work, all the same to him. But Tom, as good a man as he is—I broke something in him."

She rises from her chair, limping slightly and rubbing her hip. "Damn rheumatism." She opens the kitchen junk drawer and shuffles around in the back of it till she finds a small box. She opens it and sets it between them on the table. "Take a look at that."

Kitty picks up a two-part gold medal. The pin section is a small banner with "St. Thomas School" engraved on it. The dangle is a Greek cross engraved with a crown of laurels, a sacred heart symbol, and the words "Christian Doctrine." The other side of the dangle is inscribed, but the words are marred by superficial scratches. "I can't make this out," she says.

"It's his name and the date, June 1894. He was eleven when he received the honor and that medal was his pride and joy. Or maybe I should say that, through the fog of those dark years, it was *my* pride and joy. Later, when I made him drop out of school, he was so angry with me, furious that I couldn't work some kind of magic to allow him a couple more years to graduate. He accused me of losing faith in him, of condemning him to the life of a laborer or an office boy. He took a pin and scratched through the engraving on the back of his medal and threw it at me. I felt sick to my stomach."

Her eyes meet Kitty's. "I truly tried to come up with an alternative. I could have left three-year-old Kate home with Mamie while I got a job as a scrubwoman or a forty-eight-year-old shop girl, but believe me when I say that Tom working as a shipping clerk for the mercantile made four times the wage of a scrubwoman or a shop-girl. We had to pay the rent."

Mother takes another swallow of her whiskey and closes her eyes. "I spent our last dollar on transporting Frank's dead body back to Catawissa so we could have a family funeral and bury him the family plot at St. Patrick's. I thought the family who was willing to give him a piece of their prosperous farm would have offered us some help, but Pa gave each of the four children a silver dollar. That was all. All I know, Kitty..." Her index finger tapped the table. "All I know is that when I die, I do not want to be buried with Frank in that godforsaken place. I told Tom to buy me a plot here in St. Louis, at Calvary. Frank and I will meet again in heaven."

It is a worrisome story for Kitty. In Tom, she sees a man in charge of his destiny, tall, muscular, with the strong jaw of determination. He succeeds in everything he sets out to do. She has never seen him as vulnerable to the whims of an unfeeling God. She looks closely at the medal in the dim light. "I think these scratches can be buffed out by a jeweler. Do you mind if I take it?"

"It's yours, dear. You are Tom's redemption."

Kitty gets up, crouches next to her mother-in-law, and hugs her close. "Thank you for sitting up with me on this terrible night. And thank you for telling me about your family. I'm so happy my child will have a grandmother."

Ellen Barrett wraps her arms around Kitty and kisses the top of her head. "Your child will have a wonderful life."

BOOK 3. BARRETT'S MARKET

Part 1. On Bayard, Trouble Ahead, 1914-1918

:: 81 ::

Sunday, August 9, 1914. Tom Barrett walks the half-mile home from six o'clock Mass at St. Mark's, enjoying the cool air before the temperature climbs back into the nineties. At 1343 Bayard, he trots up the concrete steps from the sidewalk, collects the newspaper, and enters their half of the duplex. He and Kitty rented the apartment after Mary Margaret was born last November—nine months ago today. The moment he saw the big blue eyes lighting up her tiny face, Tom was gripped with the fear of losing her. The apartment above the store was too dangerous, too exposed to every fever and cough a customer might walk in with, so he found them an airy apartment just around the corner. Kitty argued against it, saying Mary would grow up in grocery stores, eating well and strengthening her resistance, but Tom won.

For now, they use the apartment over the store to warehouse bulk purchases when his wholesalers have good deals, but maintaining all that inventory hasn't paid off. They get stuck with too many cases of unpopular items they have to sell below cost. As soon as the heat breaks, he'll clean it up, have a sale, and put up a *For Rent* sign.

Dropping his suitcoat on its hook, he catches a glint of gold on the inside pocket. He smiles. It is the medal he received for "Christian Doctrine" at the age of eleven. Kitty had his angry scratches polished away and returned it to him as a Christmas gift. It means everything to him. He spent too much of his young life resenting the burden of his father's death and regretting the education it cost him. But Kitty changed his perspective from the weight of the past to the lightness of the future. He keeps it pinned to the inside of his coat to remind him every day how lucky he is.

In the kitchen, he rolls up his sleeves, makes coffee, then sits down to read the paper. It is full of war. Since the June assassination of Archduke Ferdinand in Sarajevo, Europe has gone up in flames. How can a whole continent succumb like that, death taking thousands a day, every man pulled from his home and enlisted in the military, dying in trenches, sacrificing themselves to the egos of royalty?

Will President Wilson pull the U.S. into the madness? Tom shakes his head. Wilson's wife Ellen has just died of kidney disease. The President and the nation are mourning her. How can a man with so much responsibility suffer such a loss and still think straight?

That reminds him. Tom takes a small notebook and fountain pen from his shirt pocket and jots down *life insurance.* At Mass he remembered that he hadn't changed the insurance beneficiary from his mother to Kitty. When he joined the Knights of Columbus seven years ago, it was to access their affordable life insurance. Too many people depended on him. If he dropped dead of a heart attack like his father, the family would be plunged back into poverty.

But the K of C has also given him many business connections. The sons of last century's Catholic immigrants now run small shops in every St. Louis neighborhood. They run the labor unions. The run the hospitals and the growing network of parochial schools. They run the political machine.

He looks out the open kitchen window. Kitty's window box is lush with scarlet geraniums, vivid against a turquoise sky. A pair of blue jays call back and forth to each other. He thinks back to the hell of getting started in business, a kid with no time for beauty. Tom didn't even go to the World's Fair because he was working seven days a week to raise money for the down payment on the Lexington Avenue property, so that his family could escape their rat-infested neighborhood downtown.

With a sigh, he touches the gold ring on his right pinkie finger. When he completed his Knights' initiation, he bought himself the ring and had it engraved with his initials and the date, 1907. As with his wedding ring, he is superstitious about ever removing it. It is more powerful than a good luck charm, more potent than a religious medal. It signifies his connection to the collective power of his fellow Catholic businessmen. It symbolizes his control over his family's destiny. It makes him proud of his accomplishments and very… modern. Very *American.*

He sits with these thoughts for a moment. Tom manages the proceeds from both stores and pays all the family bills. He will be thirty-two this year and has been doing that since he was sixteen—half his life.

He jots down another note: *speak to Francis*. It's time to spin off the store at 5530. Francis is thirty and still living with Mother and the girls. Between Francis and Mamie, they can easily assume the expenses at the Lexington house. But wait. He scratches his chin. Francis has been seeing Molly Curran. If Francis marries her and moves out… Tom decides it is better to continue paying for Lexington. Francis should be able to focus on building his business and starting his own family.

He goes back to his paper. Amid the pages of dire news about Europe are the displays of fall fashions. Kitty's birthday is coming up on the twelfth. He sees an ad from Grand Leader about their August fur sales. Oh, wouldn't Kitty just die for a fur coat! He studies the ad. Price-reduced seal-skin coats range from $275 to $775. What a fortune. Even the dyed-muskrat coat was only reduced to $285. Maybe she'd be happy with a hat or a muff. Or maybe he can find a fabulous fur second-hand. He jots down another note for himself.

Tom continues to study the paper, visualizing the war's battlefields on a mental map. How fast Europe has descended into chaos. The idea of that insanity spreading to America makes his stomach tighten.

He fixes an egg for himself, then hears Kitty coming down the stairs. He checks his pocket watch. 10:45. She'll be late for the eleven o'clock Mass.

"Jesus, Mary, and Joseph, it's hot," she says as she breezes into the kitchen with the baby in her arms. She glances at the newspaper on the table as she hands the nine-month-old into his open arms and kisses the top of his head. "She loves it when you read the funnies to her. Hey, it's birthday week for the Flanagans. I told Papa we'd have the party here. What do you think, Friday night?" She grabs a broadbrimmed straw hat from the coat rack. "Okay, I'll be right back."

Before he has a chance to react, she's out the door.

"Mama. Bye-bye," Mary calls out.

"You're so smart," he says, turning the paper to the comics section. "Looky here, Mary-Mary."

He starts to explain what's going on in the drawings, but Mary points to the cartoon buffoon being played a trick on and squeals, "Dada! Dada!" Then she wriggles off his lap, much more interested in exploring the kitchen than reading the funnies.

Mary Margaret is pure Barrett, with her bright blue eyes and white-blonde hair, already tall for her age. He smiles as she pulls pots from a cabinet, shouting "No!" when he tells her to put them back. Okay, she does have Kitty's feisty personality. "Full of piss and vinegar," as Papa Flanagan likes to say.

Oh, the Flanagans. Kitty's affection as a wife and brilliance as a business partner comes with a price. Her family.

In the Irish-Catholic families Tom knows, losing your farm, a parent, a spouse, a child means that you bow your head in humility to God, work harder, find more rules to follow, seek more organizations to join. The family stays close and the oldest son accepts his obligations.

The Flanagans are different. Unnerving. No one gave them the rule book. The wheels of the family wagon wobble. Nellie and Kitty, leaving home so young. Nellie's mysterious and horrifying death. The terrible step-mother. Ethel's fits. Julie's frailty and lack of schooling. The third wife May, always two seconds from a breakdown. The boys, underemployed. The young one, Modie, doing odd jobs for politicians and saloon owners—destined for trouble.

Kitty loves to attribute her organizational skills to Moses, pointing out how many planing mills owe their success to his talents. But Tom only sees a blustering man in his fifties, telling long-winded stories and dropping his cigarette ashes on the floor. If he was once a brilliant job estimator and operations expert, he's now been reduced to inside sales, checking boxes on order forms from the big mercantiles.

Family gatherings are stressful for Tom but a tonic for Kitty. She loves the laughter, the spontaneous singing, the edge of craziness.

So party they will.

Kitty is back before noon.

When she sees his raised eyebrow, she says, "So I left during Communion. Forgot my fan. That church is an oven." She tosses her hat on the coat rack, strips off the light jacket covering her bare arms, and dons an apron. "Besides, I have a lot to do."

She sweeps Mary off the floor and plops her into the highchair. From the back porch, she hauls in a half-bushel basket of over-ripe peaches. "Move your paper."

Tom puts his notebook back into his shirt pocket and folds up the newspaper. "Anyone ever tell you what beautiful hands you have?"

She leans toward him, puts her hands on either side of his face, and rubs her nose against his. Then, with a quick kiss to his forehead, she's back to business.

"Unless you want to help cut these up, out with you." She chops a peach in half, tosses the pit in the garbage pail, and sets the fruit on the high-chair tray. Mary squishes the fruit against her face and slurps in the juices.

"She's making a mess," Tom says, standing up and getting a bib from the kitchen drawer. He ties it around Mary's neck.

"Nothing that can't be cleaned up. She loves watching me make cobblers."

"You're baking cobblers in this heat?"

"Got a better idea for soft fruit? No one wants to turn on their ovens in this heat. That's why these will sell out in no time tomorrow." She fills a large pot halfway with water and sets it over a flame. Then she fills the sink with cold water. "And we'll get our money back on these expensive peaches."

He watches Mary get the peach all over herself and give him a defiant grin.

"Do you want to read me the paper?" Kitty asks. "Or do you want to get out of my hair?"

"It's all about the war. Belgium is toppling to Germany. Some locals are caught behind the lines and we're trying to get them to safety."

She cuts an X in the bottom of each peach, puts them in a basket that holds six, and settles the basket into the boiling water. Almost immediately, she pulls it out and dumps the peaches into the cold water—a familiar routine. She'll blanch them, skin them, slice them, pile them into glass baking dishes, and drizzle them with lemon juice to keep them from turning brown. Then she'll start on the biscuit dough for the topping. She'll be at it all afternoon.

"There's cold chicken in the icebox if you're hungry," she says.

"I'm heading over to the store. Say, I'm thinking we're not getting much advantage using the apartment upstairs for storage. Maybe rent it out? Might be good to have someone keep an eye on things."

Kitty doesn't look up from her peaches. "Tommy turned twenty-two last week. Maybe he could stay there, pay a little rent."

"No," Tom says, dreading that kind of entanglement with a brother-in-law who spends his free time playing pool and shooting craps. Kitty gives him a look, forcing him to add: "I mean, I was thinking of a young couple, someone who would be in at night, someone willing to pay a premium rent for the advantage of living on the streetcar line."

She nods and he can hear her sigh as she returns to her peaches. Maybe he better think again about buying that fur coat.

:: 82 ::

Spring, 1916. Kitty is behind the cash register at 4841 watching Mary Margaret stack soup cans on the floor. Tom comes in from the storeroom, sweeps the two-and-a-half-year-old into his arms and sets her on the counter. He takes a handful of dry beans from his apron pocket and scatters them on the counter.

"Here, line these soldiers up," he tells Mary, then stoops to put her cans back on the shelf. "Francis rented a second storefront at Arlington and Wabada."

"He's on the move," Kitty says. "Energized by a wife and their own flat. And probably goaded on by marrying into a well-to-do family. Needs to impress the old man."

Tom bristled. "The Currans are no different from the Barretts. Both families did their time in St. Patrick's parish."

Kitty knows the story, a familiar tale of two brothers, sons of Irish immigrants, figuring out a business together. For the Currans it was commercial printing. Brother Cornelius was the dynamo who partnered with small printers downtown, then bought them out. His older brother Florance—Molly's father—figured out the financials. Con P. Curran Printing boomed and Florance was able to move his family of twelve children from the Seventh-Street tenements to a spacious nine-room home on

Romaine Place.

"No reason why our business won't grow, why we won't have a home in a wealthier parish," he says.

Kitty adds, "Without the twelve children."

Tom smiles. The Currans aside, Kitty had taken to heart Nellie's harsh observation that rich women were not saddled with a houseful of children. And her own mother had been all the proof she needed that a woman's insides could tolerate only so much. So she and Tom kept a calendar and put a pillow between them during certain days of the month.

"Anyway," he says. "Francis's move makes me want to start looking for a second store too. We need something on a busy residential corner."

"We can use the extra income, if you can keep your costs down," Kitty says. "I want to have our living room furniture reupholstered and we need a bigger refrigerator." Kitty has discovered her taste for fine goods—good business has allowed her to buy second-hand silverware and Noritake china from classified ads. And Tom found her a heavy brilliant-cut glass pitcher from Corning, New York, not practical for water, but perfect for cut flowers.

"Let's not get ahead of ourselves," Tom says.

"I know, I know," she says, "but my mind is on entertaining. We're going to have Easter at our place this year. It's Molly's first visit here and I want her to be impressed. We don't have a grand dining table so we're going to have to eat off our laps like bums."

Laughing, he leans over and kisses her forehead. "Molly is already impressed by you."

Tom helps a customer gather her groceries and Kitty checks her out. A second store is still on her mind.

"If we get a second store, I'd like us to live upstairs. As long as there aren't rats."

Tom considers the question as he checks potatoes for sprouts.

"And I'd like the apartment big enough so we can bring Ethel home from the Sanitarium to live with us." She's been waiting for the right moment to make this request.

"What?"

"She's sixteen now and they moved her to the adult wing. Papa is heartbroken over it. They keep her all doped up, telling him she's too dangerous otherwise. But she's a real human being—funny and smart.

She could entertain Mary and do small jobs in the store, couldn't she?"

"Oh, Kitty," he says, "I know you love her and I'm the first one to understand family obligation, but… but I've witnessed her fits. The family may know how to get her through them, but—"

Kitty bangs a roll of quarters on the side of the cash register drawer, letting them spill into their compartment. "But! *But* onlookers are horrified and a few morons think she's possessed by the devil, right." Her eyes well with tears. "God forbid our customers might witness a seizure." Kitty knows in her gut that grown-up Ethel's sudden eye-rolling, twisted, shuddering swoons would be a problem in the community. Ethel under heavy medication is no less spooky. Her speech is slurred and she has difficulty with her hygiene. But Kitty's heart makes her keep arguing.

"Don't you think that having a sister-in-law on Arsenal is a greater stigma for the family?" Kitty asks. "Everyone calls it the *insane asylum*. Doesn't matter if you're there for a brain injury. Insanity marks a family as… as weak."

"Don't make me feel worse about this than I already do," Tom begs her. "I think she is where she needs to be, to hell with what the neighbors call the place. Ethel's story is tragic, but we can't undo the deed."

Kitty orders a ham for Easter. She'll serve it cold, with rye rolls and mustard, along with cold side dishes from the Barrett women, a fruit salad from Molly, dyed eggs from Aunt Delia, and sweets from May. Kitty makes a note to bring home ice cream for Papa and orders a double-layer box of bonbons from Mavrakos to ensure enough chocolate for all.

She's excited about having Molly over. She reminds Kitty of Nellie, pretty and sharp-witted. How bittersweet it is that each holiday without Nellie is a little less sad. Soon Nellie, like Mama, will simply be a spirit that sits among them, enriching their time together without words.

She thinks of Ethel again, neither fully human in that awful place nor elevated to spirit. She calls Papa.

"I feel terrible that Ethel can't join us for Easter. It's that terrible place, all those drugs. I really want her to come live with us, to have a real life. But Tom won't hear of it. Can't you talk to him?"

She hears him sigh.

"Don't you think that if there were any way in hell I could have avoided that place for my child, I would have? Don't you think there isn't a day, I don't miss that bright girl reading stories to me from the newspaper? And a day where I don't curse myself for her fate? And it terrifies me to think that Ethel's fate also sealed Nellie's, that she couldn't bear the thought of a child for fear of all that could go awry. Don't burden yourself with the sins of your father, Catherine. This is America. You are young. Look forward, not back."

:: 83 ::

April 23. Easter. Kitty awakes early to dress in her new suit, a spring-green skirt and jacket of silk-lined linen, with a white voile blouse over a new petticoat and slimming corset. She twists her hair into a loose bun and pins on a brimless green hat trimmed with pink roses. Then she helps Mary slip on her lacy white frock and ties a big pink bow in her hair.

After strolling to nine o'clock Mass, chatting with neighbors along the way, the couple flies into action, organizing the buffet dinner.

The Barretts arrive first, followed by Pat and Delia Keville with their two girls, Peggy and baby Delia, ages four and three, perfect playmates for Mary.

The guests are helping themselves to ginger ale punch, spiked with a bit of brandy, when Papa and May arrive, along with Tommy, Joe, and Julie. They all look distressed. Joe's left hand is wrapped in bandages.

"Jesus, Mary, and Joseph, what happened?" Kitty asks.

Joe hesitates and Papa speaks sharply. "Apparently, at the Riverside mill, they think Good Friday is an occasion for drink. Your clever brother lost two fingers repairing a band saw."

"Oh!" Kitty feels the pain shiver through her as she pulls her hand to her chest.

"And they fired me on top of it," Joe says in a slur.

"He's loopy on laudanum," Tommy says with a snicker. "He may need a nap."

"My buddies and I are moving to Chicago," Joe continues, his gray eyes blinking. "Plenty of work up there. I'm done with this town."

"Prohibition can't come soon enough," Papa mutters. He hands Kitty the basket of May's sweets and clears his throat. "Shall we try to enjoy ourselves then? Howdy-do, Mrs. Barrett!" He begins to work the room, speaking warmly to each guest. He makes much ado over Molly, launching into a long-winded description of how he designed customized wooden bays for some of her uncle Con's printing equipment.

Fifteen-year-old Julie hands Kitty a smaller basket. "Apple tarts. Sweetened with pear juice concentrate I boiled down myself. Better for my sugar."

Kitty gives her a big kiss and asks her to help put the food out. "Is Modie coming by?" she asks.

Julie shrugs. May overhears.

"Don't expect that one today, hon," she says. "He's been running wild. Another thorn in your papa's side. Nineteen, no job, and he thinks he owns the world."

"Modie has a lot of money," Julie protests. "He gave me ten dollars last week to buy this new shirtwaist for Easter."

"He's very good to you, dear," May says. "Why don't you run and get a cup of punch for your papa."

As Julie turns away, May tilts her head toward Kitty. "I'm afraid Modie is bumming around with some local characters, if you know what I mean."

Kitty shakes her head. "What 'characters'?"

May lowers her voice. "Gangsters. Guys like Cherries Dunn and Baldy Schoenborn. You see their names in the paper. Spending time at Bev Brown's saloon, you know, the whatchamacallit, Fifth Precinct Democratic Club. They might have him doing some political dirty work. And don't ask me what's up with Joe moving to Chicago. Can't be good. Let me help you get that ham on the table, hon."

Kitty is left with a terrible feeling as her guests chat and laugh. She hates hearing that news about her youngest brother. He is so handsome, so charming, grown tall as Joe now. How does such a sweet kid get involved with hoodlums? As she fills small bowls with mustard and horseradish, she can't stop thinking about him. He is gregarious, like her, but where she is the leader, the organizer, he is the willing follower—anything to get approval. If she'd realized that years earlier, she could have asserted herself more with him, given him a boss. But for years, all eyes were on Julie, then Ethel. Papa was always distracted. Then Nellie was gone too. Now Modie's bosses are a bunch of small-time gang leaders.

As she brings the toppings to the table, she looks at Katie Barrett, who is Modie's age. What a contrast. Tom found the money to get her through a secretarial course at Bryant and Stratton and she's already much in demand as a stenographer. Kitty doesn't understand how the fatherless

Barrett children all turned out so perfectly skilled and in charge of their lives. She prays that Mamie and Katie will inspire her little Mary to work hard and have her own set of talents to develop.

:: 84 ::

Saturday, May 27. Kitty is bustling to get out of the house and around to the store before opening time. Tom has already taken the delivery truck over to the new shop on Newstead. She hasn't quite forgiven him for renting a storefront with no upstairs apartment. Both of them are always dashing from home to store like a couple of squirrels.

The phone rings. It's Papa.

"Catherine, can you spare a minute?"

"What is it, Papa? I'm on my way out the door."

"Just to let you know, May and I have a new address. Do you have a pencil? 3931 St. Ferdinand. Carting truck coming tomorrow. You needn't bother yourself. We're fine."

But his voice isn't fine at all.

"What happened?" she asks.

"Well, um, now that you mention it, we did have a bit of a problem."

Kitty sets Mary on the floor, handing her the keys to play with. Customers will be standing on the sidewalk in front of the store if she doesn't leave shortly. "What?"

"Wednesday. May and Julie were here alone. Police swarmed in for Modie, looking for Modie. Created a ruckus. Then stood outside waiting for him to come home. Arrested him. Made a terrible fuss and got the neighbors all riled up. The landlord, he went crazy and suggested we find a different place to live." He was talking fast now. "I should have protested and made apologies to everyone, but..."

Kitty interrupted. "Why was Modie arrested?" Her legs trembled and she had to sit down.

"Suspected burglaries. Didn't come home Tuesday night and the police said there was a rash of burglaries. Petty things like cigarettes and candy from a confectionery. But then jewelry from a house. And a gun."

"Jesus, Mary, and Joseph."

"I spent all night at the police station with him. I gave them hell and they finally decided the charges wouldn't stick. Let him go. But they reeled off a list of his 'known associates' and believe me, Catherine, it isn't good.

I've run into some of these characters over the years. Their names get in the newspaper, in stories about lid joints and gambling rings, and political arm twisting. Egan's Rats—the gang, have you heard of those sons of bitches? Modie is playing with fire. What am I going to do, Catherine? What *can* I do?"

Is her father really asking her that question? Does he really expect his twenty-five-year-old daughter to have the answer to the local Irish mob, minutes before she needs to open her store? Her eye is on Mary, crawling toward an electrical outlet, two keys poised to plug herself in. As she snaps her fingers to get the baby's attention, she finds herself beginning to cry.

"Papa, hang on." She scoops Mary into her arms, the baby squirming and screaming. "Papa, I don't have the answer. But I have to—the store—can we sort this out later?" Mary slams the keys on Kitty's nose. "Oh!"

"Of course—I didn't mean to—you run now." The line goes dead.

With tears streaming down her face, Kitty wipes the blood off her nose, drapes her handbag over her shoulder, puts the baby under one arm, and grabs the collapsed carriage in the other. Down the front steps and out on the sidewalk, Kitty wrestles one-handed with the buggy to get it open, plops the wailing child into it, and trots down Bayard to Easton.

She unlocks the front door of the store thirty seconds before the first shopper shows up.

:: 85 ::

On Sunday afternoon, Kitty tells Tom she has to check on Papa's move.

"Why the change of address?" Tom asks. "The Evans apartment was good."

"Something with the landlord," Kitty says, evading the issue with Modie. "You know how Papa gets his back up."

"I'll come with you."

"No, no. Enjoy your day off and keep an eye on Mary. I'm taking the truck in case they need me to carry boxes for them."

Tom jumps to his feet. "The truck? You're driving?"

Kitty is not a skilled driver, impatient and easily distracted, but it's a fine day to practice—stalling out on a Sunday afternoon doesn't slow down traffic for miles.

"Remember to put on the parking brake before you—"

She slams the door. She knows all the steps, one, two, three, four, before she jumps out to give the engine a firm hand-crank. It's keeping the car going that befuddles her—too many foot pedals and hand controls. But sooner or later, she has to learn.

She stalls only once on her way to Evans Avenue, so she arrives in a good mood.

It looks like the carting truck has come and gone. She walks through the empty apartment and is surprised to find Modie standing at the sink, carving the orange meat out of a muskmelon with his pocket knife.

"Kitty!" He rinses his hands before he gives her a hug.

"I was hoping I'd run into you," she says, hugging him back. He is a big man now, not as tall as Tom Barrett, but muscular. She pulls back. "And look at you, wearing your cap inside the house."

Instead of smiling at her jibe, his eyes narrow. "What do you want?"

"I heard the police picked you up Wednesday."

"Yeah, what of it? They couldn't pin nothing on me."

"They must have had a reason to cause such a spectacle, to make the landlord ask Papa to leave."

"Landlord don't care. It's Papa. He's ashamed of me." Modie sniffs, stabbing the melon with his blade. He carves another piece and holds it out, dripping, toward Kitty. "You want it?"

She shakes her head.

"Have you joined a gang?"

He scoffs. "They're not exactly the Knights of Columbus, you know. You don't 'join up.' I hang out with people who like me, who think I got guts, who pay me to take care of some business for them, that's all. I get cash, no fussing with taxes or banks." He slurps down the chunk of melon, wiping his chin with the back of his hand. "The dames love me."

"The *dames*?"

He turns to slice another piece of melon. "Dames love a guy with rough hands, a little blood under his fingernails. A guy with a reputation. They're lining up for me."

Kitty doesn't like how this is going. "If all you want is a girlfriend—"

He spins around and points his knife at her. Too close. She rears back. "I don't want a stupid girlfriend. I want respect. Respect!"

She takes a step away and raises her hands to her chest. He lowers the knife.

"Just like your Mr. Thomas P. Barrett, living on the strength of his reputation for fresh meat, for clean produce. Banking on the loyalty of his customers. Guys I work for, no different. Me, no different."

"What about Papa? He has a name to protect too, a salary to earn, a family to worry about."

"Give me a break. The old man's losing his marbles. You don't see him more than, what, once a month anymore? He gets it together for his precious Catherine. Yeah, don't look at me like that. His hands tremble, he has headaches, can't sleep. He's starting to see plots against him everywhere. I can't stand him like this. He didn't have to move. I could have smoothed things out with the landlord." Modie rubs his hands together and smirks. "These days, I have more than my Irish charm to persuade guys to see things my way."

Kitty doesn't like this tough guy act. "You're scaring me, Modie."

"That's the point, Catherine." He gazes at her with his big brown eyes. "Nobody messes with little *Modie* anymore. Little *Modie* is dead. They know me as Muhoney now. Sometimes Maroney. I change it up, keep 'em guessing. Makes it tough for the coppers to track me down."

"You sound ridiculous," Kitty says.

Modie—or this new Muhoney person—raises his knife again and takes a step toward her. "Just watch me," he says. "Go home to your good man and your beautiful baby, to your tidy little apartment and your well-stocked store. Read the newspapers. Keep an eye on the saloons and clubs. There's going to be a war this summer. And every time you see the murder of some disloyal thug, of some lowlife who can't honor the code, who betrays his brother, you'll see me there."

Kitty looks into his eyes again, searching for some sign that it's all a blustering joke from an anxious nineteen-year-old who's read too many Zane Grey novels. But she sees nothing, gets nothing but a cold chill down her spine. With a shake of her head, she says no more and walks away.

Back in the truck, Kitty is upset and confused. She grips the steering wheel to steady her hands. She sets her controls, then gets out to lift the crank. The car backfires. She curses, repinning her hat as she wishes she'd taken a taxi.

Modie appears.

"Get in the truck, Kitty. I'll get it going for you."

He cranks and the car starts.

"Can I give you a lift?" Kitty asks.

He shakes his head and disappears into a gangway between buildings.

She heads down Evans, planning to check in on Papa. But at Vandeventer, she turns right instead of left. Slowly, she drives south to Kingshighway, makes a right at Arsenal, and parks in front of the City Sanitarium.

Kitty and Ethel sit on a park bench in the sanitarium garden. Kitty puts her arm around Ethel and pulls her close. Her sister lays her head on Kitty's shoulder. Together, they spend the afternoon watching pigeons.

:: 86 ::

The run-in with Modie rattles Kitty. When they all lived under the same roof, she fought all the time with her kid brothers, yelling, shoving, hairpulling, even punching, till the boys hit adolescence and Papa drew the line. Still, they had screaming matches over who left the mess in the kitchen or who ate all the bananas. Their quarrels were summer storms, a few minutes of thunder and lightning, then back to muggy sunshine, the tempest quickly forgotten.

But Modie, with his pocketknife in hand and his humorless eyes, feels menacing. She is afraid of him.

Then she feels afraid *for* him. Who does he think he is, acting so tough? He had an easy childhood compared to thugs who grew up as lost boys on the streets. He's acting the part, playing a game, striving to fit in with people who will use him. This is not her Modie.

She doesn't tell Tom about the encounter, hoping it's all a phase.

The next Sunday, she dresses up Mary and takes a cab to Saint Ferdinand Street. Papa is thrilled to visit with the baby. Everything seems fine.

As Papa bounces Mary on his knee, Kitty says, "I ran into Modie when I was looking for you last Sunday. He says you're having headaches, trouble sleeping."

"Don't you worry, Catherine. I'm hunky-dory. Modie caught me one bad night and you know he takes everything to heart. And this new apartment is really much better than the one on Evans."

"I visited with Ethel too. She seems okay, well adjusted," Kitty says, even though her heart breaks every time she sees Ethel in a phenobarbital haze.

He nods. "Very peaceful she is, very calm."

Kitty asks about Joe.

"Got a postcard with his Chicago address. He's working, not writing home for money, so I guess losing a couple of fingers isn't slowing him down. What more can his old man ask for?"

On her way home, Kitty tells herself it's okay to make believe all is well because otherwise, how do you wake up and go to work in the morning if all you see are problems you're powerless to fix?

As summer gets underway, however, Modie's words linger in Kitty's mind, his words about being involved in *wars* and in some kind of honor killings. She scans the newspapers for crime stories.

In August, she picks up on the story of Harry Romani, murdered in the Fifth Ward Democratic Club on North Twelfth and Chestnut. Kitty remembers it as one of the places where May said Modie hung out. According to the paper, Romani was twenty-three, a part-time prizefighter and full-time hood. The club manager told the police that Romani was having a drink when two men joined him at the bar. Another came up from behind and they gunned Romani down. Of course, the manager was out of the room at the time and couldn't identify any of the shooters.

The account makes Kitty's skin prickle. Could Modie have been there?

In September, she spots another big murder, another name May mentioned. Harry "Cherries" Dunn is gunned down in the Typo Press Club. Kitty remembers a birthday of hers long ago, on Farlin, when Papa blew his top at Modie for being picked up in a police raid at the Typo Press Club.

October brings a couple more high-profile murders. Edward "Baldy" Schoenborn is gunned down at the Fifth Precinct Club. Then a pal of Romani's is shot to death at a saloon on Chouteau.

Kitty reads each story carefully, praying she won't see her brother's name.

At the family gathering on Thanksgiving, after the meal, Kitty fills a pot with water to start a soup. Her brother Tommy sets the turkey carcass on the counter.

"Grab a knife and cut off the good parts," she says. "We'll have sandwiches later." She plops a leg bone into the water. "And while you're here, tell me what's going on with Modie."

Tommy rolls his eyes. "What's to tell? We hardly see him anymore unless we catch him at dawn before he flops into bed. Gone before Papa and I get home from work. Talks to Julie, that's about it. Maybe he'll show up for his birthday on Saturday, but I wouldn't bet a nickel on it."

"What about these gangs, these clubs? I read about the murders at the Fifth Precinct Club, at the Typo Press Club. Modie have anything to do with those?"

He stacks slices of turkey onto a plate. "Jesus Christ, Catherine, how am I supposed to know about that stuff?"

But he does seem to know.

"Look. You got Egan's Rats and the remnants of the old Bottoms Gang. They're into voter intimidation, robbery, murder, gambling, you name it. They get in each other's way. They steal each other's loot. They bribe police and politicians against each other. The lines blur. One day, a punk is working for the Rats. The next day, he's working for the Bottoms. Too often, the punk hisself don't know who he's working for. He's told to do a job. He does it. He gets his money."

"And Modie?"

"Modie's that punk." Tommy's black eyes suddenly look tired. "He's all bluster and charm like our old man, so he pitches himself as more important, more dangerous than he really is. He'll either grow out of it or—"

"Or what?"

Tommy cracks the second leg bone to release the marrow and drops it into the pot. "Nothing. Nevermind. He'll grow out of it. Maybe one of his floozies will turn out to be wife material."

"And Joe in Chicago? Is he a punk too?"

He shrugs. "Seems okay. Papa gets a card from him once in a while. Working as a machine hand for a trucker. Dan Hern Teaming Company, something like that." He tips the platter of bone, skin, and grease into the pot.

Kitty hands him a rag to wipe his hands. He is shorter than her other two brothers. Slim but solid. His hair, thick and black. "How about you, Tommy? How are you doing?"

"Can't complain. Schaffer Brothers is a decent place to work. Short walk from the flat."

She lays a damp towel over the sliced meat and slides the dish into the icebox. "I have the whipped cream here. Take those pies out."

Tommy catches her sleeve. "Kitty, I—" He hesitates.

"What is it?"

Whatever he has in his mind to say, whatever furrows his forehead, vanishes with a crooked smile. "Little Mary. She's really adorable."

:: 87 ::

Moses Flanagan prides himself on being able to do his job through any family crisis. He keeps his mustache trimmed, his shirt collars starched, his suits brushed. He shows up, ready with a smile, a wink, and endless small talk about the weather, baseball, and music. And yet something in him is gradually being gnawed away—his optimism, his hope. Is it age? Is this what happens to a man as he approaches sixty?

He thought losing Nellie was the final blow, one last kick in the gut from a cruel God. But he carried on. Modie needed him.

Modie is his heartburn, his toothache. Modie is the slow-rising river in springtime, the devastating flood inevitable and unavoidable.

But as Christmas of 1916 approaches, Moses grapples with another worry: the increasing disability of his sugar-sick Julie, who will turn sixteen in January. Moses reads that scientists have connected diabetes to a malfunction of the pancreas, but the only remedies publicized are worthless nostrums and ridiculous starvation regimens.

Since Julie came home from Guardian Angel, the Flanagans have muddled through. May has been a godsend for his frail child, providing companionship, helping her through textbooks sent over by the school district, and teaching her to eat meat and nuts to avoid the diabetic swoons that occur after too much fruit or bread.

May has also helped Julie pick out sturdy, well-fitting shoes to relieve her foot pain, encouraging her not to run around barefoot because every nicked toe sets off a round of foot infections.

But now, Julie complains about her vision—spots and floaters and cobwebs appearing in her eyes. The doctor warns Moses that her eyes will worsen as the months and years go by.

In the face of unbearable truth, Moses does the only thing within his power to do. He decides to buy Julie a piano.

She loves playing her growing record collection on the Victrola. She has a good ear and a voice almost as strong as Kitty's. He will teach her all the tricks he knows for sounding out a tune and adding chord progressions to make it sound like she knows what she's doing. She won't have to bother using her spotty eyes to decipher the code of sheet music.

Twice over the years, Moses surprised his family with a piano, in Leclaire and then on Farlin. Both times, watching Kitty and Nellie jump and scream with excitement was a thrill for him. Now, on Christmas Eve, with a light snow falling outside, the family's third piano is being rolled into place and tuned. He is struck with a sudden nostalgia for those past joyful moments. The knifelike longing for his dear Maggie catches him by surprise. And poor lost Nellie. He chokes up, even as May prattles on in the background about rearranging furniture and carpets. He loves May. He needs her. But she buzzes like a bee from subject to subject, never really expecting a response and often losing her train of thought.

Julie is radiant as she puts her arms around him and lays her mop of curly hair against his shoulder. "Are you really going to teach me, Papa? Really? This is the most amazing present I've ever received!"

True to his word, Moses and Julie spend every spare minute of the holiday break sitting side by side on the piano bench. Julie catches on fast and they move quickly from "Twinkle, Twinkle, Little Star" to sounding out the melodies of the recordings she loves. When Tommy is home, he teaches her "Chopsticks" and they roar with laughter at their harmonious success.

When Kitty comes by, she protests that she can't play a thing without sheet music but manages to play "There's a Tavern in the Town" from memory, much to Julie's delight.

Moses is concerned that his old fingers don't hit the keys the way they used to, back when he could sound out rags and blues progressions by instinct. He writes it off to arthritis, refusing to let it spoil his fun with Julie. Teaching her is all that matters. Watching her come to life at discovering what she can do fills him with love and pride. It is the happiest he has been in a long time.

:: 88 ::

Monday, January 1, 1917. Moses awakes feeling good. There was no party the night before. He didn't even have a drink. New Year's Eve was all about music with Julie, either sitting at the piano or playing their favorites on the Victrola, singing along while May cooked and worried that the neighbors would start complaining about the racket.

As Moses dresses, it crosses his mind to wake Julie and go to Mass with her on this Feast of the Circumcision of Jesus in the Temple, a holy day of obligation for Catholics. His mind travels back to the two holiday seasons when he and Maggie marched their entire bundled-up brood of seven to Christmas and New Year's Day Masses. 1901-02—Julie was a toddler. 1902-03—Maggie was in pain, the beginning of the end.

But the idea of church-going vanishes with the aroma of coffee from the kitchen, where May is mixing the ingredients for waffles.

Later, as Moses and May finish their first helping of waffles, the phone rings.

"My name is Daniel Hogan, Mr. Flanagan. I'm the attorney for your son Moses Rafael. He asked me to give you a call."

"What is it?" Moses asks, dreading the answer.

"He's on his way home. Hate to have to tell you this, but young Moses was arraigned this morning on a charge of forgery. Long story short, Mr. Flanagan, your son showed up at the Laclede Avenue Police Station with a $1,500 bond for the release of a burglar named Tony Ortell. After they left the premises, a clerk discovered that Judge Kern's signature was bogus. Police picked your son up at one of Bev Brown's saloons."

Forgery? On a bail bond? Is that the kind of shite Modie is involved in?

"You said he's on his way home?"

"Yes. He entered a plea of guilty and, seeing he's just twenty, living with his family, the judge released him to your care and custody, awaiting a sentencing hearing in March."

Minutes after Moses hangs up the phone, Modie walks into the apartment, disheveled in his tweed suit, cap askew, unshaven.

"What the hell is going on?" Moses demands.

Modie pushes past him. "Nothing. Let me wash up."

From behind the closed bathroom door, rising above the sound of the water running in the sink, Moses hears his son retching.

When Modie comes out and starts toward the bedroom, Moses says, "Wait. Sit down here at the table and talk to me."

Modie balls up his shirt and jacket, tossing them into the bedroom, then pulls up his suspenders over his union suit. "I'm tired, Papa. Let me go to bed."

"Not till you spill the beans. A lawyer by the name of Hogan called.

You're in my 'care and custody,' so have a seat."

Modie sits, elbows on the table, hands covering his eyes, the stench of jailhouse piss clinging to his clothes. May pours him a cup of coffee.

"I didn't do what they say. I didn't forge that judge's name. I've been driving for—" He hesitates. "For this guy and he gives me the bond and tells me to go pick up Ortell. Next thing I know, the police are hauling me in and I spend the night in lockup." He sniffs, wiping his eyes on the dirty edge of his sleeve, then taking a drink of coffee. "They deliver me to the courthouse this morning and that Hogan guy shows up, tells me he's my lawyer and that I should plead guilty. I was ready to do anything to get the hell out of there."

May sets a plate of waffles in front of him, topped with scoops of cinnamon butter. Modie takes a bite, closing his eyes as he chews. "Thank you," he says to her. "I guess I'm starving."

Moses is impatient. "This guilty plea—doesn't that mean prison?"

Modie shrugs. "Hogan says they'll drop the case. Or knock it down to a violation, charge me a fine. Guy I did the errand for, he'll pay it off."

March comes around and the case hasn't been dropped. Both in their well-brushed suits and starched collars, Moses and Modie take the streetcar downtown to the courthouse.

Hogan greets them. "Nothing to worry about," he says.

In front of Judge George H. Shields, Modie pleads guilty to forgery in the fourth degree. Hogan makes a case for leniency: first offense, barely twenty years old, good Catholic family.

The judge squints at Modie. "Six months in the Workhouse." He bangs his gavel. "Next case."

"No!" Moses cries as Modie turns to him, eyes wide with surprise and horror, cops coming out of nowhere, grabbing Modie's arms.

"Papa!" Modie shouts, flailing, resisting, his legs collapsing from under him. "Don't let them take me. It was supposed to be a fine. Papa!" He is dragged through a set of swinging doors behind the judge.

Hogan takes Moses by the elbow, nudging him out of the courtroom, into the corridor. "I'll have the paperwork sent to your residence. It'll be a few days before they let him have visitors."

Moses yanks his arm away. "What the hell just happened, you son of a bitch? And who is paying your bill?"

Hogan stiffens. "Muhoney's employer takes care of his people. He'll be well compensated for his time."

"*Muhoney*, my ass. You made my son your fall guy and now he'll go through life with a police record." Moses winds up for a roundhouse punch at the lawyer, but his swing misses by a mile, throwing him off balance and landing him on the floor, room spinning, bystanders crowding around him, helping him to his feet, guiding him to a bench. When his eyes re-focus, the lawyer is gone.

He trudges out of the courts building over to the Wellston streetcar, his mind a muddle. When he misses his stop at Vandeventer, he stays on the car till Kitty's store, deciding to tell her in person that her kid brother is a jailbird.

:: 89 ::

Thursday, March 15. Kitty is lying on her side in bed, staring into the darkness. She has slept fitfully, wondering how to tell Tom about her brother going to the workhouse for six months. Tom's biggest fear is financial ruin. And financial ruin for a small business is driven by the loss of customer loyalty. And, according to Tom, loyalty is lost through scandal, a black mark on your name.

Kitty likes to argue that spoiled milk and rancid oils drive customers away faster than private personal problems, but he says he can't help what people think. Family trouble—sickness, divorce, insanity—they all cause people to look away, to avoid interaction, to buy their groceries elsewhere even if they sympathize. It's like they believe the taint is catching.

They already have two family secrets, kept hidden with public lies. Nellie died of a kidney infection, don't you know. And Ethel is working as a live-in domestic in south St. Louis. Will her brother's jail time be a third? Will they tell people he went to work with Joe in Chicago?

Tom stirs. The luminous dial of the clock on the nightstand says 4 a.m. He removes the pillow between them, laying a hand on her hip, moving it to her waist, snuggling closer, purring in her ear. She catches the hand before he goes further.

"Bad time," she says softly, even as she loves his warmth. "Next week."

He kisses the back of her head. "Molly brought the baby by the store yesterday. Cute as the dickens." Francis and Molly had their first child in January—Francis Junior. "I was thinking…" He tries to move his hand again, but she holds it in place.

"We agreed," she says. "Five or six years, to give us time to establish the business. We go by the calendar."

"I know," he says, nuzzling her neck.

"I need to tell you something else though." She tightens her grip on his hand so he doesn't pull away. "Papa came by the store yesterday. Modie's in trouble. They didn't think it would come to this—I didn't know a thing—but yesterday he was sentenced to six months at the City Workhouse for forgery."

She hears Tom sigh as he rolls away onto his back. She moves with him so she doesn't have to let go of his hand.

"Jesus wept. Forgery? Does the idiot even own a pen?"

Kitty drops Tom's hand at the insult and pulls the covers up around her. "He delivered a bail bond to the Laclede Avenue police station. Turns out the judge's signature on it was phony. He had no idea. Papa says they played him, made him the fall guy for someone else's work."

"Who the hell are *they*?"

"I don't know." Kitty feels a sudden blush of shame. She wants to be angry with Modie, but she doesn't need Tom to pile on. "Modie's been doing odd jobs for some fellow out of the Fifth Precinct Democratic Club." Maybe Tom will think he's working for an elected official.

But it's Tom's turn to pull the covers snug around himself. "That's one of those lid joints, an after-hours club. Owned by Bev Brown. I see it in the news. Police raids. Murders. He has a saloon on Chestnut, same deal. That's who your brother is involved with?"

"Honestly, no idea. I think it's just where he meets his… whoever he works for." She sighs. "I don't even know where the City Workhouse is."

"Way down on South Broadway, on the river, near where we went to school at St. Thomas. Sits on top of big limestone cliffs and the convicts are put to work pounding boulders into macadam for road repair. I guess six months of that will teach him to be a man."

Kitty twists back to her side and buries her face in her pillow. How horrible. What kind of man emerges from six months of hard labor on the banks of the Mississippi? From cold, rainy spring through the sweltering summer, eaten alive by mosquitos, cheek by jowl with men older, bigger, tougher than he is. She wants to weep for him, without the judgment from Tom.

Weeks go by. The papers are full of news about the devastating war in Europe and America's growing involvement. After much debate, Congress finally approves drafting an army to drive back the Germans. Every able-bodied man in his twenties is expected to register in June, millions of them to be shipped overseas. Leaders of the impending railroad strike are accused of treason by people worried about hobbling the war effort. The Russian czar has abdicated and what looks like a revolution is under way.

Locally, all eyes are on the Viviano kidnapping and a police slush fund scandal. Debate rages about the likely effects of alcohol prohibition on local breweries and distilleries, rippling back to all the farmers who supply them with barley, corn, and rye. Thousands will be thrown out of work. Thousands will lose their farms.

These are the topics their neighbors discuss in the aisles of Barrett's Market as they gather their groceries.

No one seems to notice the tiny article in the evening *Star* that one Moses Flanagan was sentenced to six months in the Workhouse for forging a judge's signature on an ex-con's bail bond.

Kitty breathes a sigh of relief.

:: 90 ::

1918 pulls the United States deeper into war. Germany is invincible. Millions of American men have received their notice that they will be activated, trained, loaded on ships to England and France, and lined up on the Western Front with guns, grenades, and gas masks, everyone praying they won't be slaughtered like their allies. November's Bolshevik revolution in Russia has thrown the eastern alliance into chaos.

Last year's abnormally cold winter depleted the country's coal supply and Washington fears there won't be enough to fuel the massive mobilization come summer. Price controls go into effect. Business hours are regulated and early bedtimes encouraged to reduce the draw on coal-fired electrical plants. Every week Kitty and Tom deal with new regulations to protect the food supply, like the ban on selling hen and pullet meat to save birds for egg production.

It is a somber time.

Kitty is grateful that her brothers are saved from the trenches—Modie by virtue of his police record, Joe by his lost fingers (though he is put on a reserve list), and Tommy by pure luck of the lottery. Too old for the first wave of registrations, Tom and Francis Barrett will have to register next summer, in case the dragon of war devours all the youth in Europe or directs its fiery maw at American shores.

Still, as the new year begins, the Barrett stores are making a profit, enough to hire a cleaning girl on Thursdays and another to watch four-year-old Mary in the afternoons, when the Easton store is busiest.

On a Wednesday evening in late January, with a frigid wind rattling a loose windowpane, Kitty stands at the kitchen table wrapping a pair of her shoes for the cobbler to resole for the second time. Tom is tinkering with an old Burroughs adding machine that one of their customers traded to pay off his account.

Out of the blue, Tom announces he wants to expand to a third store.

"I have my eye on a property at Cote Brilliante and Hamilton. Francis tells me out toward Wellston people have more money, buy more groceries, better cuts of meat."

"Why would you even think about expansion when all we hear about are food and coal shortages, with half the population of young men getting ready to march off to war?"

"People still need to eat. And we're the ones to feed them. Hey, where do we keep that can of 3-in-One oil?"

Kitty rummages through a drawer and hands it to him. "Who'll manage store number three? You and I are stretched to the limit as it is."

"There is a good apartment above the Cote Brilliante storefront, cheaper than this place," he says. "If you take charge there, I can split my time between the Newstead and Easton Avenue stores. And we can keep renting the space above Easton."

"You've done all the math? Oh, look, you're dripping the oil on the table." She grabs a rag and hands it to him.

He grabs her hand. "I figured it all out," he says. "I even factored in the cost of having another child in a year or two."

Kitty blinks, then laughs. "While you're at it, could you project when we'll be able to afford new shoes?"

:: 91 ::

The Barretts subscribe to three city newspapers, ever watchful for what's coming next. Tom focuses on issues that affect the grocery business: weather patterns, commodities trading, transportation, and war.

Kitty enjoys local news, studies the classifieds for bargains, and keeps an eye out for gang activities—stories that might involve Modie. Lying low since his September release from the workhouse, he drifts in and out of holiday gatherings without much to say to anyone but Julie. Apparently, her brother Tommy tried to give him a talking to and got cut off. Papa says he leaves money for rent but is rarely home.

On February 13, Kitty glances at the evening *Star* before Tom arrives home. There, on page three, is Modie. In trouble. There was a riot at a ball of the Theatrical Brotherhood held at the New Club Hall downtown. Police were on hand to make sure liquor sales stopped at 1 a.m., but cases of beer had been sold in advance to each table. Things got rowdy. Beer bottles got thrown. Dozens of men and women were piled into patrol wagons and taken to Soulard station. Seven of them got charged with disturbing the peace in a public place. Modie was one of them. Luckily, Judge Hogan dismissed the case on a technicality: the New Club Hall was private property, not a public place.

Kitty might have chuckled over the fracas, but damn that Modie, smack in the middle of it.

Tom passes over the article as he chats with her about the war in Europe, a threatened telegraph worker strike, and the price of wheat. When he's done with the paper, Kitty snips out the article, not for Modie's name but for the names of his associates. She tucks the clipping into a makeshift folder cut from cereal-box cardboard, her library of information about the Irish gangs, hidden among papers on her desk.

The dance hall incident is minor. Seven weeks later, the worst happens. Not only is Modie back in trouble, but Tom spots it before she does.

It is April 8, a typical Monday morning. Tom and Kitty are up early bustling around, getting a few chores done, eating their oatmeal, scanning the *Globe-Democrat*. As Kitty scolds Mary for dumping too much brown sugar on her cereal, Tom leans forward, focused on a short piece at the bottom of page two. He folds the paper and hands it to Kitty.

The headline reads, *MEN CAPTURED WHILE ROBBING SALOON*

SAFE. Her stomach sinks.

> Thomas Rowe, 28 years old, 4432 Garfield Avenue, and Moses Flanagan, 21, 3931 St. Ferdinand Street, were arrested yesterday morning when they were discovered in the saloon of Joe Mochesky, 3201 Pine Street. A lookout who was posted outside the saloon escaped.
>
> The two men, police say, were engaged in forcing the safe when captured. The men fled through a rear door on approach of the police and six shots were fired before they halted. The prisoners are suspected of robbing the Ferguson, Mo., post office a few weeks ago.

"Jesus, Mary, and Joseph," she says in a low voice, zeroing in on the people and the addresses. *Rowe* got picked up with Modie on that disturbance of the peace charge. *Garfield Avenue*, not far from St. Ferdinand. Does Rowe live with his mother? Does she shop at Barrett's Market? The *Pine Street* address is downtown, but west of Jefferson. And *Ferguson*? That cow town? Modie doesn't have a car. Does Rowe?

"Safecracking, for God's sake," Tom says. "Shots fired—he's lucky to be alive."

Handing back the newspaper, she shakes her head. "Let's see what the day brings. Papa will give me a call when they sort it out. Try not to worry."

He stands up and wraps his arms around her. Her long hair is pinned up into a neat roll around her head and he smooths a few loose strands behind her ear. "I want to tell you everything will be okay, but this feels serious."

"I know," she says with a sigh. "I know."

About eleven, Papa shows up at the store. Kitty is stacking cartons of cigarettes behind the counter. Mary is playing with some girls out on the sidewalk, trying to learn hopscotch. The butcher is in the back behind the meat counter, waiting on a line of customers.

"You saw the paper?" Papa asks.

She nods.

"I just came from the arraignment. Same charlatan for a lawyer as last time. The police could have killed him, you know, firing shots after him like that. He wasn't committing murder."

"What's the upshot?"

"Trial date set for May. Released on a common law bond till then. Caught red-handed—I can't see any defense."

The phone rings with an order for delivery.

"Sit here behind the counter, Papa," she says, pushing the stool in his direction. He takes off his hat and sits.

List in hand, she races around the store, up and down the ladders, collecting the order into a box. As she finishes, the clatter of a bicycle against the front window announces the return of her delivery boy.

As he comes through the front door, she points to the box, "Mrs. Powers up on Wabada."

"Got it!"

The butcher's customers are beginning to line up at the cash register. As Mrs. Hempel places her wrapped package of meat on the counter, she studies the baked goods and asks, "Got any day-old bread?"

"Not today, but how about half a loaf of this rye? It'll be a treat with your corn beef here. Need mustard? Horseradish?"

Mrs. Hempel hesitates, then nods. "Maybe a small jar of French's too."

With her customers taken care of, Kitty turns back to Papa, who is staring out the window. A Liberty Bond poster is flapping loose from the telephone pole in the breeze, but he seems to be looking way past it.

"I've been talking to your mother," he says, "and she's worried I'm not spending enough time with Modie. He was always the one who needed the most attention."

Kitty frowns. "You mean *May*? You were talking to *May*?" She lays a hand on his forehead, worried he might have the flu so many had this spring, but it's cool.

He takes her hand in his. "Not May. With my dear Margaret. She's warning me about Modie's friends. Did you read about the riot at the New Hall Club? Maggie's very upset with me."

Her first impulse is to tell him to stop sounding like an old fool, but she squeezes his hand and says, "Mama knows you've done your best."

He looks up into her eyes. "I may have to quit my job. Every time *Moses Flanagan* appears in the news, they pull me further back from dealing with customers. I hate it. I'd like to go back to carpentry, have my own shop. May could have part of it, sell her pastries with Julie. I'd have Modie working right alongside me, doing some good with his hands, not cracking safes with no-good hoods."

The door opens and Papa glances up at the shopkeeper's bell that announces each customer.

"I rang a bell like that once," he says, gazing out toward the street again. "When I was a conductor on the cable car. Rang a bell every time I collected a fare. The sound of money, the sound of opportunity. I met your mother there. Caught her hand, took her nickel, rang the bell. Luckiest moment of my life."

Kitty kisses the side of his head. "Don't worry, Papa. Modie will be all right."

:: 92 ::

The week before Modie's trial date, on Saturday, May 18, Modie's name gets in the paper again. He was picked up at dawn forty miles south of St. Louis in DeSoto. He and three buddies were arrested on suspicion that they were the robbers who held up the Tri-City Bank in Illinois on Thursday.

Her brother and his friends claimed they were going on a fishing trip—each with a revolver under his jacket "for protection."

When she calls Papa to see if he knows more, he says the boys were released. The Illinois troopers tracked the bank robbers to Indiana.

"They're targeting our Modie now, that's clear," Papa insists. "The police have his name and they're going to pick him up for every damn thing. And those gangs, they're gunning for him, making him the fall guy, smearing the good name of *Moses Flanagan*. I can't let that happen."

With her brow furrowed, Kitty lets him ramble on for a while, then promises she'll go with him to the trial.

He has more to tell her.

"I'm looking at a couple of storefronts on Easton. 3837 and 3835, just west of Vandeventer, a scant few blocks from our flat. Rent's cheap and a lot of folks are doing work on the old houses in that neighborhood. May and I, we want to set up two shops."

"Sounds interesting." Is he serious or fantasizing? She'd have to sort it out later. "Look, I got customers lining up. Let's talk more next week. Tom can take a look. You know how he loves checking out properties."

Monday, May 27. The trial of Moses R. Flanagan is brief. Kitty holds Papa's hand as they watch the prosecutor present evidence of breaking and entering, attempted burglary, and fleeing arrest. Modie's lawyer has little to offer except that his young client suffers from undue influence, perhaps even coercion, by the twenty-eight-year-old Thomas Rowe. He begs for the mercy of the court.

They are allowed to wait with Modie while the jury is out. Her brother is full of nervous braggadocio as he flips through Papa's newspaper and its stories about the first wave of Americans engaging with Germans in the trenches.

"I should have enlisted when I turned sixteen," he says. "I like being a soldier, you know, having comrades, doing stuff. In war, soldiers are heroes. At home, guys being good soldiers are branded as hoodlums."

"Claptrap," Papa snaps. "There's no soldiering like being in the trades, being part of a crew, building something with your hands, putting in a God's honest day of work instead of strutting around like a banty rooster, being an errand boy for sons of bitches who'll chop your head off the minute you become inconvenient to them."

Kitty starts to jump into the argument, but Modie's lawyer pops in to say the jury is back.

Guilty.

"One year in the workhouse," the judge pronounces and pounds his gavel.

"Damn," Moses whispers.

As the court adjourns, Kitty runs to Modie, hoping to give him a hug before he's escorted away. His eyes start to tear up, but he quickly stiffens and shakes his head. "I'll be fine. A soldier," he says in a low voice. "Stay safe, Catherine. Don't get involved."

She bites her lip and returns to the bench where Papa sits staring at the floor. He takes her hand in his and presses it to his cheek. "You were right, Maggie. I wasn't paying enough attention. I lost track of our boy."

"Papa, it's me, Kitty. We need to leave the courtroom and catch the streetcar home."

He gets to his feet and takes a moment to find his balance. Then he looks her in the eye. "All right, dear. Let's go. I have a lot to do."

The day is warm and muggy. Kitty and Papa trudge toward the streetcar stop, opening their umbrellas against a soft rain.

"I'm going ahead with opening my own shop," he says as they take their seats, his voice flat and sad. "It's something I should have done years ago. I'd have trained your three brothers in woodwork methods and machinery. Joe wouldn't have lost his fingers in any shop of mine and Modie wouldn't have sought fellowship with safecrackers. And Tommy—Joe wouldn't have bullied him so much if they both operated a lathe with equal skill. Tommy's a drunkard now—that'll be the end of him one day. All my fault. A father should have a business for his sons to inherit, a gift to future generations, something they can be proud of."

"Don't be ridiculous. You had important jobs, with big salaries. You could never have afforded the nice things we had out of a small shop."

"People do. That husband of yours will."

Part 2. On Cote Brilliante, Murders and Plagues, 1918-1920

:: 93 ::

Food shortages and intermittent rationing are a challenge for the grocery business, but Tom and Francis both know how to hoard their working capital and pounce when wholesalers offer hard-to-get meats, grains, and produce. Trusting their discipline, Kitty gives the nod to a third store.

In early June of 1918, Tom leases the building on the corner of Cote Brilliante and Hamilton, hiring a crew to build out the interior to his specifications. Kitty takes charge of moving their household from the Bayard flat to the apartment above the store, scheduled for July first.

By now, Kitty observes, the Barretts are a well-oiled machine. The brothers work in tandem to keep their stores well-stocked. Kitty and Tom fly through the day, then sit together at the kitchen table after dinner to update their lists. Kitty focuses on keeping the customers happy with fast check-out and speedy delivery. She screens and hires the help, usually teenage boys, now that most young men are either fighting in Europe or training at Fort Dunston in Kansas. With no patience for stupidity, laziness, or petty theft, she fires as quickly as she hires.

In bed at night, she falls asleep in Tom's arms as they talk through their plans. Then, he nudges her awake before five to review the day's agenda. By the time she puts her feet on the floor, her mind is buzzing with tasks to be completed before the stores open at nine.

The Saturday before they're scheduled to move, Kitty is directing a couple of boys packing boxes when the mail arrives. Two letters catch her eye.

The first is from Papa. The envelope is imprinted with a business address: *M.M. Flanagan, Carpenter and Builder, Office and Store: 3837 Easton Ave., St. Louis, Missouri.*

"What the hell?" She tears open the letter. The stationery has a bold letterhead. Name, address, phone number, and these tag lines: *Carpenter and Builder, WILL DO ALL KINDS OF ALTERATION WORK, Door and Window Screens Set Up, Plans Details and Specifications Made for All Kinds of Work.* She reads his letter.

> My dear daughter, Mrs. Tom Barrett—I am pleased to let you know the shop is open. Already I have work and have hired a boy to help. As soon as business picks up, I trust your brothers will find steady employment with me and I can change the logo to "M.M. Flanagan & Sons."
>
> We have also rented the tiny shop next door. May and Julie will run a tearoom. I am praying we will be able to bring Ethel home to work with them.
>
> I know you are busy, Mrs. Barrett. Please give my love to your husband and beautiful daughter. Your father, M.M. Flanagan

She sits down at the kitchen table and re-reads the letter. Her papa is a brilliant man, a man she worshipped and admired her entire life. Organized, thoughtful, detail-oriented. So why does this letter alarm her? If anyone can start a new business at the age of sixty, he should be able to. She hasn't laid eyes on him since the day Modie was sentenced, that day he was acting so strange, confusing her with Mama. She wrote off his confusion as the heartbreak and guilt of seeing his son marched off to hard labor for the second time. But setting up a shop—two shops—on the Easton Avenue business corridor, having expensive stationery printed, to fix screens in a word-of-mouth business? Why didn't he involve her?

But of course, he did mention it, twice, and she brushed him off, her mind ever-focused on her own business.

She puts aside Papa's letter for the moment to open the one from her Aunt Delia Walsh in Chicago. Inside the envelope is a folded card with a black border.

> My dear Catherine, it is with a heavy heart that I must let you know of the passing of your beloved cousin Mary on June 10. Beginning in January, an unfortunate series of illnesses resulted in endocarditis—a heart problem. She passed away peacefully at home, fortified by the sacraments, at the age of 24.
>
> I have delayed writing you and your Uncle Pat because I did not want you to drop everything and travel to Chicago. With the War, trains are expensive or impossible.
>
> Please know that Peg and I are fine. Your Uncle Charles is a great help to me. My best regards to your family, Aunt Delia.

Tears spring to Kitty's eyes. What terrible news. Ill since *January*? She remembers how Aunt Delia traveled to St. Louis when her mother faced surgery, and held the family together when Mama died. Now Kitty has missed the opportunity to repay that kindness in her godmother's hour of sorrow.

Kitty lays her head on the table, refusing to cry in front of the help.

She is exhausted. She has lost track of everyone important to her except Tom and Mary. She hasn't seen Uncle Pat or Aunt Delia Keville or their growing girls since Christmas. Why didn't she have them over for Easter? When was the last time she visited Ethel? Does she know what her brothers are up to? Has her father lost his mind?

The grocery business owns her now.

The voices of the movers soften into a lullaby. The world spins gently—till she twitches awake from her moment of slumber. Popping up from the chair, she shakes off the sleep and barks at a boy to label the box he's closing, pitching a china marker at him.

Tomorrow they move. The next day, she will take charge of a new store, in a new neighborhood, hiring a new butcher, a new delivery boy, a new cash register clerk, figuring out sales and loss leaders to attract new customers. And in two months, Mary needs to be ready to start first grade at Notre Dame.

How will she survive?

That night, as the clock approaches midnight and they dress for bed, she shares her worries and her grief with Tom. He holds her while she suffers a bout of weeping. Then he fetches two glasses of brandy for them to sip as they crawl into bed. The windows are open wide to catch the breeze. A weeklong fuel-saving curfew has closed the businesses along Easton Avenue, making the neighborhood unusually quiet, quiet enough to hear the evensong of crickets and katydids in the shrubbery.

The brandy goes down easy. The boundary between who is Kitty and who is Tom blurs, floating them together. The thought of her safe-time calendar drifts past, too trivial to catch in this sea of love.

:: 94 ::

It is hot July. Moses sits in the office of Dr. Henry W. Hermann on the second floor of a building on Delmar at Grand. Despite the oscillations of a small fan, he needs to mop the sweat from his face and neck.

He is ill. Since Modie's sentencing, increasing confusion, insomnia, and headaches have turned him into a dunderhead. Quitting his job to fulfill the dream of running his own shop has only added to his distress, causing fumbles and errors intolerable for a man of his experience.

Last week, his pharmacist recommended Dr. Hermann, who specializes in psychological complaints. Moses visited in hopes of getting a sleeping draft or some other medication to get him through the day. But Dr. Hermann went overboard, probing him about his symptoms, prying into his personal life, making him strip to examine his private parts, and poking him with a large hypodermic for a blood sample.

This morning, he's is back for a follow-up, perspiring while Dr. Hermann sits behind his desk scribbling notes.

Without looking up, he asks, "Did the pills help with your sleep?"

"Yes, they did, thank you," Moses says.

"I'm not going to beat around the bush, Mr. Flanagan. The Wasserman test confirmed my suspicion." Dr. Hermann finally looks up. "You're suffering from an advanced case of syphilis."

"Excuse me, what?" Moses leans forward. "What did you say?"

"It is syphilis. Your neurological symptoms suggest it is quite advanced."

Moses shakes his head. He hears the words but they don't make sense. "I don't understand."

"Do you know what a venereal disease is, Mr. Flanagan?"

Moses pulls back. "I'm not a damn fool, but where in God's name would I get a venereal disease?" The sweat trickling down his back turns cold.

The doctor raises an eyebrow. "You've been married three times. Twice to women who were married before. There is an epidemic of the disease in this country, Mr. Flanagan. There is really no prevention except for abstinence—and prophylactics, hard to find in these United States because of the Comstock law. The Christian powers of this nation disapprove of protecting men from their own bad behaviors. Did you know our boys in the trenches of Europe are the only soldiers among the Allies not provided with condoms? It's a crime."

What Moses knows about the disease he gathered in disjointed chunks, spoken in whispers late at night among worried men in saloons. "I, um, never noticed any sores on my, um, nether regions. Surely, I would have noticed…" His mind speeds back through time, trying to think of every woman he ever touched, every mysterious itch and ailment. "God help me, I can't remember…"

Hermann shrugs. "Not uncommon. The chancre is painless. Disappears quickly. You might have noticed stage two—feels like the flu, maybe a low-grade fever. Maybe you remember a rash on your hands, your feet…"

"Jesus." He thinks back. That February before he married May. That flu he had. She said she'd had it too. And she told him she once had a similar rash on her hands and feet, *dermatitis* she called it. But he used a condom. He used a condom because he didn't want more children. Then he remembers: that first crazy afternoon, that *one* time when he lost his head. "Yes, um, I believe it was my current wife… she suffered the symptoms before I did…" He mops his brow again, feeling faint. "Flu… rash… before her husband died. Said he lost his mind before his stroke, assumed it was all the lead fumes from his plumbing work."

Hermann makes a note. "You'll want to bring her in for a blood test, then. How is her health? Does she suffer from any neurological or psychological symptoms?"

Moses compares the sharp, energetic woman he fell in love with seven years ago to the fretful, flaky woman May is now, the woman who can't seem to do anything but bake pastries and who is as dependent on Julie as Julie is dependent on her.

"Hard to say," he mumbles. With a deep breath, he asks, "What next, doctor? Is there treatment?"

"Can't offer you a cure, but I can start you on neosalvarsan injections. They're painful, expensive. No guarantees, but they might slow down the damage the spirochetes are doing to your nervous system … buy you time."

The physician begins fooling with papers on his desk, to Moses's annoyance.

He reaches out to tap the doctor's desk with his index finger. "Look a dying man in the eye, Dr. Hermann."

The doctor faces him.

"Tell me what to expect. How will I go?"

"Everyone is different," Hermann says. "You may lose control of your thought processes, suffer from delusions. You may lose control of your physical functions, experience weakness and seizures. Tomorrow or years from now. Treatment might prevent your needing long-term hospitalization in the end."

Dabbing his nose and eyes with the handkerchief, Moses squares his shoulders and sits a little taller in the chair. "I have a lot to do. My children still need me. I've neglected some things I need to make up for. Let's begin those treatments."

Arriving late due to the time it took to prepare his injection, Moses finds his apprentice Walter standing on the sidewalk in front of the shop, waiting for his lesson in making window screens.

"Are you all right, Mr. Flanagan?" the boy asks as Moses unlocks the door. "You're white as a sheet."

Shaking his head, Moses hurries to the toilet at the back of the shop and vomits, an aftereffect of the injection, as Dr. Hermann warned. *This is shite*, he thinks. *People can't know I'm sick*. He washes his face, combs his hair, and makes sure his mustache is clean.

He and Walter begin their work.

At eleven, May and Julie arrive with their baskets of pastries. Her tearoom next door consists of a hot plate for heating water, a table for laying out the baked goods, a collection of second-hand-store cups and spoons, and assorted mismatched tables and chairs for patrons. It's a start. Every day they sell out all the goodies they made that morning, saving their profits to install a kitchen where they can continue to bake on the premises during the day.

At eleven-fifteen, same as every day, May walks through the open door of the carpentry shop in her white apron, holding her tray of tea and pastries for Moses and Walter. Same as every day, she calls out, "Sweets for the sweets!"

But today, Moses can't find his smile. He looks at May with new eyes. She poisoned him. She not only stole his attention from his children during a time when they needed a strong parent, but she also snatched away his health from his children's future, threatening to turn him into a drooling cripple, both a scandal and a burden.

No, wait a minute, he tells himself, blinking the thought away. *That's an exaggeration*. He needs to train himself to recognize crazy ideas. He needs to discipline himself to think rationally. Focus.

She sets her tray on his desk.

"Thank you, my dear," he says. "Tell Julie to come give her papa a hug when you finish setting up."

May blows him a kiss as she leaves.

:: 95 ::

October, 1918, begins with a tide of gossip rising through the neighborhoods where the Barretts operate their three stores. The flu that killed a few St. Louisans in the spring is predicted to flare up into a highly contagious second wave. Worried about how it will affect their business, Kitty and Tom search the papers for news and share what they hear from their customers.

The papers are packed with news of the war, details of the massive American assault on Germany along the western front, and the swirl of speculation over how it will end. Over dinner on October 3, Tom finds word of the epidemic buried on page four of the *Post-Dispatch* and reads it aloud. One death has been reported in St. Louis, but eastern states are being ravaged—80,000 cases in Philadelphia alone.

The next day, at the cash register in the new Cote Brilliante store, Kitty quizzes her customers about what they're hearing.

Mrs. Schultz, a physician's wife, is stocking up on canned goods and dried beans. "It's going to be bad," she says. "The health commissioner—Starkloff—he ordered all the docs to report every case to him. All eyes are on Jefferson Barracks." She lowers her voice. "It's spreading by way of the military bases. Believe you me, no one's keen to let that cat out of the bag—because of the war effort, dontcha know. They don't want us turning against our boys."

"How do you die from the flu, for godsake?" Kitty asks.

"Oh, it's the pneumonia, honey. Young or old, this Spanish influenza thing settles smack dab in the lungs and, boom, you're dead."

A chill ripples down Kitty's arms as she enters Mrs. Schultz's purchases on the adding machine. "So many cases in Philadelphia, so suddenly," she says. "That's terrifying."

"Well, you know what happened there." Mrs. Dubrowsky is standing in line with her five pounds of Quaker oats. "Big outbreak in the navy yard and the *meshuggeneh* town fathers go right ahead with their giant Liberty Loan parade. People dropping like flies. What a shame."

That evening, while Kitty heats up her stew, Tom points out a letter in the *Post-Dispatch* from Max Starkloff. It urges people to prevent the flu by avoiding fatigue, alcohol, and crowds, and cautions St. Louisans to get plenty of fresh air and to stay away from anyone sick.

"I wonder if you should take a break from working downstairs," Tom suggests. "I think we can afford to hire another clerk."

"Are you kidding?" she says. She is happy to be settled in the apartment above the store and delighted that the store is so busy. But the new location does need constant attention to make sure the shelves are stocked with preferred brands and any complaints are promptly resolved. As with their Easton Avenue store, their competitive edge is selling fresh meat along with dry goods, so they have to worry about butcher competence, health department inspections, refrigeration temperatures, and hygiene protocols.

"But your delicate condition," he says.

She puts the lid back on her stew and turns to see the worry in his blue eyes. Laying a hand on her belly, she leans over to kiss his head. "We have a long way till April. How about if I just follow the advice to get more sleep. I'll wear a mask if I have to."

Kitty continues to interrogate customers with political or medical connections. Several mention an outbreak at Jefferson Barracks, with soldiers now confined to quarters. After the noon Mass on Sunday, October 6, Mrs. McMurphy, whose son works for the city, tells her that yesterday a family with seven cases was reported to Dr. Starkloff's office.

"Jerry rang me again this morning to say there are already fifty more called in."

Mrs. Lohan tells her that the Board of Alderman held an emergency meeting to officially declare Spanish flu a communicable disease, giving the mayor authority to call a public health emergency.

It is no surprise, then, when the October 8 morning paper reports that, after a powwow of city officials, hospital administrators, and business leaders, the city is closing down. Theaters, movie houses, pool halls—all entertainment venues shuttered, all public gatherings canceled, all churches dark, effective immediately. School districts are ordered to suspend classes as of Friday.

What *is* a surprise is the news that city physicians have already reported a hundred cases to Starkloff's office and that Jefferson Barracks has called in nine hundred.

It also shocks Kitty and Tom to hear that private-hospital emergency rooms are turning away flu patients, declaring they can't risk contagion to inpatients. So, by October 11, the City Hospital is full, sending its overflow to the Arsenal sanitarium, where Ethel resides.

The Red Cross jumps in with a plan to care for quarantined patients at home by deploying nurses with volunteer drivers.

Police cars and cabs double as ambulances.

Within a week, St. Louis is transformed, from a community excited about the end of war, homecomings, and holidays to a town in crisis, out of work, hoarding food, fearing for their lives.

With Notre Dame parochial school shut down, Tom takes Mary over to Lexington, where she can stay safely with his mother and sisters for a few days.

The grocery business goes nuts.

Shelves are emptied as soon as the Barretts can stock them. Kitty is forced to hire extra help for the cash register so she can spend her days on the phone with wholesalers, bargaining for more deliveries and searching for new vendors where there are shortages. And in the evenings, she sits at her sewing machine making masks from old sheets. Or she goes down to the basement to boil and bleach a perpetual mountain of aprons, shirts, skirts, and trousers. Tom tries to help but often falls asleep in his chair before they're done with their late suppers.

The epidemic gets worse. With women now showing up to shop

in mourning clothes, tearfully sharing their tales of losing sons and daughters, the Barretts become frightened that their crowded stores are contributing to the spread. They ask customers to line up outside and wear masks. If customers admit to having coughs or chills, they are asked to sit on a bench outdoors while employees fetch what they need. The Barretts encourage call-in orders and home deliveries. They hire another couple of boys with bikes and rent an additional truck to get the work done.

The customers are their friends and neighbors. Everyone cooperates.

Kitty and Tom keep their stores open for as long as there are customers in line outside. Their employees disinfect counters and doors when the store closes. After putting the day's receipts in pouches, Kitty and Tom wipe down the cash registers. Upstairs, their aprons and masks are stuffed down the laundry chute. When they finish their tally at the kitchen table and lock the cash in the safe, they scrub the table and bathe.

As much as they miss her, they are grateful Mary is staying with her aunts and grandmother—for her, an adventure full of books and games.

By Monday, October 21, the mayor has closed most of the retail businesses downtown. In the rest of the city, shops are allowed to open a couple of hours for urgent business. Only grocers and pharmacies may remain open all day.

That afternoon, Kitty is upstairs, working the phone, talking to their suppliers. About three, she answers a call and is surprised to hear her brother Tommy.

His voice is thick and slow. "We've been sick here, Catherine. Papa and May, Julie and me. We're quarantined."

"Mother of God," Kitty says, suddenly longing for Mary in her arms. "I had no idea. Tell me, what can I do?"

"A nurse from the Red Cross comes by every day and someone—a volunteer—drops off food." He pauses to cough, his lungs wheezing. "We've been doing good, getting by, but today Julie took a turn. Hard time breathing. Began looking a little blue. The nurse came in and said she needed to go to the hospital. A volunteer took her down to City. I hope we did the right thing."

"When was this?" Kitty feels that familiar wave of guilt that she's been paying attention to all the wrong things.

"Just now. I wanted to go with her, but they said no. Said the hospital will call us after she's admitted or if she's in good enough shape to be sent over to the sanitarium to convalesce. I feel terrible. She looked so scared. The volunteer was a big guy wearing a white gown and a mask. Just picked her up and carried her away."

"Oh, my Jesus." Her poor baby sister, a skin-and-bones seventeen-year-old, alone in an overcrowded public hospital with hundreds of other flu victims. "And Papa? The nurse thinks Papa is okay to stay home?"

"Yeah. He was up all night by Julie's side talking to her, singing his songs. A little delirious maybe, talking to Mama, praying to her to get her baby through this. But his breathing is okay and now he can sleep."

"You'll call me when you hear from the hospital, okay?"

"Sure thing."

After hanging up, her anxiety through the roof, Kitty calls her mother-in-law's house. Mamie answers, reassuring her that they are all fine. Mamie and Katie are staying home while their jobs are suspended. Mother is healthy. Francis delivers groceries to them every couple of days. Little Mary is having the time of her life at the center of their world.

Next, Kitty tries City Hospital, but their switchboard is jammed. What about the sanitarium? Is Ethel all right? No one answers there either.

Modie. She calls the City Workhouse. A guard answers. "Flanagan is present," he says. "Any of 'em get sick, we transport 'em up to City. Then we notify next of kin."

Kitty goes back to worrying about her father and Julie. She has a meatloaf in the icebox and could grab a bag of potatoes from downstairs and run them over to Papa's place. With a knot in her stomach, she scans the work spread across her table. With beef already scarce, if she doesn't get the poultry ordered this afternoon, they'll be short come the weekend. And she still needs to find someone with toilet paper. Wiping the tears from her eyes, blowing her nose, she picks up the phone. "Let's get this done."

When Kitty hears the door slam, she realizes she's been stretched over the kitchen table, sound asleep. It is Tom, coming in after closing up each of the three stores.

She sits back, staring at the piles of paper, trying to remember what was on her mind before she conked out.

"What time is it?" she croaks.

Tom lays the three money pouches on a chair and scrubs his hands at the sink. "After ten," he says.

"I stopped at Mother's for a minute to check on Mary. She was already asleep. Katie says she's learning how to read. Our little girl is something else, isn't she?"

"I miss her so much," Kitty says, then yawns.

Tom lays his hands on her shoulders and bends over to kiss her neck. "Why don't you gather up your papers and head on to bed. I'll do the receipts and clean the table. Anything I need to know?"

"Oh." She rubs her eyes and consults her list. "Catanzaro says plenty of apples. He can deliver tomorrow. Poultry order's in, but Jones says no turkeys for Thanksgiving. If he finds any, they'll be small and expensive." Then she remembers Tommy's call. "Oh, Jesus, yes. The Flanagans are all down with the flu. Julie got taken to City Hospital this afternoon." She pushes away from the table, piles up her papers, and moves the phone to its stand against the wall. "I'll make you a sandwich."

Tom catches her in his arms and pulls her close. "That's awful to hear. Terrible. She's such a frail girl. I hope—" He lets the thought dangle, but Kitty can finish it. He hopes Julie lives. Or he hopes she dies easy.

Kitty is grateful for her healthy little girl, so curious and high-spirited, capable of entertaining herself for hours on end and equally capable of holding her own with older girls in the neighborhood. While she grills Tom a cheese and tomato sandwich, she prays to the Blessed Mother to get her sister home soon and to keep Papa, May, and Tommy on the road to recovery.

:: 96 ::

As the days go by, the reported cases of Spanish influenza begin to subside and the mayor lifts some restrictions and schedules the school reopening. Kitty is glad to hear that Papa, May, and Tommy are up and about, even if still dragging. Tommy has returned to work at Schaffer's, doing emergency repairs during their limited hours. Papa and May keep their shops closed. The bad news is that Julie is not responding to treatment.

Papa has cajoled a nurse at City Hospital into calling him every evening when her shift ends. Day after day, he calls Kitty with the same report: Julie is weak and barely conscious, drifting between this world and the next. He begs to visit, to sit with her, to read to her, to sing her songs, but no visitors are allowed till Dr. Starkloff declares the public health crisis is over.

In international news, it appears that the war in Europe is coming to a rapid end as American troops swarm into Germany, declaring victory as they go. It is only a matter of time before the Kaiser abdicates and the Germans surrender. Tom gets his final draft classification on a postcard—a permanent deferment—one less worry.

St. Louis businesses agitate for full re-opening, but according to Starkloff, the statistical projections point to a spike in the infection rate, so the mayor orders *increased* restrictions. When armistice is declared on Monday, November 11, most businesses are closed and police patrol the streets to disperse the celebrating crowds.

On Sunday, November 13, Kitty and Tom visit Mother's to celebrate Mary's fifth birthday and to bring her home for school on Monday.

At home, Mary arranges all her new books on a shelf, except for *The Secret Garden*, which she hands to Tom.

"I can read *you* a story now," she says. "Aunt Mamie taught me to read."

Kitty's heart sings as she sees the adoration in Tom's eyes for his brilliant girl.

For Thanksgiving, Mamie plans a feast at Lexington Avenue. But on the day before, the newspaper announces that the dreaded spike in flu has materialized, spreading especially fast among children. Kitty calls Mamie and they rejigger the plan. Mamie already intended to pack a food basket for the convalescing Flanagans, so she expands the project to food baskets for all.

Thanksgiving is a bone-chilling, rainy day and the Barretts are thankful for the chance to sleep late, eat pancakes and sausages, and play the Scott Joplin records Papa gave them. Kitty putters in the kitchen while Tom teaches Mary to play parcheesi. The afternoon *Post-Dispatch* reports that the flu infections continue to soar. More cancellations and closures are ordered. The Red Cross nurses are brought back on duty and an army of volunteers is requested to help sanitize the streetcars and enforce their proper ventilation. Schools are closed indefinitely.

At three, Kitty announces she's going to pick up the baskets from

Lexington and deliver one to the Flanagans. "Toss me those keys."

"You're driving? No, no, I'll do it," says Tom. "It's going to be dark soon and the roads are slick."

Driving is still not one of Kitty's better skills, but ever since they bought a used truck with an electric starter for the Cote Brilliante store, she manages to get from point A to point B without stalling at every corner.

"I have to see my family," she says, pinning a warm hat to her hair.

"Then at least take a cab."

"Well, I'm not taking a filthy cab anywhere, that's for sure. The police commandeer cabs to take flu patients down to City Hospital. If you're worried about your unborn child, my driving is much safer."

"I want to go," Mary says. "I miss grandmother and my aunties. School is canceled, so can I go live with them again? They're way more fun than you two."

"Mary Margaret!" Kitty says, as she fastens her luscious second-hand sealskin coat around her expanding middle. "It's Thanksgiving. Be grateful for what your parents can provide for you, a lovely home above our very own store."

Mary frowns. "They buy me stuff. They make me cookies every day."

"You're staying here with *your* father while I go check on *my* father."

Tom says, "You know I'm going to worry about you till you get home."

"I know," she says, pulling on her gloves. "I'll be fine."

In a slow drive full of jumps and jerks, Kitty makes it the four miles to the Lexington Avenue house. The place is redolent with the aroma of roasted chicken, sage, and rosemary and the fireplace crackles with hospitality. Kitty can't resist the offer of brandy. They talk about war shortages and pandemic layoffs, then about their precious Mary. Mother and the aunties love having her stay with them and can't wait for the next little Barrett to spoil.

When Kitty leaves Lexington Avenue with her food baskets, it is dark, rain mixing with pellets of sleet. Kitty secures the two baskets in the enclosed truck bed, pulls the fur coat snug, and re-pins her hat against the wind. She takes brightly lit Vandeventer for the mile drive to St. Ferdinand. The brandy evidently enhanced her ability to coordinate the clutch and gear shift. She arrives at the Flanagan apartment feeling a rare glow of relaxation.

Papa opens the door. His face is pale and his cheeks sunken behind his waxed walrus mustache, but his smile is broad.

"Oh, my darling Catherine. How wonderful to see your face!"

"You too, Papa."

She waves to May seated in an easy chair across the room while Tommy steps forward to kiss her cheek and take the heavy basket of food.

"Everything's cold. Needs reheating." As Tommy disappears into the kitchen, she embraces her papa, thrilled to see him. "Tell me how you all are. Have you heard anything about Julie? Did I tell you I was able to talk to Ethel the other day? She sounded all right. Her nurse said she's working in the laundry facility there on Arsenal, keeping sheets and gowns sanitized."

As Kitty babbles to her papa, she catches the rich fragrance of cigars and sees a tall, dark figure emerge from the shadows. Her jaw drops.

It is her brother Modie.

He gives her a shy smile. He is bundled in a dark overcoat, unshaven, but more handsome than ever.

"Oh, my heart!" she cries and throws her arms around him, on second thought praying he doesn't have the flu.

He hugs her back. "Glad I got to see you," he says.

Still clutching his arms, she pulls back to look into his brown eyes. "So, what is it? Did they commute your sentence? Did they give you leave for the holiday?" She senses the sudden stiffening of her father and May. "What is it?"

"I escaped," Modie says. "Got fed up with pounding rocks into gravel. I'm headed for Chicago. Came here to see Papa and to say goodbye for a while. I'm really sad not to see Julie. I can't stand it she's so sick."

"Escaped?" is all Kitty can manage to say.

He winks at her. "Pays to have friends. I'm plenty strong now and climbed up a quarry wall to the street outside the workhouse. We had it all planned out. My buddies picked me up there right on Broadway and Meramec. They're waiting for me now, in that Packard you probably parked next to."

"But the police—" Kitty starts to say.

Modie laughs. "Cops are too busy with flu patrol to bother with a workhouse con."

He peels away from her and digs something out of his coat pocket. It's a thick stack of currency. He stuffs it into Papa's jacket. "Don't worry. It's all mine. Fair and square. Didn't rob any banks, didn't blow any safes on the way here." He chuckles. "I want you to have it, Papa, for all the hell I put you through last couple of years."

Papa tears up as Modie gives him a big kiss on his cheek and a hug. "Oh, my boy, can't you stay here? Can't you lay low with us… for a few days… till after Christmas?"

"Gotta work, Papa. Earn my keep. This town doesn't love me anymore. But I'll be back. Don't you worry."

Modie takes a step and pecks May on the forehead, then gives Tommy a bear hug. "Take care of Papa, Tommy boy. I'll give Joe a punch for you when I see him in Chi-town."

Tommy bites his lip and gives his brother a jab on the shoulder.

Modie turns to Kitty, who is still gaping at him. With a hug and a kiss, he says, "I miss you, sis. Miss you bossing me around, telling me to do what's right. I'm going to be okay from here on in, you'll see." He heads for the door. "And that's a swell coat you got there. I knew you'd be successful!"

With that, he's through the door, disappearing into the night.

She hears her papa sigh and turns back to him. He is mopping his face with his handkerchief. Their eyes meet.

"It's been a helluva year, Catherine," he says. "Helluva year."

:: 97 ::

Chicago. December 25, 1918. Joe Flanagan is roused from a deep sleep by knocking at the apartment door. One eye opens. The room is bright. The clock says noon. The three other cots are empty and he remembers his roommates are away visiting their families in Skokie and in Calumet. He wanted to go back to St. Louis for Christmas, but the Spanish flu got him.

The knocking grows louder. He stumbles out of bed in his union suit and opens the door.

His brother Modie stands there, the last person Joe expects to see, a big grin on his face, a full-length fur coat around his shoulders, and a fine felt fedora with a small feather in the hatband, giant smile on his face.

"Merry Christmas! Santa's here!" he bellows.

Joe wonders if he's hallucinating.

"You gonna let me in, ya big goof?"

Joe steps aside. Modie enters the apartment, drops his two big carpet bags, and hugs his brother.

"Come on, let's fix breakfast," Modie says, tossing his hat on a chair, his energy filling the room. "I brought chicken, bread, eggs, cookies, coffee..." Taking the grocery-filled bag into the tiny kitchen, he makes himself at home. "You look like shit, old man. You sit, I'll cook. Where's your coffee pot? Tommy gave me your address. Sorry I haven't looked you up till now, but I've been working."

"Yeah, Tommy sent me a card, said you broke out of the workhouse, heading this way. That was weeks ago, but I got the flu, lost track of time. You need a place to stay?"

"Hell, no. I have my own place, just north of here on Madison, twelve-thirty. One two three zero, easy."

"You kidding? That's right at the intersection with North Ann, right where I work at the teaming company," Joe says, surprised Modie lives so near.

Modie nods. "Small world," he says. "But they've been shut down all month because of the flu, or I would have caught up with you sooner. Hey, how do you like my snazzy new coat?" He twirls around. "Racoon. I brought you one too. These are big with the college boys. They're going to be all the rage, you'll see." He takes off his coat and drapes it over a living room chair. He's wearing a tweed suit underneath, with a white shirt and tie. "Let me get some food started." He finds the can of bacon grease on top of the stove, scoops a dollop into the frying pan, then adds half a dozen chicken legs.

From his second carpet bag, Modie pulls out a giant coat. "Try this on!"

Joe stands up, wobbly and coughing. Slipping on the coat, he catches the label: *Joseph Klein, Fine Furs, 5207 South Michigan Blvd, Chicago, Illinois.*

"Pretty swank furrier you got this from," he says.

"Aw, I don't buy retail. Got them from a pawn shop on South Clark. Friends of mine own it."

"It's fabulous," Joe says, "but I can't really see wearing it to the machine shop."

Modie laughs. "It's for going to football games. For ice-skating. For walking your sweetie home on a January night. It'll fit you better with your suit on."

"It's quite a gift." Joe tucks his hands into the deep pockets, thinking of it more as a fine robe for his frigid apartment. What's this? He pulls out a roll of hundred-dollar bills.

Modie grins. "You're out of work at least a month. Figured you could use some dough. Buy yourself a pair of good leather gloves for that ugly hand of yours, stuff the two empty fingers with cotton."

Joe chuckles. "Sorry I don't have a present for you, Modie. If I knew—"

Modie waves away Joe's apology. "By the way, nobody calls me 'Modie' anymore. I'm 'Maroney' here in Chicago. Jack, John, Tom, Frank—any first name will do. I like changing them up, keeps the coppers on their toes." He laughs. "You know I have a second police record in St. Louis under the name 'John Flannigan.' Flannigan with two 'n's and an 'i.' How's that for keeping everybody guessing?"

Joe hardly knows what to say. His kid brother is on the lam from the St. Louis workhouse, but instead of lying low, here he is, a puffed-up prankster, in his fancy suit and fur coat. Joe shakes his head.

On the other hand, here he is, fixing breakfast for his sick brother, understanding that Joe might be short on cash.

"Who are you working for?" Joe dares ask.

Modie shrugs. "My buddies—Dwyer and Weaver —my buddies and me, we work with Charlie Stillwell, a fellow St. Louie kid. We call him the 'Chancellor.' Hey! Maybe you want to pick up some extra work, get out of this dump. We hang out at Barney Grogan's most nights. Look me up."

"You mean the Democratic Club on Madison?" Grogan is a ward heeler and popular character in the neighborhood. His Saturday night dances draw hundreds of couples.

"That's the place. Find me there almost any night."

Joe doesn't pry any further into Modie's new friends. Instead, they catch up on the family and talk old times till late into the evening, when Joe's eyes won't stay open. Modie walks him to his bed and covers him with the raccoon coat.

Even as his flu lingers, Modie's visit leaves Joe lighthearted and the cash gift lets him sleep easy, knowing he'll be able to pay his share of the January rent.

:: 98 ::

The new year brings the re-opening of the city, including the Herr Teaming Company, where twenty-six-year-old Joe Flanagan works as a machine hand keeping the delivery trucks in good repair.

Like his papa, Joe is an early riser who enjoys breakfast and a newspaper before walking the three blocks north from his place on Jackson, to the shop on Madison.

On Monday, January 20, after his daily dash to the corner newsstand, Joe fries his eggs, pours his coffee, and sits down to his *Tribune*, as his roommates begin to stir—water running, toilet flushing.

Skipping over the usual headlines obsessed with the rippling aftereffects of the Great War, Joe's eye catches a local piece: *ART INSTITUTE GEMS CLEW TO CLUB MURDER. Slaying at Grogan's Is Traced by Mystery Phone Calls.*

There was a murder at Grogan's Democratic Club early Sunday morning. He's surprised to see that the victim is the guy Modie said he worked for—Charles Stillwell, described in paragraph one as a burglar. Joe sits up straight and uses his finger to follow the words in the rambling speculation about Stillwell snitching on the burglars of a 1915 jewel heist at the Art Institute. After an anonymous phone call, the police made some arrests and, bam, Stillwell was shot.

The story goes on to describe the shooting, which occurred at the tail end of a big dance.

> Stillwell, as nearly as the police can make out, was sitting in the rear of the hall, talking with three men—Frank Weaver, Jack Maroney, and Patrick Dwyer. Weaver has a record as a safe blower. Both he and Maroney are said to hold memberships in the Grogan Eighteenth ward organization.

Joe finds he's holding his breath. *Maroney* is Modie's alias. *Weaver* and *Dwyer* are the names of the buddies he talked about at Christmas. He reads on.

> About three weeks ago, Dwyer, Stillwell and Weaver, and later Maroney were arrested as suspects in a number of burglary cases. They were thought by the police to be members of a band that robbed retail stores by loading merchandise on automobile trucks.
>
> Dwyer and Weaver were indicted. Maroney was held but later released. Stillwell obtained his liberty almost immediately and

> made no effort, it is said, to supply bonds or attorneys for Dwyer and Weaver.
>
> They believed from this that he had turned stool pigeon, the story goes. They later found a bondsman and the four met for the first time, it is believed, at the Grogan clubrooms.
>
> There was no intimation of trouble, according to the police version. The music and general amenities were going so loud that voices were muffled by the din.
>
> Suddenly there were a number of revolver shots. The music stopped and the crowd fled. Dwyer and Weaver ran out the front door, Maroney out the back. It is believed now that Stillwell fired before being killed and wounded Dwyer and Maroney, as there were drops of blood leading from the spot where he lay to both the front and rear exits. The police are still seeking Dwyer, Maroney, and Weaver.

Joe lights a cigarette to settle his stomach, churning at the thought of Modie being connected to a cold-blooded execution and possibly wounded in the process.

One of his roommates appears and pours himself a cup of coffee. "You okay, Flanagan?" he asks. "You look like you seen a ghost."

Joe mumbles, "I'm fine." He stands, folds the paper, and goes to the bedroom, hiding it under the mattress. He looks at the raccoon coat, his wonderful, warm blanket. Was it stolen?

He rushes out before his usual time, so he can see if Modie's at his flat, to check if he's wounded or not. But he stops when he sees two patrolmen nearby. It signals to him that Modie isn't home but that the police are waiting for him to show up. Joe walks on by. He doesn't want to be associated with *Jack Maroney*, in case Modie shows up at Joe's flat needing help. Joe can't approve of Modie's friends, but a brother's a brother.

Joe is up early on Tuesday, anxious for more news. There it is, an entire column on page thirteen. *BLAME THIEVES' FEAR FOR DEATH OF STILLWELL,* the headline screams. Today, Stillwell is described as a small-time gangster on the west side, leading a double life as a respectable, newly remarried barber on the south side. Modie and his pals are mentioned halfway down.

> Three men, Frank Maroney, Frank Weaver, and Patrick Dwyer, all members of Grogan's club and hangers-on at his saloon, are being hunted. Dwyer is a former convict. Maroney was arrested Jan.

> 15 in connection with the Dressel Commercial and Savings bank robbery and released on bonds of $1,000 signed by Clarence White, one of Grogan's henchmen.

Modie! Joe thought, *what the hell are you into?* The article went on to describe the rumor that Stillwell was meeting with police and that this motivated the shooting.

Modie is more deeply involved with the underworld than Joe wants to believe. What should he do? He wishes he told Modie where he keeps an extra latchkey in case his brother needs a place to hide. The article mentions several St. Louisans relocated to Chicago in recent years, all associated with Stillwell, all murdered. Joe imagines himself renting a car, and driving Modie back to St. Louis, back to safety. Or hightailing it out west like the heroes of the Zane Grey novels they loved as boys, starting fresh in Texas or Montana, warming themselves under buffalo skins instead of stolen raccoon coats.

The news on Wednesday alarms him even more: three new murders yesterday alone, with growing evidence of war and revenge killings among rival gangs. When they aren't murdering one another, they're being knocked off in police shoot-outs.

On Thursday, Joe is actually relieved to see that Modie, a.k.a. John Maroney, along with his pals Dwyer and Weaver, were arrested on Wednesday "without resistance." At least his brother is alive. Now Joe faces a new problem. Should he tell Papa that Modie has been arrested again? That he is in police custody, this time for murder? As he tucks another day's paper under his mattress, he prays to his patron saint, to Saint Joseph, for guidance.

At their Christmas reunion, Modie told Joe that Papa seemed fragile after his bout of flu and wasn't working, and that he was overwrought with Julie's continued decline.

Joe can't bring himself to make it worse.

He could call Kitty. She'd know what to do. He sighs. No, he needs to be a man, make his own decisions, find his own way.

The saga of "Maroney" continues on Saturday with a police informant's revelation of a "trust," a network of Chicago burglars stealing expensive furs, directed by a brother-sister team running pawn shops on

South Clark. One of the theft victims is Joseph Klein, a furrier on South Michigan, the furrier whose label is in Joe's raccoon coat. Stillwell, Weaver, Dwyer, and Maroney are named as members of the ring.

Joe sits on his bed, head in his hands. The flu has left him listless, with a chronic cough. He can't fathom the energy needed to play cops and robbers, but that's Modie, the enthusiastic follower.

The roll of cash Modie gave him is hidden in one of the fur coat's deep side pockets. Joe digs it out and counts how much is left. Nearly a thousand dollars. He doesn't need it now that he's working again. He wraps the money in brown paper, with a note to Papa saying he is doing great and hopes to make it home soon, maybe for Easter. He binds it up with strong twine, addresses it, and walks the package to the post office. Might as well make someone happy.

February is a long, miserable month, with bitter winds and sidewalks caked with lumpy ice and hardened gray snow. A winter's worth of smoke and coal dust hangs in the air. The newspapers are full of nations jockeying for power in Europe, labor union troubles, and the threat of Bolshevism in the West. Nothing more about Modie, who is still in jail awaiting trial.

Joe receives a note from Papa on his new business stationery, thanking him for his "investment" in M.M. Flanagan and expresses hope that he and Modie will return to St. Louis before long to join the business. Joe tucks the letter under his mattress with his clippings.

On March 5, in the gray light of dawn, Joe is squinting at the newspaper over his morning coffee and eggs. There! He finally spots what he's been praying for, in a tiny article on page five. Judge McKinley has dismissed the murder charges against Maroney, Dwyer, and Weaver for lack of evidence.

"Whoopee!" He is happier and more relieved than he thought he would be. Maybe Papa was on to something. Maybe he and Modie should return to St. Louis and live out their days doing simple work for their neighbors along Easton Avenue.

:: 99 ::

Meanwhile, in St. Louis, twenty-eight-year-old Kitty Barrett is focused on her own life. While she and Tom are relieved that the pandemic has passed, the war is over, and business is back to normal, she is nearing the end of her second pregnancy—or, as she likes to call it, her fifty-pound sack of potatoes. During her last doctor visit, the physician pressed a pinard horn to her belly and listened from various spots.

"I believe... yes, I believe I'm hearing two sets of heartbeats. Any twins in your family?"

Oh, no. She isn't sure *two* bundles of joy are accounted for in their careful planning. "Yes, my husband's sister was a twin, but the twin was stillborn."

"Well, Mrs. Barrett, unfortunate events can happen at the time of birth, but I hear two very strong heartbeats."

On April 1, those very strong heartbeats turn out to be two blue-eyed boys. They are fraternal twins, one slightly longer, the other slightly heavier. Thomas William and Robert Patrick. Bill and Bob.

Five-year-old Mary is delighted and volunteers to quit school to take care of them.

Tom is also thrilled. He can't stop talking about the idea of training the two boys to take over the Barrett grocery empire in twenty years.

"I'm not very good at ball games," he says, cradling a boy in each arm. "But I can teach them board games. And I'll invent one especially for them, to teach them strategy, without the frustrating complications of chess."

Kitty laughs. "How will you find time for that?"

He thinks. No remark is ever too casual for serious consideration. "Well, for starters, we can move the Newstead store farther west. That would save me an hour every day. Just think what I could do with an extra hour."

Looking at the two hungry boys, she says, "Just think..."

When she calls Papa with the news about the twins, she is frustrated to find the St. Ferdinand Street phone disconnected. She tries calling his shop a couple of times, but no one answers, forcing her to send him a note with the birth announcement and inviting him, May, and Tommy to their brunch after the baptism on April 13.

She is disappointed and worried when the Flanagans fail to show up at the brunch. Sunday evening, she scribbles a postcard to him. Exhausted from lack of sleep and the christening rigmarole, she tells herself that Tommy would have let her know if the absence was due to anything more dire than Papa's increasing forgetfulness—assuming Tommy was even told about the brunch.

On Thursday, the mail brings a letter from Papa, handwritten under his heroic letterhead.

> My Dear Daughter—Mrs. Tom Barrett, I was most pleased to receive your letter 4/14 *ultimo* this month and am most exceeding glad to learn by it that you became the mother of twin sons. And I presume that both of you are extremely overjoyed, and I hope that the Father & Mother of the twin sons and also the twin sons, that is best wish from me to Tom Barrett, his wife and hope it will come to pass.
>
> Again, my Dear Mrs. Barrett, I was not sick at all, only in this way. I had a man working for me and while I laid out all the work for him and showed him how to erect it, when I returned after one (1) day and a half, I found that he had all the work spoiled and I remained up three (3) consecutive days which losing so much sleep until 2 o'clock in the morning for several days made me act queerly and sleepy even in cars and traveled too much too far on account of losing so much sleep. I again wish you and your husband and your babies good luck happiness from Your Father M.M. Flanagan (over)

On the back is a note.

> I am no longer living at 3931 St. Ferdinand. If you want to write again, address as per card & letterhead.

She sits down to re-read the letter. For the meticulous Moses Flanagan, the letter is a muddled mess, with many cross-outs and corrections. He refers to her postcard of the fourteenth, but had he mislaid or forgotten the invitation sent ten days before? And losing his way on the streetcar, blaming lack of sleep? And what happened with their apartment? Where was May?

When the twins start squalling to be fed, she sticks the letter into a cubby hole on her desk. She'll have Tom stop by Papa's shop on his way home from the Newstead store.

After Tom checks in on Papa, he tells Kitty that, yes, Moses and May had some kind of falling out. But he is fixing up the small apartment above the shop, so that she can vacate the St. Ferdinand flat and move there with him.

"He says there's room for Tommy and for Julie, when she comes home, 'God willing.' He seemed…" Tom squints. "A little twitchy. We should probably keep a better eye on him. He says Tommy's helping him out evenings, so…"

Kitty nods and tries to put her worries on hold as she needs to review the produce order with him before Mr. Catanzaro calls. Strawberries are in season, but the prices are high this year. And, as her boys scream to be fed, she asks Tom to tell her how the radishes are selling at his two stores.

The days go by.

:: 100 ::

Monday, May 12. Joe Flanagan sits down with his coffee, his eggs, and his newspaper. A page-one headline catches his eye. The police are dealing with two shootings that happened overnight. The first is a labor leader, but the second tells of another murder at Grogan's.

He skims down the page.

> Victim No. 2 is believed by the police to be a jailbird mixed up in a gunman's war which led to a fatal shooting in Barney Grogan's Eighteenth Ward Democratic club last January. The police are investigating the possibility of a connection between the two crimes.

The front page is full of *Case No. 1*, so he shuffles the pages open to page six. There. Near the bottom of the first column is *Case No. 2.*

> Thomas Marooney of 1230 West Madison Street was found on a porch at 1842 West Monroe Street at 1:20 o'clock this morning. He had been shot eight times. He was taken to the county hospital and physicians say he will die within a few hours.

"No!"

Tears spring to Joe's eyes as he rereads the paragraph again and again, realizing he's been waiting to see this news for months. He rolls up the newspaper and races out the door. On the corner, he uses the phone booth to call work, letting them know he won't be in, his voice shaking as he says his brother is in the hospital.

He sprints the mile to Cook County Hospital, a massive eight-story edifice on West Harrison. Inside, he gasps for air and struggles to talk through his fit of coughing. Where can he find Moses Flanagan?

The desk clerk flips back and forth through a card file and shakes her head. "I don't see—"

"Maroney. Marooney!" He slaps the paper on the desk and points. "Thomas Marooney. Gunshot wounds."

He is directed to an emergency surgery ward but is blocked by a patrolman standing guard.

"Marooney. He's my brother." Joe, still gasping, waves the newspaper. "My brother."

They let him in.

Modie is lying there, his torso swaddled in bloody bandages, his eyes half-open. "Joe," he whispers.

A nurse comes by and pulls a sheet up over the wounds. "Are you related to Mr. Marooney?" she asks.

"His brother, Joseph Flanagan. And his name isn't fucking Marooney. It is Moses Rafael Flanagan, born November twenty-fifth, 1896, in Leclaire, Illinois." Joe's voice cracks, but he can't stop talking. His kid brother cannot go down as this made-up character *Marooney*. "He is the fifth of seven children. Our father is Moses McCarty Flanagan, who lives in St. Louis. Our mother, God rest her soul, was Margaret Keville. Both our parents emigrated from Ireland."

The nurse stares at him. "You best be praying for his immortal soul now. The priest gave him last rites a few hours ago."

"I can stay with him?"

She nods. "If he comes to, the police will be in. He wouldn't say who did this to him. Maybe he'll tell you."

Modie's eyes flutter closed, his chest heaving and rasping. Joe pulls a high-back wooden chair close to the bed, watches his brother's torture for minutes, then hours. He finally looks again at the newspaper account.

> Residents along Monroe Street heard shouts and shots for several blocks and, opening the windows of their flats, saw a black touring car speeding up the street without lights and without license plates. It is believed Marooney was shot while fighting the other occupants of the machine.
>
> A streak on the pavement forty feet long showed how the autoists had put on the brakes and locked the wheels so they could get rid of the victim in a hurry. They rushed the wounded man up onto

> the porch and a shot was heard just before they sped away, indicating they had fired a last bullet into his body just before they left him.
>
> Fred Ordway of 1814 Monroe street said he saw the automobile speeding by with a man's feet hanging out of the *tonneau*.
>
> Mrs. Helen Elliot of 1836 West Monroe street said the murder machine was a black one with a white stripe around the body of the car. She was the first to call the police.
>
> A letter was found by the police in Marooney's room addressed to him care of the county jail.
>
> The police of the Warren Avenue station believe Marooney was a victim of a gunman's war. When questioned by detectives, Marooney refused to talk further than to reiterate:
>
> "Ask Pat Dwyer; perhaps he'll tell you."
>
> He gave Dwyer's address as 230 South Wood Street. Dwyer is a leader in Barney Grogan's club.

The article goes on to list the names of several underworld figures whose recent deaths were thought to be connected. Joe can't follow the cast of characters.

Joe sits with Modie all day and all night. He thinks he should call Papa but puts it off, sure that Modie will charm his way out of the devil's grip and wake up.

On Tuesday, there's no change. Joe takes a break to find some food, to call his boss again, to buy a newspaper. The story of the shooting is reported once more, but without any new information.

That afternoon, a couple of women barge into the ward, scanning the beds, calling out, "Marooney! Where are you?."

The cops corner them immediately, demanding their names.

"We thought he was someone we knew. A Yellow Cab driver," the one called Lillian Hand says.

Her pal Florence Dunn chimes in. "Yeah, wrong guy! Not who we thought it was!"

The police grab their elbows and push them toward the corridor.

"We'll see about that, ladies," one of them says, "down at the Warren Avenue station."

Except for that, the ward is quiet. Occasionally, Modie groans, drifting up to the surface, then sinking back into his oceanic sleep.

Night comes. Joe falls asleep in his chair, arms crossed, chin on his chest. At some point, Modie mumbles something and Joe curls forward to lay his head next to Modie's and to clasp Modie's warm hand in his.

When the room brightens with first light, Joe stirs and blinks his eyes open. It is then that he realizes the hand he clasps is cold.

His brother is dead.

He sobs till the nurses come in and tell him he needs to step out of the room.

Joe sits on a bench in the hallway, without a clue about what comes next.

Before long, he is joined by a priest, the Catholic chaplain, he says. He has white hair and kind eyes.

"St. Louis," Joe says. "We need to get home."

:: 101 ::

Wednesday, May 14. At breakfast, Tom and five-year-old Mary talk through the day ahead and practice some spelling till it's time for Mary to jump into the delivery truck, proud to be chauffeured to school when the other children have to walk.

The image lingers on Kitty's mind as she feeds the six-week-old twins. She smiles.

Laying each boy in his own basket, watching them sleep for a moment, wishing Tom stood behind her to massage her aching shoulders, Kitty tries to ignore how bone-tired she is. The boys are hungry every two or three hours all day, all night. She has read articles about keeping them to a schedule—a double challenge with twins. Women in the know have advised her of the trend to ween babies quickly from breastmilk in favor of commercial formula, which the Barretts now stock. She tries it, but mixing the powder and sterilizing bottles is one more chore she'd rather avoid.

As she wolfs down a corn muffin, with a sip of cold tea, the phone rings.

A long-distance call. "Catherine?"

She hears her brother's voice through the static on the line. "Joe! What is it? Are you sick? Hurt?" She drags the phone over to the table.

"It's Modie. He—" His voice cracks.

Another voice. "I'm Father Brennan, Catholic chaplain here at the Cook County Hospital. We've just come from the bedside of your brother Moses Rafael."

"Yes?" She holds her breath.

"I regret to tell you he passed away early this morning. We've been trying to reach your father."

"What?" Her heart is pounding. "Modie?"

"Your brother Joe was at his side when he died."

"Let me talk to Joe."

A pause, then Joe's voice. "He was murdered. Murdered!" Kitty hears snuffling, nose blowing. "Gunned down. Nobody knows who or why."

"Oh, Modie!" Kitty covers her eyes.

"Happened early Monday morning. I got here as soon as I saw it in the paper. Stayed with him. Wasn't conscious. But he hung on. Till this morning." He takes a moment to find his voice again. "I'm coming home with him. To stay. I have to sign for his personal belongings and pack up my own stuff, talk to my boss, let him know. We'll be on the train tomorrow. Can you tell Papa? Tell him I'm so sorry I didn't watch over Modie better, so sorry I didn't stop this from happening."

Kitty squeezes her eyes shut against the tears. "We'll be so happy to see you."

The priest comes back on the line. "Don't you worry about a thing, Mrs. Barrett. We'll take care of your brothers till they board the train." He fills her in on the details: train arriving at 5 p.m. tomorrow, Donnelly funeral parlor taking over the process, and something about Modie's savings paying for it all. "Another thing I need to mention. This, er, incident has made quite a bit of news here in Chicago. No doubt the St. Louis papers will pick up the story tonight or tomorrow. Reading about it will be very hard on you. Just a warning."

"Jesus. Okay. Thanks. Thanks for everything."

Tightening her jaw against the tide of grief, Kitty makes phone calls, first to bring an extra clerk into the store, then to ask her neighbor Birdie Bialick to watch the boys. She resists the temptation to call Tom, fending off the fantasy that he could somehow make everything all right, knowing she has to find her father first.

With a couple of hours before the twins will be hungry again, she takes the streetcar down Easton Avenue to Papa's shop. Both his and May's storefronts are locked. Walking around to the alley, she finds a back door open, hikes up her skirt, and climbs the stairs. She walks through a galley kitchen, spotting a broken dish in the sink. The living room is sparse—table and chairs, a rocking chair, a floor lamp. Doors open to two small bedrooms, one empty and one with a daybed. Papa lies on the bed, asleep in his clothes.

"Papa!" She lays a hand on his shoulder to shake him, surprised to feel bone instead of his thick carpenter's muscle. "Wake up, Papa."

His eyes flutter open, staring blankly at her. "Nurse? Are you the nurse? Is the treatment ready?"

"What nurse? It's me, Catherine. I need you to wake up."

"Oh, Christ." He struggles into a sitting position, planting his feet on the floor. "I wanted to get the rooms finished before you got here. But I'm either too jangled to get anything done or I'm dead on my feet." He straightens his collar. "That May poisoned me, you know. It's playing havoc with my projects. Did your mother tell you I'm working on the World's Fair? All the woodwork for one of the big pavilions."

"Jesus, Mary, and Joseph, nobody's poisoning you. You need to wake up. When did you last eat?"

"My appetite is shot." He tries to stand but collapses back on the bed. "Where's that damn Walter? He should be here to work on the screens by now."

Kitty finds a bag of apples in the icebox, cuts one up, and puts it in a bowl on the table, where his papers and checkbook are piled up. She glances through them, noting the sum of money going to May and the St. Ferdinand flat. She yells at him that she'll be back soon.

As anger overpowers her shock and confusion, she mumbles to herself. "What the hell is going on? Can't I enjoy my goddamn babies without the whole goddamn world falling apart?"

Outside, she marches up Vandeventer to St. Ferdinand as fast as the narrow width of her skirt will allow. She bangs on May's door.

Papa's wife answers in her dressing gown.

"What's going on with Papa? I just came from the shop."

May lets her in. "He's gone crazy, honey. Stopped wanting anything to do with me." She shrugs her shoulders.

"Look, May, we have a lot going on." Kitty's voice shakes. She wags her hand at May. "Gather some things. You're coming back with me to the shop. You're going to take care of him or find somewhere else to live. I'm notifying your landlord that you'll be vacating by the end of the month."

"But, honey, that apartment over the shop, it's—"

"Has my father abused you, beat you?"

"Why no!"

"Then get your arse moving. He needs you.. I'll have Tommy get the rest packed up."

When they get back to the shop apartment, Moses is dozing in his rocking chair. It looks like he shaved and ate half the apple slices. Good.

May begins to whine about the tiny kitchen and unreliable oven.

"Be quiet, May." She scoots a chair next to Papa and takes his hand in hers.

"You're back," he says. "I apologize— May! Welcome home, my dear. The place is a mess—"

"Papa," Kitty interrupts. "I have bad news. Modie has been killed. Modie is dead."

Papa's eyes widen. "Dead? My poor boy! Killed, you say?" He looks wildly around the room. "First Nellie, then my two babies hospitalized, now— Why is God doing this to us, smiting my children one by one? Maggie said I would take us all to the promised land, but by God, I failed."

She squeezes his hand. "Look, the good news is that Joe is coming home. Home. To stay. That's why you have to get this place cleaned up. They will both be back here from Chicago tomorrow evening. There will be a funeral. You need to get yourself cleaned up with some fresh clothes." She shoots May a look. May nods.

Mindful of the time and her boys' next feeding, Kitty's heads down the street to Shaffer Brothers, the building supply company where Tommy works.

She waits in a small office while someone fetches him from the machine shop. He enters, dressed in stained overalls, wiping his blackened hands with a rag. Eyes watery and bloodshot, he is surprised to see her. She stands up.

"I just came from Papa. Haven't you been living with him?"

He shakes his head and looks out the window. "I'm going to. Gotta get my bed moved. It's been so busy… Easier to flop nights at St. Ferdinand… you know… till I get some time."

"Look at me," she says. "Today is the day. Joe is coming home. You need to borrow a truck and move everything from St. Ferdinand to the shop apartment. And I mean today. I just rousted May from there. Joe will be here tomorrow night." She takes a breath. "He's coming in on the evening train with Modie—with Modie's body." Her voice catches. "Modie's been killed."

"Oh, my Jesus." He takes a step toward her, his arms outstretched, but then looks down at his greasy clothes. Turning his palms up in a gesture of hopelessness, he repeats, "Oh, my Jesus."

They discuss a few more details, Kitty instructing, Tommy agreeing. Then, Kitty is back on Easton Avenue, waving down a streetcar for the three-mile ride back home. Too full of nerves to sit, she stands. It is easier to be angry than to be sad. Passing their Easton Avenue store, Kitty spots Tom's truck out front but doesn't get off. Her babies need her now. She'll tell him about the wreckage of her family tonight when she can rant at full volume. Didn't Tom say he was going to check in on her father more often? He certainly checks in regularly with his mother and sisters, who aren't on his route at all. God forbid he should spend an extra ten minutes with Papa.

She hears a fellow passenger clear his throat and realizes she's been talking out loud to herself.

When Tom arrives home, Kitty gives him the news in a loud outpouring of rage. Not only has her brother suffered a senseless death, but also her father has fallen apart in the midst of a family claiming to care for one another.

"I understand why we didn't bring Ethel to live with us," she says, "but I should have realized it was Modie who needed a stable, disciplined family. I should have insisted he live with us when we got married. He would have been a tremendous help in the store, using his charms on good folks, not on gangsters. I had the chance again when Nellie died, when he was so broken up, so vulnerable, that's when—"

"Kitty." Tom says as he lifts Mary onto his knee.

"And when I saw him at Thanksgiving, when he was on his way to Chicago and so cocky about escaping the workhouse—"

From the other room, Bill starts crying. She can already tell her boys' voices apart. Her hand touches her bosom. He is hungry.

"I was always so busy," she murmurs.

Tom just looks at her with his serious blue eyes as Mary lays her head on his shoulder.

This, she thinks, *this is what I chose to do.* She could have insisted on getting into Nellie's business and maybe Nellie would be alive. She could have insisted on taking in Ethel and Modie, incorporating their lives into hers come hell or high water. She could have called her father every evening.

In the bedroom, she unbuttons her shirt and picks up Bill. "I chose you," she whispers. "I chose you."

:: 102 ::

On Thursday, the two evening papers have long stories about the Chicago shooting of "local gangster" Moses Flanagan. Kitty glances at them but seeing the ugliness in print wounds her heart. Tom takes more time to study them as they wait to hear that Joe has arrived with Modie's remains.

At 7 p.m., they get the phone call from Donnelly's. They take Mary and the babies next door to the Bialik's. In the truck, before starting the engine, Tom leans over to Kitty, squeezes her hand and kisses her cheek. "We'll get through this," he says.

At the funeral home, Joe greets Kitty with a big hug.

"Oh, Joe." She sags into his arms, powerless to hold back her sobs.

"I saw him at Christmas," Joe says. "He was so full of life. But he got into trouble, got tangled up in a bad crowd, thought he was so damn smart. I couldn't do anything. I failed him."

Kitty pushes him back and looks into his watery gray eyes. "I know." She wants to comfort him, but has nothing to add, no explanations to give, no excuses to make. "I know."

Tom touches her arm. The mortician wants to review the arrangements with them. Kitty is surprised to see how Joe takes the lead in the conversation, how protective he is of Modie, how anxious he is that everything go just right for his brother's final passage.

She hasn't seen Joe in three years, not since the Easter when his two fingers were lopped off and he announced his departure for Chicago. Now, at the age of twenty-four, he looks decades older than the cocky young brawler she knew. His shoulders have rounded. His cheeks have hollowed. His voice, softened. His pale eyes, saddened.

When they get to Papa's apartment, Kitty is relieved to find that

Tommy has also risen to the occasion. The apartment is full of furnishings from the St. Ferdinand flat, including beds for the spare room. Food is on the table. Tommy and a fellow named Walter, introduced as Papa's apprentice, are hard at work cleaning and reorganizing the small living space. Papa is directing from his rocking chair.

It takes a beat for Papa to recognize Joe, but then he struggles to his feet, arms outstretched, tears springing to his eyes.

The funeral is held early on Saturday, May 17—a private prayer service at Donnelly's downtown, followed by the long motorcade drive to Calvary cemetery. Joe pays for the funeral out of what he refers to as Modie's "estate," but in reality is a small valise stuffed with cash.

The long newspaper stories about Modie's life of crime eliminate the need for a family cover story. Everyone knows. But it is 1919. Every family in their Irish neighborhood has a brother or an uncle or a cousin enmeshed in the seamy side of lid clubs, ward politics, labor union agitation, or the soon-to-be illegal production and distribution of alcoholic beverages. It's a small comfort.

After the burial, the family and friends come by the Flanagan apartment with generous platters of food and cases of cold beer. Tommy has turned the shabby apartment into a welcoming habitat, with rugs and lamps and a few old pictures on the walls. Papa is in his glory with all the company.

The afternoon wears on. People drift away. Francis Barrett ferries Mother, Mamie, and Katie back to Lexington Avenue, then returns for pregnant Molly and their two-year-old. He will close up the stores so that Tom can stay with the Flanagans. Kitty and the twins retire to her brothers' newly organized bedroom. Feeding time turns into a long nap.

When she wakes up, she leaves the twins to sleep and finds the five remaining men seated around the table with beer bottles and half-eaten sandwiches. May is fussing in the kitchen. Mary is sitting on Tom's lap, taking in the conversation.

Fixing a plate of food for herself and finding a glass for her beer, Kitty overhears their discussion of Modie. Uncle Pat Keville has on his reading glasses and Papa is holding a large magnifier as they pass around Joe's newspapers clippings.

"I can't make heads or tails of this reporting, Joe," Papa says. "It's a jumble of names. Who killed my son?" His finger taps on the table. "And why?"

Joe starts to explain for the umpteenth time what he knows about the small circle of Stillwell, Dwyer, Weaver, and Flanagan, a.k.a. Maroney. From her day bag, Kitty digs out her own set of articles in their makeshift folder, which she'd packed intending to show Joe. She lays it on the table.

"These are from the St. Louis papers. Maybe there's a connection."

Her clippings are eagerly examined.

They provoke more questions than answers.

Stillwell was killed because "they" thought he might have been a stool pigeon, snitching on his fellow thieves.

Did someone suspect Modie was a snitch? Then why was he so adamant about keeping his mouth shut on his deathbed? What was stopping him? Did they threaten to kill his family?

That idea made the group quiet, each taking long swallows of their beer.

"Who is this Jennie Kraft they are after?" Papa asks. "She was with him that night. A girlfriend? Or a seductress leading the lamb to slaughter?"

Joe shakes his head. "No idea. And no idea who those girls were who barged into his hospital ward."

"And who lives in the house where his body was thrown on the porch? Isn't that important?" Tommy Flanagan asks.

"Why is that being kept a secret?" Papa adds. "Who are the police protecting? Who is paying off the paper not to publish the name?"

"So many names!" Uncle Pat starts calling out names of men in the reports. "Harry Romaine, Cherries Dunn, Arthur Fineberg, the twins Tom and Dave Rowe, Gutter Newman, Tony Ortel. The cast of characters goes on and on! Chicago, St. Louis. In one article, a man is suspected of murder. In the next, he's murdered himself. I can't keep the buggers straight."

Tom Barrett speaks up. "We could turn them into pieces on a game board. They are marching across a battlefield. Competing for territory of one kind or another. Killing the guys who get in their way."

"You'd have to make it a six-sided board," Papa says. "With game pieces that can flip sides. Like coins. One day a young man is moving as *heads*. The next day he finds himself moving as *tails.*"

Little Mary chimes in. "I want one of those games, grandpapa! Can you make me one from your wood?"

Papa smiles at his little sweetheart, but Kitty is distressed. "Mary, go help May in the kitchen." Standing up, she begins gathering plates. "This is ridiculous. It all adds up to nothing. Modie didn't belong among those murderers. He was a dupe, a fall guy, a small-time thrill-seeker tangled up in some… some… *game* that he didn't know the rules of. Yes, Papa, life became a flip of a coin for him. One day, heads. The next day, tails. And, yes, it's all about as insane as a six-sided checkers game."

:: 103 ::

The summer of 1919 is quiet. For Kitty, the jolt of Modie's death gives way to chronic, low-grade worry about her father's health. He gives up all pretext of running a business out of the 3837 storefront, angry at Tommy and Joe for not taking over the enterprise. But they are machinists, not carpenters. Joe finds a job at a planing mill, a better fit for his skills than installing woodwork or making window frames.

Without a source of income, May begins baking again, opening her tearoom in the afternoons with Walter's assistance. Tom Barrett finds her a deal on commercial appliances from a recently closed restaurant—refrigerator, stovetop, and ovens, along with some butcherblock counters.

When Kitty stops by one evening, she finds Papa with his tape measure, stubby pencil, and pad, trying to plan the placement of the counter, but his own numbers seem to confuse him.

She is alarmed. Calculations were always Papa's genius. When he throws his pad on the floor, she sees it's covered with meaningless scribble.

"Walter," he barks, "take these measurements. This headache is driving me crazy."

"Tell me about your headache," Kitty says.

He dismisses the request with a wave of his hand. "May poisoned me. She's making me lose my mind," he mutters.

Kitty looks at May.

"Oh, Moze, you're such a pistol," May says, then turns to Kitty. "Don't you worry, honey. He's seeing a doctor. We both are. That Spanish flu wrecked our lungs, and the air in this city—nothing but coal dust and gasoline fumes."

Neither of them has the cough Kitty hears daily from customers with chronic respiratory conditions, but she can't get a straight answer.

So she carries on, running the Cote Brilliante store, bargaining with wholesalers, and minding her children. Tom finally finds a new location for the Newstead store, farther west on Union, conveniently halfway between Easton and Cote Brilliante. But Kitty talks him into waiting till fall for the move, till Mary is back in school and the weather is cooler.

Wednesday, September 10. The weather is already a blistering eighty degrees as the day begins. Despite the big exhaust fans in their second-floor apartment, Kitty is sweating, glad to have weaned her two five-month-olds, sweet as their warm skin was back on cool spring days. With Mary and Tom out the door, and the boys in their baskets ready to charm shoppers all day, the phone rings.

It is May.

"City Hospital just called, honey," she says. "It's our dear Julie. They say she's taken a turn for the worse. She won't last through the day. Moses is beside himself. The boys have already left for work and he wants us to take the streetcar to be with her."

"Mother of God," Kitty says. "Tell him to stay put. I'll get a taxi and come by for you. And you have the boys' work numbers, right? Call and see if they can get away, meet us there."

With the twins dropped off at Birdie's, Tom called, and the store clerk told to make do without her, Kitty arrives at City Hospital with Papa and May about ten. Julie is in a large ward of patients whose underlying illnesses allowed the flu virus to turn their lungs into jungles of chronic bacterial infections. Despite the open windows, the place is stifling hot and laden with disinfectant.

Eighteen-year-old Julie is already a ghost—her skin bluish, her eyes glazed and sunken. It has been weeks since Kitty has visited her baby sister. No, months, not since May, not since the day she came with Joe after Modie's funeral. Where did the summer go?

A priest comes by to bless Julie. He leads the family in a mumbled Hail Mary.

Dr. Herb Langsdorf, the resident surgeon, joins them briefly. "With her diabetes, the influenza should have killed her immediately. But she has a great spirit, a powerful will. Nevertheless, with every new infection, more of her lungs turned to scar tissue. We tried everything—surgery, exercises, and experimental medications. But now, with scarcely any lung capacity left, the rest of her organs are shutting down."

Papa pulls a chair close to Julie and clasps her hand. "I'm so sorry, my beautiful child. I'm so sorry for the pale semblance of a life we gave you. You never really knew your mother. But you'll get to be with her soon. Along with Nellie and Modie. It won't be long before I join you and we'll play the piano again together."

Kitty stands behind her father, hands on his bony shoulders, praying that he can endure another heartbreak. She feels numb.

Tommy and Joe arrive separately, looking horrified and helpless. They kneel by Julie's side and beg her to come back to them.

About one o'clock, Kitty is surprised to see Tom Barrett.

"The store was quiet," he says, putting one arm around her and reaching out the other to squeeze Papa's shoulder.

At 1:30, Julie's wheezy breath stops. She is gone.

After allowing the family a few minutes to weep and kiss their Julie goodbye, nurses usher the family to a waiting room near the ward.

Here, without warning, Papa collapses to the floor.

His arms and legs stiffen and flail like one of Ethel's seizures while he weeps and babbles incoherently, his eyes bright with terror.

"Papa!"

Kitty drops to his side to calm him, but managing a fit in a grown man is beyond her. Her brothers and Tom don't do any better.

May's quiet tears of grief turn hysterical. "Moze! Moze, don't do this!"

Large men in white rush in, lift Papa onto a gurney, and strap him down. A nurse follows and gives him an injection that knocks him out.

Dr. Langsdorf dashes in and gives Papa a cursory exam, including lifting his eyelids and shining a light into his eyes.

"Does your father have a physician?"

Kitty starts to say she doesn't know, but May speaks up. "He goes to Dr. Hermann. Office on Delmar."

Langsdorf nods. "Oh, I know Henry. I'll give him a call." He turns to go, then looks back. "I'm so sorry about Julia."

:: 104 ::

Looking around at the devastated family, Tom Barrett steps into the breech. While the death of his young brothers and father scarred him as a boy, now he knows death only through the heartbreak of the Flanagans—first Nellie, then Modie, now Julie. Moses has finally broken down and the rest of them look dazed and exhausted.

"Wait," Tom Barrett says to the physician. "We need to make arrangements—how—?"

"I believe Mr. Flanagan already left instructions. There is a note in her chart."

The Catholic chaplain comes by. His attention goes immediately to Moses, still in a twitchy sleep, strapped to the gurney. "The angels have your baby. May you find peace now, Mr. Flanagan." He performs a blessing, then turns to offer condolences to the family.

"Where do we go from here?" Tom asks.

"Someone from Cullen and Kelly is on his way for Julia. They'll walk you through the process."

In short order, Dr. Langsdorf returns. "I've spoken to Henry Hermann," he says, pressing his fingers to Moses's wrist and looking at his watch. "Given Mr. Flanagan's condition and his current symptoms, he recommends that Mr. Flanagan transfer immediately to St. Vincent's. That's where Henry admits his patients."

May sinks back in her chair, eyes closed.

"What condition?" Kitty asks. "I've never heard of St. Vincent's."

"It's a beautiful facility out St. Charles Rock Road. Run by the Daughters of Charity. It, um, specializes in mental and nervous disorders. You'll need to have a conversation with Dr. Hermann once your father is settled there."

"*Settled* there? I'm not following," Kitty says. "He just needs a good meal. We've been watching over my sister since morning without a bite to eat or drink. He's probably dehydrated."

Tom puts a hand on her shoulder and addresses the physician. "Do you have an ambulance that can take him there?"

"Of course," says Langsdorf. "And Dr. Hermann will be on duty there this evening. I'm sorry, I have other patients who need my attention. Again, my heart is with you on this sad occasion."

"This is out of control," Kitty mumbles as Langsdorf disappears. "May, what *condition* is he talking about?"

But May only shakes her head.

Tom gives Kitty's shoulder a quick squeeze, then runs after the doctor. He catches up, matching his pace with the physician rushing to his next obligation. "I'm Tom Barrett. Flanagan's son-in-law. What is it you're not saying to our family?"

Langsdorf stops and looks Tom in the eye. "Confidentially, Mr. Barrett..." He takes a deep breath. "Henry Hermann tells me your father-in-law is suffering from the nervous system collapse of advanced syphilis. He apparently got it from his current wife, that woman May. They have both been under treatment with neosalvarsan. Mrs. Flanagan is doing passably well, but Mr. Flanagan has not responded as one might wish."

Tom wants to take a moment to process this bombshell, but the doctor is turning away. "Wait... what does that mean?"

"It means he needs to be at St. Vincent's. And it likely means he'll never leave there. This is the breakdown Dr. Hermann has been dreading. You would do well to prepare the family for that." He pats Tom on the arm. "Now I really have to run."

Tom trudges back to the waiting room. The mortician from Cullen and Kelly is there.

"Let's have something simple," Tom says. "This has been very hard on her father and we need to—" He looks at Kitty, her sad eyes staring into space. It seems like only yesterday they went through the terrible ordeal of Modie's murder and funeral. And now Moses faces a grim spiral of his own. "Yes," he says. "Let's keep it simple. We need to tend to the living this week."

When the mortician leaves, ambulance attendants show up to take Moses out to St. Vincent's.

"Joe and I will go with him," Tommy Flanagan says, "so he doesn't wake up alone."

May starts to speak, but Tom interrupts her. "You stay with Kitty and me," he says. "We'll take you to St. Vincent's, but we need to stop by the flat first, tend to the children."

Tom's clear voice pulls Kitty out of her daze. "You need to call Francis, too—get him to close up the stores."

:: 105 ::

The day shimmers with temperatures in the nineties. The truck is an oven. The Cote Brilliante apartment is suffocating. Tom switches on the exhaust fans and seats May at the kitchen table with a glass of lemonade as Kitty splashes her face, neck, and arms with cold water.

While Tom talks to Francis, Kitty heads next door to Birdie Bialik's. The children are out back with her husband Jake, playing in the spray of the hose. Kitty looks down at them through Birdie's kitchen window and smiles. Jake's parents, Jewish immigrants from Russia, who live in the flat downstairs, are laughing with the children and, in their Yiddish, encouraging Mary and the two Bialik girls to run through the water. Bill and Bobby, in their diapers, are up on their hands and knees on a blanket, almost ready to crawl, squealing with delight at the girls getting splashed. For a moment, trouble seems far away. Seeing her children so joyful soothes Kitty as she tells Birdie about her sister's death and Papa's collapse.

"We bury Julie on Friday. I pray my father will have snapped out of this spell he's having by then and we can get back to normal. Get whatever you need from the store—extra food—how about some ice cream? I'll let them know to put it on the store tab. And you have the key in case you need anything from upstairs."

"I am sure everything will be just fine," Birdie says, giving Kitty a quick hug. "I love your little ones. And they love my cooking. They can come with us to temple on Friday evening if you are still occupied. We will pray for your family."

Back in the apartment, Kitty puts out a platter of cold potatoes and chicken. May starts rambling about poor Julie, their cooking together, her piano playing, how horrible her suffering has been, then Modie, and now Moses, crumpling under the weight of it all.

Tom comforts her in the Catholic way, assuring May that Julie is in a better place and that everything happens for a reason.

Pushing back from the table, Kitty can't listen to Tom's God talk. Yes, Julie's suffering is over, but there is no reason, no meaning to any of it, not in the gangs who killed Modie or the thousands who died of the flu before Julie, or the brain injury condemning Ethel to a sanitarium, or the malignant pain that killed her mother. If there is a God, his power is pitiless as a steam roller.

Before they leave, Kitty packs a few things for her father in a small valise—a shaving kit, a comb, a newspaper, and a bag of chocolate Kisses.

St. Vincent's is in the town of Normandy, a two-mile drive west, the late summer sun hanging low in the sky. The hospital is an enormous castle, with turrets and spires, built on a hill, surrounded by a hundred acres of green countryside.

Papa is in a small private room, lying on a bed in his BVDs, with a light sheet covering him. He appears semi-conscious, speaking in a soft voice, incoherently, Tommy and Joe sitting on either side of him like stone guardians. Joe says the doctor is waiting for them all to arrive.

Kitty can hardly give Papa a kiss before May throws herself over him, head on his chest, hands hugging his arms. "Look at you, just look at you. What's to become of us, Moze? How do we get you out of this snake pit?"

Papa barely responds to either of them.

Dr. Henry Hermann, a short, silver-haired man in a gray linen suit, enters. He greets May with a familiar handshake, then leans over Moses, patting his arm and whispering something to him. Then he turns to the family.

"Mr. Flanagan is very ill. He is entering a state we call 'general paresis.' He has an infection in his brain. You've heard of *encephalitis*, I'm sure. The brain becomes inflamed and can't function normally. *Meningoencephalitis* expands that to the brain lining and spinal cord. This is what Mr. Flanagan has"

Tommy says, "I heard of encephalitis. I heard it's an epidemic. Sleepy sickness. Is that what you're talking about?"

"Same idea, son," Dr. Hermann responds. "Yes. It's somewhat like *encephalitis lethargica*, what you call sleepy sickness, affecting the nervous system, very debilitating. Moses will need to be hospitalized for quite some time."

May plops into a chair and begins to cry.

"An epidemic? Is it contagious?" Kitty asks, thinking of all the hugging and crying at the hospital with Julie—was it only this morning?

Dr. Hermann blinks. "Um, no ma'am, well not exactly, not like the flu. But it is wise to use precautions, if only for his protection, in his weakened state."

Tom Barrett is frowning. Kitty nudges him and says, "Do you have a question? Ask."

Tom looks at Moses, shakes his head. "I thought, um…"

Distracted by May weeping in her chair, Tom looks around at all the family members, then addresses the physician. "Nothing...," he says, then adds, "It sounds crass, but this place, it can't be cheap. Not that we don't want Moses to get the best care."

Dr. Hermann raises an eyebrow. "You can work out something with the Sisters, Mr. Barrett. Mr. Flanagan is a long-time patient of mine for his sleep difficulties and other complaints. I'd like to continue with his care. You can move him down to the public sanitarium on Arsenal, of course, but the treatment here is more personal, more compassionate for the severely impaired. The nuns do a wonderful job."

The family drives back into the city after dark, the five of them squeezed into the Barrett delivery truck. They are all quiet, all exhausted. Tom drops Kitty off at their flat, before taking May, Tommy, and Joe back to their apartment.

Kitty takes a bath before she gets the children from Birdie, a ritual to wash away the sticky stench of sadness that permeates everything, her dress, her skin, her soul. She is sick about Papa's sudden collapse, but as she washes, she finds some relief knowing he'll be under the care of Dr. Hermann and the Daughters of Charity instead of being subjected to May's moods and her brothers' inattentiveness. Kitty is sad that Julie had to die so young, but also understands that she is now liberated from the agonizing deterioration of diabetes and the devilish impact of chronic pneumonia on her lungs. As she puts on a clean dress, Kitty is refreshed.

Birdie volunteers to keep the children overnight since the twins are already asleep, but Kitty needs them near her, needs them with her when she wakes up, needs to dress them in clean clothes and comb their fine hair, needs to watch her five-month-olds learn to crawl, needs to listen to Mary's bright conversation with Tom over breakfast. As her past disintegrates behind her, she needs to see the future.

:: 106 ::

Thursday, September 11, is another warm morning. Kitty retrieves the day-old pastries from the store for their breakfast as Mary runs alongside her to pick up the newspaper for Tom.

At the breakfast table, Tom tries to explain to Mary about her grandpapa's hospitalization.

"I've been waiting for this," Mary says, in a perfect imitation of Kitty's tone, picking a cherry off the top of a danish and popping it into her mouth. Looking back and forth at the surprised faces of her parents, she continues. "Well, he's been saying all along that May poisoned him. What did you expect?"

Kitty sits back in her chair and says, "Oh, that's just grandpapa's way of being silly. He's just teasing." But as she says the words, she hears Tom's small gasp and sees the shadow cross his face. "What is it?" she asks.

He stands and nods his head toward their bedroom. They leave Mary at the table. Out of Mary's earshot, Kitty asks, "What? What is it?"

He takes a deep breath. "Dr. Hermann wasn't fully honest with us last night. Yes, Moses has meningoencephalitis. But it has nothing to do with sleepy sickness. In effect, May did poison him. He won't recover."

"What the hell are you talking about?"

"Dr. Langsdorf gave me the facts yesterday at City Hospital. Facts he got from Dr. Hermann." Tom speaks in a low voice. "Papa has an advanced case of syphilis, which he supposedly got from May, who supposedly got it from her second husband. It is destroying his brain. He's not going to come out of this."

"What are you saying?" Her voice gets loud. "What in God's name are you saying? That he picked up VD like some degenerate hiring prostitutes? From goddamn May?" She picks up a pillow and throws it at Tom. "That's the most disgusting thing I ever heard of! Is that who Dr. Hermann is, some kind of whore's doctor?" She picks up a second pillow and slams it on the floor. "He let that idiot May give him a pox? What is wrong with him? He marries that bitch Aunt Bridget who destroys Ethel, then falls for a tramp who gives him a death sentence? This is outrageous!" Tears spring from her eyes. Weeping, she sits on the edge of the bed and folds over around the ache in her stomach.

Tom starts to approach her, but she jumps to her feet and wags her finger at him. "You will never tell this to another soul, do you understand? Not to Tommy, not to Joe, not to Francis. We are going to our grave with this ugly secret, do you hear me?"

He nods.

Mary peeks around the doorway.

"Mother of God." Kitty's voice softens. "Come here, baby." She sits on the bed again and pulls Mary into her arms. "Mother just needed to blow off some steam. Grownups get upset sometimes when we don't understand things. But we're okay. Everything is okay."

The next day, Kitty takes time out from the store to go to Papa's apartment. She collects all his papers into one of her hat boxes—some piled on the table, more in big envelopes from a bottom drawer. She takes note that May's tearoom is open and filled with customers. Walter Barry is helping her.

That evening, she asks Tom to look over Papa's papers to figure out how much money he has. She has already figured out that his savings account is empty and his checking account has a balance of less than $50. However, he has several envelopes stuffed with cash, including one labeled "from Joe" and one labeled "Modie's estate." The rest are cash receipts from his carpentry business.

"Sure," he says. "I spoke to the nuns today at St. Vincent's. We have to work out what we can pay for his treatment." He switches on a small oscillating fan. "I also arranged for five gravesites at Calvary. One for Julie. One for your father, God help him. And, thinking about the future, two for you and me. When that terrible day comes, our children won't have to scramble."

"The fifth one?"

"Ethel."

"Good. Thank you," she says. Kitty gazes out the window at the busy evening traffic along Hamilton Avenue under the glow of street lamps. Her jaw tightens as she thinks ahead to the holidays. "Another thing: I want May out of our lives. If Papa isn't going home, then she can pay her own rent. Tommy and Joe should clear out of that apartment, think about their own lives. See what you can figure out."

She doesn't want May and her nasty disease in her family, touching her children, putting a taint on everything. That woman cursed her father, turned a lonely man into a drooling symbol of the wages of sin. She is poison.

These feelings of desecration and ruin haunt Kitty through the rest of the year. Everything is dirty.

The war in Europe was a slaughter, leaving too many young men in their neighborhood shellshocked or without legs. Now, in news stories and among community groups, conjuring up ways to make Germany pay, to crush the German spirit, and to dismantle the German military machinery is all the rage.

She gets tracts in the mail from the Women's Christian Temperance Union celebrating Prohibition and the final passage of the Volstead Act. If it isn't the Germans, it's the alcohol that gets blamed for everything—war, crime, sin.

The Nineteenth Amendment is being ratified state by state. Women will finally get the vote. Will that be a good thing, or will women simply be left holding the bag for a society gone to hell?

She hires a crew to scrub their apartment, to tackle the tedious job of cleaning coal smoke off the wallpaper, to wash and restring the Venetian blinds, to shampoo the rugs, to oil the woodwork, to scour away the grease caked up in the kitchen, and to wash all the windows. The results are sparkling but don't really cheer her up.

The holidays will be somber. She has lost Modie to crime. She has lost Julie to influenza and pneumonia. Ethel will turn twenty-one on December 21, once a normal child with fits, now a heavily medicated woman socialized into the routines and habits of psychotics and mental defectives, terrified of leaving the safety of the Arsenal campus. She is lost. And Papa is lost, as he pays for his lust with a degenerating nervous system.

When Tommy and Joe move out of the Easton Avenue flat, May is shunned by the family. Yet she manages to land on her feet, one of those perpetual survivors. Her tearoom continues to operate. The grapevine tells Kitty that young Walter Barry has moved into the upstairs apartment with her.

Kitty sees the ravages of grief reflected in her brothers' eyes as they join the holiday rituals, bringing toy blocks and trucks to the nine-month-old twins and storybooks to six-year-old Mary. Kitty wishes they could speak to one another about the dissolution of their family over the year, but instead, they all wind up cracking lame jokes and drinking too much.

The Barrett family's good cheer carries them through. Francis and Molly, still glowing from the August birth of their second son, bring Tom and Kitty a Christmas tree. Mobilizing Mary as their little assistant, Mamie and Katie decorate the tree and festoon the newly scrubbed apartment with colorful decorations. Christmas Eve is always a double holiday for the Barretts because it is also Tom Barrett's birthday. Especially because last year's pandemic canceled the celebration, this year the party must go on.

Kitty does her best to add to the cheer. As she watches her husband blow out the inferno of thirty-seven candles on his cake, everyone singing and applauding, she admires how youthful and robust he is, even as he approaches forty.

She thinks of her father, withering away at St. Vincent's. At thirty-seven, he was also on top of the world as the newly installed Superintendent of Cabinetry in utopian Leclaire, Illinois. She and Nellie were Mary's age and Papa bought them a piano and tickled the ivories with Irish ditties for them while Mama tended her rose garden. How many lifetimes has she lived since those innocent days? And yet, she is only twenty-nine years old.

The guests begin to sing, "For he's a jolly good fellow." She raises her voice, hoping no one sees her brush away the tears.

:: 107 ::

Over the long months, Kitty half-persuades herself that what Papa really has is sleepy sickness, *encephalitis lethargica*. It prevents her from dwelling on his contamination—his "poisoning"—by May Gaines. It allows her to fantasize that he might recover.

Papa's escalating delusions and diminishing control over bodily functions makes it painful for Kitty to visit. Quickly, he fails to recognize her. Kept in restraints to prevent injury, he wastes to skin and bones.

At home, life demands so much of her. On weekday evenings, Mary has homework. As the twins learn to walk, they develop two distinct personalities. Bill is focused, figuring out how to open drawers and how to jiggle knickknacks off shelves. Bobby is more athletic, jumping on furniture and turning small objects into missiles. Tom has little patience with their hijinks.

"We're running a business, Kitty," he pleads with her. "If I can't get quiet time in the evening to catch up on the markets and strategize, we'll lose our shirts."

So, with pangs of guilt, her visits with Papa shrink to those Sunday afternoons when Tom takes the children to visit his mother.

In April, Kitty brings a cake out to St. Vincent's to celebrate Papa's birthday, but he is heavily sedated, a dry husk of the father she so adored.

On Wednesday, May 7, 1920, at 2:45 a.m., Moses McCarty Flanagan passes away. Awakened with the news at 4 a.m., Kitty returns to bed and sobs in Tom's arms.

Kitty has prepared for this moment. The next morning, the family attends a private service at Cullen and Kelly's funeral chapel on North Taylor, followed by the burial at Calvary. May shows up with Walter Barry but gets little more than a polite nod from the family.

The obituary says simply "husband of May Flanagan and our dear father." Kitty doesn't want obituary-watching customers to needle her with sympathetic inquiries about how Papa died. She doesn't want to talk about St. Vincent's.

She also declines Mother Barrett's kind invitation to have lunch for the family after the service. Instead, Tommy and Joe come back with her to Cote Brilliante and she picks up Bill and Bobby from Birdie's. The twins, now thirteen months old, are delighted to play silly games with their uncles, but Kitty prefers to go back to work downstairs, to operate the cash register and make chit-chat with her customers as if the world hasn't just become a slightly colder place.

In the afternoon, after school, Mary comes running into the store full of glee. She won a double-Dutch jump-rope contest in the schoolyard, taking devilish delight in the pitiful tears of her arch-rival. Kitty smiles at her girl's strong personality and blossoming talents.

That evening after dinner, she takes Mary into the master bedroom to explain about Grandpapa's going to heaven. Kitty pulls out her old treasure box from the bottom drawer of her dresser—the box she assembled after Mama died in 1903.

She shows Mary the few photos she has. Grandpapa as a young man. Her Grandmama Maggie. Auntie Nellie. Uncle Modie with Grandpapa at the World's Fair. All in heaven now. Kitty chokes up, but Mary's nearness and her curiosity console her.

Mary is fascinated by the hair mementos. She unwraps Kitty's childhood braids from their tissue paper and lays them across her lap.

"The color is like roasted coffee beans, almost black," she says in awe. "How come my hair is blond?"

"The Flanagans were darker, with brown hair and greenish-brown eyes. The Barretts are lighter, with blond hair and blue eyes. You take after

Daddy's side of the family, including that little cleft in your chin. Bill and Bobby have blue eyes but brown hair, so they are more of a mix between Mother and Daddy."

Mary considers this and nods. Then she unwraps Maggie's hair. "This hair is lighter. This looks like Bill's color of brown and the braids look like Bobby's color of brown."

"Very good," says Kitty. "That hair belonged to your Grandmama. Women in those days wove their cut hair into hairpieces to be more stylish." She showed Mary how the hairpiece formed Mama's bangs in the old photograph.

"She's so pretty," Mary says.

At the bottom of the box is Mama's autograph book, with its yellowed pages and faded red velveteen cover. As Mary pages through it, Kitty explains how she and Nellie got to write love notes to their mother in it. Mary's reading is good, but she hasn't yet learned to decipher longhand.

Returning to the first pages, Mary says, "This writing is the prettiest. Read me those."

She points to a verse Papa wrote to Mama on January 7, 1888, a few days before they got married.

Kitty reads:

> No regent pearl that crested fortune wears
> Nor gem that twinkling hangs from beauties ears
> Nor pale moon which night's blue arch adorn
> Nor rising sun which gilds the vernal morn
> Shines with such lustre as the tear that breaks
> For others' woes down woman's lovely cheeks.
> M.M. Flanagan

Mary frowns. "I don't get it," she says.

"It's a quote from a poet. Papa told me who, but now I forget. It's about the beauty of shedding a tear with someone when they are sad," she explains, heaving a great sigh, putting her arm around Mary, pulling her close. "He was very well-read. Very proud of his schooling in Dublin. And it's an excellent lesson for you to learn, to sympathize with other people."

Mary lays her head against Kitty's chest and flips to another page, dated April 28, 1888. "Now this one."

Kitty reads.

> Remember well & bear in mind

A worthy friend tis hard to find
And when you find one just & true
Never change her for the new
M.M.Flanagan

"You know what this one means, don't you?"

"If you have a good friend, keep her, right?"

"That's right."

Mary flips back to January 14. "Now this one."

Kitty reads.

I wish there was mountains of sugar
And rivers of wine
Plantations of tea leaves
And you to be mine
M.M. Flanagan

"I love that one!" Mary cries. She jumps down on the floor and spins in a circle. "Mountains of sugar and rivers of wine, plantations of *chocolate* and you to be mine."

Kitty laughs at her improvisation.

Mary dances around the bedroom. "Mountains of sugar and rivers of wine, plantations of chocolate and *you* to be *mine*." Then she prances out. "Daddy, listen to this, listen to this..."

Kitty closes the autograph book and hugs it to her chest as she curls onto the bed. Her tears run freely. *Thank you, Papa*, she thinks. *Thank you for my life.*

:: 108 ::

Papa's death leaves a great hole in Kitty's heart. But she tells herself that he lives through her now and through her children.

The post-War economy is good and the Barretts dare to feel prosperous. Tom begins to assess how soon he can add a fourth store. Francis has already beat him to it, joining forces with an old friend Paul Matthews.

"Matthews was struggling," Tom says one evening as he studies his ledgers at the kitchen table. "I'm not sure Francis did himself a favor jumping into that mess."

"Molly's expecting again," Kitty says. "He must be anxious about money." She puts a pot of coffee on the stove. The children are settled in bed and she has a pile of wilted vegetables to chop into the soup pot on the back of the stove.

Tom shakes his head and makes another note on his pad.

"Mary spent nearly all afternoon in the store with one of her little friends," Kitty tells him. "They were pretending to be housewives stocking up their kitchens, having a serious discussion about what kinds of food their children would or wouldn't eat. Then they were looking at the prices and talking about their food budget. And didn't our little Bill and Bobby follow them right around wherever they went!"

Tom smiles, then looks up at her. "How about you, Kitty? Are you having fun?"

The question surprises her. She loves the hurly-burly of running a store, of working side-by-side with Tom, of watching her children grow up surrounded by abundance and friendly neighbors.

She has to laugh. "As much fun as an exhausted storekeeper-mother-of-three can possibly have."

"I'm tired too," he says—a rare admission. "We have no life beyond the walls of our business. I used to go to civic meetings. I used to design games. When did we last go anywhere but church on Sundays?"

Kitty puts his cup of coffee on the table. "Wouldn't it be nice to spend Saturday afternoon at the show or take the children to the park in the cool of the evening?" she says. "How do other men grow their businesses? How did Mr. Kroger do it when he started out in Cincinnati?"

She stands at the stove, rough-chopping the wizened carrots and wilted celery and tossing them into the boiling broth.

Tom shakes his head. "Dunno. Must have formed a corporation, got the dough somehow—investors or a bank loan—money to hire store managers for the day-to-day while he sat in an office somewhere."

"Is that you in five years?" she asks.

He squints at her for a moment. "I used to think so. When I started at Luyties Mercantile as a kid, I hated the rough and tumble of the merchant class. I wanted a priestly life. A scholarly life. If I had to make a living in business, then I wanted it to be in that quiet corner office, overseeing the madness from behind my glass wall."

"And look what happened to August Luyties," Kitty says, "for all his family's brains and energy, winding up bankrupt and under investigation, killing himself with a bottle of poison. Remember that?"

"I do. Right before Mary was born. His problem was he kept expanding, kept reinventing his business, but kept lousy books. Everything on the back of an envelope. It crushed him. I'm no August Luyties, but I'm no Barney Kroger either. I like the hands-on, the control."

As Kitty rinses her knife, he turns to a page in his ledger. "I took a look at our numbers from a different angle and you know what I found? Our easiest profit comes from renting the flat above the Easton Avenue store, the only property we own. The new store on Union—we're not making a dime and it's killing me. I'm thinking—"

"Dump it," Kitty says. "We can do fine with two stores. I don't want to see you going to an early grave. We don't need an empire like Kroger's."

Tom nods and takes a drink of coffee. "I think we should put what we're spending on Union into additional rental property."

Mulling over the idea, Kitty puts a plate of cookies on the table and lifts a basket of diapers to be folded onto a kitchen chair. "Being a landlord doesn't sound like easy money." She lays a diaper on her end of the table and folds it to fit her boys' bottoms. "But with the right tenants…" She starts a stack of folded diapers on another chair. "With the right tenants, it could be a monthly checklist of things to do, instead of a daily one."

At the end of the month, Tom closes the Union Boulevard store.

:: 109 ::

On Sunday, August 1, Kitty scoops ice cream on cake in Molly Barrett's kitchen on Highland Avenue. She is there with Mary and the twins for an impromptu celebration of Florrie Barrett's first birthday later that week.

"In the Flanagan household," Kitty says, "we had a big family picnic every August for all the Flanagan summer birthdays. Me, Nellie, Joe, Tommy. August makes me sentimental, especially this year, with Papa gone. So many of us, gone."

August 12 also marks her thirtieth birthday, which is making her feel old.

"Oh, Kitty, let's have a picnic! I have a summer child too now. And brothers with August birthdays. I'd love to start a family tradition like that. I bet your brothers could using cheering up too."

Kitty hesitates, then agrees.

Molly brims with enthusiasm. "I'll take charge. The sixteenth is my brother Doug's birthday. And the fifteenth is Harry's. You'll like his wife

Fran. Their baby Eileen was born between your twins and our Florrie in '19, so another toddler to entertain us."

"The more, the merrier," Kitty says, with a laugh, "especially if you're organizing it."

"Oh, I'm so excited!" Molly says. "Let's have it away from the city this year, out at Creve Coeur, where it's more private—where we can knock back some 5% beer without the cops looking over our shoulders."

"You know where to get 5%? Our hoard ran out by Thanksgiving last year," Kitty says. "We've been reduced to drinking that swill Bevo."

"Don't tell Tom," Molly says, "but last year August Busch filled the basement storage room at the Curran's with barrels of beer he couldn't sell anymore. My brothers turned the room into an icehouse, with straw and block ice deliveries to keep the beer from getting skunked. Then they pitched in for a contraption to bottle it." Molly lines up cups for lemonade. "Francis's partner in the Arlington store—Paul Matthews, you met him that time, remember? He has a source for delicious home brew, but somebody's gotta pay for that."

Kitty is sold. They agree on Sunday, August 15, for the picnic.

On Thursday, August 12, Kitty's actual birthday, she and Tom take a rare afternoon off. They have lunch in a stylish café.

Kitty also wants new clothes. 1920 has brought a major shift in women's fashion. In her adult life, Kitty's wardrobe evolved from the curvaceous, hourglass silhouette of the Edwardian era, to the flowing, draped silhouette of art nouveau. Now, with women getting the vote and preparing to take their place beside men in elected office, styles are simplifying fast. Flatter profiles, fewer layers, less cumbersome sleeves, shorter hemlines—perfect for a woman on the run.

So Tom patiently waits while she picks out a couple of summery cotton voile dresses with organdy cuffs and collars, adding shoes to show off the turn of her ankle, plus a couple of new hats to top off her look.

On Saturday night, with Kitty dolled up in her new clothes, they continue the celebration at the latest Mary Pickford movie.

:: 110 ::

August 15 is a breezy day, cool for late-summer St. Louis. Kitty and Tom pack up the children for a day in the countryside.

With so many family and friends attending their picnic on the edge of Creve Coeur Lake, Kitty is in her element—lots of people, everyone laughing. A couple of friends bring their ukuleles, adding music to the festive atmosphere. Tom raises an eyebrow that so much 5% beer appears in coolers of chipped ice, but Francis tells him to loosen up and enjoy the bounty.

Kitty relaxes, observing the differences among the families. Her side—the Flanagan brothers and Uncle Pat Keville—are laborers, muscular men with big hands and a solid physical presence, the kind of men who greet toddlers by lifting them up over their heads and spinning around, leaving the children dizzy and squealing with laughter, begging for more.

The Barretts are tall and stout, with a quieter presence, more cerebral, more task-oriented. Mamie and Katie take out embroidery projects to work on as they relax and chat. Francis, his hair already gray at thirty-six, manages the grill and cooks dozens of sausages. Tom brings binoculars and a bird book for himself and Mary, but is crestfallen when Mary is more interested in organizing games with cousins Mary and Delia Keville, games where the trio can boss around the younger children.

The Currans are wiry bundles of energy. There are twelve siblings in Molly Curran's Irish family, three girls and nine boys—a baseball team and three cheerleaders, she likes to say. For the birthday picnic, five brothers plus one wife and baby piled into old man Curran's machine for the drive out to Creve Coeur. The youngest brother, Delaney, has just turned six and, without shyness, runs off to play with the other children. Harry, Douglas, Westlyn, and Ewald are younger than Kitty's crowd. Wes and Ewald are still in their teens. Doug turns twenty tomorrow and Harry turns twenty-five as of today. After lugging their coolers of ice and beer out of the car trunk, the brothers introduced themselves to everyone, then made themselves useful setting up the horseshoe pit, leveling the picnic tables, shepherding stray children back to the picnic area, disposing of a wasp nest from under the pavilion roof, and repairing the oarlocks of an old boat so that the picnickers could go out on the lake.

What an amiable bunch, Kitty thinks of the Currans. She must have met them all at Molly's wedding but the memory is a blur. Today, they remind her of Papa, the man who knew how to work a room.

Kitty strikes up a conversation with Harry's young wife Fanny, anxious about letting her fourteen-month-old wander off in the direction of Florrie and the twins. But then Uncle Ewald swoops in with a soccer ball for the toddlers to chase. He kicks it a short distance and the four run screaming after it.

"I'll give them a good workout," he shouts. "They'll have long naps this afternoon!"

"She never stops," Fanny says to Kitty. "How do you manage with twins?"

Kitty hands her a cold bottle of beer.

It turns out Fanny grew up in O'Fallon, Illinois, near Edwardsville, so they enjoy a good chinwag about growing up in small-town Illinois. But where Kitty can reminisce about idyllic Leclaire and its sparkling, well-ventilated factories, Fanny's father and now her brother are coal miners, so her memories rise through the haze of coal dust and chronic fear of mine collapses and explosions.

After the big lunch and copious amounts of birthday cake, the picnickers settle into Sunday afternoon relaxation. The children nap on blankets. Some of the men play horseshoes. Doug and Wes Curran take turns rowing guests around the lake. The women sit in circles, chatting and enjoying the rare August breeze and the ukulele tunes. Kitty leads them in a few songs and they laugh at how the beer improves their voices.

Kitty drifts from circle to circle, tuning into the conversations and making sure all have drinks in their hands.

She is surprised to see her brothers in an intense conversation with Ewald down by the boat dock, with much nodding and gesturing and the occasional guffaw. When she strolls down to join them, Ewald is telling a story.

"So these guys are so nervous carrying their whiskey, trying to get it out of the truck, down the alley into this garage, they start dropping cases and breaking bottles. And the neighbors are starting to smell the whiskey." He slaps his thigh. "Can you believe these fellows have hauled *fifteen hundred cases* up from a government warehouse in Owensboro, Kentucky! Made by a distillery for medicinal purposes only. Haha! Medicinal purposes!"

The Flanagan brothers laugh along with Ewald.

"Damn clever, these guys. At least they started out that way. Listen to this. The drivers have papers with the forged signature of Shrader Howell, *Shrader Howell*, the state Director of Prohibition in Kansas City, so they walk right into this warehouse and carry out the hooch. And who rents the garages they are delivering to? Harry Levin, a constable for Judge Miles. A *constable*! Can you believe these guys? The government is stealing from themselves!"

He steps back to make room for Kitty to join the conversation. "So, Catherine, I'm telling Tommy and Joe here about the big whiskey heist. These fellows are trying to get the cases down the alley, spilling as they go, and somebody drops a dime on them. The feds only have to follow the smell of whiskey to catch 'em red-handed, haha!"

"They don't sound too bright," Kitty says.

"Maybe not those two, but somebody's got some brains. Fifteen hundred cases of whiskey walked out of that warehouse. Fifteen hundred! They could have got two-hundred-fifty simoleons a case! Know how much that adds up to? I hear they only recovered a couple hundred cases so far, so if you see any bottles with labels from Thompson Distilling, Louisville, Kentucky, remember it's for *medicinal purposes only*. Ha, ha, ha!"

Kitty laughs out loud. What an entertaining young man.

"You're certainly well informed," she says.

"My buddy Matt O'Neill, his brother joined the police force. He tells us all his stories. I'll be sixteen in a couple of weeks. Might join the police force myself, but in the meantime, I'm heading to Chicago. Our brother Jim just got married up there. Thought I'd take a look around. Lot of printing jobs open, Jim says."

Joe asks, "So, Ewald, are they really bothering to enforce the Volstead Act? I mean the local police, not the feds."

Ewald raises his bottle of 5% beer. "You tell me, Joe. You tell me."

:: 111 ::

With their stores now consolidated in two locations, Tom is the main beneficiary. He resumes going to Knights of Columbus meetings, takes more interest in politics, researches rental properties, and finishes the design of a board game he started years ago. He calls the game "Skirmish" and hires his attorney friend Hugh Wagner to file papers with the U.S. patent office.

It is Election Day when Tom signs the final documents to be mailed to Washington. He and Kitty walk down the street to their polling place.

"Wouldn't it be wonderful if the game caught on, like 'Monopoly'?" he says. "We'd be rich."

She laughs. "We'll have a house in the country. With flower gardens. And a pond. And a gazebo! Wouldn't you love a gazebo! We'd have picnics every Sunday."

They join the long line. Kitty is thrilled and nervous about her first presidential election since women got the vote.

"Still going to vote for Cox?" Tom asks her.

"Of course. Harding is full of bull trying to sell the idea of going backward to some 'golden age' before the War."

"But I can't convince you to vote for Debs?"

"Oh, Tom!"

Eugene Debs was the Socialist candidate and one of the founders of the Industrial Workers of the World trade union organization.

"He's fighting for the little guy, the common working man. And against war."

"The man is in jail!"

"That's only because of his war protest. He's a political prisoner, just like some of the Irish freedom fighters."

"He doesn't have a chance in hell."

Both are disappointed when Warren G. Harding, the Republican, wins the election. Kitty wonders if the women's vote was responsible. In the run-up to the election, she heard too many women say they were going to vote for whichever candidate their husbands supported. Maybe Kitty should have worked harder to persuade Tom not to waste his vote on Debs.

On Sunday, November 7, Harding will celebrate his victory with a stop at Union Station to thank Missourians for their votes. But Tom and Kitty turn their attention to Mary's seventh birthday, with her first "girls only" birthday party, followed by a family dinner.

Kitty's brothers arrive for dinner in Joe's new Model T Ford. Both are tipsy. With a wink, Joe hands her two bottles of whiskey labeled "Thompson Distillery, Louisville, Kentucky."

"Shall we get out the shot glasses for a little medicinal tonic?" he asks with a snicker.

Kitty laughs and opens the cabinet for the glasses. "When are you boys going to get girlfriends and settle down?"

"And be like Papa?" Tommy asks. "Saddled with a bunch of whining little brats?"

"What a small-minded thing to say," she snaps.

"Sorry," he says, dropping the silly attitude. "I don't know what the hell I want."

Ten days later, on Wednesday, November 17, she's surprised to get a call from Tommy while she's working in the store.

"Hate to call you like this, Catherine."

She takes a breath. "What is it?"

"Joe got picked up by the police last night."

"Jesus, Mary, and Joseph."

"I think it was a big mistake. He just got swept up with a bunch of people. He was at an East St. Louis saloon after hours Saturday night, well, Sunday morning. Some kind of craps game going on. Then the craps game got held up by a couple of highwaymen. A police detective was there and somehow he got himself killed. They found and arrested the stick-up men, but, I don't know, the guys started naming names and the police went on a tear, arresting everybody in their path. Joe got picked up."

"Mother of God." Kitty feels her jaw tightening.

"His name was in the paper this morning, front page of the *Globe*. Describes the whole incident, the big round-up."

"Damn, I didn't see it." She pulls her stomach taut and stands straight, not knowing whether she is facing another tragedy or a sick comedy. "What do you need me to do?"

"He's down at the Central District lockup. Says he has a lawyer, but I don't want him being a fall guy like Modie was. I want to go down there and get him out. Can you go with me? You're smarter than me. You know the right words. The St. Louis police picked him up as a favor for the East St. Louis police. That's across state lines. They just can't hand him over without some kind of, you know, legal papers."

"It's called *extradition*," she says. Years of scanning newspapers for clues to Modie's gang activities taught her a thing or two. And she knows that if the St. Louis police have nothing to charge Joe with, filing a writ of *habeas corpus* would get a judge to release him. "When are you going downtown?"

"Now. The lawyer's going to meet me. Got somebody to watch the store? I'll come by for you. I have Joe's car."

"I'll be ready."

Downtown, they are seated in a room where Joe is escorted in, wearing shackles. Horror crosses his face when he sees Kitty glowering at him.

"I didn't do anything! I swear!" He has a coughing fit as the cop pushes him into a chair. "I was curious about those joints across the river. I was bored. They have games, booze. Some fellows I work with recommended the place—the Palace Bar—on St. Louis Avenue. I checked it out is all, got in the game. Had my ten bucks stolen."

Kitty has nothing to say. His eyes are shifty. He isn't telling her everything. When the lawyer strolls in, she is disheartened to find that he is the same kind of shyster Modie had, flunky to political bosses and bootleggers. He starts to say that he can work a deal to get Joe thirty days, but Kitty interrupts.

"You'll do nothing of the kind till I see the extradition papers from Illinois."

The lawyer rears back and squints at her. "And where did you get *your* law degree, little lady?"

"Do you even know what *extradition* means?" she shoots back. "Meanwhile, you'll file a writ to get him out of this damn place. Unless you show me extradition papers, Joe Flanagan is out of here by tomorrow afternoon or I'm reporting you to the Missouri bar association. Are we clear?"

He nods.

That evening, she pulls the morning paper from the stack by the back door. Under the headline "Prisoner Names Four in Big Bank Robberies," the rambling full-column story describes a variety of possibly intertwined crimes and arrests. Joe Flanagan and his address on North Seventeenth are buried in the middle. Like Tommy said, it looked like he was swept up as an "associate" of men arrested for serious crimes.

The next morning's paper has another long page-one story, mentioning Joe among those who refused to return to East St. Louis without extradition papers. But there is another name in the same paragraph, a name that sets off alarm bells with Kitty—David Rowe.

"Son of a gun," she mutters. Rowe's twin Tom was the one arrested with Modie for safecracking when Modie got sentenced to a year at the City Workhouse. Not much older than she is, Tom and Dave are familiar names in the St. Louis underworld, known as the *Heavenly Twins*. They are career criminals, in and out of the penitentiary. Kitty notices every time one of their names hits the papers. Tonight's article doesn't draw a direct line between Joe and Rowe, but the mention of their names in the same paragraph makes her skin crawl.

That afternoon, Kitty gets a call from Joe, saying he's been released and thanking her for speaking up for him.

"Some of the other guys, they knew about the extradition process, but I would have been railroaded if you weren't there for me. And I swear, I swear my only crime was going to that saloon."

Joe is not out of jeopardy. There's an outside chance one of the East St. Louis witnesses will finger his photo and extradition papers will be drawn up. Meantime, Kitty decides not to mention it to Tom. Her family has already given the Barretts enough grief.

When Tom puts on his new reading glasses and picks up the paper after dinner, she distracts his attention from the crime stories by pointing to one on Ireland's struggle to get out from under the heel of Great Britain.

"Look," she says, "there's a new organization being formed to supplant the Friends of Irish Freedom."

Tom has been a longtime supporter and donor to the F.I.F., but it recently ran afoul of the Irish provisional president Éamon de Valera for ineffectiveness and misuse of funds. The new organization is called the American Association for the Recognition of the Irish Republic.

Tom spends an hour studying the long article and making notes. "Really interesting," he says. "I'd like to work on forming the Missouri chapter of this organization."

"I have my scissors right here," she says. "Let me clip the article for you."

He stands up and hands her the newspaper. "I'm going to kiss the children goodnight and read in bed for a while. I'm bushed."

Kitty cuts out Tom's story of American involvement in the Irish freedom fight, then snips out the Joe Flanagan story for her crime file.

She goes to bed feeling small. The world has become too complicated. Tom is more capable of being a citizen of the world, of balancing grocery orders, property management, game design, fraternal organizations, and politics. He is still reading, halfway through *The Magnificent Ambersons*, as she snuggles close to him, wiggles her head under his arm, and circles her own arm around his waist.

"We have a good life," she says.

He takes his hand away from the book and rubs her back. "That we do, Kitty. That we do."

Part 3. On Rowan, Blessings and Curses 1923-1926

:: 112 ::

Friday, November 9, 1923. It is Mary's tenth birthday. When Mary returns to school after lunch, Kitty accepts delivery on a second-hand baby grand piano. It is the best gift Kitty can think of for her clever girl—music. With a smile, she remembers Leclaire and the delirious thrill of the Flanagans' first piano. That's the kind of family enjoyment she wants for her own children. The Barretts were farmers out in Catawissa, then dirt-poor tenement dwellers, so Tom didn't have any such luxury growing up. When she proposed buying a piano, he was charmed by the idea of music in their home.

Their home. After eleven years of marriage, Kitty and Tom are finally homeowners, even if it is still an apartment above a store. But it is *their* flat, *their* store, *their* building, *their* lot with a garage and a chicken coup, at 1401 Rowan Place on the corner of Ridge, just two blocks from St. Barbara's Church and parochial school. It even has a rectangle of lawn in front, where Kitty can plant flowers if she ever has a free minute.

Buying the twelve-year-old brick building in February of 1921 was initially part of Tom's real estate plan. He easily got tenants for the spacious six-room apartment upstairs, but couldn't rent the retail space on this quiet residential corner, so he stocked it with dry goods and once again opened a third store.

Kitty wasn't happy. The children needed her constant attention. The third store expanded and complicated her weekly orders. And Tom refused to give up his work with the Missouri chapter of the American Association for the Recognition of the Irish Republic. When his patent for "Skirmish" was granted, he stayed up for nights designing prototype game boards to test with friends and family.

"Tom! What is the hurry?" she said one typical night. "The Irish will win their fight without you. You have your whole life to work on game boards. Why in hell do we have three stores again?"

His response was to slam doors and exclaim she didn't understand. "Our children need to have what I didn't—prosperity, a roadmap to self-sufficiency and a good education, a sense of community, a sense of the world."

Kitty snapped back. "Some nights, they just need a daddy."

It went on like this. A rollercoaster of petty explosions followed by profuse apologies and expensive gifts. Kitty loved the brooches and the cut glass, but something needed to change.

In June of '22, he took out a loan to buy a commercial building on the same block as the Easton store. It rented and immediately became profitable. When the upstairs tenants of the Rowan property moved out, he finally had to admit its purchase was a mistake. He put ads in the September papers to sell it.

Kitty's epiphany came when she decided to save a few pennies and clean the Rowan apartment herself. She brought the children, who ran from room to room, their footfalls and giggles echoing and making her smile. It was clearly a better space than their Cote Brilliante apartment. The rooms were airy, with high ceilings, tall windows, and shiny oak floors. The basement was gigantic and full of possibilities.

Despite her loving the Cote Brilliante neighbors (what would she do without Birdie Bialik next door?), she persuaded Tom to terminate the lease on Cote Brilliante and move the store and their family to Rowan Place.

Now, with their lives more compact, she is happy. Now she can have a piano. Now her family will have the gift of music.

But when Mary comes home from school, the girl takes one look at the piano and says, "I wanted a ukulele."

Kitty is deflated. "Why would you want a silly instrument like that?"

"I can take it to parties and picnics. I can be popular. Now you're going to make me take boring old piano lessons."

But the four-year-old boys are very interested in the piano and start banging on the keys.

Mary stomps her foot. "And we're going to listen to those little monsters making noise all the time." She marches off to her room.

Hours later, when Tom arrives home from the Easton Avenue store, he walks up the long staircase to the sound of piano music and Kitty singing "Let Me Call You Sweetheart." He reaches the landing with a smile on his face, but when he peeks around the corner, he is surprised to see, not Mary, but Bobby sharing the piano bench with Kitty. The room is November dark, with only a piano lamp lighting up the sheet music.

He backs away and walks down the hallway, past the dining room, past the doors of the master bedroom on the left, bathroom on the right, past the back stairs, past the icebox nook, into the kitchen. Bill is sitting at the kitchen table, putting together a small wooden jigsaw puzzle. A pot of stew sits cold on the stove. Mary's room is off the kitchen to the left. She is sitting on her bed against a pile of pillows, reading *The Secret Garden*.

He sits on the side of the bed. "How's my birthday girl?"

"Fine."

"I thought you'd be learning about the piano with your mother."

"She's mad at me." Mary closes her book and leans forward. "Really, daddy, I'd rather have a ukulele."

He sighs. "Look, if you learn your music on the piano, I'll buy you a ukulele. But you have to go apologize to your mother now. People are coming by for cake and ice cream later.

She rolls her eyes. "All right."

After dinner, the Barretts arrive in the sisters' new car—Mother, Mamie, Katie, and Katie's beau Chas Dyer. In his mid-twenties, Chas is on the lowest rung in the dry goods business. With his father recently passed away, he's looking to improve the family income by starting his own store, so he's eager to get Tom's advice. And Tom is always ready to talk shop.

Mother knows Mary's love of fantasy and strange creatures, so she brings her a Frank Baum book about sea fairies. Mary loves it and gives Mother the hug Kitty wishes she would have received for the piano.

Then Joe and Tommy show up. They bring Mary a new jump rope and a bag of sidewalk chalk. She gives them each big, giggly smooches on their cheeks.

The group would usually crowd around the kitchen table for their ice cream and cake, but tonight they get to sit in the living room with the new piano. Kitty plays "Happy Birthday" and then shows off her rusty talents with some of the sheet music she's been accumulating. As Kitty gets everyone singing to "Barney Google" and "Yes, We Have No Bananas," she spots Mary moving closer, looking back and forth between Kitty's hands and the happy singing.

When Kitty takes a break, Uncle Tommy pulls Mary onto the piano bench with him and, to everyone's wild applause, quickly teaches her to play "Chopsticks." Now Mary is grinning ear to ear.

:: 113 ::

While everyone's spirits are high, Kitty notices that her brother Joe is quieter than usual, his gray eyes tired. He does a little fake boxing with Bill and Bob, but he stops when a coughing fit forces him to excuse himself to the bathroom. When Kitty sees the door opening, she crosses the stair landing into the hall to intercept him.

"Come with me to the kitchen," she says, "while I put on the water for more tea."

He follows her.

As she runs the water, Kitty asks, "How come so quiet? You all right? I see your cough is back."

"Been out of work," he says as he glances around her kitchen. "Planing mill laid off a bunch of guys. Lot of the work is moving south." He looks out the back-door window to the screened-in porch. "Been picking up odd jobs, but it's wearing me down."

Turning up the flame under the tea kettle, she wants to ask if by "odd jobs" he means work with the gangs, transporting booze from bootleggers to the private clubs springing up all over, but part of her doesn't want to know. "Have you been checked out for TB? That cough doesn't sound good."

"It's not TB. I took a test. That flu, it scarred my lungs or something. Now, weather gets chilly and damp, coal smoke clogs the air, cough comes back." He grabs an apple from a bowl on the counter and takes a bite. His eyes close. "Oh, this tastes good." He looks through the window again. "But you know what I loved? You brought them to the picnic, the green grapes, so full of juice, sweet as candy."

In a rush of affection, Kitty puts her hands on Joe's shoulders and presses the side of her head against his chest, surprised at the rattling she hears in his lungs. The tea kettle whistles and draws her back to the stove, her brain racing, calculating, making a quick decision. "Look, I can use some extra help downstairs, at least through the holidays. I'm still getting it organized and the twins are running me ragged. How about coming to work for me?"

Joe's sad face brightens. "A job?" He breaks into a smile. "That would be fantastic, a lifesaver. I can start tomorrow." Then he grabs the door jamb for balance as he bends over with another coughing fit.

Joe quickly learns the process for keeping the shelves of the Rowan store stocked, but his most valuable contribution is tuning up all the motors on Kitty's refrigeration units, from the milk cooler to the meat locker.

But over the three-week run-up to Thanksgiving, his cough gets worse and he loses his appetite.

On Thanksgiving, when Kitty and Tom have their first big dinner party in the spacious formal dining room, Joe winds up on the twins' bed, sleeping all afternoon and into the evening. That night, to avoid having to rouse Uncle Joe, Kitty piles blankets and pillows on her bedroom floor as a "camp out" for her boys.

Early the next morning, as Kitty prepares breakfast, she hears Joe cough. She turns to see him walking out of the boys' room, through Mary's room, into the kitchen, trousers and suspenders over his ratty union suit.

"That bacon smells good enough to wake the dead," he says. Then his eyes roll back and his legs crumple to the floor. Unconscious.

Kitty rushes to his side. He's burning up.

"Tom!" she screams. Mary pops up from her bed and Tom rushes out of their bedroom. "Tom, call the ambulance. Mary, get me the rubbing alcohol, then keep your brothers away from here. Run now."

Joe comes to in a state of delirium, flailing his arms and legs, talking gibberish.

Sing-songing to Joe that everything was going to be all right, splashing a dishrag with rubbing alcohol, Kitty wipes his brow and cheeks. The doorbell rings and Tom dashes downstairs to let in the ambulance drivers. They wear masks.

They manage to get Joe to his feet, so he can walk down the stairs.

"We need to take him to City Hospital," one of them says. "The private hospitals won't take him if it looks like influenza."

"Okay," says Kitty. "I'll get down there as soon as I can."

When they leave, Tom ties a handkerchief around his nose and mouth and starts throwing open windows. "Get the bed linens off the bed," he instructs her. "Carefully, so you don't raise a lot of dust. We need to get this place disinfected. Get some handkerchiefs from my drawer to mask yourself and the children."

Kitty bristles at his tone of voice, but at the same time, she remembers Julie's long slow death from the flu and can't think of anything worse. Instead of handkerchiefs, she digs out the cotton masks they wore during the pandemic.

By this time, the children are all crying, upset at seeing their uncle hauled into an ambulance and at watching their parents fly around stripping bed linens and filling buckets with hot water and disinfectant. As the late November wind sweeps dead leaves through the apartment's open windows, they huddle under blankets on the settee in the living room, pulling at the masks tied hastily to their faces.

"I'll open the stores," Tom says as he retrieves the cash pouches from the safe. "I know you want to get to the hospital, but if the children have been exposed to the flu, you can't leave them playing in the store downstairs." He gives Kitty a quick kiss on the top of her head. "I'll get back here as soon as I make sure everything's covered."

"I had Joe scheduled to work downstairs today," she calls after him, "so we got nobody. Let me open up, makes some calls."

He tosses Kitty the cash pouch. "Mary," he calls. "Get out a game you and the boys can play till one of us gets back. You're ten years old now.

You can be captain of the ship for a while." With that, he's down the steps and out the front door.

It is late afternoon by the time Kitty arrives at City Hospital. Everything is back under reasonable control at home and in the stores, but what's upsetting her now is that she can't locate her brother Tommy to tell him what's going on.

Joe is lying in a crowded ward, semi-conscious, his breathing labored. A nurse tells her it's not the flu, but an x-ray shows he has lobar pneumonia.

Kitty takes his warm hand in hers. "So, what can you do for him?"

"It's a holiday weekend, you know," the nurse says. "What staff we have are overwhelmed. You can't believe how many gunshot wounds we're getting. We'll keep him comfortable till Monday when things quiet down and the staff doctors are all back on duty. We're giving him aspirin for the fever. Meantime, he should be trying to sit up to clear the congestion. Maybe you can get him to eat.

When Kitty gets home, she's relieved to be able to tell Tom that Joe doesn't have the flu, but she worries that Joe's pneumonia will get worse over the long weekend. Tom calls over to his family to let them know what's going on and his sister Katie volunteers to come mind the children till she has to go back to work on Monday.

It is Monday morning before Kitty finds Tommy Flanagan at home in his apartment, his voice stilted and heavy, like someone coming off a bender.

"Shit," he growls when he hears the news about Joe. "Let me—I'm supposed to be at work—I gotta call. I'll meet you there. Shit."

Kitty doesn't arrive at the hospital till early afternoon. Tommy is there looking hungover and distressed. Joe is propped up with pillows, conscious but glassy-eyed and slow to respond when he sees Kitty. A nurse pulls her aside.

"The doctors were in to see him earlier, Mrs. Barrett. I hate to tell you this, but they don't think he'll make it through the night."

"What?" Kitty is dumbfounded. She has mentally prepared for a long siege but expected his full recovery. "He's a healthy young man, only twenty-eight years old."

The nurse shakes her head. "His lungs are scarred. Smoking and coal soot don't help. Pity." She squeezes Kitty's arm before she rushes away.

Kitty pulls up a chair to Joe's side and runs her fingers through his damp disheveled hair. "You have to pull yourself together, Joe. You have to eat something and fight this damn pneumonia."

He reaches for her hand and presses it to the side of his face. "Mmm… you know what I'd love?" he murmurs. "I keep thinking about those grapes. Those big green grapes you brought to the picnic. They were so cool, so sweet. Can you bring me some grapes, Catherine?"

"If you promise to eat them all, I'll find you some grapes. Do you promise?"

"Yes, okay. I promise."

With Joe brightening up toward the end of the afternoon, she runs home to put dinner on. Grapes are out of season in Missouri, but she calls Mr. Catanzaro, her produce man, and explains the situation to him.

"Oh, I still have a lotta grapes up from the south. People like them for their Thanksgiving tables. How about I bring you a bunch?"

Kitty finds herself delaying her return to the hospital. In their warm apartment, Tom is puzzling over some discrepancy in the day's receipts and the boys want a story before they go to sleep. Mary is actually practicing her piano lesson. Kitty hates to leave.

At last, she wraps the grapes in a checkered napkin, nestling them in a basket, and heads out into the cold drizzle of early December.

It is quarter to nine when the taxi drops her off, technically past visiting hours, but she walks authoritatively past the nurses' station into the brightly lit ward. Nurses stand around Joe's bed. Tommy sits close with his arms stretched out across Joe's chest. He is sobbing.

Joe is dead.

"No!"

She drops the basket on the floor and puts her hands on Tommy's shoulders, rubbing his back, choking down her own tears. How does this happen? There is no war, no famine, no pandemic. They live in a city with clean water and working sewerage. Of the nine Flanagans, she and Tommy are the only ones left now, except for poor Ethel, who is fading into her own tiny world.

While Kitty is devastated by the sight of her dead Joe, she is suddenly furious with Tommy—hungover and crying like a baby. Then anger turns to terror. What if this *thing*, this death, comes for her babies?

On Thursday, they bury Joe in the third of the gravesites Tom purchased for the family.

On Friday, Mary awakes with a fever.

On Saturday, the boys have fevers.

:: 114 ::

Their children are sick, stuffed up and coughing. Both Kitty and Tom are paralyzed with fear. Of course, the children have had chest colds before. Mary had measles, chickenpox, and mumps before the twins were even born. But this feels different.

Tom arranges a house call from a young physician in the neighborhood, Frank Murphy, who tells Kitty and Tom that the children simply have bad colds and will be right as rain in a couple of weeks. He raises an eyebrow when Kitty mentions that she runs the store downstairs and usually keeps the twins with her there.

"You can't bring sick four-year-olds into a public shop. What, are you going to set up cots for them behind the butcher counter?"

Before she can tell him that she isn't stupid, he scribbles on his notepad. "Here's the number of a service that can send over a practical nurse." He hands the note to Tom. "If Mrs. Barrett is too busy to care for your children herself."

When Murphy leaves, Tom says he's reassured the children will be fine, but still makes another round of opening windows and wiping down door handles and drawer pulls with disinfectant. Kitty bristles over the doctor's rudeness. She slams Tom's open windows and retreats to the kitchen to find her clippings on poultices and herbal steam therapies.

On Monday, she calls the nursing service, which sends over an Irish girl in a white uniform and cap.

Bobby is first to recover. In quiet moments behind the cash register, Kitty can hear him upstairs plinking on the piano, sounding out simple tunes.

Mary is wiped out with a cough that keeps her awake at night. It's two weeks before she's out of bed and playing with her dolls again. By then, it's nearly Christmas, so Kitty decides to keep her home till the new year.

At the same time, Bill's cold has turned into croup. On Christmas Eve, his fever spikes. Over the phone, Dr. Murphy recommends they take Bill to St. John's, but Tom cajoles him into another house call.

The doctor arrives in a merry mood, the scent of wine on his breath. After examining Bill, he sobers up. "I'm afraid it's pneumonia, streptococcal by the smell of it, but we can be more definitive at the hospital."

"He's not going to the hospital," Kitty says. "We just went through this at Thanksgiving with my brother. Had a cough and fever. Went to City Hospital and—" Her voice catches. "And he died three days later."

"Mrs. Barrett, St. John's is not City Hospital. The boy needs an x-ray so we can see what's going on. It's early. We have serum treatments and other interventions if his lungs fill up."

She looks at Tom, whose face has gone ashen. "I think we need to listen to the doctor, Kitty."

Her heart is pounding. Hospitals are where people go to die. But she also remembers the story Mother Barrett told her, of Tom witnessing the death at home of two younger brothers from scarlet fever. She doesn't want Mary or Bobby to suffer that trauma either.

She agrees.

The nightmare begins. During the week between Christmas and New Year's Day, Kitty and Tom spend every minute they can with Bill at St. John's.

Bill turns deathly ill. Kitty clenches a rosary in her hand while she and Tom watch every move by nurses and doctors to keep their son on this side of death's door.

Physicians rush in and out of his room, brandishing words like "empyema" and "pneumothorax" and injecting him with this and that. When asked what's going on, their explanations sound like a foreign language.

As Bill fights to breathe, Dr. Murphy makes an incision in her boy's back, to insert a drainage tube.

Meanwhile, the Barretts have quietly stepped in to keep the rest of the family going. Katie and Mamie take turns watching Mary and Bob. Kitty and Tom arrive home late, barely able to wash off the hospital stench before they collapse beside their sleeping children, murmuring to them that everything is all right, everything is just fine.

Francis manages the stores. As the days of Bill's hospitalization pile up, Francis winds up hiring his brother-in-law Ewald Curran to help out. Ewald is nineteen, back from a stint working in Chicago, and looking for work outside the family printing business.

"Ewald is young," Francis reassures them, "but he's about as energetic, smart, and honest a kid as I've ever known."

In tiny steps, Bill improves. His fever breaks. His drainage tube is removed. His breathing becomes easier. His appetite returns. And he wants to go home.

Bill's return home is a big morale booster all around. But with a collapsed lung and a drainage wound through his chest wall, he's not out of the woods. Kitty and Tom are under strict instructions to keep him in bed. Compared to Bobby, he is a hollow-eyed rag doll.

Tom hovers, letting Francis manage the stores, badgering Mary and Bobby to entertain Bill with endless hours of cards and board games. Kitty finally has to give him the boot.

"You're depriving Francis of time with his own children," she says. "And we have hospital bills to pay off. We'll keep Ewald on downstairs. Bill only needs one of us."

Tom returns to work.

The world revolves around Bill, as weeks of recuperation turn into months.

:: 115 ::

The twins' fifth birthday on April 1 is a small but lively celebration, with Bobby standing on a kitchen chair belting out "Happy Birthday to me," while Bill is snuggled in his father's lap, smiling but listless. Mary leads the boys in singing nursery rhymes, which Kitty swears is good for exercising Bill's lungs.

Kitty decided not to have guests, to limit Bill's exposure to new germs. But just as they are finishing up their cake and ice cream, Tommy Flanagan shows up, drunk. Kitty hears the slur in his voice as he walks down the hallway with Tom to the kitchen.

"Hey, I couldn't miss the birthday of my two little heroes, could I?" he says as he staggers into the kitchen. "I brought presents!" Out of his jacket pockets, he produces tattered copies of *Tarzan of the Apes* and *Beasts of Tarzan*. He hands one each to Bill and Bobby. "I know you guys can't read yet, but I betcha Mary will love reading these to you."

Bill smiles as he takes his book. "I can read some. I love adventure stories!"

Bobby hands his book to Mary as he stands up on the chair. "I can't read but I can dance!" He does a silly little shuffle and they all laugh before Kitty scolds him to get down before he breaks his neck.

It is a Tuesday evening, so Mary has school in the morning. Tom begins herding the children toward their rooms as Kitty makes up a bowl of cake and ice cream for her brother.

"I have a pot of coffee on. How about a cup?"

Tommy nods. When Kitty sets it in front of him, he takes a small flask from his hip pocket and pours in a generous shot of what smells like rum. With Tom Barrett out of earshot, Kitty makes an issue of it.

"So what's with the heavy drinking and showing up at a children's birthday party loaded?"

He stares into his cup. "Shit, I'm sorry."

She starts filling the dishpan with hot water and pulls on her rubber gloves. "Is that all you have to say?"

"I'm sorry that I'm such a screw-up, sorry for it all. I'm sorry I couldn't have been a better brother. I should have gotten Joe to a doctor sooner. Maybe he wouldn't have died. Maybe little Billy wouldn't be half-dead now if he didn't catch a bug from Joe." He takes a drink from his cup. His eyes redden.

Kitty starts washing dishes.

In a slightly louder voice, Tommy continues. "I'm sorry I didn't make Papa go to the doctor as soon as he started losing his train of thought. They could have stalled out the disease if he started treatment earlier. He told me what it was. I knew and I couldn't help him. I'm so, so sorry."

Now he is sniveling. Kitty needs this like she needs a wooden nickel. She throws a towel at him. "Here. Start drying these dishes."

He takes another drink and stands up. Closer to her, with a dish in hand, he lowers his voice. "I knew Auntie Bridget was slapping around the babies. I should have spoken up. I could have saved Ethel. I live every day being sorry about that too. And Modie—Jesus! I should have knocked some sense into that knucklehead when he was thirteen years old and following me to the pool hall and running off with those hoods."

Kitty feels the muscles in her neck tighten as she scrubs the cake pan. "I suppose you could have saved Nellie too."

"I might have." He pauses his drying and looks at the coffee cup. "I knew she was in a family way. I was fixing her stove and overheard her and Harry arguing in the bedroom. I should have told you, but I thought it was her business, you know. But I should have told you." He rubs his sleeve across his eyes.

Kitty takes off the rubber gloves and wipes her hands on her apron. "Don't be a damn fool," she says, her voice low and sharp. "We all second-guess ourselves, blame ourselves for what we should have, could have done. But most of us can't afford to drink ourselves into oblivion over it."

He throws down the towel and takes a gulp of the rum-laced coffee. "I'm sorry. I'm sorry."

"Stop being *sorry* and start being helpful. Did it ever cross your mind to come over and sit with the children or help out in the store? To use the brain God gave you instead of pickling it in rum?"

He stares at her for a long moment, then says, "I gotta go."

He turns and Kitty watches him weave down the dark hallway. She hears him pound down the stairs. She hears the front door slam.

She stands still, aware of her heartbeat and a tremble in her arms and legs. In the quiet, she hears the low rumble of Tom Barrett's voice reading to the children in the boys' room. She takes a deep breath and picks up the dish towel.

:: 116 ::

As spring turns into summer, Tommy and his alcohol problem are far from Kitty's mind. Although his breathing is all right, Bill is still sickly, failing to gain weight, constantly running a low-grade fever, as the incision on his back refuses to heal. Ewald has been a godsend in the store, allowing her to spend all her time upstairs coddling her invalid and barely attending to her other motherly chores.

Dr. Murphy is impatient with her calls, offering little more than a prescription for an antimicrobial wash and brusque reassurances that "time heals" and young Bill is "lucky to be alive." Despite the daily sponge baths, dressing changes, and the wash that stains Bill's skin and makes him scream, the wound continues its foul discharge.

On a day when Bill is particularly whiny and she is particularly fed up, Kitty lays the boy across her knees and begins scrubbing dead skin and pus out of the wound. Bill screams and she weeps.

"Oh my God!" Much to her horror, what she thinks is a hunk of dead tissue deep inside him turns out to be a square of surgical sponge. She drops it into the wash basin to show Tom.

By the next day, Bill's fever is gone.

With the incision finally healing properly, Bill is up and around, progressively better and, despite having only one lung and weakened back muscles, learning to be a little boy again.

With Ewald still managing the day-to-day in the store, Kitty resumes responsibility for ordering. But she's on the warpath against the physician.

Thursday, July 24. Kitty wakes up in a mood, snapping at the children and rushing to get them fed before she heads downstairs to the store with her lists. While she bustles around, Tom sits with the paper in front of his face.

"So, did you call Dr. Murphy yet? About the sponge?" she asks.

"I will," he says. "I'm reading about the Leopold and Loeb trial. What a couple of cold characters they are."

"Dr. Murphy," she insists. "When I called to give him a piece of my mind, all he said was 'these things happen.' Apparently, he needs a man to tell him off."

Tom folds his paper. "These things do happen, Kitty. And you did heroic work getting to the bottom of the problem, literally. Dr. Murphy is a rising young physician and surgeon in the community. He should be held accountable, but I want to do it right, at the right time, in the right way. And he did save Bill's life with his treatments, I'm sure of that. Remember how grateful you were when we brought Billy home."

Kitty squints at him, annoyed that Tom is arguing the doctor's case.

The phone rings.

"Who the heck is calling at this hour?" Throwing down her dish towel, she parks herself on the chair at the phone table, snugged into the niche over the back stairway, next to the icebox. She grabs the phone earpiece in one hand and a pencil in the other.

"Mrs. Thomas Barrett, Catherine Barrett, please." A man's voice.

"This is she."

"This is Father McClellan, a Catholic chaplain at City Hospital. Am I correct in understanding you have a brother Thomas Flanagan?"

Kitty sags. *What now?* She hasn't seen Tommy since their confrontation in April and dreads planning the yearly birthday picnic, with Joe gone and Tommy so besotted.

"Yes."

"I have the sad duty to inform you that your brother Thomas Flanagan passed away this morning."

A shiver runs through her.

"Mother of God." Her voice drops low as she scoots her chair closer to the table so the family can't see her face. "What are you saying? Wait a minute."

She turns to Tom, whose face immediately lights with concern. "Get the children outside. Now, all right?"

She turns back to the phone. "What happened?"

"He's been here for a couple of weeks. Police picked him up off the street one Saturday night. He'd been on quite a bender." McClellan paused. "I know this is hard for you to hear, Mrs. Barrett."

"Tell me," she barked.

"The police figured he just needed to dry out, but he was quite physically debilitated. As he sobered up, he began suffering from *delirium tremens*. It's a severe—"

"I know what DTs are. You're not going to tell me he died from seeing pink elephants."

"It happens pretty often at City. You can talk to Dr. O'Malley here—Eugene O'Malley—for the full picture. At its worst, the condition causes what they call cardiovascular collapse. Once that happens, the doctors can't reverse it. Mr. Flanagan gave us a bit of information, including your name as next of kin. But he didn't want us to contact you. He said you had a sick child, didn't want to worry you, didn't want you to have to come here."

Jesus, he was all alone. For two weeks. Kitty drops her pen and covers her eyes, choking down the lump in her throat. What a stupid ass her brother was.

"Are you all right, Mrs. Barrett? I can call back later. The undertaker, Geraghty, he needs a few details."

"I'm fine," she says and takes a deep breath. "I've been here before. Get your pencil out. Calvary Cemetery, a lot under the name of Thomas Barrett. A pine box will do. Burial on Saturday if possible. No services required. Give us a time and we'll meet the casket graveside. No notice in the paper." It felt cruel saying that, but who was going to mourn him?

Herself. And maybe Mary because he taught her to play "Chopsticks."

When she hangs up, she feels Tom's hands on her shoulders, tender, holding her together. "Tommy?"

She nods and breaks down.

:: 117 ::

Weeks later, after a couple of half-hearted stabs at celebrating her thirty-fourth birthday, Kitty is working in the store with Ewald. She enjoys working with him. He's good company with his funny, rambling stories and he never needs to be told what to do.

When there is a lull in shoppers, she lights up a cigarette, something she hasn't done in years. Ewald is sitting on a crate, stocking shelves near the cash register.

"What's this, you're smoking now?"

"Just in the past few weeks. I used to smoke now and then, years ago, to keep up with the boys."

"You don't say. I didn't take you to be a smoker."

"My secret sin," she says. "Settles my stomach."

"Aw, jeez, what's wrong with your stomach? It's still August—not flu season—bad piece of fish?"

She takes a drag. "I'm… expecting," she says, surprised at hearing herself say it out loud.

He pauses his work to look at her. "A baby? How come you're not smiling?"

"Because I'm not happy about it," she says. "I haven't even told Tom yet. Bad luck to tell anyone till you're three months along."

He does kind of an abbreviated double-take. "How come you're telling me?"

"I don't know. You're sitting there. You asked me a question. And I'm standing here, wondering how in the world I can manage another child."

He turns back to the box of cans. "Women got the vote now, wearing short skirts, bobbing their hair," he says. "You can do anything you want, make your own decisions."

"I was thinking the same thing," she says. "It's been a helluva year. Lost two brothers, almost lost a child. I'm whipped. Last thing I need is to start all over with a baby."

"I guess I'm the last person to talk to about that. I'm number ten of twelve kids and my mother lost three others at birth, one right before I came along."

"*Your* mother is a saint," Kitty says. "And, she has a husband who is a salaried executive at one of the biggest companies in St. Louis. She doesn't have to roll coins into paper sleeves at the end of every day. She can be a mother to her dear dozen."

Ewald laughs. "I think they were running out of names when I came along. There's this guy my father knows, old guy, never married, no kids, no namesakes. He begs my father to name a kid after him. *Ewald*, haha. Well, I guess I did okay by that because now every year on my birthday, the original Ewald gives me a gold dollar coin. How about that? And I'm going to be twenty next week. I'll have twenty gold coins!"

With a chuckle, Kitty says, "What a lucky fellow you are."

She takes another drag on her cigarette and watches Ewald stamp the top of every can with the price, remembering her first days of romance with Tom Barrett when she balked at having to write every price with a wax pencil.

"I'm not going to do anything," she says.

He stops stamping but keeps his eyes on the shelf of cans.

"I wouldn't try anything. My sister Nellie, she thought she could have everything her way, you know. Women have all these remedies, all these little tricks. And she did herself in. Killed herself trying to be clever."

Ewald looks up at her. "Jeez," he says, "that happened in my family too. Did Molly ever tell you about Marguerite?"

"John's wife, right? I remember Molly being upset, going to her funeral a couple of years back."

Ewald nods. "Big family secret. She couldn't deal with the idea of a fourth child, did something bad to herself. The way I figure it, she got a fever, chills, knew she needed help, and got herself to City Hospital. You know, they won't touch a married woman without notifying the husband, so she gave them a bogus address and said she was divorced. They didn't know diddly about her till she passed away and they went through her bag. Everything fell apart. John's living back home with little Johnnie and their two girls went to live with the Kramers, Marguerite's family. What a mess."

"That's heartbreaking," Kitty says, then holds out the pack of cigarettes. "Have a smoke with me?"

Ewald gets up from his seat and she lights his cigarette.

"I'm nobody's fool," Kitty says. "I don't play games with God."

:: 118 ::

On March 23, 1925, in her bedroom at 1401 Rowan, to the delight of Tom, Mary, Bill, and Bobby, Kitty gives birth to Kathleen Ellen.

As much as Kitty dreads starting over with another child, Kathleen is easy. Mary was a challenge because every day of her pregnancy, every day of motherhood was a new experience, requiring imagination and problem-solving. The twins needed double or triple the physical and mental effort—two different personalities from the get-go, eating and sleeping on their own divergent schedules. Her brain had to get used to operating on two tracks all the time, coordinating like a railway switchman, so the carloads of demand did not collide. Layered onto that was the six months of icy terror that Bill would be a lifelong invalid or die an early death.

By contrast, Kathleen is plump, hungry, and doesn't take long to sleep through the night. During the spring of 1925, Kitty luxuriates in motherhood.

Mary is eleven, able to walk the six-year-old twins the two blocks to St. Barbara's school. Kitty pays the extra fee for them to eat lunch at the school cafeteria. Although she tells Tom it's because she worries about Bill exerting himself on his way home or, worse, stopping to catch his breath in the middle of Hamilton Boulevard, the truth is that not having to prepare lunch for her school-age children gives her extra quiet time with her little sweetheart.

Ewald manages the store. Her cleaning lady adds another day to keep the Barrett flat spic and span and to wash diapers. Kitty spends time in bed with her magazines and her baby. She even has an hour or two in the afternoons when she can plan meals and cook. A quick phone call and Ewald dashes upstairs with a bag of potatoes or a wrapped cut of meat.

In the evening, Mary is happy to play little mother and learns to change the baby's diapers. All three children love keeping Kathleen entertained with rattles and puppet shows and songs. Tom is attentive, sacrificing his reading time to get the older children into bed. And Kitty is getting used to Tom's shoulder rubs while she sits at the kitchen table with her newspaper after dinner.

On the first warm Saturday evening in May, Kitty and Tom sit on their screened-in porch, at the northwest corner of their apartment, with the kitchen behind them and the boys' room to the left. Tom opens the door and windows to the boys' room, so they catch the breeze blowing in from the southwest.

It is 10 p.m., dark. Kitty pours glasses of beer for the two of them. Like everyone else now, they keep a private stash of local home brew. Tom pushes their metal chairs up to the windows, giving them a second-floor crow's nest over the streets, to watch the neighbors, to gaze at the traffic, to monitor the firehouse at the corner of Ridge and Hamilton.

"They're just about done with the new bank building on the corner of Union," Tom says. "Art Blase asked me to be on the Advisory Board."

"Sounds like a feather in your cap," Kitty says. "What's it mean?"

"Times are good. I think it's a way of encouraging neighborhood businesses to bank with them and to take out loans, mortgages. I'm happy they think I have some influence."

They sit quietly, listening to the faint sound of a piano and distant laughter. A party.

"Do you think the twins are too young to go see a photoplay?" Tom asks. "There's a Tom Mix movie showing at the Delmonte. *The Rainbow Trail*. Based on a Zane Grey novel."

"If Bobby can stand on his seat and if Bill can read the titles to him." Kitty laughs. "I forget if the Delmonte has a piano or organ for music. Bobby will be curious about that." She remembers back. "My brothers loved reading Zane Grey stories." She takes a drink of her beer, surprised at the pleasure of her memory: those funny, rambunctious little boys with their cowboy books. But now—all three are gone. The warmth of her memory turns to a sudden chill, which she shakes off. "Oh, that was such a long, long time ago. Yes, you should take them to see Tom Mix."

Tom reaches a hand out and massages her neck. He says, "I don't think I've ever seen you happier or more relaxed."

She leans toward him, enjoying his touch. "It's been kind of a dream time," Kitty says, "thanks to everyone pitching in. The children will be out of school next month, so it'll be back to chaos. Ewald turns twenty-one in September and is talking about joining the police force, so I don't know how long we'll have him to help."

"I've been thinking," Tom says. "Maybe it's time you got out of the grocery rat race and enjoyed raising a family. Like Molly. I've been looking at ads for houses. Saw one in University City today. Seven rooms in a quiet neighborhood. We could swing something like that."

Kitty sits up, filled with a rush of joy. A house! Liberation from the daily juggle of running a retail business and giving enough attention to her family. But then the thrill drains away. She doesn't want to be Molly Barrett. Why not, she wonders.

"It's a fabulous idea," she says. "But let's think it through. Schools. St. Barbara's is the third school Mary's attended. I don't think we should move out of the parish till she graduates from eighth grade. And we talked about sending her to high school. That might be a factor in where we live."

"We'll send her to St. Joe's Academy," Tom says. Two of his Geatley cousins teach there, Sister Hortensia and Sister Beatrice—country cousins from Catawissa. The school caters to bright girls and lets them graduate to Fontbonne College, on the same campus. "Our girl is damn smart. She should plan on college."

Kitty gets up to fetch another bottle of beer from the icebox. She thinks about Molly Barrett again. Molly, Francis, and their four children live over on Semple, a sleepy residential street divided into tiny lots, crowded with small frame houses. Molly's life revolves around those children, without a whit of interest in the grocery business.

Back on the porch, she uncaps the beer and splits the brew between their two glasses.

"I like it here for now," she says. "God knows I've enjoyed the past couple months of leisure with the baby, but I'm itching to get back to the store. I miss our customers—the gossip, the politics. My magazine stories are dull compared to real life. Mary and the twins learned to walk by pulling themselves up on cracker barrels and fruit crates. So can Kathleen."

She sets her beer on the window sill and reaches out for Tom's hand, a big mitt for her slender fingers. They hear the fire horn go off at the firehouse. They look. Within a minute, the doors fly open. The pump and the hook-and-ladder pull out, bells clanging, sirens wailing. They turn north, toward Easton Avenue.

Kitty and Tom hear another alarm and sirens from the east, the station at Ridge and Goodfellow.

"Two-alarm fire," Tom says. They sit holding hands till all is silent again.

"The swimming pool at the Forest Park Highlands opens tomorrow,"

Kitty says. "How about if we take the children, have a picnic?"

Tom squeezes her hand. "Sounds good."

Kitty prepares for her return to the cash register by updating her wardrobe. While 1920's style has gone flat and boxy, her pregnancy, her extra time in bed, and her weakness for rich chocolates have left her round and soft. She invests in a Bien Jolie Corsette, an all-in-one foundation garment made of pink satin coutil, easily stepped into and wiggled on over her drawers-and-camisole combination. Garters along the edge hold up her silk stockings, Her wardrobe makeover is completed with a couple of new frocks, their hemlines just below the knee. She shortens her other dresses by hand to match the new style.

Now for her hair. Over Tom's objections, Kitty goes to the hairdresser and has her hair bobbed, a style that brings out her natural waves.

On the first Monday morning working again full-time, Kitty gives herself a once-over in the long vanity mirror. Spreading her arms, she does a little dance step. "Yessir, that's my baby," she sings. "No, sir, I don't mean maybe." Still dancing, still singing, she sweeps Kathleen's baby basket into her arms and heads downstairs to the store.

:: 119 ::

Not long after Kitty returns to the store full-time, Ewald announces that he's leaving to join the police force.

"Yeah, I'm going to visit my brother for a few weeks in Chicago, do a little swimming in Lake Michigan, then I'll go to the training school."

Kitty is disappointed to see her right-hand man go, but she can clearly imagine Ewald as the friendly beat cop, strolling down Easton Avenue, cajoling pickpockets back into school, patching clues together on break-ins, and catching babies dropped out of windows.

But at Christmas, Molly tells her that Ewald quit the police force on the very day he was supposed to receive his badge and gun. "Pop is furious at him," Molly says. "He's up on his 'nobody loves a quitter' high horse, doesn't even want to hear what E has to say about it. I think you'll be hearing from my brother after the first of the year.

And sure enough, on January 2, Ewald turns up at Kitty's store.

"Where's my apron?" he says with a big grin. "I need a job. Hey, look at this one!" He scoops the nine-month-old baby into his arms. "What's your name, young lady?"

The baby slaps his shoulders with her hands. "Kash-a-leen!" she shouts.

"Oh, a little smarty-pants. Kash it is."

Kitty is thrilled to see him. "Well, tell me what the hell happened with the police."

He bounces the baby on his hip. "Aw, jeez, I thought I'd make a good policeman, you know? But they put me on a couple practice patrols and damn if they didn't partner me up with cops who were shaking down the speakeasies. Collecting payoffs to turn a blind eye. How is that any better than the gangs, Catherine, you tell me that."

She can only shake her head.

"Maybe I should have joined the fire department. But I don't know—they like big guys at the fire department and you see me, I'm on the scrawny side."

"Why don't you work in the printing business, like your brothers? Make a good living, for Pete's sake."

"You sound like my old man. He's ready to frog-march me into the pressroom, chain me to a machine."

"So, what's the problem? Other than your darn pride."

He scoffs and sits Kathleen on the counter. "I can do that. I got the head for it." He takes out a pack of cigarettes and offers Kitty one. "Maybe I don't have the heart for it. Gigantic, loud machinery. Paper snarls and self-destructing plates. Mechanical breakdowns. Men shouting at men, day in day out." He strikes a match and she leans her head toward it to light up. "I enjoy the store. The people. The talk. Every day is different."

Kathleen reaches for Kitty's cigarette, but Kitty puts her on the floor, pointing her to a cardboard box. "Back to your play house, baby." As Kathleen crawls away, Kitty picks a shred of tobacco off her tongue. "We haven't found anyone who can do what you do, E, so… welcome back."

With that, twenty-one-year-old Ewald Curran becomes the Barretts' utility man—trusted to manage cash and lock up at night, handy with a plumber's wrench or a screwdriver, willing to work wherever needed.

:: 120 ::

With the arrival of summer, the Barretts organize a slate of Sunday activities. The boys are seven and discovering sports, so Tom takes them to a Browns game and a Cardinals game. Bobby is a natural athlete. Bill doesn't have the stamina for running, so Tom teaches him about the umpire's job and about how to keep score on each batter up.

Tom also buys tickets for performances at the big outdoor Municipal Opera in Forest Park. Starting the evenings with picnic dinners by the lagoon, they see three operas: *The Red Mill*, *The Pink Lady*, and *Iolanthe*. Driving through the park, Kitty always points out buildings that were part of the 1904 World's Fair, reminding her children about how her papa contributed his carpentry skills to the grand project.

And, of course, they make a couple of Sunday excursions to the Forest Park Highlands, where they can swim, visit the funhouse, and ride the big roller coaster.

But for the final Sunday of summer, they all pile into the car and head for the newer amusement park at Westlake, out Natural Bridge, where it joins the old Rock Road.

After lunch, Kitty notices Tom rubbing his right side and grimacing, his face pale in the bright sunlight. She's sitting at the picnic table, watching Kathleen explore. Mary and the boys have run off to ride the Tumble Bug.

"Something bothering you there?" she asks.

"A little indigestion." He pats his belly. "Getting fat from your good cooking. Maybe eating too fast."

"Bothering you how long?"

"Maybe a couple of weeks. These things come and go. I'm forty-three. Getting old."

She frowns. "We carry indigestion tablets at the store."

"Been taking them," he says. "Don't worry about it."

When she crawls into bed with him that night, she is alarmed at the heat he's radiating and presses a hand to his forehead. "You have a fever," she says.

"Just sunburn."

"Tom."

"All right. Tomorrow's Labor Day. If I'm still warm on Tuesday, I'll get it checked out. Promise."

Kitty knows he will. Tom likes to proclaim that good health is the key to long-term business success. Since the Spanish flu era, he continues to wipe down door handles and countertops with Lysol. He keeps clipboards in both stores to log the refrigerator and freezer temperatures at opening and closing. Community health and personal health are one and the same to him.

On Tuesday, with a big pancake breakfast, they make a grand ceremony of the first day of school. Kitty catches Tom rubbing his right side again.

"Today," he reassures her.

That afternoon Kitty takes time off to dress up Kathleen for an eighteen-month photograph at a studio in Wellston. Every day, the baby reminds her more of her mother Maggie and her sister Nellie. The other children, with their cleft chins and sky-blue eyes, are clearly Barretts. But Kathleen's round face, button nose, and greenish eyes are very Flanagan, very Keville.

After dinner, out of earshot of the children, Tom tells Kitty that he visited the doctor, who is ninety percent sure his problem is gall bladder.

"He gave me some pills and recommended a liquid diet for a few days. If it doesn't clear up, he wants to schedule surgery to remove it."

"Mother of God," Kitty says. "Not another hospital."

Tom reassures her. "It's a simple procedure. Thousands are done successfully every day. The bile duct is probably blocked with stones. If I ignore it, the duct could rupture and emergency surgery would be dangerous."

Kitty starts scraping the dinner dishes into the garbage pail. "Who did you go to?"

Tom picks up a crust of bread from the floor and pitches it into the pail. "Frank Murphy."

She stops her work and stares at him. "Not the Frank Murphy who nearly killed our Bill—tell me it isn't."

"Yes, the Frank Murphy who saved Bill from dying with pneumonia."

Kitty sets down the plate and puts her fists on her hips, aware of her pulse starting to race. "What in God's name are you thinking? There isn't another damn doctor in town you can go to, one who hasn't left a sponge in a child's surgical wound?"

"I knew you'd be on my back about this," Tom says as he raises his hands in mock surrender. "But he's a good guy. Our paths cross now and then at K of C meetings and political events. I spoke to him about the damn sponge months ago, remember? He said an intern was responsible for that and was duly mortified that Bill's recovery time got prolonged. I told you that, didn't I? A man shouldn't be punished for life because of a lapse in attention."

"A lapse in attention? Your son almost died!"

"We've been over this. He's a respected physician. He *saved* Bill's life. Why, he has twins of his own their age. And if you have to know, I did check with the local Medical Society after Bill's troubles and no other complaints have ever been lodged against him."

She turns back to her dishes.

He goes on. "I thought you trusted me."

From the front room, she hears Mary start her piano practice, then some clanging on the treble keys, boys laughing, Mary screaming, Kathleen crying. Kitty takes off her apron, throws it on the table, and marches down the hall to settle whatever the hell is going on. Of course she trusts Tom, but she really doesn't understand why he trusts Murphy.

:: 121 ::

Tom says little, but Kitty sees the pain scrawled on his face as the week goes by. The procedure is scheduled.

Tom enters St. John's hospital on Thursday afternoon to be prepped for surgery on Saturday, September 18.

Kitty is relieved when the surgery goes well and Tom wakes up from the anesthesia without a fever.

Even with the discomfort of the surgical wound, Tom insists that his week of recovery in the hospital not be wasted. He doesn't want visitors. With a pile of books and trade publications to read, he doesn't want Kitty or Francis to take time away from work for hours of idle chitchat. He even shoos away his mother.

All is well.

With Mary now old enough to watch the other children, Kitty takes a taxi over to spend time with him after dinner, to go over orders and cash flow. She is pleased to see that in no time the drainage tube is out and the wound is healing.

But on Thursday, Kitty arrives to find that Tom's fever has returned. When the staff physician stops by, he is reassuring.

"We're keeping a watchful eye on it. Sometimes the road to recovery is a bit rockier than we'd like."

Where has she heard that before? she grumbles to herself.

Tom is in a surgical ward with five other men, all with visitors, half the visitors coughing or blowing their noses. She takes Tom's dry, warm hand in hers. "Then we'd like to be moved to a private room, please. We like an open window. Fresh air."

Tom squeezes her hand. "Kitty, the expense."

She insists. "The faster you can leave this place, the cheaper it will be. Can you arrange that, doctor?"

"Yes, of course."

On Friday evening, to save money, Kitty decides to drive herself to the hospital. As Ewald empties the cash drawer, she asks him to get large deliveries done with one truck, so she can use the other to travel back and forth to St. John's.

"You're driving?" he asks. "I can take you, bring you back home too—"

"Mind the store. That's what I need you for!" She hears the edge in her voice, but she's in no mood for a discussion. She needs to get Tom the hell home.

Ewald hovers. "At least let me give you a lesson, some pointers about shifting gears, like we've been talking about."

"Ewald! I've been driving since you were a baby! I need you to take care of today's receipts. Please!"

He backs away. "Got it. No problem." But his eyes are worried. "Just try to remember to ease off the clutch—"

"Goodbye!" She slams the door behind her.

Kitty is a terrible driver, jerking and stalling nearly every time she has to shift. She curses and talks out loud to herself and to the drivers honking at her, but in a crazy way, the driving is a distraction from fretting about Tom.

She finds her husband in his private room but is alarmed to find his fever has spiked and his pain is worse.

"I want some answers," she says.

"Kitty, please. Everything is under control. Let me deal with the doctors. I had a long talk with Murphy this morning. I don't want you fighting my battles. You need to be doing double duty at the stores and with the children. I'll get through this. You being upset doesn't help."

Tom's voice is soft but leaves no room for argument.

With a sigh, she backs off.

"Speaking of the children, I brought the proofs of Kathleen's photos." She digs them out of her handbag. "I want you to pick out the one you like and we'll have some printed for your mother and sisters."

He goes through them slowly. "What a beauty. Every picture is stunning. Get them all. Yes, get them all."

She stashes the photos back in her purse. "Ewald figured out how to hook up our radio. He said it needed an antenna out through the window, something like that. The boys were all excited about listening to a fight being radioed from Philadelphia. Dempsey versus Tunney."

Tom's eyes widen. "No kidding! That was the big heavyweight title match. Who won?"

Kitty has to laugh. She was so enthralled with the whoops and hollers of her dear little boys that she paid no attention to the boxing match. "Gosh, Tunney, I think. The challenger. Anyway, if the Cardinals win the pennant tonight, they told me the World Series would be on the radio. That's next week. You'll be home by then, won't you?"

"Wouldn't miss it for the world," he says.

:: 122 ::

On Saturday evening, she has to drive through the bedlam of St. Louisans celebrating the Cardinals' first National League pennant. There are so many broken beer bottles and so many drunks staggering across Page and Kingshighway, a person wouldn't think Prohibition was still the law of the land. The melee means she can often roll through stop signs and glide for blocks in first gear, easing her stress.

But the merriment is infectious, so she arrives at St. John's with a spring in her step.

Tom's room is dark. She raises the shade. She thought he was sleeping but finds him in some kind of semi-conscious stupor, his eyes following her but with no expression.

"It's a madhouse out there," she says to him but feels the catch in her voice as fear rises in her throat. She swallows. "Cardinals are the National League champs."

She pulls the chair close and grasps his hand. Hot. Limp. "What's going on, Tom? You're supposed to be getting better."

"You're so beautiful," he whispers. "Is Mary with you?"

"No, honey. They don't allow children in the hospital."

"I'm in the…" His voice trails off.

A nun with a starched white apron over her habit pushes a cart into the room.

Kitty speaks to her. "I need someone to tell me what's going on."

The nun glances at her, then swabs Tom's upper arm with alcohol and gives him a shot. She says, "I'm afraid your husband has developed peritonitis, an abdominal infection."

"What? No!" Peritonitis is what killed Nellie, the result of a dirty, back-alley procedure. "We're in a hospital. Everything clean, sterile. How—possible—?"

The nun glances at Kitty again, then turns back to Tom with a thermometer in her hand. "Gall bladder surgery can be messy. A bowel gets nicked. Impossible to see. It's all in the hands of God."

Her pulse racing, Kitty shakes her head. If it were in God's damn hands, Tom could have gone to a faith healer. The nun takes Tom's temperature and pulse, recording her findings on the chart attached to the foot of the bed.

"Dr. Murphy only sees patients in the early morning, before the day's surgeries, but I'll send in a staff physician to give you more information." She pushes her cart halfway out the door, then turns back. "Do you want me to find a priest to come pray with you?"

Kitty frowns. "The doctor, please."

An elderly staff doctor comes by and stands at the foot of the bed.

"What's this about peritonitis?" she asks.

"Yes, Mrs. Barrett. An unfortunate turn of events, indeed." He takes a glance at Tom's vitals on the clipboard. "All we can do is give him increasing amounts of morphine for the pain. And pray."

"I'm not following," Kitty says, despite the sense of dread spreading like floodwater from her fingers and toes, swirling ice cold into her chest. "He's healthy, takes care of himself. A little infection, that's all, right? He's strong. Very strong."

He stares at her. "What I'm saying, Mrs. Barrett, is that your husband is going to die. Because he is such a big strong man, it may take a few days for… for the infection to take its toll. But you need to prepare your family, think about your arrangements. This is God's plan. I'm sorry. I'll find the priest to come sit with you."

He leaves.

Kitty squeezes Tom's hand and curls over to lay her head on his warm shoulder. "They're wrong," she says. "Pay no attention to these quacks. Do you hear me?"

But he is asleep.

Kitty stands, then walks over to the tall window and pushes it open. The air is refreshing and a brisk wind from the north fills the room, riffling the papers on the clipboard. She can see the lights and traffic along Kingshighway. She can hear the horns and cowbells and whoops of people celebrating.

She begins to cry.

She returns to Tom's bedside, lays her head down, stretches her arms across his chest, and sobs. Her mind is blank. All she feels is her heart breaking. She weeps until her tears are dried out, then she hangs onto him, silent. He stirs and she feels his hand on her head, smoothing her hair.

When she gets home, the children are asleep, the twins in their back bedroom, Mary and the baby on her bed. She sits at the phone table and dials Francis' number. Her voice is calm as she tells him things aren't looking good for Tom and that Francis might want to have his mother and sisters visit the hospital tomorrow. She gives vague answers to his questions. He offers to keep the children with his family for as long as she needs to, but she wants them with her. Mary is nearly thirteen and knows which neighbor to call if she needs help.

When she's done with her phone call, Kitty bathes, telling herself that if she goes through all the motions of a normal life, Tom will be pulled back into his proper role of husband and father.

After kissing each of the boys and adjusting their blankets, she carries Kathleen to her crib, then wakes Mary up to get her out of her street clothes.

"Is Daddy coming home tomorrow?" she asks as she gets her nightgown from the adjoining room.

"No, my dear," Kitty says. "It's going to be another long week. I am counting on you to take care of things here while I look after your daddy. He's very sick. Don't leave your dress on the floor."

After tossing her dress on the bed, Mary hugs Kitty. "I miss him so much." Mary is almost as tall as Kitty now and naturally slender, just right for the skinny flapper fashion now in vogue.

Kitty picks up the brush from her dresser. "Let me do your hair." Kitty runs a brush through Mary's long straight hair, darkened from the white blonde of her childhood. "We'll all get dressed up tomorrow and go to Mass together. And then I'll make waffles. How does that sound?"

"And we'll pray for Daddy?"

"Yes, lots of prayers for Daddy."

:: 123 ::

Tom drifts between restless, sweaty nightmares and the vacant stares of semi-consciousness. The hospital is strict about visitors, no more than two at a time, no children ever. So the Barretts—Mother, Mamie, Katie, and Francis—take turns sitting with Kitty, who spends the afternoons there, returns home to put dinner on for the children, and comes back for the evening. Molly, Aunt Delia, and friends keep them supplied with casseroles and stews.

Kitty is numb, focused on the minutia of getting through the days and nights, trying to telegraph her strength to Tom, to push him through this crisis and back into her arms.

The family makes hours of small talk in the hospital room, pretending Tom is taking part. Francis is following the preparations for the World Series, which begins on Saturday, October 2. And he also goes into great detail about the aftermath of storms that swept through Illinois the other day and the imminent flooding of the Mississippi. Mamie and Katie can't get enough of gossip about the drama of Aimee Semple McPherson, a California preacher and radio evangelist who faked her own drowning, only to be found with a lover. By contrast, Mother doesn't have much to say. She sits close to Tom and prays her rosary. Father Lemkes, the pastor at St. Barbara's, stops by every evening.

Kitty would have preferred to be alone with Tom, to lay her head next to his, to whisper stories about the children, to tell him how much they need him to get better and return home. But the Barretts need time with him too. They all hope their company will summon the miracle that pulls him back from the edge.

On Saturday, October 2, Kitty leaves early for the hospital because of the expected traffic jams as everyone in town looks for venues with radios to hear the afternoon's first game of the World Series.

There are also more storms brewing. Yesterday's tornado-like winds knocked down trees and phone lines, blew bricks off buildings, and devastated a lumber yard on Easton. The threat of high winds and drenching rain today persuades Mother and the Barrett sisters to stay home, allowing Kitty precious time alone with her darling.

Arriving at Tom's room, Kitty is surprised to run into Dr. Murphy.

"Ah, Mrs. Barrett. Such terrible misfortune has befallen your husband. He was an interesting man, so well-read, so patriotic."

Misfortune, my ass, Kitty is about to say but stops herself. In her younger days, she might have lunged at him or slapped his face. But she is a businesswoman now, with a name to protect, so she stands perfectly still, staring at him.

"He *is* an interesting man."

He blinks and his eyes dance away. "Oh, my. I'm sorry for..." He takes a deep breath. "But I fear he is at the end now, his suffering nearly over. A day or two at most. Has the priest been here? If he hasn't had Last Rites, now—"

"It's been taken care of," she snaps.

"All right, then," he says. "My best to you and your family."

She watches him scuttle away.

Tom lies motionless, his eyes closed, his breathing shallow and raspy.

"I want you to tell me what to do," she says aloud to him. "What should I be doing?"

He is silent.

"Yes, I know. Be practical. Take care of business. Eye on detail," she says and walks out to the nurse's station. "Is there a mortician's office here?" she asks.

The nurse checks a card on the desk. "Geraghty is here on Saturdays. Office is downstairs next to the chapel."

With a tight jaw, Kitty sits with Mr. Geraghty, explaining her situation.

"I'd like to be prepared in advance. When the time comes, the children will need my full attention."

He nods. "A wise move, Mrs. Barrett."

She sits up very straight, massaging her hands to hide their trembling. "The wake will be in our apartment. He's a fourth-degree Knight of Columbus at the Phil Sheridan Council, so he's entitled to an honor guard, if you can let Bill Hogan know."

Geraghty is writing down her instructions. "Bill, yes, I know him well."

"And I want a Requiem Mass at St. Barbara's, a High Mass, with a choir."

"I'll share your wishes with Father Lemkes."

"Tom purchased a few lots at Calvary six or seven years ago, but they were all used by my family. I think he bought more, but—"

"I'll check on that. Not a problem."

"And a beautiful coffin. Pick something out. Mid-range. With a wooden exterior. Cherry. No, oak."

"Very good. The staff will let me know when the time comes and I'll have everything ready to set into motion, so you can be with your children."

She marches back up to Tom's room.

At four o'clock, the sky darkens. Heavy rain begins, driven by a strong wind out of the west. She stands at the window and watches the traffic on Kingshighway grind to a halt.

Before five, the evening shift starts arriving, the lay nurses shaking their umbrellas and removing galoshes. "What a mess out there," she hears someone exclaim. "Vehicles are stalling, ignitions shorting out."

"You said it," says someone else. "Whew! The water's so deep up between Lindell and Delmar that cars are getting stuck. Wooden paving blocks are floating up off of Pershing. They're crashing into car fenders and landing on running boards. It's a nightmare."

Kitty realizes she isn't going to get home for dinner. She finds a public phone to call Mary.

"We heard the World Series on the radio, Mother!" Mary says. "The radio! Even if our team did lose, it was so, so exciting."

"That's good, now can you settle down and put dinner on the table? The streets are flooded along Kingshighway. Flash floods like this go away fast, so I'll be there later on. Don't worry, okay?"

"We're fine, Mother!" With that, Mary hangs up.

The nurses are still gabbing about the storm as she passes their station on the way back to Tom.

In the doorway of Tom's small room, she sees that the bit of pink in his cheeks has drained away, that his chest is no longer rising and falling. She steadies herself against the doorway. He is gone.

"No!" She rushes to his side, flinging herself on the bed, throwing her arms and head across his chest, as if her tears will start his heart beating again. "Please don't leave me. Please!"

But the voice in her head says, *This is it, Catherine. It's your show from here on in.*

Who knows how much time passes before someone lays her hands on Kitty's shoulders and says, "Oh, honey! Let me call the chaplain for you!"

Kitty rises, shrugging off the comforting touch and putting her feet back on the floor. Rain is still pelting the window. Kitty takes the handkerchief from her pocket and dabs her face. "No chaplain," she says. "Just let Mr. Geraghty know. Geraghty. The undertaker. He has my instructions."

Kitty finds her way to the public phone again, glancing at the hall clock. It is 5:30 p.m. She calls Francis, who is still at his Easton store.

"It's over," she says, "He's gone."

"Oh, God," he says, taking a moment to absorb the news. "God help us. Are you—?"

"Everything is arranged. I just need to get home to the children."

"The storm—please don't drive in this storm," he says. "The police have been in and out of here, talking. That whole area, Kingshighway to Delmar, Delmar west to DeBaliviere, it's all flooded. When it looks clear to go, take a cab, okay?"

"I understand," she says mechanically.

"When the streets stop flooding, I'll pick up Mother and the girls. You shouldn't be alone tonight."

"No, don't. Please. I don't know how long I'll be and I don't want the children all upset tonight. Tomorrow, okay?"

She sits by the window in Tom's room, watching the whipping rain and traffic snarls, while the nuns and lay nurses take care of Tom. She refuses to be consoled by any of them. She just wants the rain to stop.

:: 124 ::

It is eight o'clock by the time she leaves the hospital. Cars are still stalled along Kingshighway. It doesn't take more than a few seconds at the cab stand to realize there won't be any taxis to get her home. She rounds the corner to the parking lot.

Relieved that her truck starts, she drives out the back of the lot, east to Taylor. Cautiously, she turns south on Taylor. The street is not flooded. She drives all the way to Manchester before she turns west, and all the way to McCausland before she turns north. Lights are on. People are out. The drive is slow, but she avoids the flooding.

It is after nine by the time she parks the Ford on Ridge. She unlocks the apartment door and climbs the long stairway. The place is dark except for the front room, where she sees Mary and Kathleen stretched out on the sofa under a blanket. She hears Duke Ellington music from the radio. Walking into the room, she's startled to see Ewald, chin to chest, dozing in a chair, then suddenly alert.

"Catherine!" He jumps to his feet.

"Ewald!" she says in a low voice. "I didn't expect—"

"I was closing up the store when the storm hit. I knew you were at the hospital, thought the kiddos might be scared, you know, if the lights went out or anything, so I came upstairs. Helped Mary warm up some corned beef and potatoes. Got the twins in bed." He looks at the sleeping girls. "I called over to Molly to see if they had any flooding. She told me… told me about Tom. Figured I better, you know, stay. In case you needed anything."

The moment hangs between them. The Ellington music continues.

"Can you shut that thing off?" she asks.

"Oh sure, sure!"

He rushes over to turn off the radio while Kitty picks up the sleeping Kathleen with a grunt.

"Let me get her for you!" he says.

"I got her. No need." She carries Kathleen down the hall, switches on the kitchen light, and takes the baby through to her crib.

As Kitty returns to the front room, Mary sits up and pulls the blanket around her. "We were worried about you, Mother."

"I'm fine, honey," Kitty says. "Off to bed with you." She follows Mary down the hall and they hug before Mary disappears into her room, pulling the pocket doors closed behind her.

Halfway down the hall, Ewald calls out. "Okay, then. I'll hit the road."

"Oh! Wait a minute." Kitty is surprised that she doesn't want to be alone. "Have a beer with me?"

Handing him a bottle of beer from the icebox, she also pulls out the platter of corned beef and a jar of horseradish. Ewald grabs a loaf of rye bread from the counter.

Kitty opens the bottle and pours it into two glasses.

They each make a sandwich and drink their beer in silence. Ewald starts to speak.

"I'm sorry—"

She raises her hand to stop him and shakes her head.

"But I want you to know—if you need anything—"

She shuts her eyes and shakes her head again. The horseradish is flooding her nose with its fumes. It feels good.

Ewald focuses on his plate, making another sandwich.

"How about a smoke?" she asks.

He nods and pulls a pack of Lucky Strikes from his shirt pocket. His matches are tucked inside the pack.

She lights up and inhales. She feels the burn in her throat and blows smoke rings up at the light. Tom hates it when she smokes. She finishes the cigarette and crushes it on her plate next to the half-eaten sandwich.

It's her game now. Her rules.

BOOK 4. KITTY RISES

Part 1. Back on Her Feet, 1926-1929

:: 125 ::

October, 1926. The beautiful vehicle that is Kitty's life has crashed. She has only one choice: to sharpen her focus and get the vehicle back on the road—back on the exact same road to the exact same destination as quickly as possible. It will stop her children's weeping and their anger at her for allowing this to happen. It will stop her in-laws from looking at her with their ashen faces. It will shut them up about God's will. It will stop friends from pitying her. It will stop the widows, young and old, nodding their understanding to her, with their doleful eyes, welcoming her to their club. It will stop the men—the bankers and lawyers, the wholesalers and priests, the Knights of Columbus fellows—it will stop them all from calling her "dear," stop them from handing her a lot of useless advice, and stop them from warning her of the perils of a "gal" trying to make decisions on her own.

Francis does not consult her about closing the stores on Monday and Tuesday—goes right ahead and tapes a sign in the windows about a "death in the family," allowing Geraghty's morticians to hang black wreaths on the doors. She planned to have Ewald keep the stores open, but now she is distracted by the worry of people coming to buy groceries for their World Series parties, finding Barrett's Market closed, and taking their business elsewhere, forever.

She wants to be annoyed with Francis for stepping in. But the brothers have worked together as partners, colleagues, and friendly competitors for twenty years. Francis is as stunned by Tom's disappearance as a brother could be. Sunday, Monday, Tuesday, he spends as much time as he can with her and the children. To the annoyance of his own four children, Kathleen is never out of his arms. He holds her as if she is the magical connection that will keep Tom alive in him.

Still, the stores are Kitty's business, *her* livelihood.

After the funeral on Tuesday, the Barretts, along with Pat and Delia Keville, all gather at the Rowan apartment to drink beer, to eat from the mountain of food brought by friends and neighbors, and to catch their collective breath before life moves on.

By late evening, all ten children are running wild through the apartment, high on cakes and cookies, banging on the piano, giggling, fighting, playing hide-and-seek.

The adults in the kitchen pay no attention to them. Kitty gets out tin foil, wax paper, and brown bags so that the mourners can take food home with them. She bustles around, scraping some dishes into the garbage pail and combining others.

"By the way, Francis," Kitty says, "I told Ewald that we're opening the stores tomorrow."

"Oh, my dear," Mother says, "surely you can afford to stay closed for the week. Don't your children need you?"

"They need to get back to school. They've been in and out, on and off since Tom went to the hospital. They need their routine back." She hears the flatness in her voice, the loss of her lilt. She'd like a cigarette.

Molly jumps in. "You have insurance, right? I know Tom was so careful about things. You shouldn't have to worry about the money for a while."

"It isn't the money," Kitty says, although she's not so sure. There are hospital bills already on her desk and getting the insurance money involves some kind of a rigmarole she barely understands. Yesterday, their lawyer pulled her aside to say that Tom's will has to go through probate. It will snarl up her cash flow.

She continues. "I have a position in the community. People know

Barrett's Market. They are used to getting what they need on the day they need it." She looks pointedly at Francis. "If something happened to Molly, how long would *you* keep your stores closed?"

Francis rears back in his chair. She could see the words forming in his eyes. *But I'm a man*, he wants to say. She tilts her head and waits for him to say something.

Molly pats her chest. "Oh my," she says. She wants to say, *what an unspeakable thought*, but she can't because Kitty is living that unspeakable thought.

The truth is that Kitty needs her community as much as they need her store. A small part of her is already looking forward to managing Tom's store on Easton, which has served the same customers since before she and Tom got married. Ewald can take care of the Rowan store till she gets the lay of the land.

Mary comes into the kitchen, throws her lanky arms around Kitty's waist, and lays her head on her mother's shoulder. Kitty rubs her back. Mary picks up Kitty's hand to look at the gold rings that had to be cut off Tom's fingers: the large wedding band and the Knights of Columbus ring, its design nearly worn away by nineteen years of wear.

"Frankie and Florrie want to come over tomorrow afternoon to listen to the baseball game with us, all right?"

"You're going back to school tomorrow," Kitty says, "and those boys have school too."

"What?" Mary pushes away, releasing Kitty's hand. "You're making me go back? *Tomorrow? Already?*"

Kitty pulls Mary back into her arms, hoping to avoid a scene in front of the family.

Mary lowers her voice. "Everybody's going to be looking at me and feeling sorry for me or not looking at me, not talking to me, like I have the plague or something."

"You'll hold your head high, my dear," Kitty says. "Your daddy wants you to go to a good high school, so you have to get back and keep your grades up, hear me?"

Mary lays her head back on Kitty's shoulder. "I guess so."

Kitty whispers in her ear. "A word to the wise is sufficient."

:: 126 ::

Kitty dresses carefully for her first day back. Black has been in fashion for several years now, so she has plenty of frocks to choose from, as well as the correct foundation garments for keeping her silhouette strong, for assuring the world that she is a prosperous and reliable businesswoman, no pity required.

Reminding the older children to stand tall and waving them off to school, Kitty drops Kathleen off with Ewald.

"You know I'd bring her with me," she says, as Kathleen toddles toward him with her arms extended, "but I have no idea what kind of mouse traps and rat poison lurk in the corners of that store. Mary will take her after school."

"Aw, she's my little buddy, aren't you, Kash?" He lifts her up to sit on the counter. "Did you show your mother how I taught you to wink?"

Kathleen scrunches her face and twists her fingers and arms in a comic effort to shut one eye but not the other. Kitty and Ewald both get a good laugh.

"All right, you jokers, I'm on my way," Kitty says.

Kitty arrives at the Easton store, eager to assess which routines need updating and which shelves need reorganizing. But the day is spent chatting with sympathetic customers and comforting the shellshocked butcher and clerks over the loss of their brilliant Mr. Barrett. Throughout these long days of public grieving, it's hard for Kitty not to choke up, but she has instructed herself that tears will be a secret between her and her pillow.

On this first day, this Wednesday after she buried the love of her life, the light of her soul, she arrives home to a silent apartment and a cold kitchen. Tossing the bag with cash and credit slips on the table, before she takes off her coat and hat, she pulls out some of the leftovers from yesterday, tosses them together in a Pyrex dish, and slides it into the oven.

Where is Tom?

Tallying the day's receipts, entering numbers into ledgers, sorting cash into pouches, while dinner cooks and children play, were all part of Kitty's life with her husband, a ritual with many variations, but forever the linchpin of their combined business and family life.

As she takes off her coat, looking out at the damp October evening, she wonders how she and the children will ever continue without Tom.

The back door opens and the twins clatter up the stairs, arguing.

"Rogers Hornsby is the greatest player ever," Bill insists, giving Kitty a quick hug around her waist then reversing course toward the living room. "We're going to turn on the radio, Mother! World Series is going into the ninth!"

Bobby hugs her too, but with a tug on her arm that scores him a kiss on the top of his head. Then he runs after Bill, yelling, "How can you say that when Babe Ruth already hit three out of the park?"

The door opens again. Mary runs up the stairs and into the kitchen. Hands on Kitty's shoulders, she pecks her cheek. "Ewald brought a radio into the store. We're listening to the game. I gotta get our radio tuned! We're getting trounced!"

As she pulls away, Kitty asks, "How did school go?"

"All right," Mary says, trotting down the hallway to the living room.

Next up the back stairs is Ewald, with Kathleen, climbing slowly, as the baby insists on scrambling up the stairs without help. When she works her way to the top, she follows the voices of her siblings toward the front room while Ewald pulls the expansion gate across the top to keep her from heading back down.

Looking fresh in his white shirt and tie, he plops the money pouch on the table. "Whatd'ya know, whatd'ya say," he says. "Let me get the machine." With an exaggerated grunt, he pulls out the adding machine from the shelf under the phone table. "Now for a little light on the subject." He turns the wall switch.

Her kitchen is suddenly bright with good cheer.

Ewald has been managing both stores and the daily accounting for nearly three weeks now.

"Gosh, E, I can't thank you enough for pitching in. But I'm back in the saddle again. I don't expect—your mother must be waiting dinner for you."

"Pop's never home till seven or eight, so we eat late. The two of us can get this done in no time." He pulls up a chair and zips open the pouch.

"In that case, let me get you a beer."

"Something I should have told you," he says as he slips on the rubber fingertip for counting bills. "When Tom went into the hospital, Pop pulled me aside about handling the money. Gave me some advice."

Ewald's father is the vice-president and assistant treasurer for Con P.

Curran Printing Company, a company he helped his brother build from scratch, now the dominant printing enterprise in St. Louis—a man whose advice is worth hearing.

"I'm listening," she says.

"He told me to stop making bank deposits till Tom was back on his feet, in case, you know." Ewald looks down at his glass of beer. "Creditors can make a fuss if they get spooked. And they don't always want to deal with a gal, no disrespect." He takes a drink. "Um, anyway, there's three weeks' worth of cash in the safe, plus the rents from Williams's shop and the two apartments."

Kitty's first reaction is an enormous wave of relief. Things have indeed gotten complicated and it hadn't occurred to her to start hanging on to the cash. But then she feels a slight slip of control, which makes her sit straight in her chair. "I wish you would have told me that."

He nods. "I should have. You're right. I should have."

:: 127 ::

A new ritual is born. Every day, Kitty and Ewald split a bottle of beer and gab about customers as the receipts get tallied and recorded and as Mary is instructed on dinner preparations.

One evening, while Kitty is relating a juicy bit of gossip, Ewald has one eye on the baby, who is standing in the hallway studying the latch on the expansion gate.

The gate pops open and Kathleen disappears downs the steps.

"Hey!" Ewald is on his feet. She is two steps down the stairs hanging precariously onto the banister. Ewald swoops her into his arms and sits back at the table. Bellowing, she squirms out of his lap and runs off to her brothers' room.

Kitty laughs. "She loves playing on those steps. I might as well throw away that gate."

"It needs a better latch—"

"Oh Jesus, she'll just figure out how to climb over it and really take a tumble."

"I've been meaning to talk to you about her. She doesn't sit still. All day long, she's pulling cans off shelves and climbing into the cookie bins. It isn't safe. I was thinking—"

"All right, I'll take her up to Easton with me, but I was hoping Mary would watch her here after school during the busy afternoon hours. Hasn't she—?"

"Oh, Mary's a good kid," Ewald says. "But I'm thinking my mother could watch Kathleen during the day. She's raised twelve children and now she has thirteen grandchildren who are in and out all the time. She'd love having baby Kathleen to watch over."

Kitty finishes punching in her numbers on the adding machine and wraps a pack of bills with a rubber band. She feels her jaw tighten.

"Don't you think I can take care of my own children?"

Saying nothing, Ewald slides a stack of quarters into a paper sleeve and folds down the end.

Kitty stands up and goes to sink, making a big production of scrubbing her hands after all the money handling. Her eyes are filled with tears.

Bill walks into the kitchen. She can see his reflection in the darkened window, tall and fair, like Tom, and at age seven, as serious and as smart.

"Find any good ones, E?" he asks.

"Look at this," Ewald says, and flips a coin into the air for Bill to catch. "A 1917 Indian head nickel. All yours."

"Wow! I need this one. You remembered!" Bill whoops and runs to his room with the coin. Tom got Bill started on coin collecting last Christmas, with kits for pennies and nickels.

Feeling a wave of emotion, Kitty turns her attention to the glassware piled up in the sink. Will the children ever learn to wash a damn glass?

"Catherine."

She grabs a dish towel to dry her hands and hastily swipes it across her eyes. She turns. "What?"

Ewald's blue eyes are serious. "I don't know much, but… but I think you have to let people help you."

:: 128 ::

Bridget Delaney Curran quickly becomes Kathleen's second grandmother. Five days a week, Mary walks her across Ridge Avenue, through a couple of yards, then across Romaine Place to the busy Curran household. The nine-room brick house is still home to five of the Curran sons, from thirteen-year-old Delaney to the thirty-eight-year-old widower John, although Doug and Wes are planning to be married before the end of the year. John's son Johnnie lives there as well, a couple years ahead of the twins at St. Barbara's. Two daughters, Ella and Catherine, as well as Bridget's unmarried sister Katie complete the roster—nine adults and two youngsters. With everyone now at work or school during the day, Mrs. Curran is delighted to have friendly little Kathleen to keep her company.

On Saturdays, it's Mary's job to watch Kathleen.

Kitty's life falls into a rhythm. Chaotic mornings getting the children up and out. Busy days at the Easton store. Speeding through the daily receipts with Ewald at the kitchen table, sharing a beer, against the backdrop of children playing and Mary's dramatic suffering at having to turn the heat up on whatever pot of stew or casserole Kitty has devised from the store's unsellable meat and produce.

Ewald is good for an adult conversation, often about local politics, including how the Democrats are recruiting his father to run for President of the Board of Aldermen against the Republican stronghold. By summer, they are talking about Charles Lindbergh and the "Spirit of St. Louis" flight across the Atlantic, the future of airmail, and the development of dirigibles.

When Ewald dashes off for dinner with his family, the Barrett children gather around the table to eat Kitty's concoctions and tell her about their day. Kitty begins to notice that her ears are not catching all of their sweet young voices, so she makes the children sit up straight and speak with voices loud and clear.

After dinner, Kitty misses Tom the most. No strong hands to massage her shoulders. No leisurely talks about the children. No strategizing about their future. No dreaming together. She sits alone at her desk near the front stairway, with order forms and account books.

Her life, her children's lives, her business—everything is hers alone to manage. She's like one of those circus performers who spins plates on top of sticks, dashing from one to the other focused on keeping her act flawless, no time to think about whether the act needs to change. Plate wobbling? Move faster, move smarter.

Ewald is the perfect employee, a jack-of-all-trades, good at spinning plates. He keeps the equipment humming. He entertains customers. He warns her about items that aren't selling and items that run out too quickly. He keeps a few chickens in the coop out back for the butcher. Ewald is the master of *today*, feet and hands always in motion, never dropping a spinning plate.

But as the months go by, who she really needs is Tom. He could mentally step back from the spinning plates and modify the act. He saw the big picture. He was master of the long view, which is where Kitty is now stuck.

Her children think she is nuts, but the only way she can work through the numbers is by talking out loud, as if Tom were sitting next to her.

"Our two residential tenants on Easton are good. Williams in the commercial space at 4867 is doing okay with his auto repair shop, selling used cars now, paying his rent on time. But the Easton store doesn't measure up to the Rowan store. Why is that? Prices are good. Customers are there, but just not buying as much."

Is it just the smaller floor space, less variety? She thinks about the neighborhoods. "Easton is mostly Irish. Men in the trades. Is construction slowing down? Am I missing something in the news?" The Rowan store is in an Irish neighborhood too, with a smattering of Italians and Germans, but economically better off. There is a conservative synagogue down the street, so Rowan is lined with families of Russian Jews, who buy their meat from a kosher butcher, but get the rest of their *Pareve*-labeled products from her.

"What don't I know that you would?" she asks Tom.

In the dark, all she can do is try an experiment. She labors over the figures to see how much they cleared from the Easton store for the past twelve months. Feeling bold, she puts an ad in the paper to lease the space for twice what the store's profit was. She informs Francis, half-hoping he'll tell her she's crazy. But Francis is preoccupied with refurbishing his Semple Avenue home to make room for a fifth child at the end of August. He doesn't say much more than good luck.

Much to her surprise, she gets several offers and awards the lease to a small publisher of psychology books, who can wait a couple months for her to sell off her inventory and say goodbye to her dear customers.

Just like that, she will be down to a single store and making more money.

"What are you going to do with the fixtures?" Ewald asks. "There's a nice counter there and some of those small shelving units you can't buy these days."

Kitty starts to say she'll put an ad in the paper, but gets an idea.

The building at Rowan and Ridge originally had two storefronts, one on the corner and one along the Ridge side. When the Barretts moved in, Tom used as much space as he could for the grocery store, installing a large walk-in meat locker that reduced the second storefront to the size of a postage stamp. Kitty always thought the petite storefront could be used as commercial space, but Tom had bigger fish to fry. It remained a junk room with whitewashed windows.

Now it called her name.

"What if we took that good old counter and a couple of shelving units and turned the Ridge Avenue storefront into, what? A little confectionery?"

"Now you're cookin'!" Ewald says. "We can bring over a refrigerator and that small ice cream freezer."

She rents the space to brothers, George and Tom Sylvia, who open their new confectionery after school and on weekends, to the delight of the neighborhood children, who stop by with their pennies for sweet treats.

Her success in reshaping the course of business to her own liking makes the first anniversary of Tom's death a shade easier to endure. She can feel sad. She can curse the empty space that Tom's love once filled. She can feel angry at God and Dr. Murphy for depriving her and her children of a good man. But she does not feel helpless. She does not have to depend on anyone but herself.

:: 129 ::

Kitty plans a celebration to bring 1927 to a close. Her business is thriving on Rowan. Fourteen-year-old Mary started high school at St. Joseph's Academy for Girls. Eight-year-old Bobby is winning praise at school for his musical talent, while Bill maintains his good health. And Kathleen is a charmer. No more gloom.

The big party is scheduled for Christmas Eve, a Saturday. Mary has been practicing carols on the piano so they can have a sing-a-long. Bobby brings his flute home from school and quickly learns to play along. Kitty sings with them from the kitchen, where she squeezes in some cookie-making between her orders and her bill-paying.

But Molly calls on Friday to say that her older children brought a bug home from school and everyone is sick. No parties for them.

Christmas Eve is quieter without Francis's brood. The Kevilles come by, of course, along with Mother, Mamie, Katie, and Katie's beau, Chas Dyer, who adds his baritone voice to Uncle Pat's tenor.

On Christmas Day, Kitty rests. The children have their own open house as friends from the neighborhood duck out of their family celebrations to play board games and make music with the Barretts.

:: 130 ::

On the following Friday, December 30, Ewald shows up at the store looking worried.

"I stopped by Molly's last night and Dr. Dougherty was there for Jack. Poor kid was screaming in pain."

Kitty feels a jab of empathy in her belly. John Joseph was Molly's and Francis's fourth child, a year older than Kathleen and just about to turn four.

"How terrible. And I'm bad—haven't called her at all this week. What's going on?"

"I guess they've all had strep throat. Looks like his settled in the kidneys. The doc gave him some painkiller and sedated him so he could sleep, but Molly's a wreck. Sat in the rocking chair with him all evening."

Kitty remembers the terrible Christmas when Bill got pneumonia. Nothing in the world mattered but that sick child.

"I can't imagine anything worse," Kitty says with a sigh.

But there is worse.

Mamie calls Kitty the next afternoon to give her the news—Jack Barrett is dead. "We're heading over there. Molly's hysterical. Francis is near collapse. The children…"

"I'll meet you there," Kitty says, her heart thumping with disbelief. She sits for a moment at the telephone table to collect herself, then gives Mary a shout. "Uncle Francis has an emergency. I need to go over there. Might be a while. You can stay up till midnight with the radio on, but stay indoors, you hear?"

Kitty races to her bedroom to get dressed. The store closed at noon for

New Year's Eve. It's been snowing all day and she was prepared to spend the evening curled up with the latest Agatha Christie.

Mary follows her to the bedroom, watching Kitty curse as she searches for her snow boots in the back of the closet.

"Who died?" Mary teases.

Kitty stops her hunt and glares at Mary. "Your cousin Jack, that's who."

Mary stares open-mouthed. "No! My little Jackie? Really?"

Kitty nods. "A strep infection. Settled in his kidneys."

Mary sits on the bed, staring at the floor, then murmurs, "Just like Uncle Johnny."

Kitty finds her boots and is pulling on her woolen stockings. "What are you talking about?"

"Three older kids, two boys and a girl, bring home strep from school. They pass it to their three-year-old brother John. And he dies. That's *Daddy's* family. The pattern is repeating itself. The baby will die next."

Kitty feels a chill on her arms and snaps at Mary. "Who's filling your head with that kind of nonsense?"

"Granny told me about Uncle Johnny and Uncle Martin. Granny told me to look for patterns, like Grandpa Barrett dying in his forties with two boys and two girls and then his son, our daddy, dying in his forties with two boys and two girls. She says I should always pay attention to signs and omens."

Jesus, Mary, and Joseph, Kitty thinks, as she wiggles into her corset and slips into a long tube of a dress. "Granny is from the Old Country, sugar, where they have lots of superstitions. We live in twentieth-century America. We don't read into things like that. We don't listen to oracles."

"How about the Gypsies? They make a lot of money telling fortunes in their little shops along Easton," Mary says.

Kitty runs a brush through her short hair. "I better not catch you going to one."

Mary stares out the window at the light snow drifting past the street lamps. "Still," she says softly, "little Jack is dead. That's really sad."

Kitty bundles up and heads down the long stairs. With taxis already jammed up for hours, she's dreading the mile-and-a-half drive through snow-clogged streets. But when she opens the front door, who does she see but Ewald, hand poised to ring the bell.

“E!”

“Thought you’d be heading over,” he says, pulling his collar up against the wind. “I’ll drive.”

Mr. Curran and Ewald’s brother Delaney are hovering on the Barretts’ front porch smoking cigarettes. The hearse is pulling away from the curb into the night. A priest exits the house and shakes Mr. Curran’s hand before he rushes down to the sidewalk.

Inside, Mrs. Curran and the sisters Ellie and Catherine are focused on Molly. Despite their reminders about her other children and their consolations about God’s plans, she is, of course, devastated and unable to stop weeping.

Mother, Mamie, and Katie arrive within minutes. Mamie and Katie sit on the sofa at Francis’s side, giving him whiskey to sip and rubbing his back.

The children Frankie, Florrie, and little Ella Rose are in shock, not knowing what to make of their family’s sudden disintegration. Ewald jumps in. He sits his niece and nephews in the kitchen, asking them about school and ice-skating in the park, letting them talk about Jack when they want. He puts bread and ham and mustard on the table. He has a knack with them. His voice makes the world feel normal.

Kitty is left watching over Mother, who is reliving the deaths of her own small children. She echoes Mary’s “pattern” finding.

“John and John Joseph, John and John Joseph. Oh, and the children sick all week with scarlatina. Where is the baby, Kitty? Where is little Delaney James? Oh thank God they didn’t name him Martin.” She pats Kitty’s arm. “Bring him to me, honey, will you?”

While Kitty heats up a bottle of formula, Mother rocks the five-month-old. Then she asks Kitty to dig out the rosary from her purse, so she can pray to the Blessed Mother for mercy on the baby and not take him before his time. Then she prays another rosary for the soul of John Joseph and for all the dearly departed members of their family.

By midnight, the four children are asleep, with aunts Katie and Mamie snugged in beside little Ella Rose. Molly, sedated into sleep, is sprawled on her bed, her two sleeping sisters by her side. Francis and Mother are snoring in their chairs, with their chins dropped to their chests. The others have gone home.

Ewald dims the lights and finds Kitty's coat. They drive through the lights and parties along Easton Avenue, not saying much of anything. The snow has stopped falling but a bitter wind blows it into swirling drifts across their path.

As they pull up in front of the Rowan building, Kitty asks, "How about having a beer with me?"

At the top of the stairs, Mary rushes down the hallway to greet them and asks how her cousins are.

"Very sad, sweetie, very sad."

In the kitchen, Kitty pulls out a bottle of beer from the icebox.

"Can I have some?" Mary asks.

Kitty pours a couple of ounces into a jelly jar for her.

"You were good with your sister's children," Kitty says to Ewald.

He nods. "Being near the tail end of a big family, there's always somebody having a hard time, who can't decide whether they want to laugh or cry." He pulls out his Lucky Strikes and offers one to Kitty. "None for you, young lady," he says to Mary. "You don't want your teeth turning yellow before you're sixteen."

"Did the twins stay up till midnight?" Kitty asks.

"Yes, we listened to dance music on KMOX. Kathleen did too," says Mary. "But, Mother, we missed you. It's the first year we didn't sing 'Auld Lang Syne' together. Can we sing it now?"

"We'll wake the baby," Kitty says, nodding toward Kathleen's crib in the next room.

Ewald says, "Yeah, I missed singing it with my family too. What do you say we sing it very, very soft? How about that?"

Kitty laughs and starts them out. "Should auld acquaintance be forgot…"

They sing barely above a whisper till they lose track of the words and Mary clinks her glass against the other two. "Out with the old, in with the new! Happy 1928!"

:: 131 ::

1928 speeds by and dissolves into 1929. Kitty gets used to being described as a widow and hits her stride as a businesswoman in a man's world.

The probate process reveals Tom had invested in several undeveloped properties in other parts of the city, speculating on St. Louis's continuing growth. Her lawyer advises that hanging onto the properties for a few years might double her money.

But Kitty doesn't want the mental clutter, the liability, one more thing to keep her awake at night. Deciding to keep the Rowan building and the pair of rental properties on Easton, she instructs the attorney to dump everything else. She put the proceeds toward reducing her mortgages.

Running a retail grocery business is complex enough. The property and all its equipment need to be maintained. It has to be safe, hygienic, and attractive at all times. Inventories, arriving from multiple supply chains, have to be managed, with multiple salesmen vying for shelf space. Beech-Nut, Procter & Gamble, Coca-Cola, Kellogg's, and Kraft are all after her business and she has to know what her customers will buy.

Tom Barrett was an early adopter of shops that combined dry goods with meat and produce. Meat, eggs, and dairy must come from approved sources and be stored under exacting conditions. Lettuce can't wilt. Tomatoes can't go mushy. Potatoes can't sprout. Cans can't be dented. Every variety of pest must be defended against, from rats to weevils, from flies to ants, from the ubiquitous cockroach to the occasional tarantula that drops out of a hanging bunch of Honduran bananas.

The Rowan shop was the first of Tom's stores intentionally designed for self-service. Instead of the shopper presenting her list to a clerk who picks merchandise off high shelves with ladders and long-handled grippers, shoppers pass through a turnstile and fill their baskets with whatever they please. Pilferage was a worry but turned out to be less of a problem than anyone guessed.

The upshot is that, once Kitty moves her workday back to the Rowan store, she doesn't need much help. Her butcher works full-time six days a week and doesn't mind doing occasional check-outs. Kitty can't carve a side of beef into roasts and steaks, but in a pinch, she can hack apart a bird carcass, grind hamburger, or slice ham. Mary is learning to work the cash register, enjoys arranging produce in pretty displays, cleans fingerprints off the door glass, and can be cajoled into sweeping.

The odd man out is Ewald. Even with collecting rents, looking after the property on Easton, and raising a few chickens, his hours shrink.

"It isn't fair just using you as a handyman," she says to him one evening after work. He still pops upstairs for a beer at the end of the day, even though Kitty's receipt-tally procedure is half what it used to be. "You deserve a real job."

Ewald takes a swig of his drink. "My Pop's been nagging at me about the same thing. Says I'll never be able to support a family working for… you know…"

Kitty bristles. "A woman?"

"No!" Ewald's cheeks turn pink. "No. Working for a small retail business—"

"One that has shrunk from three stores to one? Less a *brothers'* enterprise, more of a *widow's* project?"

"Aw, Catherine, you're the one who's telling me I *deserve a real job.* And Pop's leaning on me to be a printer, even if it's not for Uncle Con. My brother Harry runs a big web press in Chicago. Florrie works a Linotype for the newspaper. It's good money, with a strong union. It's not about you."

Kitty pushes away from the table and stands. She takes off her store apron and scrubs her hands at the sink. Picking up a towel, she says, "Bill is going to miss you finding pennies and nickels for his collection."

Ewald chuckles. "Maybe he better start rolling coins and finding them himself. Anyway, I won't go far. I'll check out the Easton property on Saturdays and collect the rent there for you. Do any repairs you need."

"I can afford that," Kitty says.

He waves it off. "No charge. I got nothing else to do. You're family."

:: 132 ::

On Thursday, October 24, 1929, Kitty sees a story in the evening paper about a big stock selloff on Wall Street. She owns no stock, so moves on to the stories about a ferry wreck at Milwaukee and the death of a lone flyer over the Atlantic—a Montana cattleman copying Lindbergh.

She goes on to scan the sales for winter coats. Mary's sixteenth birthday is coming up and wouldn't she just love one of those stylish long coats with the plush fur collars.

On Tuesday, October 29, the headlines are again about stocks, but, look, Vandervoort's is having an anniversary sale on fur-collared coats. She picks out one with a curly caracul collar, making a note to have one in Mary's size sent over.

During a break in Kitty's Friday night bridge game, a couple of the women talk quietly in the kitchen about withdrawing their money from the bank, their husbands worried something deep is rattling the economy. Since Tom's death and the ordeal of probate, Kitty has always maintained enough cash in her safe to tide her over for a month or two. She checks with Ewald the next time he stops by.

"I have savings in Union-Easton, not much but—"

"Pop and Uncle Con moved their accounts to a federal bank," Ewald says. "The family had some dough at Union-Easton, but Pop doesn't like the president, that guy Blase. Rumor has it he's been siphoning funds to shore up a second bank that does a high-risk business in second and third mortgages. Pop says all the local banks are way over-extended."

That's all Kitty needs to hear. She takes her money out and goes all-cash.

Within a few weeks, she notices that tough chunks of stew meat are selling faster than usual. The butcher is grinding up unsold roasts with crackers for hamburger. A few regulars stop buying meat altogether and ask for the butcher's trimmings to flavor their beans.

Throughout the neighborhood, family breadwinners are losing their jobs. A surprising number of families lose their houses. Those who can't double up with brothers or cousins begin clustering on public land along the river. As winter sets in, men who helped build the mansions on Portland Place are piecing together shacks from crate wood, sheet metal scraps, and canvas. Women are quickly learning how to set up communal kitchens.

Some families, like the Currans, are unaffected. Their cash is Kitty's lifeblood. Others ask for credit extensions. A few women who raise chickens offer Kitty fresh eggs in exchange for flour and oatmeal.

Kitty adjusts. Their fortune is her fortune.

Her tenants Tom and George Sylvia close their confectionery business, as no one has spare change for candy. Kitty rents the space to a German neighbor, Maizie Braun, who stocks it with notions—needles, thread, straight pins, ribbon, and other sundries women need quickly and in small amounts.

Joe and Bessie Fishman, who operate their little Psychology Press out of 4865 Easton, go broke as colleges and libraries stop buying books. Their business closes and Kitty forgives their deposit. The only tenant she can find to fill the vacancy wants to install a pool hall.

“What do you think,” Kitty says to Ewald when he stops by with rent money from Williams’s auto repair. “The only offer I have for 4865 comes from a fellow who wants to open a pool hall.”

Ewald raises an eyebrow. “Gambling.”

“That’s what I’m worried about. Gambling and gangsters.”

“How about if I check around, see if they have a reputation?”

“Yes,” she says. “Check with your police friends too.”

Ewald wastes no time getting back to her. The prospective tenant has kept his nose clean., Relying on Ewald’s promise to keep tabs on the place, Kitty moves ahead with the rental.

March 29, 1930. The front-page banner of the Saturday *Star* blares: “UNION-EASTON TRUST CO. CLOSES DOORS.” Accounts of 6,000 depositors are frozen, as Missouri orders the bank directors to come up with the money to cover bad debts. Thankful she got her money out in time, Kitty also faces the fact that many of those 6,000 families are her customers. All anyone can talk about is money.

Kitty stays focused. She uses her cash to upgrade the furnishings in the apartment, buying from neighbors who need cash more than their oak and cherry bedroom suite or their pecan dining room set or their cane and walnut living room furniture. Her cash helps save homes, helps keep her customers in the neighborhood and buying groceries.

The Great War and the pandemic taught her a lot about managing through food shortages and rollercoaster prices. Now, alone, she keeps the store stocked, with no waste. What cast-off vegetables and stale bread her children can’t eat get transported to Hooverville, what people are calling the mile-long community of shacks along the Mississippi near the free bridge.

This becomes Mary’s job. Ewald teaches her to drive, but to earn weekend driving privileges, every day after school she takes crates of food downtown to Fourth and Chouteau, to the Welcome Inn, a makeshift soup kitchen and food pantry staffed by volunteers and Hooverville residents.

One snowy afternoon, as Mary buttons her long coat with the curly caracul collar, she complains. “Lugging these crates into that so-called inn is making my coat smell like cabbage.”

Kitty is sharp with her. “You need to carry your weight, young lady. You need to see how those people are getting by and thank God you have a roof over your head and a coat to pull tight against the cold."

:: 133 ::

On November 11, 1930, thirty-four-year-old Katie Barrett is wed to her longtime beau Chas Dyer. Everyone is thrilled for her. Chas owns a furniture business now and has so far weathered the economic tumult. Her sister Mamie is enthusiastic about fighting off the hard times with love. At forty-five, she has also found a suitor, Mickey Coleman.

Kitty isn't so sure about the "love conquers all" perspective. Both Mamie and Mickey support widowed mothers. There will be no marriage till one of the mothers is in her grave. Mamie claims that a man devoted to his mother is a sign of his kindness. Kitty isn't so sure. Chas Dyer also supports his widowed mother. What marriage means for Katie is giving up her stenography career to keep house for Chas and the ailing old woman.

"Nothing would make me happier," Mamie tells Kitty at Thanksgiving, "than to see you find love again. And I know Tom is looking down on you feeling the same."

And so, when the Barretts hold a Christmas open house, Mamie introduces Kitty to Dennis Pedrotti.

Pedrotti is a widower with four children.

With him is his sister-in-law Ella Timlin, one of the Barretts' country cousins, a spinster about Kitty's age. When her sister Mary Jane—Pedrotti's wife—died of heart trouble in '29, Ella moved in to help with the children. As the rural farm economy crashed, the grieving family picked up stakes and moved to St. Rita's parish in Vinita Park, just outside the city.

It's clear that Ella is wholeheartedly committed to the Pedrotti children. She can't talk enough about their talents and accomplishments. But Kitty can tell a mile away that Mamie wants to fix her—Kitty—up with Dennis, entertaining some fool notion about amalgamating the Barrett cousins into combined family. Mamie means well, but didn't she listen to Kitty's tales of the disastrous attempt by her father to do the same for the Flanagan cousins?

How would that even work? Kitty owns property, runs a business. Pedrotti is a carpenter. How long it will be before he's jobless? Then what? Would a husband get to claim half of her business? Does he have any aptitude as a partner? Would she wind up supporting eight children rampaging through her well-outfitted flat above her well-run store?

No, thank you.

Kitty is forty now, and as she diligently touches up her gray hairs, the only man she longs for is Tom Barrett.

But now she has to ask herself: if Tom Barrett appeared magically in her bedroom tonight, would he find the same woman he left behind? Together, Tom and Kitty operated like one of the fine-tuned multi-purpose woodwork machines her father adored. Tom and Kitty ran their family and their business with routines and schedules, making fine adjustments on a daily basis. There was a time and a place for everything.

Now, in four short years, everything is an improvisation, with a little theatrics thrown in. She has allowed herself to grow stout, so that the world sees a well-fed woman in command. She trades groceries for second-hand furs, eye-catching costume jewelry, and hats she can update with a little netting or new hatband. But she's careful not to appear too prosperous. She doesn't want anyone to think they don't need to pay their bills, even though too many already know they can cut a deal with her.

She directs a chaotic system of arrangements with shoppers, vendors, and tenants. Every morning she wakes up calculating who she needs to pay and who she needs to collect from. Sometimes she profits, sometimes she sacrifices. In the long run, the fewer neighbors who are hungry and homeless, the better the lives of her children will be. That is her form of strategic thinking.

Tom dabbled in the idea of socialism as a form of government. Kitty lives it—if her neighbors can't afford groceries, she is out of business. If her tenants can't pay rent and her Easton building is abandoned for back taxes and unpaid utility bills, it will become an eyesore and drive more people and businesses out to University City and Wellston. She likes the city. She needs to stay in business. But she can only do it in her own style.

It chills her to think she has moved beyond her beloved Tom. But her pile of ledgers and her four healthy children tell her it's working out.

Part 2. Course Corrections, 1931-1933

:: 134 ::

As the economy continues to worsen and the spring of 1931 rolls around, Mary decides she's had enough of school.

"I'm bored," she claims, sitting at the kitchen table chopping scallions. "The girls there are all idiots with rich daddies."

"Mary Margaret! Your father wanted you to go to college. Don't you want to go to Fontbonne? With your good grades, maybe they'll let you start early. We could talk to the nuns—"

"Puh-leeze." Mary rolls her eyes. "Last thing I need is those old biddies on my case. The girls are bad, but I really hate the nuns."

Dumping a pot of red potatoes into a colander at the sink, Kitty says, "Don't be sacrilegious." But she doesn't care much for the nuns either. Only a few months ago, she read the riot act to the principal at St. Barbara's. Kathleen, one of the youngest children in her second-grade class, had asked to be excused to the bathroom. Her teacher said *no* and Kathleen wound up peeing in her pants at her desk. Banished from the classroom, Kathleen walked home through a winter rain in wet pants, sobbing. Kitty consoled her baby as she got her cleaned up and settled with a jigsaw puzzle. Then, she marched up to the school and chewed out the principal for allowing such cruelty. The nun was huffy about it, insisting that children must learn self-control.

Kitty might have pulled her children out of St. Barbara's, and sent them to Hempstead, but yanking her sixth-grade twins away from their friends felt wrong. And she knew that her papa regretted that Mama and he had turned away from parochial schools in the heat of anger.

With lots of coaxing, her embarrassed little girl returned to school. "You're as good as the best and better than the rest," Kitty kept telling her. "Don't you forget."

Kitty lifts the colander out of the sink and sets the steaming potatoes on the table for Mary to peel.

"Can't I help you in the store?" Mary persists. "The world is a flaming mess. People are starving and I have to learn trigonometry and medieval history? Where the heck is that going to get me?"

"You'll finish the year. Over the summer, if you show me how you can work full-time in the store and share housework responsibilities, I'll consider you an adult and you won't have to go back in the fall."

"Woohoo," Mary shouts. "I promise, I promise!"

Kitty shakes her head. Tom is turning over in his grave, she thinks.

:: 135 ::

Sunday, May 3. Kitty's day of rest. She hears the children get up and dress for Mass. The twins are altar boys for today's nine o'clock Mass. She hears them run down the steps early.

In the next room, Mary brushes Kathleen's hair.

"Stand still. It's full of knots."

"Ow! I want you to pin it up like you did yesterday."

"Oh, all right, but that's so old-fashioned. You should get your hair bobbed, with a Marcel permanent like I have. Hand me those hairpins. Stand still."

"I can't jump rope," Kathleen says. "Will you teach me how? Bill says I'm too fat to jump."

"That's a silly thing to say, as if skinny old Bill could jump," Mary says. "You just have to get the rhythm of it, that's all. Remember what Mother always says: 'You're as good as the best and better than the rest.' Don't forget."

Kitty smiles and turns her pillow over for another hour's sleep. She'll go to eleven o'clock Mass. She'll wear the silk print with the chiffon ruffle along the neckline—perfect for May. She thinks of Tom, the ghost who inhabits her bed. He'd frown at her vivid pinks and greens. He'd be quick to say that widows were supposed to wear black or navy or brown, but Kitty would point out that times have changed and that women can't live looking backward. Today's woman is too busy for that.

Later, after Mass, she parks the car on Ridge and sees that the cellar doors are open. The boys have only recently figured out the trick of getting the heavy steel plates lifted from the sidewalk and locked open. The basement is cool and has a smooth earthen floor, good for roller skating and other games. She grabs the railing and descends a couple of steps. The sunlight blinds her from seeing into the dark cellar. She smells gasoline.

"Billy, Bobby, you down there? What are you up to?"

"Nothing," comes the answer.

"Where are your sisters?"

"Kash is with us. Mary went across the street to talk to the boys."

"I want you outside. It's a beautiful day."

"Okay."

Kitty rounds the store and enters the apartment, thinking about the pot of stew meat on the back of the stove. It needs to cook for another couple of hours to get it tender enough for the children to eat. She heads straight for the kitchen, pulls the pot to a front burner, checks the water level, switches on the gas, then goes back down the hall to change her clothes. She hears the front door open and Kathleen's voice singing as she runs up the stairs. Kitty drops her hat in its box and pauses to listen.

"Wish I could shimmy like my sister Kate," her baby is singing in a loud voice as she passes the bedroom door, trotting toward the kitchen. Kitty hears a kitchen chair scrape along the floor and is about to shout *what are you doing?* when she hears Kathleen scream.

In an instant that lasts a hundred years, Kitty flies into the kitchen. Flames! Kathleen's face is twisted in pain and terror. The side of her long-sleeved dress is on fire.

Kitty lunges.

As she sweeps the six-year-old into her arms, her mind reels back to a frigid January morning. Farlin Street house on fire. Papa yelling to her *Blankets! Suffocate it! Smother it!*

With two steps into the girls' bedroom, Kitty drops her screaming child on a throw rug and rolls her up in it. The fire is out.

Kathleen's screams turn into weeping. "I'm sorry, Mama," she keeps repeating between the sobs and the moans of pain.

Kitty is sprawled over her child, shaking, unable to find her voice to scream for help. All she sees is Kathleen's beautiful face, hair pinned up and away from danger, perfect and undamaged, and she knows everything will be all right… if she can just…

She hears the boys pounding up the front steps, rushing toward the screams. She sees their shocked faces.

“Everything’s going to be okay,” she hears herself say in a trembling voice. “Kathleen’s been burned, but everything’s going to be fine. Bobby, go find Mary.” Bobby turns and disappears down the hall. From the jumble of her brain, she lines up more words to say, “Bill, turn off the stove, please.”

With her baby still crying and shuddering, Kitty rises up on her knees, her mind racing to what next.

The gas flame switched off, Bill says, “Ambulance? I’ll call an ambulance?”

“Wait.” She gently eases Kathleen from her carpet cocoon. The left side of her baby’s dress is burned away, as well as the underside of her sleeve. Her skin beneath, along her sweet baby’s side and inner arm, is seared black. Kitty fights off a wave of nausea. She turns to Bill, who is staring wide-eyed at the burns.

“Get Dr. McLarty.” She makes her voice loud to reassure everyone, including herself that she knows what she’s doing. “His number is in my address book there. Tell his answering service it’s an emergency.”

It is a long afternoon as Dr. McLarty eases Kathleen’s shock and pain with laudanum, picks burnt rayon from her wounds, applies compresses of linseed oil and lime water, and instructs Kitty about Kathleen’s care, which will require weeks of quiet healing in bed.

Finally, drying his hands at the kitchen sink, he asks, “Mrs. Barrett, how are you doing? Do you have any burns?” His eyes glance pointedly at the bodice of her dress.

She looks down. The embrace of her flaming child burned away the ruffles, revealing her ivory slip below.

“Mother of God!” She folds her arms to cover herself.

He smiles and nods. “Kathleen will sleep through the night. You need to take care of yourself now. The days ahead won’t be easy.”

With the doctor gone, she pours herself a glass of beer and sits at the kitchen table facing the bed where Kathleen sleeps. She’ll change her dress in a minute. Mary and the boys hover.

She takes a drink of her beer and says, “How about running down to the store and bringing up some ice cream? We might just have ice cream for dinner. And pull the phone over here.”

After stretching the phone’s long cord to the table, Mary puts a hand on each boy’s shoulder and all three disappear down the back stairs.

Kitty picks up the phone to call Francis but decides she doesn't want to get Molly ruffled up with memories of Jack. She starts to dial Mamie's number, but dials the Curran house instead, and asks for Ewald.

"What d'ya know," he answers.

"How about coming over," she says.

"Be there in five."

:: 136 ::

It takes a couple of days for Kathleen to emerge from her drug-induced sleep and to get past mewling about pain and discomfort.

On Wednesday, after the daily ordeal of bathing the burns in Carron oil liniment—lime water and linseed oil—and applying clean dressings, she treats Kathleen to a bowl of chocolate pudding. Kitty can finally quiz her about the fire.

"Now I want you to tell me what happened. Why in the world were you up on a chair at the stove?"

Kathleen starts crying.

"You have to talk to me, sugar. It will make you feel better. Crying doesn't make the pain go away."

Kathleen stammers over the words, confessing that she was reaching over the burners to get a box of matches from the shelf above.

"What for?"

"Bobby and Bill were playing a game down in the basement. They had gasoline." She gulps back her tears. "They made trails, then set them on fire. It was really neat."

"Jesus, Mary, and Joseph," Kitty mutters. "Go on."

"They ran out of matches," Kathleen says. "They said they were going outside to play marbles. But…" Her face dissolves into tears again. "But I liked the fire. I wanted to get more matches so we could keep playing. I'm sorry, Mama."

Kitty runs her fingers through Kathleen's tangled hair, longing to hug her close, wondering when that will ever happen again. "You learned a good lesson, then, didn't you? No more looking back."

It is a long summer. Kathleen has good days and bad days as her deep burns begin to heal, forming dense, painful webs of scar tissue. Mary enjoys cooking, so flits between helping Kitty in the store and making family meals. At Kathleen's command, every night before bed, she repeats the story of Rumpelstiltskin in her most dramatic voice.

Mother Barrett comes over often for the first few pain-filled weeks, telling Kathleen her stories, and helping with her compresses. Ewald stops by to see his Kash nearly every day after work, chatting up a storm as he re-papers the kitchen walls and regrouts the tile to clear away all traces of smoke and fire.

Kitty appreciates the help, puts on a cheerful face for everyone, but can't shake her gloom. For the second time, she has nearly lost a child. Because she was in a hurry and cranked the flame too high under her stew. Because her six-year-old didn't have the good sense not to reach over it. Because her ten-year-olds thought it was fun to see how gasoline lights up the basement, the basement with wooden joists, under the store that puts food on their table. Because her seventeen-year-old was flirting with the boy down the street. Because she was a distracted mother. Because Tom Barrett was dead.

She thinks about her papa, that proud man, so talented, so ambitious, the same kind of busy, distracted parent, slowly losing track of his children, till they were all lost, all of them.

Except for her and his four grandchildren. Now, teetering.

:: 137 ::

In August, the family picnic is planned for the backyard at the Lexington house because Mother has been unsteady on her feet and wants to stay home.

On picnic day, while Mary shreds cabbage for coleslaw, Kitty scans the newspaper at the kitchen table. After skipping over the news of more bank closings and the ongoing tales of Lindbergh derring-do, her eye catches a small report of an overflow crowd at the Municipal Opera for Ziegfeld's *Rio Rita*.

"Weren't you at the Muny last night?" she asks Mary.

"It was a gas. We sat in the free seats. Best place to be on a summer night."

"Says here there were 9,500 in seats and another thousand standing."

"The music really got us going and, of course, the big dance numbers were amazing."

Kitty's spirits droop. She spent the evening laboring over her ledgers, then darning a patch over a new hole in her silk stocking.

"Last time I went to the Muny was 1926, that summer before your daddy died. Five years ago."

Now she can't even remember the last time she had a good laugh.

Later, at Mother's, she catches Francis alone in the kitchen.

"How's your business going?" she asks him.

He grunts. "I need to close one of the stores. Even with Frankie and Florrie on board and Molly pitching in when she can, we can't figure out how to pay the rent in a neighborhood where a third of the men are out of work and just as many have had their wages cut. You?"

"The bills are getting paid, but I'm whipped. The children are suffering. School is starting soon. Mary doesn't want to go back but isn't crazy about working in the store. The boys are wild. They need someone supervising their homework or they'll never make it to high school. And my poor baby… I'm starting Kathleen over in second grade. I pushed her into school too young, for my own convenience. She needs a fresh start, still wobbly from her trauma. She needs her mama."

Francis hands her a glass of lemonade. "Can you afford a manager? Somebody like Ewald?"

She frowns. "There's only one Ewald and he has a good-paying union job. Besides, it isn't the hours in the store that are killing me. It's all night staring at the books, and making phone calls to see who can pay how much on their tabs. They're my neighbors. I don't have the heart to cut them off from feeding their families."

But as she speaks, an idea forms. She loves the business that she and Tom built and wants it to be her sons' inheritance, the future Barrett Brothers Market. But it will be years before they can take over.

"What if I lease the business?" she asks Francis. "Can I do that? Find someone who has the time? Someone who can benefit from the Barrett name and our loyal customers?"

"Like someone buying a Kroger franchise?"

"Yes!" she says. "But renting. I'm going to want it back in a few years."

It's a crazy idea. But Kitty lets it ripen in the back of her mind.

:: 138 ::

September comes. On Saturday afternoon, September 12, with a line of shoppers at the cash register, Mary rushes into the store, tears streaming down her face.

"Oh, Mother!" In front of everyone, she throws her arms around Kitty. "Aunt Mamie just called. Grandmother is dead! Aunt Mamie was out shopping and the milkman found her dead on the kitchen floor. I can't believe it!"

Kitty is embarrassed to have such a sad event announced in front of her customers, who murmur sympathetically but are still impatient to finish their business. Fighting back her own tears, Kitty gives Mary a squeeze. "You'll make dinner then," she says. "I'll go over to Lexington as soon as the store closes."

Ellen Barrett's death is a blow. No one knows how old she was, but she must have been at least twenty when she arrived from Ireland, in time to witness the Great Fire in Chicago, so she might have been eighty. She was their anchor, their elder, their old soul, their link to ancient Ireland.

Then again, it releases Kitty from an obligation. Supporting his mother was Tom's lifelong commitment. The house had been paid for decades ago and would go to Mamie now. But there always loomed the possibility of having to pay for Mother's hospitalization or nursing care. Now, to put it hard-heartedly, there was one less worry.

At the funeral on Tuesday, Kitty is approached by a couple who introduce themselves as Charles and Sidonia Winther. They are older, about Francis' age, and say they knew Tom Barrett from his first store on Easton, when Charlie worked for a wholesale bakery that supplied the store with bread.

"After that, Sid and I moved out to California where I tried my fortune in the oil business, then I became a locomotive engineer for Southern Pacific and we moved back to Saint Louis."

"Did you know Mrs. Barrett?" Kitty asks.

"No," he says, "but I happened into one of Francis's stores last week. Got reacquainted, exchanged our stories. He told me you might be looking for someone to operate your store."

"Maybe," she says.

"I made pretty good change on the railroad, but they're laying guys off now. Sid and I have some savings and a little property but we need work, something we can really dig our teeth into. We weren't blessed with children, so we have lots of time." He reaches an arm around Sid's shoulders. "When I got to talking with Francis about needing work, he said to talk to his sister-in-law, that you were interested in some arrangement till your sons were old enough to take over the store. Appealed to me—something wholehearted, but with an endgame. Saw Mrs. Barrett's death notice and thought, well, if I stop by and if I run into Mrs. Kitty Barrett, maybe the idea will bear fruit."

Bear fruit it does. Over the next week, Kitty spends many hours with Charlie and Sid negotiating a deal, introducing them to her vendors, and organizing their recordkeeping. In a burst of generosity and relief at getting out from under the daily pressure of the store, Kitty tears up all the credit slips. A gift to her faithful customers.

Everyone gets a fresh start.

:: 139 ::

It is a strange feeling to hand the keys of her business to someone else. For twenty years, the store hours have been Kitty's clock. Now, still living upstairs, she hovers over it like a goddess. Charlie and Sid are hard workers and eager students of the business. Kitty sweeps through Barrett's Market as she wishes, chatting with her neighbors, putting groceries on her tab, and giving the Winthers her words of wisdom about where to get sawdust for the meat department floor or how to prepare for the health department inspection.

Then she retreats to her motherly domain.

The economic depression continues to worsen and Mary takes a job in an office downtown, but forty-one-year-old Kitty Barrett focuses on domestic joys. She makes hearty family breakfasts. She turns beans, potatoes, and cheap cuts of meat into a variety of meals her children enjoy, meals followed by a bounty of homemade pies and cakes. She arranges the apartment and its beautiful second-hand furnishings so that she can easily host dinner parties, sing-a-longs, and bridge club nights. She finally allows the boys to get a puppy, a white spitz they called Boots. Mary buys Kitty a pair of canaries, delightful creatures who fill the apartment with their joyous song.

But by summer, Kitty sees that the Winthers are in distress. July's rent is late and some shelves are not being restocked. The butcher is working only two days a week and the meat counter is filled with hot dogs and long rounds of bologna. Panicking that they will lose customers with money to spend and run the store into the ground, Kitty invites them upstairs to troubleshoot.

Their money problems turn out to be deeper than slow business at Barrett's Market.

"We want to make a go of it," Charlie tells her. "We truly love the work. But we have this property on Penrose—a four-family flat. We paid too much for it. Now the rents aren't coming in like we expected. The mortgage payments, the taxes, it's all piling up. We keep trying to make one more payment hoping that good times are just around the corner but the bank is threatening to foreclose. It's a mess."

"How about letting me see the Penrose property," Kitty suggests. "Maybe I'll have an idea."

The Penrose building is in her old neighborhood, Holy Rosary parish. She makes a quick assessment. The four-thousand square-foot brick structure is only ten years old with four compact apartments, a spacious basement, and a narrow but grassy L-shaped yard—the kind of place where newlyweds love to start their families. She thinks of her children, growing up so fast. Wouldn't it be perfect to give them a quiet street to start married life, instead of a noisy apartment above a pool hall on Easton Avenue? She feels Tom Barrett with her, getting her to think long-range, planning for their children's future, making sure they get off on the right foot.

"Let's talk about what you need to get out from under your bad investment here," Kitty says.

The Winthurs are eager to deal.

Kitty contacts a friend in the real estate business to work the angles. With too many abandoned properties and foreclosure costs already on their books, the bank itself is teetering on collapse. The manager willingly strikes a bargain.

By Labor Day, the property is hers. She knows she has scored big, that she pulled off something Tom would have done, something the Winthurs could have done themselves if they were half as savvy as the Barretts. The Winthurs can now restock their grocery shelves and Kitty has rescued her sons' future business.

:: 140 ::

In the fall of '32, election fever goes into full swing. With his sons and son-in-law now operating the printing business, Con P. Curran takes over as head of the Democratic party in St. Louis County. The Dems are hellbent on breaking the Republican stranglehold on local politics and electing Franklin D. Roosevelt president. Uncle Con encourages Ewald to join the effort for the Twenty-Seventh Ward, in their local precinct.

Ewald is enthusiastic. "Hoover's made a mess of this country," he says, giving Mary and Kitty his pitch to join the campaign. "Just look at all the starving families in this city, families with no work, no homes. It's the most important election of our lifetime and I ain't lyin.'"

"Mother, let's open our basement as campaign headquarters for the precinct!" Mary says, catching Ewald's enthusiasm. "We have acres of unused space. My pals would love to join in. What a gas!"

Kitty latches on to the idea. Too many nights of "freedom" from her account books are piling up, leaving her starved for companionship, no matter how many games of Parcheesi she plays with her children. And wasn't that always her intention, to turn the basement into a money-maker with holiday parties and wedding receptions catered by Barrett's Market?

Kitty works fast, clearing away years of junk and checking out bankrupt restaurants and saloons for tables and chairs. She hits the jackpot with a long oak bar being sold for firewood. She hires a couple of out-of-work carpenters to dismantle it and reinstall it in her basement.

Ewald connects new overhead lights to the main switch. After making sure the toilet works, he installs a small sink in the powder room behind the washing machine. A broken old refrigeration unit from the store gets a new life when Ewald repairs it to hold beverages for campaign workers. Kitty persuades a distributor to keep it stocked with donated Vess soda.

As quickly as Kitty adds tables, Ewald fills them with volunteers—housewives and out-of-work men during the day, the younger crowd at night—assembling lists, stuffing envelopes, recording information from their canvassing forays, the air thick with cigarette smoke and conversation. The twins run errands for the campaign after school and after dinner. Seven-year-old Kathleen trails after Ewald, eager to be his assistant, keeping papers neat, fetching tools, and running upstairs for bags of snacks.

Hobnobbing with the campaign workers, Kitty keeps an eye out for men suitable to keep her company. She's tired of the occasional fix-up with whatever friend's brother or cousin is depressed or recently divorced or shy-around-women. How many times is Molly Barrett going to introduce Kitty to her widowed brother John Curran before she gets the hint that Kitty isn't interested? He's a nice man. Kitty knows John and his fifteen-year-old Johnnie from the store, but from Ewald, she also knows the dark secret of his wife's abortion-induced death, along with the warring in-laws seizing custody of his two young daughters.

At one of their envelope-stuffing sessions in the basement, Molly brings him up again. "He's such a good man," she says. "And he's gone through so much. The two of you would have a lot to commiserate about."

"For Pete's sake," Kitty responds. "I'm not interested in a lonely hearts club. I've suffered my losses, but I keep them to myself. I'm not a damn bit interested in hearing somebody else's sob story. I don't want somebody else dripping their tears on my pillow." She stands up and brushes the creases out of her skirt.

Molly sniffs. "Well, you don't have to bite my head off."

"Sorry," Kitty says. "The world is such a dreary place. I can hardly look at the newspaper anymore. I'm not a social worker. I can't afford the sorrow. It sounds selfish, but I need a fella who can give me some laughs."

:: 141 ::

November 8. Election day. Everyone is optimistic that Democrats will steamroll the Republicans for their pitiless attitude toward the millions out of work and losing their homes. Kitty suggests they have an election night celebration in her basement headquarters. Ewald and Mary are on board.

After work on election day, Mary and a couple of girlfriends cut crêpe paper into streamers and tack them to the basement ceiling joists. Ewald brings over a big Philco radio and, with Bill's help, gets it positioned and tuned just right to hear KSD, the station owned by the *Post-Dispatch*, starting its broadcast of election returns from their newsroom when the polls close at 7 p.m. Kitty splurges on a ham and makes a mountain of sandwiches for their volunteers. Ewald gets his hands on a keg of 5% beer.

The basement is quickly crowded with campaign workers, either coming from work or, if not working, coming from their service as poll watchers. They turn the radio up full volume to hear the latest bulletins gathered by Associated Press reporters in every precinct of the country, as well as by *Post-Dispatch* reporters at the St. Louis Election Board headquarters. By 7:20, with early returns announced from twelve states, it is clear that Roosevelt is headed for a landslide. Soon after, the Missouri vote count points to a Democratic avalanche locally.

The gang starts celebrating.

In between election updates, KSD plays live band music. Mary starts the group dancing by grabbing the hand of Lester Hohmann, an amiable young man from the neighborhood, tall and gangly like Mary. Soon everyone is in the swing. Kitty's foxtrot is rusty, but she pulls Bill, then Bob, onto the dance floor with her. She winds up dancing a few circuits with all who reach their arms out to her, playing the perfect hostess. She floats on a sea of energy.

At 9:30, the Senate flips Democratic and the House increases its Democratic majority. By 10:30, they hear the news that Roosevelt is amassing the biggest landslide in American history and that the anti-Prohibition forces have gained enough power to repeal the Eighteenth Amendment and nullify the Volstead Act.

At 11:17 p.m., Hoover concedes defeat.

The group cheers. Couples hug amid the whoops and hollers. The radio blasts Roosevelt's campaign song "Happy Days Are Here Again."

Kitty is standing next to Ewald and is surprised when he pulls her into his arms for a big hug, pressing his cheek against hers, holding the hug for a moment longer than she expects.

"We did it," he says. "We did it."

As he draws away, she catches his hand and squeezes it. He glances down, then winks at her before he's clapped on the shoulder by a fellow asking where the john is.

The party winds down. Against the backdrop of dance music from the radio—volume now turned low, the volunteers find their coats and chat about what Roosevelt should do first, while the twins pack leftover sandwiches into paper bags for them to take home.

Kitty looks for Kathleen and finds her asleep on a pile of coats. She hears Ewald's laugh and spots him rinsing glasses behind the bar.

"Come on, baby," she says, smoothing Kathleen's hair. "Let's get you upstairs. School tomorrow." She calls to Bill and Bobby. "Time for bed. Let's go, boys."

Kitty is annoyed to see Mary in the dark end of the basement slow-dancing with Lester. He's been part of Mary's crowd forever, since they met at the drug store on Hamilton, where the Hempstead and St. Barbara's youth mingle after school. He's a nice enough boy but the family isn't Catholic, and German to boot, like that awful Harry Kralemann that Nellie tangled with.

"Mary!" she barks. "I need to put these three to bed. They have school. Get the garbage outside. I'll be back shortly."

"Yes, Mother."

She hears Ewald's laugh again as they climb the stairs.

Kathleen begs for cookies and milk before bed, which delays Kitty's return to the basement. Before she knows it, the back door squeaks open, then bangs shut, followed by Mary's footsteps. She carries a tray of serving plates into the kitchen.

"All cleaned up. Everyone's out," she calls to Kitty.

"That was fast. I was going back down to say goodbye."

"Oh, they all pitched in. Got the garbage out. Put the glasses in a washtub. I'll do those tomorrow after work when I take down the crêpe paper. Lights are out and the doors, locked." She piles the dishes into the sink. "It was a great night, wasn't it? What a gas to *win*!"

It was a gas all right, Kitty thinks, as she changes from her dress to a nightgown. Tomorrow the world will be a brighter place.

And Ewald. That moment. What was that? The neighborly hug that, for a second, felt like an embrace. The warmth of his cheek. The impulse that made her hold onto his hand for that extra second. The wink.

There was a spark.

And she can feel it now. A tingle. Like an old friend at the door. She runs her fingers through her hair. It has to be a ghost. Tom passing through on this triumphant evening. Not Ewald.

Ewald is like everyone's favorite kid brother, always good for an entertaining story, always good to bum a cigarette off of. The one she calls when…

The one she calls.

The one she doesn't have to call.

The one who shows up.

Well, this is ridiculous. She has finally spent too much time alone and is reading into the innocent gestures of her brother-in-law's brother-in-law, who isn't even thirty years old.

Still… that spark…

On Saturday morning, Ewald stops by with rent money he picked up from the Easton Avenue property. He sits at the kitchen table and Kitty pours him a cup of coffee. While Bobby plays the piano in the front room, Bill shows Ewald some of the new pennies he's found.

Kathleen pops in. She gives Ewald a hug. "Mother made biscuits this morning to go with grape jam. Want some?"

"Sounds dee-lish," Ewald says. "Let me see how you're stretching that arm of yours."

Kathleen's burn scars are still an issue. Their tightness makes her hold her arm close to her side. Kitty massages the scars daily with salve and pushes Kathleen to stretch the new tissue and strengthen the underlying muscles. The ritual makes her baby cry.

But Ewald plays a game with her, making her stretch to touch his raised fist ten times before she can see what's in it. This morning it's an acorn. She giggles and runs to get the jam and biscuits off the counter.

"I keep meaning to say," he says to Kitty, "I can pick up the rents at Penrose, if you want."

"Nah, that's a drive. I don't mind going over there, getting to know the tenants. It's my old stomping grounds."

Kathleen spreads jam on a biscuit for him and he takes a bite. "Mmm-mmm. Did you help make these biscuits?"

She nods. "And the jam too." She pulls her chair up to the table next to his.

"You know, Catherine, they're already talking about Congress authorizing the sale of 5% beer. Missouri's going to be all over it, with new licensing for retail sellers and new taxes. Keep your eye on it, for the store."

Kitty is taking measure of her interactions with him. Did something shift on Tuesday night? Does he see her with new eyes?

No evidence of that this morning. Same old E. Full of chat. Brain going a mile a minute. Ready with a laugh.

The question hangs with her.

:: 142 ::

Kitty's New Year's resolution for 1933 is to jazz up her social life. If she's going to start having romantic fantasies, let them be about a forty-some-odd *bon vivant*. Wouldn't it be fun to dress up for the show or a concert? Wouldn't it be fun to go to one of those private clubs where men and women dance and drink together instead of sitting up late waiting for her vivacious night-owl Mary to come home?

What she doesn't want is to fall asleep at night wondering if Ewald will stop by the next day. It feels inappropriate. And maybe a little pathetic. Like a lonely old woman standing at the window to say hi to the mailman or the delivery boy.

But since those middle-aged *bon vivants* are not lined up outside her door, she initiates her plan to open the basement for parties, to cast a wide net for all fun-lovers. She hosts a wonderful wedding reception in February for Mamie Barrett and Mickey Coleman. The word gets around. As long as her friends arrange the food and drink, as long as they clean up after, and as long as she is invited, they can use her space for receptions and birthday parties and holiday reunions.

For "live" music, she finds a second-hand pianola—a player piano—with a collection of rolls, including foxtrots, waltzes, and ragtime jazz melodies.

And, because her basement is part of her private home, there's no official objection when she acquires a couple of used slot machines, one for pennies, the other for nickels.

Kitty's social life does pick up. She tangos and waltzes with every neighbor's cousin. When a guest can play the piano, she brings down her sheet music and leads sing-a-longs, harmonizing with every tenor and baritone in the crowd. She accepts dates and sees popular movies—*Dinner at Eight, 42nd Street, Golddiggers of 1933*, and more. She goes to clubs in groups with other couples and dances to the best local bands.

But the men are laughably unacceptable.

"This one nearly broke my foot, his dancing was so clumsy," Kitty says one evening as she watches Ewald replace a burnt-out tube in the Philco. "And I swear, he had egg on his tie."

Ewald laughs. "Gotta watch out for those old bachelors. Lot of them are mama's boys, looking for someone who will scrub that egg out of their ties."

She takes a drink of her beer and lowers her voice. "Their mamas should have taught them how to behave on a date." She leans toward him. "Too many gropers and slobberers out there. Ladies don't want a spit bath."

Ewald's blue eyes widen and he sits back in his chair. "You know, Catherine, you have to be careful dating strangers. A lot of men aren't just … you know… sloppy kissers. They're animals. Women-haters. Guys who never got over some pretty girl teasing them for their buck teeth in the third grade. I hear them talking at work, talking about giving a girl what she's asking for, if you know what I mean. There are a lot of angry men in this world right now." His cheeks turn pink and his eyes dart toward the icebox. "Got another beer in there?"

His words sober her. She fetches another beer and pops the cap. "I don't worry about myself and those old farts," she says as she divides the beer between their two glasses. "It's Mary who keeps me awake at night. She goes with a nice enough bunch, I think, but I don't know them all. Too much drink, too many late nights, not enough responsibility to keep them on the straight and narrow. She's out every night."

"They can't party downstairs?"

"Oh, they do. And if it gets too quiet, I stick my head in the laundry chute to hear what's going on. She caught me at it once and blew her stack." She sighs. "Hasn't your mother stayed up plenty of nights worrying about her brood?"

"*My* mom?" He chuckles. "I'm her tenth child, her eighth boy. She's gone through every worry in the Encyclopedia Britannica. I heard her crying her eyes out or cursing up a storm many a night when my brothers were kids. But by the time it was my turn to make mischief, she had the whole script down to one line: *don't break your mother's heart.*"

Kitty nods. "A word to the wise," she says.

:: 143 ::

Despite the flush of optimism about the Roosevelt administration, the world is still a mess. As national economies struggle to lift themselves out of the long depression, Mussolini establishes his Fascist regime in Italy. The Nazis take over Germany. Hitler moves from Chancellor to *Führer*, demanding that his new unified armed forces—the *Wehrmacht*—

sign loyalty oaths to him personally, not to the German constitution. Stalin, General Secretary of the Communist Party in the Soviet Union, is running amok, with his five-year plans playing havoc with the food supply, causing famines, and triggering political purges that execute tens of thousands as enemies of the working class.

Americans fear war will be piled onto poverty. Most people think Roosevelt's New Deal isn't working fast enough to promote jobs, while a powerful minority preaches that the New Deal is bad for business and will kill economic expansion.

Kitty reads the headlines for national and world events because she's in business and they help her know what's coming down the pike, but attention to her children comes first.

What pride she feels when her boys graduate from St. Barbara's. Even though she has secured a livelihood for them in the grocery business, they are lucky they don't have to go straight to work. She can give them what her dear Tom lacked and longed for—a high school education. While there are several Catholic boys' schools in the city, her friends with money suggest a five-day boarding program, where the boys can be immersed in learning all week, with music lessons, hobby clubs, and religious devotions late into every evening. Chaminade in west St. Louis County gives her the best deal—both boys for the price of one.

September comes around. Leaving Bill and Bobby with their small bags at the Chaminade dormitory is painful. Kitty has a terrible flashback to that Easter Sunday in 1910 when the Flanagans dropped off their sisters at the Guardian Angel Industrial School. Fighting back her tears, she reminds herself that Chaminade is not a concession to disability and parental exhaustion. It's a sign of success—her boys brimming with talent and their mother living like a duchess off the rent of her commercial and residential properties.

But two months into the first semester, she's surprised at how relieved she is when the boys tell her they hate it at Chaminade.

"We're fighting out of our weight class," Bill tells her one Saturday at the breakfast table. "We don't spend our weekends at the county club playing golf or tennis."

Bobby chimes in. "I thought I was hot stuff with my own second-hand saxophone, but Chaminade boys have their own polo ponies."

"And their families are all Republicans," Bill adds.

They beg her to let them transfer to McBride in January. McBride is also run by the Brothers of Mary but is located on Kingshighway near her Easton Avenue properties—a neighborhood where half the men are out of work and tuitions are paid with the help of generous neighbors and spinster aunts. But that's where their St. Barbara friends are and that's where they want to be—with the regular guys.

She arranges the transfer.

:: 144 ::

The prospect of having her boys living back home by Christmas, not to mention the end of Prohibition on December fifth, puts Kitty in a festive mood. She decides to ring in 1934 with a grand New Year's Eve party. Since Roosevelt hasn't performed any economic miracles his first year as president, everyone is still poor. But dancing, singing, and noisemaking in glittery get-ups, no matter how tattered and patched underneath, will be a sign of hope for the year to come.

Kitty is tickled at the variety of people who stream through the basement door on party night, from old Mr. and Mrs. Curran, who walk over through the rain, to Mary's Charleston-dancing crowd. When the radio isn't blasting dance music, Bobby plays the piano, no sheet music needed for that boy. Bill gets a card game going in a corner away from the dance floor. Uncle Pat and Aunt Delia sit with the old folks, while their teenage daughters join Mary's crowd on the dance floor. Katie and Chas, Mamie and Mickey, Francis and Molly with their four children—the Barretts all arrive in full costume. Eight-year-old Kathleen and her eleven-year-old cousin Ella Rose take it upon themselves to act as serving girls, giggling as they balance their trays, weaving their way between the guests and the bar. Kitty has hired a bartender for the occasion, partly to allow her to socialize and partly to protect her precious cache of newly legal booze from disappearing too fast.

As the evening draws toward midnight, Kitty is bothered by one conspicuous absence: Ewald. She sidles up to Molly. "Have you seen Ewald?" she asks his sister.

"Oh didn't he tell you?" She takes a glass of beer from Ella Rose's tray as Bobby starts playing "Stormy Weather." "Thank you, sugar. Oh, I love this song. *Don' know why-y-y-y there's no sun up in the sky.* Oh, anyway, Ewald's girl wanted to go down to the Fox. They're having a bunch of live acts and showing a couple of movies. Zazu Pitts. Who'd cross the street to see that silly thing? Anyway, that's the story. I'm surprised he didn't mention it."

Kitty is surprised too.

Ewald was by yesterday morning with a little rent money from Easton Avenue and spent time adjusting one of the gas burners on the stove and helping Bobby tighten up the mechanism in the player piano. He joked about her and Kathleen being up to their elbows in cookie dough, baking for the party, but didn't mention that he wouldn't be here.

And he has never mentioned a girl. With all her blather about the screwy men she dates, he has never talked at all about his own dating. And she has never asked.

To hear he has a girlfriend should make her happy for him, but she is surprised at herself that it does not.

"Who's his girl?" Kitty asks as she reaches for a cigarette from a pack someone left on the bar.

"Oh my God, Zoe Jane Desloge, didn't you know?"

"Not one of *the* Desloges, is she?" The recently deceased Firmin Desloge was a Missouri lead-mine magnate and one of the richest men in the world. His grandson's family used to live across the street from the Currans before they snubbed the city for Clayton.

"Yes, ma'am, she certainly is. Our mother has warned E that "her type" doesn't marry "our type," but I don't know. Zoe keeps popping up on his social calendar. My sister Ellie thinks she might be the one."

"The one what?" Kitty lights up and takes a drag.

"*The. One.* Stay tuned for an engagement announcement. I think the Currans are plenty good enough for the Desloges."

"No kidding," Kitty says, as she feels the air being kicked out of her lungs. She coughs and stubs out the cigarette. For all the hours she and Ewald sit at her kitchen table chewing the fat, why hasn't she heard about Zoe Desloge?

Kathleen comes by and pulls on her sleeve. "Mother, we're running low on pretzels."

"Okay, sugar, let's run up to the store and get some more."

Kitty feels her party glow drain away. She tosses her glittery mask on the bar and smooths down her hair. She can't stop thinking about Ewald. She follows Kathleen up the steps to a back door in the store.

They flip on a light and grab two big bags of pretzels. As she jots down the take on her tab, a clipboard hanging from a nail by the door, she says to Kathleen, "I guess you miss your buddy Ewald tonight."

"Yes I do," Kathleen says. "But he had to do what Zoe wanted."

"So you know Zoe?"

"Not really. We ran into her once when Ewald and I were out bumming on Easton Avenue. She was all over him. He told me the coat she was wearing was real mink, not some dyed must rat. Can I lock the door?"

Her cheeks burning, Kitty pulls the door shut and hands Kathleen the key. "Muskrat. Dyed muskrat."

"I wouldn't like it if Ewald got married or something," Kathleen says as she struggles with the deadbolt. "I want him to be all ours."

Kitty has to laugh. "You make it sound like he's your dog."

"He's my donkey!" Kathleen giggles. "I told him he's my donkey."

Midnight comes. Glittery masks come off. The air is filled with noisemakers—clackers and blowouts and cowbells—and guests singing *Auld Lang Syne*. Kitty takes part, awarding her New Year's smooch to Kathleen, at the same time feeling an emptiness in the pit of her stomach.

The party continues. The radio orchestras play slow dances and couples pair off. The bartender leaves at one, so Kitty takes over. In addition to pouring drinks, she makes pots of coffee, which she dresses with whiskey and dollops of whipped cream.

By 3 a.m., the twins and Kathleen have gone up to bed and the last guests leave. Alone, she begins to collect glasses and throw food waste and ashtray contents into a garbage pail.

The basement door blows open. Kitty hears the heavy steel plates at the sidewalk drop shut and the bar-lock slide into place. Mary appears and slams the inside door. "Damn, it's cold out there. Snowflakes in the air."

Kitty assumes Mary was outdoors kissing Lester goodnight and is happy to see her safely back inside.

"Jesus, Mary, and Joseph, this floor is a sticky mess." Mary begins turning chairs upside down onto the tables. "What jaboney was spilling his drinks all over? I'll get the mop bucket."

As they work, they make small talk about what a success the party was and gossip about the guests.

After running through her friends, which couples are steady and which couples are bound to break up, Mary says, "I didn't see Ewald."

"Molly says he went to the Fox. With Zoe Desloge. You know her?"

Mary's eyes widen. "Ooooo, Miss Zoe Jane. Ain't he grand. Yeah, I kind of knew who she was when they lived in St. Barbara's. I think she went to Maryville College."

Kitty doesn't want to hear any more about Zoe, so changes the subject.

The basement is cleaned up by 5 a.m., so the two decide to stay up for six o'clock Mass, to get their New Year's Day obligation out of the way.

St. Barbara's is crowded with merrymakers who have the same idea, stumbling and mumbling their Latin prayer responses. The pews are full, so Kitty and Mary stand in the side aisle near the confession booth. Few people have been fasting since midnight, so the line for communion is short. But, look, at the head of the line is Ewald Curran, with his father and mother, his sister Catherine, and his brother Delaney.

Kitty scolds herself for being excited to see him and to see him with his family, not with a rich girl Molly thinks he's on his way to marry. She turns to catch Mary's eye, nodding toward the rear entrance. Their religious duty met, they scoot out into the dark morning.

As Mary starts the car, she asks, "Why didn't you have a date for your own party?"

"Oh, honey, I knew I'd be too busy entertaining to fuss over a man. Besides…" She hesitates, not sure she wants to share details of her ludicrous, middle-aged dating life with her twenty-year-old daughter.

But Mary picks up on her tone. "Besides, all the fellows you're going out with are someone's pathetic widower brother or depressed bachelor cousin, right?"

Kitty laughs. "I keep hoping for a winner. Aunt Mamie and Aunt Katie did all right for themselves, finding good men in their thirties and forties."

"Oh my God, Uncle Chas and Uncle Mickey are all wet. They can barely dance a two-step. You need to stop settling for scraps, Mother. Don't you realize how lucky a man is to be seen on the town with you? Everyone in this godawful community is dirt poor. Single women, divorcees, and widows are all out trolling for men, most of them looking for a fellow with a job to save them from having to get a shack in Hooverville. But you're independent. You own property, this automobile. You dress like a million bucks. You can have any man you want!"

Kitty smiles as they pull up to their usual parking spot on Ridge. She's tickled with her daughter's vote of confidence, as well as her modern wisdom that first-class women should not settle for second-class men.

As they slam the car doors and head for the warmth of their apartment, Mary adds, "It's not like I think you should get married again. No one can replace Daddy. But you should at least be having fun with somebody who is his own man, somebody who appreciates you, who thinks you're aces."

Upstairs in her bedroom, after wishing Mary sweet dreams, Kitty unbuttons her dress and lets it drop to the floor. She wiggles out of her corset and tosses it on the chair. Standing there in her lacy silk slip, still in her stockings and high heels, she gazes into the vanity mirror. She isn't the wisp of a girl she used to be, but her skin is like porcelain and her bosom is still full and high. Her arms are strong but not lumpy with muscle like a scrubwoman. Her hair is cut short with a stylish permanent wave and she keeps it a dark chocolate brown. She nods her head. Still first-class.

She takes off her shoes and stockings and crawls into bed with this thought: how can she make 1934 an interesting year?

Part 3. Bearcat, 1934

:: 145 ::

The following Saturday morning, Kitty makes a mountain of waffles, with whipped butter and real maple syrup. Mary and the boys eat and run. Kitty and Kathleen are still at the table when they hear Ewald coming up the back stairs at his usual time. Kitty gets up to fetch him a cup of coffee and a plate of waffles.

"Hiya, Kash," he says, as he lays a few bucks of collected rent money on the counter, "what d'ya know?"

"Not much," is Kathleen's pat response. Then: "We missed you at the big party."

"Aw, sorry I didn't make it. Heard it was the berries."

Kitty's cheeks burn at her baby's innocent question but it gives her an opening. "Molly says you went to the Fox with your girlfriend."

"My *who*? You mean Zoe?" He shakes his head and stirs some sugar into his coffee. "I wouldn't call her my girlfriend."

"According to Molly, Ellie thinks you're going to give her a ring."

"What? For chrissake, those sisters of mine aren't happy unless they're pairing everybody up. And if you want to know, Zoe asked *me* out. Some fellow dumped her at Christmas and she needed a quick date because her whole crowd had tickets for the thing at the Fox."

Kitty feels an inexplicable wave of relief as Ewald sips his coffee.

"She's a little sweet on me," he goes on, "chased after me when I was in eighth grade. Now I think she just looks me up to annoy her old man. I can't stand that Clayton crowd anyway. Bunch of college snots, don't know shit from Shinola." He glances at Kathleen. "Pardon my French."

Kathleen gets up from her chair and lays her head on Ewald's shoulder.

"You belong to the Rowan and Ridge crowd." Then she looks him in the eye. "You're *my* donkey, right?"

"That's right, kiddo. But you're so pretty, it won't be long before you have a mule train of donkeys lined up outside your door ready to follow your orders."

"I'll be queen of the mule train." She pulls away and prances around the kitchen. "Heehaw! Heehaw!"

"Go bundle up, my dear," Kitty says. "I want you to take some of these waffles over to Mrs. O'Leary."

Kathleen runs into the bedroom for her coat.

As Kitty wraps six of the waffles in waxed paper, she says to Ewald, "She'll be nine in a couple of months and you've been the closest thing she has to a father. I don't know if I've ever told you how much that means to me."

Ewald looks surprised at the compliment and chuckles. "Well, she's a pistol."

Packing the waffles into a paper bag, along with a vial of maple syrup, Kitty goes on, "You're a good friend. The one who shows up. Don't know what I'd do without you."

Ewald squints as if he's judging the truth in her praise, then nods.

When Kathleen dashes back into the kitchen, he advises her to put on her gloves and to go out the back way to minimize her steps across the alley to the O'Leary's.

"It's blistering cold out there."

They listen to Kathleen run down the back steps, then open and slam the back door. Ewald eats his waffles while Kitty makes a plate for herself.

She sits down at the table. "I was thinking," she says, "do you play bridge?"

He swallows his drink of coffee. "Sure. Ellie is crazy about it and makes us play with her so she can master the new contract bridge rules. I'm no champ, but at least I'm to the point where she doesn't yell at me anymore."

Kitty has had this idea percolating in the back of her mind all week. "I play almost every week with the Gessels and a few others. Mary's been my partner but she has no patience with it and would rather be out with her friends. I thought—if you enjoy the game—maybe you could join me. Might be fun."

Ewald grins. "Just don't yell at me if I'm not the player you expected."

With Ewald as her regular bridge partner, Kitty feels like the toast of the town. Wearing a well-fitted dark suit and tie, his curly hair slicked back, Ewald looks older than his twenty-nine years. Even though he can never get the black ink fully scrubbed off his printer's hands, everyone knows the Curran family to be prosperous and politically connected.

Kitty and Ewald are middling players, but good losers and fast learners. Kitty is the better strategist, but Ewald has a sharp memory and knows the rules cold. Their drives home are full of discussion about what they did right and wrong and how they might coordinate better.

On a bitterly cold night in February, they win their first rubber.

As Ewald opens the car door for her, Kitty grabs his hand. "Are you sure you don't want to come up for a nightcap?"

"I'm bushed. Been up since five. I'll be by for breakfast tomorrow."

Saturday breakfast has become a ritual between them, no longer a chance drop-in. He takes her arm as they walk through the swirling pellets of snow.

"Is your mother waiting up for you?"

"Mom? Aw, I don't know when she sleeps."

"What does she think of us playing so much bridge together?"

Ewald chuckles. "She thinks you're aces, always has. She told me to let you know John plays bridge too."

John again. The lonely old widower Kitty's age. "When was that?"

"Aw, weeks ago, I must have forgot."

At the doorstep, Ewald leans his head toward her, rubbing his nose against hers, letting his hands rest on her shoulders. Their lips brush. Kitty feels the *zing* down to her freezing toes.

"We really trounced the Gessels tonight, didn't we?" he says.

With his hands still on her shoulders, her legs feel rubbery as she fumbles for her key. "We sure did."

:: 146 ::

On Tuesday evening, Kitty is working in the kitchen with Mary.

"So tell me, Mother, is Ewald your hired man at the bridge table like he was in the store or are you two going steady?" She is sitting at their recently installed electric mangle, feeding through damp linens, already an expert at the controls.

Kitty looks up from the peeled apples she's chopping for a pie. "*Hired* man?"

"Not that you'd *pay* him, but you do boss him around, *fix this, hang this, tighten that*. Is he your *donkey*, like Kathleen would say, or are you actually sweet on him?"

Squeezing half a lemon over the chopped apples, Kitty gets her back up. "Is it any of your business what's going on between Ewald and me?"

"Of course it is! You're the one who's always so worried about her reputation. And I'm the one having to hear what a bearcat I have for a mother."

"*Bearcat*! What kind of word is that?"

"Come on, you've heard it. A stylish older woman who beguiles young men?"

"Ugh. So you want me to wear dreary widow's weeds and carry around my rosary beads?"

Mary jams the mangle in reverse and catches the pillowcase.

"Wouldn't that be a sight," she says.

"Weren't you the one telling me on New Year's Day that I could have any man I wanted?"

"Well, I didn't mean *Ewald*."

"What's wrong with Ewald?"

"Nothing. He's young and you're old. Except for not going to college, he's the most eligible bachelor in the parish. My friends would die for a date with him and here he is keeping company with an old lady, with my *mother*." She stands and begins folding the pillowcases she'd draped over a chair, snapping them into sharp creases. "It's a scandal."

"Scandal? Scandal, my ass!" Kitty scrapes back her chair. She slides a bowl under the wall-mounted bin and sifts in the flour she needs for her pie, giving it a glance for weevils. "Ewald is my best friend."

Mary stops folding and looks at Kitty. "But what happens when he gets bored with your stuffy old bridge games? What happens when he breaks your heart?"

This conversation jangles Kitty. Mary is forcing her to confront categories—young, old, bearcat, bachelor. Forcing her to think about scandal and heartache. But she is a Flanagan. Scandal and heartache have plagued her like moths in her woolens, silently eating small holes in her psyche. But strife has also taught her to mend those holes with invisible stitches and clever re-weaving, using the yarn of laughter and song and, yes, her womanly charms. Whatever lies ahead, she damn well won't be bullied into humble retreat now.

:: 147 ::

In March, Kitty is invited to the Currans for a Sunday afternoon card party, hosted by Ewald's sister Ella Rose, who is in her mid-thirties. Ellie has recently become engaged to Will Schanbacher, an accountant who lives with his sister's family a couple of doors down from the Currans. It's an easy crowd of casual bridge players, more interested in talking politics than focusing on their cards. Kitty and Ewald win most of their games.

Afterward, as the guests mill around the buffet table of sandwiches and sweets, Kitty chats with Mrs. Curran, who asks about her dear little Kathleen, then launches into a long-winded story about one of her many grandchildren. Kitty half-listens, while she eavesdrops on the conversation behind her between Ellie and Ewald.

"Easter is in a couple of weeks, April first," Ellie is saying. "We're going to have the usual shebang. I'm starting a headcount. Any chance you'll want to invite your sweet Zoe Jane?"

Kitty freezes, breath trapped in her lungs, waiting to hear Ewald's answer.

"For chrissake, El, Zoe's not my sweet anything. Aren't you paying attention? Anyway, I'm having Easter dinner over at Kitty's. April first is the twins' birthday too, so it'll be a big day."

With a deep sigh of relief, Kitty smiles. She hasn't started planning for Easter yet, didn't even remember it's on the boys' birthday this year. But now she's looking forward to it.

:: 148 ::

Later that month, on a Saturday afternoon, Kitty hosts a party for Kathleen's ninth birthday, with eight of her school friends plus her cousin Ella Rose. While Bob plays the piano in the front room and Mary leads the girls in a giggle-filled game of musical chairs, Molly Barrett washes the baking pans at the kitchen sink and Kitty finishes adding pink roses to the chocolate birthday cake.

Molly gossips about her sister Ellie postponing her wedding to Will Schanbacher till next January, then, at a lull in the conversation says, "If you don't mind me asking, Kitty, what's the lowdown on you and my kid brother?"

Kitty squeezes another big rose petal from the frosting bag. "Oh gosh, we do enjoy each other's company."

Molly stops scrubbing, staring into the dishwater. "But you aren't actually *dating* or *going steady*, as the youngsters would say."

Kitty pauses her work for a drink of coffee, not sure how she wants to answer.

"I guess what I'm asking is, are you two romantically involved?" Molly puts a pan on the drainboard and turns around, wiping her hands on her apron.

"And why do you need to ask?"

Kathleen interrupts them. She's wearing a pink ruffled dress, long enough to hit her knees, which makes her look very grown up. "Mother, we're going to play Twenty Questions but Mary told me to ask when you want to serve the cake."

"Go start playing your game at the dining room table. We'll bring in the cake and ice cream when it's ready."

Kathleen dashes away. Kitty asks Molly to toss her the box of candles, hoping they can change the subject.

But Molly persists. "I need to ask because I love you both. I see the looks, the touches, the private jokes. Of course, I'm glad the two of you get along so well. But I don't want to see either of you get hurt."

"Who's getting hurt?" Kitty asks, counting out nine candles.

Molly gazes down the hall, tuning in to the laughter of little girls. "Don't you think E deserves to marry to someone his own age and have his own family, instead of—"

"Instead of wasting his time with a *bearcat*, playing bridge instead of tennis, still living with his parents?"

"Oh, Kitty, I didn't call you a bearcat. I don't judge—"

Kitty balls her hands on her hips. "But that's how I'm being judged and maybe that's what I am. It's the 1930s. What's the latest song? 'Anything Goes,' right?"

:: 149 ::

The next week, after Easter Sunday dinner and the twins' fifteenth birthday celebration, while the children entertain friends with cards and dominoes in the basement, Kitty and Ewald sit in the dark on the screened-in porch off the kitchen. It's a chilly evening for spring, but they bundle up in their sweaters and turn on the electric heater Ewald rigged up during the winter, so the boys would have more space for their games and hobbies.

Like she did with Tom so many years ago, she and Ewald enjoy watching the comings and goings of neighbors along Ridge and the traffic up on Hamilton. Kitty keeps a pair of opera glasses on the sill next to the ashtray in case something needs a closer look. Their chairs are pushed together near the windows, with Irish coffees on small tables to the side. Their arms touch.

They watch two police cars speeding south on Hamilton, lights flashing, sirens screaming.

"Did you see the paper this morning?" Ewald asks. "I can't believe that son-of-a-gun John Dillinger escaped the police again."

"Too busy getting dolled up for Easter Mass, then cooking dinner and baking the cake. Didn't even glance at the headlines."

"Yeah, up in St. Paul. Police thought they had him trapped. But, no sir. He came out with his machine gun blazing, his gang of thugs by his side. They escaped in a waiting car."

Kitty sighs. "I used to track organized crime when my brothers were alive, local crime anyway. I'll have to point out the story to the boys. They love that cops-and-robbers kind of stuff." She takes a drink of her coffee, wondering whatever happened to that thick folder of clippings she kept in her desk drawer. "I'm so lucky to have good boys, smart boys who enjoy school and have wholesome friends."

Ewald pulls out his pack of cigarettes, lights one up, then lights a second from the tip of the first and hands it to her. She takes a drag. With a slight flutter in her belly, she asks, "What about you, E? Do you want children? Sons? Daughters?"

He leans forward, choking on his smoke. "Jesus Christ!" He clears his throat, dropping his cigarette on the ashtray. "Where did that question come from? *You* want more children?"

"Mother of God, no," she says, leaning forward to stub out her cigarette. "But people are talking, you know, about me taking up all your time. That you'll get tired of it. That you need the chance to find the right girl, start your own family."

"Holy crow, Catherine. Who was it, Molly or Ellie?"

She is silent. He takes her hand in his. She turns to see his profile in the light of the streetlamps—straight nose, a curl on his forehead, pale eyes wide.

"I could be anywhere," he says in a soft voice. "I got looks, I got skill, connections, money in the bank." He gives her hand a squeeze. "I'm exactly where I want to be."

:: 150 ::

Decoration Day, the official start of summer in St. Louis, is on a Thursday in 1934. On Wednesday, Mary announces that she and her girlfriends are taking both Thursday and Friday off, going away for the weekend.

Kitty is in the adjoining bedroom, putting on makeup for a special holiday bridge night at the church hall. Dabbing her cheeks with rouge, she asks for details, *with whom*, *where to*, and *how*.

"Oh, Mother, I'm twenty years old. Quit grilling me. I can go wherever I want."

Kitty looks around the corner to see Mary stuff a bathing suit, a nightgown, and two sundresses into her bag. "Tell me. Where. You're going."

"Out to Castlewood, all right? With Jane and Lucille. There's a bus from Maplewood out Manchester to the new Ballwin Road. From there, we can hitch a ride south to the clubhouse area, easy."

Kitty is familiar with the summer resort of Castlewood. It's about twenty miles out, on the Meramec River. She knows people who take the train out there from Kirkwood. There's an artificial beach created from river dredging operations and the secluded location made it popular with bootleggers during Prohibition.

"Whose club are you staying at?"

"It's the Bobolinks, but don't you worry. See you Sunday night!" With that, she bounds down the back stairs and out the door.

But Kitty does worry. Mary and Lester have been going steady for months now and she can't imagine Mary spending her precious holiday weekend with girls only. Her worries are confirmed when Mary drags into the apartment Sunday night and collapses into bed, reeking of cigarettes and beer.

The scene is repeated the following Friday night.

"You can't be going out there again," Kitty says. "Where is Lester in all this?"

Mary rolls her eyes. "Well, if you must know, Lester and his pals rented Bobolinks for the summer. But everything is jake. Girls sleep dormitory-style on the second floor and boys stay on the first. Last week, we even went to Mass on Sunday. There's a quaint little church down the road. I love being out of this damnable hot city."

Later, on the drive to their bridge game, Kitty shares her anxiety with Ewald. "That girl is too headstrong, too confident she can handle any situation."

"I wonder where she gets that from," Ewald says, as he turns right on Easton Avenue.

"When I was twenty, a girl who'd be seen with a man in a saloon was a tramp. Now taverns are springing up all over and a good girl doesn't think twice about sashaying in on the arm of her fella."

"You're showing your age, Catherine. I thought you wanted to throw out all the old rule books."

She glances at him. "That's for me. But I'm still a mother. I don't want her to get in trouble. I'm not about to pay for a shotgun wedding, and I'd die if she did something to herself, something tragic, like my sister Nellie. Is that so old-fashioned?"

"I get it," Ewald says, pulling up in front of the Gessels' place. "How about if we take a drive out there tomorrow, check things out. We can take Kash, the boys, the dog—make a day of it. We get to Castlewood, I bet we find somebody to point out the Bobolinks. Own a pair of walking shoes?"

:: 151 ::

On Saturday at noon, with the three children and Boots in the back seat, Ewald's 1928 Chevrolet hits the crunchy gravel of New Ballwin Road. They creep along the three miles till they begin to see taverns on both sides of the road. Finally, they come to a fork: Castlewood Road to the right, East Hill Drive straight ahead. Kitty sees the church on the knoll between them.

"This has to be the place," Kitty says. "She mentioned the church nearby."

Ewald pulls in front of a tavern called Crossroads. "We'll check here." He switches off the engine and trots up the steps to the open door.

The car turning into an oven, Kitty climbs out and the children follow. They watch Boots run in circles around the other cars and stop at a small oak tree to pee.

"It's so quiet here," Kathleen says.

"I bet there are snakes!" Bobby says, making his sister frown.

Kitty's glad she had Kathleen wear long pants.

Bill is bending over the sharp stones on the road. "Look at this one." He picks it up and holds it to the light. "Quartz. Look how it sparkles."

Ewald exits the tavern and points to East Hill Drive. "That way. Bobolinks is just up the hill, on the right."

They pile back into the car and Ewald starts the engine. "Owner of the tavern, guy named Nig McDaniels." He catches Kitty's eye. "Knows Mary well."

She shakes her head. Great.

They drive past the church on their right and a sign for The Grove Dance Floor on the left. At the hill, Ewald downshifts to second, but the wheels start spinning on the loose stone halfway up, and, with Kathleen screaming in the back seat, he has to back down.

"Holy crow," he mumbles.

"This isn't safe," Kitty says. "Maybe we should walk."

"I got it." He downshifts to first and guns the engine. Kathleen screams again and the boys whoop as the car roars up the short hill. Where the hill levels off, a clubhouse appears. *Bobolinks* is painted on a sign.

With her arms braced against the dashboard, Kitty gasps, then laughs with relief. "Well, this is fun," she says.

They open the car doors and get out.

The Bobolinks is a two-story clapboard cabin, stained black with creosote, the trim painted lead white. It is surrounded by tall oak trees and the air is rich with the aroma of composting leaves and oil stoves. Kitty looks up the hill to see more clubhouses, all in black and white. A breeze ruffles the leaves and a pair of blue jays call to each other.

The screen door of the Bobolinks club flies open and six young people pour out, including Mary and Lester, who quickly take their hands off each other when they realize who the guests are.

"Mrs. Barrett! Ewald! What a surprise!" It is a fellow Kitty knows as Joe and he raises his bottle of beer to greet them.

Mary is furious. "What, are you spying on me now?" She turns on her heel and stomps back into the club, letting the screen door slam behind her.

Kitty tries to ignore her daughter's rude behavior by turning to Lester. "We've heard a lot about Castlewood, wanted to check it out. Nice day for a drive."

"Sure, Mrs. Barrett, come on in and take a look," he says. "It's a swell place."

She follows him inside, where Mary is curled in a wicker chair looking out the back window, smoking a cigarette. The place is a wreck. Three unmade cots. Empty beer bottles and overflowing ashtrays. Dirty dishes everywhere. Clothes on the floor.

"It's all screened, so we get a cool breeze at night and the June bugs stay outside. The girls sleep upstairs. Want to see?"

"Yes, please," Kitty says. They go back outside and up an open staircase to the second floor. It is a mess of unmade beds, beer bottles, and ashtrays. Stamping out a smoldering cigarette on the floor next to one of the beds and taking note of the faint whiff of sex, Kitty takes a moment to appreciate the fresh breeze streaming through the windows. She recognizes the call of a whippoorwill.

"You can stay for lunch, right?" Lester says. "We got hotdogs to throw on the grill, plenty for everybody."

"We brought a cooler of sandwiches and drinks too," she says. "But I'm not sure Mary wants us to stick around."

"Ah, she'll get over it. Stay, why dontcha. Do some walking. Keep going up this road and there's a path into the woods overlooking the river. You gotta check it out."

Much to Kitty's relief, Mary gives up her pout when she sees how much her friends are enjoying the visit. Lunch is a lot of laughs.

Afterward, Kitty and Ewald start their walk up the hill. Bill and Bobby run ahead, with Kathleen and Boots chasing after. To their right, the hill sweeps downward with clubs below East Hill Drive. To their left, the hill rises steeply, with two clubs nestled into its side before the slope continues into the dense woods. They see cars and people at the first club. The second is empty. It has a name painted on a board nailed to the side: *All-Inn*. Tacked to it is a *For Rent* sign.

"Let's take a look," Kitty says.

They tackle the steep climb through piles of leaves, fallen branches, and rotted logs among the young oaks towering over them, providing dappled shade. Ewald offers his hand to help her balance as they climb. Her stockings are snagged and she's out of breath by the time they reach the club. She keeps Ewald's hand in hers.

"It's gorgeous," she says, despite the disarray of rusted lawn chairs out front. Like the others, the wood is creosoted black with chipped white trim. The structure is three stories high, with a screened-in porch and a basement. "Let's see if we can get in."

The front door is unlocked. The place doesn't look like it's been cleaned since the last tenant. The furnishings are old but usable. The squat coal-burning stove and the old ice box need a good cleaning. There is no electricity but they are glad to see spigots for running water.

"Would you look at this," she exclaims, looking through an open door to a big shower room behind the narrow kitchen. There is no toilet, but out the window they spot the outhouse, well away from the house.

Her mind buzzing with the possibilities, Kitty climbs the steps to the second floor. Four iron-frame beds, two doubles and two singles. She flips over a mattress to check for bedbugs. All clear. Upstairs on the smaller third floor, oven-hot with all the windows closed, there are also a couple of double beds and a cot.

Back outside, Kitty jots down the rental sign phone number. "I wonder how much they get for this. It'd be a great place for the girls to stay, away from that Bobolinks mess," she says, giving Ewald a light backhand nudge on his arm. "Don't you think?"

They pull two of the metal chairs side by side, brushing away the dry leaves and acorns before they sit down. It is late afternoon and the cicada song rises as they enjoy the warm breeze without saying much. Ewald puts his hand on her shoulder, finding the tension with his thumb and massaging it away.

"I could get used to a place like this," he says.

Kitty hears Bill's voice coming from the direction of the woods. "Mother!" he yells and she can tell it's a shout of excitement, not alarm. He runs toward her on the raised roadway to the other side of the club. "Mother, you should see this place!"

"Where's Bobby? Kathleen?"

"Coming. He's helping her over some logs. But you have to see, we found the most amazing place. The path leads to the top of a row of cliffs. An overlook. You can see the river and how it winds for miles east and west. People were walking up from below. They said there were steps, all the way down to Lincoln Beach. You have to see it!"

She slaps Ewald's knee. "Listen to him, listen to the energy in his voice. Look at him running. My sickly boy, blooming in the country air. He's the spitting image of his father when I see him so excited."

Bobby and Kathleen appear, holding hands. Bobby calls out: "E! You should see the railroad tracks from up there. We saw a freight train, must have been a mile long."

Kathleen races over to Ewald and throws her arms around his neck, "Fifty cars, E. We counted 'em."

Bill looks up at the All-Inn club. "What's this place? Are we staying here? That would be mighty keen if we did."

"No, honey, we have to head back to the city. Long drive ahead, so we better get going. But I have a feeling we'll be back. Whadd'ya say, E?"

Ewald smiles. "That would be mighty keen, yessiree."

As they walk back down the hill to say goodbye to the Bobolinks crew, Kitty says to Ewald, "I'm so tempted. But, you know I couldn't manage a place like this by myself. Too much can go wrong way out here. I couldn't even gun my car up the hill like you did, so what do you think, are you in?"

He nods his head. "All in."

:: 152 ::

Kitty calls the owner of the All-Inn as soon as she gets home. The summer rental price is cheap.

"But you gotta take care of things," the owner says. "I been out of work and my vehicle is broke down so I can't get out there. In fact, if you want to buy the place, a hundred dollars cash and it's yours. You'd be doing me a favor."

"Let's see how it goes," she says.

The next Friday, when Ewald comes by after work, Kitty and the gang are ready to pack the trunk of his car with food, linens, toiletries, cleaning supplies, candles, flashlights, and a case of beer. Kitty plans to spend the first weekend scrubbing.

"What did you tell your mother you're doing?" Kitty asks Ewald during their drive.

He shrugs. "Told her about Castlewood. Told her you got a summer rental. That I was helping out."

"And she said?"

"And she said remember to kneel by the side of my bed to say my prayers at night and don't forget to go to Mass on Sunday."

Kitty turns toward her window and smiles as the scenery rushes by.

Mary sulks about the invasion of her family into Castlewood and the insistence of her mother that she and her girlfriends sleep at All-Inn instead of the Bobolinks, but the arrangements quickly work out. The girls are thrilled to have a shower room with clean towels. Kitty assigns them second-floor beds, fresh with bleached-white sheets. For herself, Kitty claims the single bed at the top of the stairs to ensure there's no overnight hanky-panky between her girls and the boys across the road. Ewald and the twins sleep upstairs on the third floor.

During that first weekend, Ewald scrounges enough bricks to set up an outdoor grill. Nig McDaniels points him to a junkyard where he finds a big metal cooler on legs. Farther down New Ballwin Road, Ewald makes the acquaintance of Russ Dickinson, a young family man starting his own tavern business who also operates an ice house. He sells blocks of ice that E chips up for the new cooler.

Whipping up big bowls of coleslaw and pans of baked beans is second nature to Kitty. Ewald grills spare ribs instead of hot dogs. With its endless supply of hearty food and beer on ice, All-Inn quickly becomes popular with the Bobolinks boys.

When the mosquitos appear at dusk, they pat their bare skin with Kitty's citronella-and-lavender repellant. After dark, crickets, katydids, and tree frogs join the afternoon cicadas to provide the perfect background music for gazing up at the astonishing starscape, mimicked all around them by the flashing of lightning bugs.

Some nights, the boys gather dry twigs and branches for a campfire. They all share their favorite ghost stories and in the silences between they listen for the howl of wolves.

On rainy nights they sit at the big table on the screened-in porch and play cards. Kitty learns poker and pinochle.

Everyone sleeps late except for Ewald and Kathleen, who take charge of breakfast. Compared to weekend breakfasts in the Curran household, All-Inn is easy—a pound of bacon fried, a dozen eggs scrambled, a loaf of bread toasted, a couple of cantaloupes sliced. Ewald cooks in the narrow kitchen. Kathleen sets the porch table.

On Sundays, Ewald takes Kathleen down to St. Elizabeth's for seven o'clock Mass. They perform their kitchen magic while the others go to Mass at nine.

After breakfast cleanup, the young folks scatter. To Kitty's surprise, her city anxieties are suspended here. Mary cruises the nearby taverns and dancehalls with her friends, but they aren't driving, so Kitty doesn't worry. The boys take Kathleen on long hikes down to the river, where they fish or pay a penny for the ferry—little more than a raft—to cross the narrows to Lincoln Beach. They have quickly learned to identify poison ivy, to differentiate garter snakes from copperheads and rattlers, and to watch for nasty little scorpions. She trusts them to be fine.

Kitty and Ewald aren't attracted to the weekend dancehalls or the crowded river beach. They enjoy the time to themselves, cooking, cleaning, repairing, having a few beers, laughing.

She loves the privacy, the lack of convention. She can leave her corsets and silk stockings at home. It doesn't matter out here that she has lived so much longer than Ewald. Under the stars, among the oaks, everyone is as young or old as they please.

June and July speed by. Kitty lives for the weekends. She rushes through her housekeeping and accounting, preferring to spend time on her Castlewood lists. She gathers second-hand tools and supplies for their projects, buys her groceries, and mends their outdoor clothing, counting the minutes till 5:30 on Friday when Ewald pulls up.

While Mary and her friends head for home on Sunday evening, by July, Kitty, Ewald, and the children are squeezing one more night in. They awake at the crack of dawn on Monday mornings and scramble into the car without breakfast so Ewald can get to work on time.

:: 153 ::

By the second weekend in August, Kitty and Ewald find themselves talking long-term about the property.

"I can install a toilet pretty easy in that shower room," Ewald tells her as they sit in the shade of an oak, beers in hand, taking a break from clearing brush. "The problem is that we need to dig a septic tank. I'd love to get one of those little cement mixers. I could pour the concrete for the septic tank myself. Then we could start making some steps down from the driveway and maybe build a retaining wall."

"I'd like to pave the area around the side door too, to keep the mud out of the kitchen," Kitty says. "Now what about a hot water tank? How hard would that be?"

"We'd have to clean out the basement, get some copper pipes…"

He squints as he looks off into the distance, the look he gets when running a problem through his mind.

She reaches out and puts her hand on Ewald's arm. "Those are big projects. Whaddya say we buy this place?"

"I was just thinking that," he says and lays his hand on hers. "A cousin of my Pop died this summer. I'm going to get a hundred bucks from his estate. Didn't you say that's what the owner wanted? I could buy this place for us."

"Ohhhhhh." Kitty's imagination runs wild with visions of lively gatherings and long conversations, a lawn with a croquet game and a horseshoe pit, and, oh yes, a few rose bushes. "But look," she says as her brain sorts through the logic. "I want to go halfsies, straight down the middle. You can take what's left from your hundred bucks to buy that cement mixer."

He squeezes her hand. "Deal."

She leans over to get a kiss.

:: 154 ::

The next day is Kitty's birthday, her forty-fourth, but her thirty-ninth to anyone who asks. Molly, who has always loved their August birthday picnics, hinted around about having the Currans and Barretts all out to Castlewood for the annual event. Kitty and Ewald talked through the logistics but in the end, they agreed: to heck with it. Molly could plan her picnic in the city, at Sherman Park.

All-Inn is their separate world, their private nest in the woods, no questions asked, no eyebrows raised. That is celebration enough.

That Sunday afternoon, the weather is hot and unsettled. The children are off on their explorations. Kitty and Ewald wander down to Nig's Crossroads Tavern for a couple of cold beers. As they start back up the hill, the sky darkens and thunder rumbles across the landscape.

"Rain!" says Ewald. "Want to dash back to Nig's?"

"No, there!" Kitty points to St. Elizabeth's church. They trot across the field, through the Queen Anne's lace, black-eyed Susans, and goldenrods to the church steps.

"Wait, I don't have a hat!" Kitty says.

A streak of lightning cracks the sky, followed by a roll of thunder, and the first giant drops of rain. She reaches into a patch of white clover, pulls up a handful of flowers, then races up after Ewald.

"Hold these, hands out." As they huddle under the eaves, Kitty piles the clover into his outstretched hands and, inserting a thumbnail into each stem as she goes, quickly chains the flowers together, a trick her mama taught her as a child in Leclaire. Connecting them into a circle, she says, "There, I have a hat."

As the wind picks up, blowing rain onto their skin, Ewald tosses away the rest of the flowers and takes the circlet from Kitty's hands. He lays it on her hair. "I crown thee Queen of Castlewood."

"Then that makes you King of Clubs," she says.

Both laughing, they pull open the doors and rush inside. They stand together, catching their breath.

St. Elizabeth's is as simple as churches come. No vestibule. Backless benches instead of pews. No statuary. A plain wooden communion rail. A small bouquet of pink roses under the crucifix in the sanctuary.

"Let's say a prayer," Kitty says.

She starts to grab Ewald's hand, but he says, "Wait." He raises his hands to fasten the top button of her sundress. "There, now you're proper."

To the sound of rain pelting the roof, they bless themselves with holy water and walk down the aisle to the communion rail, where they kneel, close enough that their arms press together. After a quiet moment, Kitty takes Ewald's hand, feeling the callouses on his ink-stained fingers. Maybe it is the dampness on her skin, but she feels a sudden shudder of fear and holds his hand tighter.

"If we buy All-Inn together—" She doesn't like the tremor in her voice, so she starts over. "Ewald Curran, if we buy All-Inn together, we will be *all in together*. Forever. Do you agree?"

"You bet," he says, glancing at her, only then catching the seriousness in her eyes. He straightens his back. "I agree, Catherine Barrett. All in. Forever."

She looks straight ahead at the altar, taking a deep breath before saying, "And if I tell you that I have fallen in love with you but hate the idea of losing my independence, will you honor that sentiment?"

"I will," he says, laying his other hand on top of their entwined fingers. "And if I tell you that, since I was eleven, since the day I met you at Molly's wedding, ever since that day, I have adored you—if I tell you that, will you accept—will you *honor the sentiment*—that I am a romantic fool?"

She smiles. "I will," she says, "all the days of my life."

Epilogue

Kitty and Ewald quietly take over the ownership of All-Inn.

Castlewood becomes the family's haven—the piece of heaven where time stops, a respite from hardship, from prying eyes and uppity judgments, from the painful creep toward war as Europe becomes engulfed in Fascism and nations become the pawns of dictators.

But the world does roll on. No one escapes the river of time.

Much to Kitty's distress, Mary and Lester run off and get married in the fall of '34. Things quickly fall apart and they divorce. Mary tries again with a Catholic fellow Arthur Backlund but learns too late that he doesn't want children. Another divorce. She reunites with her true love, Lester. Kitty provides them with an apartment in her building at 4251 Penrose, where they have the first two of their four children.

Bill and Bob Barrett don't finish their studies at McBride, so Kitty gets them working in the store and Charles Winthur gradually turns it over to them. Briefly, Barrett's Market becomes Barrett *Brothers* Market, but the two young men don't get along as business partners. Bill is bossy and organized like his mother. Bob is a musician, a free spirit, who decides to leave the grocery business altogether. He gets a job at Carter Carburetor and falls in love with his co-worker Alice McKenna.

Meanwhile, Kathleen becomes the first family member to graduate from high school, from the girls' academy at St. Aloysius Rock. She follows her Aunt Katie's career path of stenography and secretarial work. Ultimately, she marries city boy Walter Price, a McBride graduate who first laid eyes on her at Nig's Crossroads Tavern in Castlewood. They also start their married life under Kitty's wing at 4251 Penrose, where the first three of their four children are born.

World War II is a tragic disruption in many American lives. Bob Barrett is drafted and assigned to his regiment's band, but is killed in an airplane crash on his way home to visit the family and his fiancée Alice. His cousins Francis Jr. and Florrie Barrett also die in the war, one in the heat of battle in Germany, the other of leukemia on Guadalcanal. Dennis

Pedrotti's son Francis dies at Pearl Harbor.

Bill Barrett takes on the family mantle as proprietor of Barrett's Market. At the age of thirty, he marries Lillian Demme, from a Sicilian family also in the retail grocery business. Like Mary and Kathleen, they start their life together on Penrose and have three children.

Ewald's father suffers a long bout with emphysema. Three months after he dies, Ewald and Kitty get married, on February 5, 1937, in a Thursday evening ceremony at St. Barbara's Church. The witnesses are their longtime bridge companions Michael and Mary Gessel.

Whatever eyebrows were raised or gossip whispered about their age difference or their years of summer fun in the secluded woods of Castlewood no longer matters. They belong together. They figure it out. At the age of thirty-three, Ewald moves from his mother's home into the Rowan apartment above Barrett's Market and continues his career as a printer.

They decide to invite Kitty's sister Ethel, long institutionalized at the Arsenal asylum, to come live with them, but her caregivers advise that her ability to live in a home environment is long gone. Ethel dies quietly of pneumonia in 1957.

In the 1940s, when Maizie Braun gives up her confectionary tucked into the side of their Rowan building, Kitty and Ewald open a small tavern in the space and they continue to offer their basement for neighborhood parties.

In 1942, as the family mourns the loss of Bob, Mary's first child George begins calling Kitty *Kitty Mom*. And because Kitty doesn't want to be called *grandma*, the nickname sticks. Across generations of extended family and friends, *Kitty Mom and Ewald, Ewald and Kitty Mom* becomes a single word for the inseparable couple, the one you want at every party, the one you turn to when you need a job done. They know everyone. Their hearts are big and their energy boundless.

Ewald and Kitty Mom entertain friends and family at Castlewood every summer weekend for over twenty-five years, till 1961. Then, when Ewald is fifty-seven and Kitty is seventy-one, with all their properties sold off, they buy a little home in south St. Louis, a bungalow with a sunny backyard where they plant dozens of rose bushes.

On September 16, 1984, Kitty passes away in her own bed at the age of ninety-three. Ewald is by her side.

Under the watchful eye of his darling Kathleen, Ewald lives another four years, restless and lonely, till he dies at the age of eighty-eight.

The story of Kitty's people has now been told.

THE END

Susan Barrett Price grew up in St. Louis, Missouri. She works now from her studio in upstate New York. Her other works include:

HEADLONG: Over the Edge in Pakistan and China (2018) A traveler's tale and memoir.

THE SUDDEN SILENCE: A Tale of Suspense and Found Treasure (2015). A novel.

TRIBE OF THE BREAKAWAY BEADS: Book of Exits and Fresh Starts (2011). Illustrated memoir and family history.

PASSION AND PERIL ON THE SILK ROAD: A Thriller in Pakistan and China (2008). A novel.

A few references are highlighted here for approximate guidance and genealogical purposes. Every mention of every name is not included. Main characters appear throughout.

Index

Made in United States
North Haven, CT
06 October 2023